Reimagining AI for Society, Organizations, and Work Environments

Editors

Eleonora Veglianti
Kedge Business School, Paris, France

Wendy Currie
Audencia Business School, Nantes, France

Luisa Varriale
University of Naples 'Parthenope', Naples, Italy

CRC Press
Taylor & Francis Group
Boca Raton London New York

CRC Press is an imprint of the
Taylor & Francis Group, an **informa** business
A SCIENCE PUBLISHERS BOOK

Cover credit: Image created by the editors.

First edition published 2027
by CRC Press
2385 NW Executive Center Drive, Suite 320, Boca Raton FL 33431

and by CRC Press
4 Park Square, Milton Park, Abingdon, Oxon, OX14 4RN

CRC Press is an imprint of Taylor & Francis Group, LLC

Library of Congress Cataloging-in-Publication Data (applied for)

ISBN: 978-1-032-84746-7 (hbk)
ISBN: 978-1-032-87917-8 (pbk)
ISBN: 978-1-003-53539-3 (ebk)

DOI: 10.1201/9781003535393

Typeset in Times New Roman
by Prime Publishing Services

Preface

In recent years, organizations have increasingly focused on a transformative force reshaping the fields of management and information systems, because of Artificial Intelligence (AI).

AI has emerged as a critical area requiring rigorous scholarly investigation to fully comprehend its multifaceted challenges and far-reaching opportunities. Notably, AI's predictive capabilities provide organizations with data-driven insights into market dynamics, risk assessment, customer preferences, and employee behavior, thereby enabling more informed and strategic decision-making. However, the impact of AI extends well beyond predictive analytics.

In this evolving landscape, Generative AI (GenAI) is redefining how governments, businesses, and citizens capture, analyze, and interact with data and information. With its intuitive and accessible interfaces, GenAI is democratizing access to advanced technologies, extending its reach across jurisdictions and fostering new forms of collaboration and problem-solving. The interplay between predictive AI and GenAI is increasingly synergistic: predictive inputs can inform generative processes, while generative outputs, in turn, enhance predictive accuracy and decision support.

Scholarly contributions in this area aim to conceptualize and critically examine both established and emerging features of AI technologies. Indeed, AI's transformative potential has profound implications for traditional management theories and practices. AI agents are poised to complement, or, in some cases, displace, substantial segments of the workforce, triggering fundamental shifts in organizational structure, workplace culture, labor dynamics, and the theoretical foundations of management information systems.

This volume responds to the urgent call to reimagine AI for society, organizations, and work environments. It adopts a multidisciplinary perspective, bringing together chapters from diverse management domains. The book appeals to a broad academic and professional audience, including scholars and practitioners interested in organizations, information and communication technologies, and human resource management. Through its contributions, the volume seeks to advance our understanding of how AI is reshaping the contemporary organizational landscape.

Contents

Preface iii

1. **OpenAI Tools for Developing Employability Skills: The SkillFusionLab** 1
Muhammad Anwar ul Haq, Francesca Di Virgilio, Antonia Puccio and *Maria Cristina Manocchio*

2. **Exploring the Pathway towards Innovation: A Meta-Synthesis of Artificial Intelligence (AI) Adoption within the Public Sector** 18
Simona Mormile, Roberta Romano, Gabriella Piscopo and *Paola Adinolfi*

3. **Digital Evolution and Information Systems to Support Decision-Making Processes in Sport** 39
Marzia Ventura, Concetta Lucia Cristofaro, Walter Vesperi and *Anna Maria Melina*

4. **A Decision Model for Aligning AI Adoption with Organizational Models and Operational Complexity** 71
Francesco Bolici, Alberto Varone and *Gabriele Diana*

5. **From Mechanical Calculation to Intelligent Machines: The Evolution of Artificial Intelligence from Management and Organization Perspective** 88
Kamran Khan and *Daniela Mancini*

6. **The Algorithmic Workplace: Artificial Intelligence and the Future of Organizational Behavior** 105
Filomena Buonocore, Davide de Gennaro, Ludovica Del Barone and *Viviana Colombi Evangelista*

7. **Responsible Marketing: When Using AI in Customer-Bank Communication Relationships** 128
Charlotte Van Hauwaert and *Monica C. Scarano*

8. **Exploring AI-Driven Solutions to Mitigate Burnout in Healthcare: A Systematic Literature Review** 147
Laura Roma, Floriana Pollio, Rocco Agrifoglio and *Concetta Metallo*

9. **Data-augmented Venture Firms: AI in Venture Capital Decision-making** 167
Sanguineti Francesca and *Previtali Pietro*

10. How AI Tools could Transform Research Methods in Organization, Business, and Management: A Review of Techniques and Emerging Trends **190**
Riccardo Coda, Arianna Ciabattoni and *Francesca Ricciardi*

11. Artificial Intelligence and Human Resource Management: Insights and Challenges through a Bibliometric Literature Review **214**
Danila Scarozza, Isabella Bonacci, Maria Menshikova and *Emanuele Gabriel Margherita*

12. Understanding the Relationship between Artificial Intelligence and Stress within Organizations **234**
Raffaele Silvestre, Mauro Romanelli and *Maria Ferrara*

Index **259**

Editors' Biographies **263**

Chapter 1

OpenAI Tools for Developing Employability Skills

The SkillFusionLab

Muhammad Anwar ul Haq,[1] *Francesca Di Virgilio,*[2] *Antonia Puccio*[2,*] and *Maria Cristina Manocchio*[2]

Introduction

The digital transformation and artificial intelligence (AI) are changing the roles of institutions, instructional strategies, and learning environments in education systems. Higher education institutions (HEIs) have to focus on the development of digital capabilities due to the expansive impact of digital technology on both personal and professional life and the rapid evolution of digital technology (Soliman et al. 2021; Soliman et al. 2023). The employment market demands that graduates possess the technical capabilities, adaptability, and interpersonal abilities necessary to thrive in dynamic professional environments (Dumitru and Halpern 2023). Digital literacy is an essential requirement for professional readiness in contemporary digital workplaces. Spurava and Kotilainen (2023) assert that digital literacy extends beyond the basic capability to use technology. It encompasses the capacity to critically evaluate digital content, collaborate using digital technologies, and rapidly adjust to sophisticated technical environments. Proficiency in digital literacy exemplifies a graduate's adaptability, a crucial skill in today's swiftly changing work environments and essential for employability (Van Laar et al. 2017). Employability refers to the capacity to function autonomously in employment prospects through

[1] Department of Management Sciences, University of Gujrat, Pakistan.
[2] Department of Economics, University of Molise, Italy.
Emails: anwar.haq@uog.edu.pk, fradivi@unimol.it, m.manocchio2@studenti.unimol.it
* Corresponding author: a.puccio@studenti.unimol.it

DOI: 10.1201/9781003535393-1

applying a range of personal characteristics, skills, and knowledge pertinent to a certain profession (Small et al. 2018). Overall, employability is considered a vital ability that aids students in college in navigating the challenges and uncertainties they may encounter in their jobs (Römgens et al. 2020; Di Virgilio 2024). The concept of employability is powerfully associated with higher education, where the center of attention is progressively on guaranteeing that students achieve both academic knowledge and practical and soft skills useful to obtain success in the workforce (Clarke 2018; Healy et al. 2022). Consequently, HEIs are instrumental in enhancing the employability of graduates prior to their entry into the workforce by cultivating critical competencies that equip them with the necessary skills to confront the challenges, ambiguities, and requirements of contemporary occupations (Picco et al. 2022). This collaboration is imperative for the implementation of employability skills that are frequently deficient among recent graduates, a gap that has been extensively discussed in academic discourse (Jackson and Bridgstock 2021; Healy et al. 2022). Graduate employment in the age of digital technology and AI encounters problems and chances for career development (Rizun et al. 2024). AI technology profoundly influences students' career pathways, necessitating the acquisition of technical AI abilities, knowledge of ethical AI concepts, problem-solving features, and a commitment to lifelong learning for success in the AI career sector (Yupelmi et al. 2024).

In this scenario, the SkillFusionLab was established at the University of Molise (Italy) in 2014 to connect academic practices with employment market demands. This curricular laboratory is an innovative program designed to cultivate critical workplace competencies, especially in domains such as digital literacy. The combined approach to academic knowledge and practical application enables students to have an extensive knowledge of the modern workplace, thereby preparing them for positions in the public sector, business, and management. SkillFusionLab adopts an organized approach to enhance employability through providing students practical experiences that considerably increase their academic education and equip them for professional challenges in the workplace. This section has the goal of showing the significance of Self-Regulated Learning (SRL) programs, such as SkillFusionLab, in the combination of academic knowledge and expertise in the workplace.

The objective of this chapter is to examine the influence of SRL theory on the development of employability skills in students, with a particular emphasis on the development of soft skills and the assistance of students' transition into the workforce through the lens of digital literacy. This chapter analyzes the SkillFusionLab experience as a practical resource for students to develop critical digital literacy skills, contextualized within a literature study that highlights the significance of digital skills in the digital age. The primary role of OpenAI Tools in enabling the development of vital job-related skills is generally recognized. This is due to their role in connecting digital literacy with innovation, flexibility, and digital collaboration. In the framework of business administration, management, and business consulting studies, the influence of these skills on the competitive pursuit of employment prospects in the public and private sectors is highlighted. These conclusions highlight the potential of educational programs that emphasize

SRL to enhance the employability of graduates in the job market by promoting the acquisition of new soft skills and identifying areas for future research in a rapidly changing professional environment.

Background

Self-Regulated Learning Approach for SkillFusionLab

SRL emphasizes the cyclical process of planning, monitoring, and adjusting academic behaviors, which are critical for maintaining productivity (Zimmerman 2002). SRL is conceptualized as a cyclical process with three main phases: forethought, performance, and self-reflection (Chiu 2024). Self-regulated scholars participate in planning, surveillance, and regulating the cognitive, motivational, emotional, and behavioral factors of learning to build knowledge and skills (Kharroubi and ElMediouni 2024). They approach learning proactively, set specific goals, use strategic methods, and reflect on their efforts. The SRL theory describes how students actively manage their learning processes. Moreover, self-regulated learners believe SRL skills can be developed and recognize the critical role that intentional strategy plays in academic success (Ateş Akdeniz 2023). Zimmerman's model underlines the importance of self-reflection and goal setting, which helps students remain productive over time.

SRL is essential for success in school, university, and beyond, particularly in blended learning environments where students must independently manage their learning process (Esnaashari et al. 2023). Yun (2024) and Esnaashari (2023) both identify distinct SRL profiles among university students, linking higher SRL engagement to better academic achievement and adaptability. In the digital age of today, SRL has become crucial for students to manage online learning environments and employ a range of digital technologies. To support their learning, self-regulated students can use digital technology, critically analyze online sources, and undertake information searches (Silva et al. 2024; Na et al. 2024).

SRL allows students to actively participate in digital educational experiences, facilitating more profound and meaningful learning. Students with high levels of SRL strategies examine online resources, seriously assess digital information, utilize digital tools for collaboration with peers, and enhance their knowledge (Kaputa et al. 2022). Boulahmel et al. (2025) provide a systematic review of how SRL is measured in digital learning environments, focusing on the use of trace data—digital footprints left by students as they interact with online platforms. The review categorizes the types of trace data and indicators used to capture SRL behaviors, such as time spent on tasks, navigation patterns, and engagement with learning resources (Boulahmel et al. 2025). Faza and Lestari (2025) systematically reviews SRL strategies—planning, monitoring, and reflection—and the technologies that support them in digital HEIs. The review identifies a range of digital tools, such as learning management systems, AI-driven feedback, and collaborative platforms, that facilitate SRL by enabling goal setting, self-monitoring, and reflective practices (Faza and Lestari 2025).

SRL promotes scholars to actively participate in the administration of their digital educational journey, therefore cultivating deeper and more significant learning. The SRL approach greatly enhances students' autonomy, self-reliance, and success as trainers, allowing them to adeptly negotiate the complexities of 21st-century knowledge (Drajati and Putra 2022). Based on the recognized basics of SRL, this chapter proposes a theoretical model that elucidates the impact of educational interventions on the professional readiness of students. The SRL ideas emphasize the necessity for students to actively manage their learning processes to acquire the knowledge and skills vital for professional development (Kharroubi and ElMediouni 2024).

AI has the potential to revolutionize traditional teaching and learning processes by introducing new instruments to the educational environment (Adiguzel et al. 2023). OpenAI tools, including DeepSeek and Chatbots, are investigated in conjunction with algorithms that are capable of simulating human interactions and generating human-like language from spoken input. For example, the use of ChatGPT allows workshop students to obtain explanations, answer questions, and receive guidance on various technical topics, acting as a virtual assistant (Farrokhnia et al. 2024). Certainly, OpenAI tools have the potential to enhance the efficiency of practical learning, provide immediate feedback on assignments, and simplify complex concepts (Bhattacharya et al. 2023).

Table 1 presents a summary of the main studies analyzed, highlighting the authors, study area and key findings.

Table 1. Summary Table.

Study area	**Key Contribution**	**Author(s)**
Core Theories and Foundational Perspectives on SRL	The cyclical model of planning, monitoring, and reflection in learning emphasizes intentional strategy and belief in skill development, linking SRL with cognitive, motivational, and behavioral learning processes.	Zimmerman 2002; Ateş Akdeniz 2023; Kharroubi and ElMediouni 2024.
SRL in Academic and University Contexts	These studies identified SRL profiles linked to achievement and adaptability, highlighted their significance in hybrid academic settings, and proposed a model linking SRL with employability and student preparedness.	Yun et al. 2024; Esnaashari et al. 2023; Kharroubi and ElMediouni 2024.
SRL and Digital Learning Environments	SRL practices foster digital readiness and autonomy in online learning, promoting deeper, collaborative learning and self-regulation through critical information evaluation and engagement with digital technologies.	Silva et al. 2024; Na et al. 2024; Kaputa et al. 2022; Drajati and Putra 2022.
SRL Measurement and Support through Digital Tools	SRL, a social work professional, has been thoroughly reviewed and updated on various tech tools, including LMSs, AI feedback, and collaboration platforms, to ensure effective monitoring and support.	Boulahmel et al. 2025; Faza and Lestari 2025
Artificial Intelligence and SRL Enhancement	The authors highlighted the transformative role of AI in learning environments, emphasizing its potential for instant feedback, simplification, and efficiency.	Adiguzel et al. 2023; Farrokhnia et al. 2024; Bhattacharya et al. 2023.

Source (s): Authors own's work

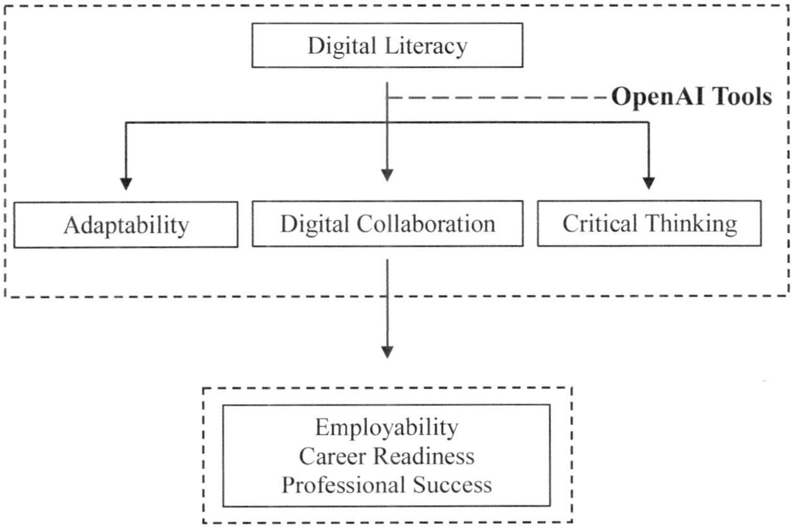

Figure 1. SkillFusionLab Model. Source (s): Authors own's work.

SkillFusionLab aims to understand how structured programs centered on SRL might enhance students' employability and prospects for professional success. Utilizing OpenAI resources, SkillFusionLab serves as an accelerator that improves students' self-regulation skills in digital literacy. SkillFusionLab precisely links specific soft skills (Adaptability, Digital Collaboration and Critical Thinking), increasingly recognized as crucial for modern workplace operations. The SkillFusionLab (Figure 1) is based on digital literacy that enhances the skills Adaptability, Digital Collaboration and Critical Thinking. These skills are crucial for adjusting to fast-paced technological changes, introducing new ideas regarding work approach in the digital era. In this framework, OpenAI tools act as a bridge between digital literacy and the development of involved skills, providing tailored feedback and customizable learning settings.

Digital Literacy

Digital literacy is the capacity to effectively utilize technology to perceive, evaluate, utilize, generate, and distribute information (González-Rico and Lluch Sintes 2024). Metacognitive knowledge, resource management, and motivational beliefs significantly and positively influence digital literacy (Wang et al. 2025). Acquiring Digital Literacy during university education is essential and widely emphasized across studies. University students require digital skills for research, communication, collaboration, and content creation (Reddy et al. 2023). Moreover, students who have a comprehensive comprehension of digital literacy are better equipped to shape the constantly evolving digital environment, which enhances their ability to compete in a technology-driven job market (Reddy et al. 2023). Digital literacy has emerged as an indispensable skill for employment in virtually every sector (Kee et al. 2023). Among employers, there is an increasing demand for graduates who possess robust digital competencies (Aničić and Bušelić 2020). Digital proficiency is a prerequisite for a variety of professional roles, as modern workplaces are significantly reliant on digital technologies (Moore and Morton 2017). Digital Literacy helps graduates shape labor market changes, learn new technologies, and remain competitive in a rapidly evolving global economy (Teng et al. 2019; Imjai et al. 2024). Digital Literacy is a foundational competence for academic achievement and professional advancement in today's digital-centric world (Antoniuk and Zasiadivko 2023). Universities are essential in fostering Digital Literacy by providing comprehensive programs and resources that equip students with essential digital competencies (Huzooree and Soupramanien 2025). This preparation is essential for students who aspire to advance in a technology-driven employment market (Murtadho et al. 2023).

Artificial Intelligence in Education

AI in education is an evolving multidisciplinary field aimed at enhancing and optimizing teaching, learning, instructional design, and assessment processes through the use of applications such as chatbots, adaptive feedback systems, and e-books. Despite its potential to support self-regulated learning (SRL), the adoption of AI in higher education faces challenges such as the need to improve digital or AI literacy among students and educators, and the risk of excessive reliance on AI tools, which could hinder student autonomy (Lan et al. 2025; Wang et al. 2025). Educational institutions are increasingly allocating money to AI technology to boost access to personalized learning opportunities and improve academic performance (Vedapradha et al. 2024). Educational systems can autonomously evaluate written assignments, quizzes, and oral presentations. Consequently, the rapid feedback is essential to encouraging self-reflection and independent learning (Babashahi et al. 2024). AI technologies like ChatGPT allow HEIs to optimize enrollment procedures, enhance student services, and boost student retention, while also presenting challenges such as privacy issues, potential misuse, and the necessity for balanced regulation (Dempere et al. 2023; Chukwuere and Handoko 2024). Moreover, programs such as Grammarly and Turnitin enhance the growth of academic writing skills by augmenting the coherence and quality of written texts. AI has an influence on scholarly research, particularly when analyzing complex data sets (Dai et al. 2023).

The integration of AI into higher education is fraught with substantial obstacles, despite its numerous benefits. Privacy and data security are of the utmost importance, as the utilization of sophisticated algorithms necessitates the collection and processing of students' personal information (Mosly 2024). HEIs need to set strict rules to safeguard information and improve transparency in AI-driven decision-making processes. Furthermore, it is essential to provide equity and accessibility in the use of these instruments, thereby lowering discrimination brought on by low digital literacy or financial background (Babashahi et al. 2024). AI markedly improves talent development in HEIs, therefore offering outstanding potential. Personalized learning, immediate feedback, the development of transferable skills, and research assistance enable students to navigate their academic paths more efficiently and prepare for the labor market. The opportunity for AI to further advance exists through appropriate and inclusive integration. The specific impact of ChatGPT on student motivation, self-regulated learning (SRL), and need satisfaction is still unclear, and there is an urgent need for research on the most effective ways to use it in education (Chiu 2024).

Adaptability in the Digital World

Digital literacy is necessary for adjusting in the constantly evolving digital job market. Students who have solid Digital Literacy can more efficiently embrace new technologies and processes, leading to desirable employees (Spurava and Kotilainen 2023). Their ability to swiftly integrate new platforms and technologies enables them to maintain competitiveness in a dynamic job market. Digital literacy promotes a sustainable approach to learning, which is crucial for ongoing career advancement in an evolving digital environment (Spurava and Kotilainen 2023). This mindset enables them to remain informed about technology advancements and adjust their skills accordingly. Furthermore, digital literacy encompasses not just technological proficiency but also an awareness of the societal ramifications of technology and its effects on relationships, knowledge, and employment opportunities (Pegalajar Palomino and Rodríguez Torres 2024). This contextual information promotes adaptability, enabling students to foresee and react to emerging digital trends. Teamwork is ultimately a component of flexibility in Digital Literacy. Students who possess digital literacy can adapt to various digital collaboration environments, proficiently utilizing multiple tools and teams, and increasing productivity, regardless of their location or technological capabilities (Alneyadi et al. 2023).

Digital Collaboration Among Students

Digital literacy comprises the knowledge, skills, procedures, and competencies required to access, engage with, and comprehend information, facilitating the proficient use of digital technologies including applications, internet-enabled computers, and mobile devices (Beaunoyer et al. 2020). Digital literacy enables university students to actively engage in online learning groups, forums, and social media platforms, therefore promoting a cooperative culture lasting learning outside the traditional classroom. It also creates among them efficient digital collaboration. The accessibility with which ideas, tools, and good teamwork—which this connectedness helps to share—may be shared promotes better learning results. Furthermore, these platforms facilitate networking, peer mentorship, and collaborative learning, thereby enhancing the educational experience. Students with elevated digital literacy can execute digital communication processes, understand various cultural viewpoints, and engage respectfully and effectively with individuals from diverse backgrounds (Deja et al. 2024). This intercultural competence is essential in today's globalized world and enhances the quality and impact of digital collaboration. Digital collaboration tools allow students to efficiently share information, coordinate tasks, and seek help from peers and educators, which can enhance learning outcomes (Wolters and Brady 2021).

Critical Thinking and Digital Tools

Digital literacy involves a deeper understanding of how to critically interact with digital content, rather than only utilizing digital tools. Digitally literate students can more efficiently access, organize, and analyze material, resulting in a deeper comprehension of topics and enhanced argumentation skills (Panduwinata and Setiawati 2024). Digital literacy skills empower students to evaluate content, identify issues, and generate innovative concepts across many contexts, hence fostering critical thinking (Reddy et al. 2023). The acquirement of analytical skills, crucial for critical analysis and problem-solving, is associated with digital literacy (Tian et al. 2023). Access to information and collaborative online platforms promotes creative thinking and improves innovative solutions (Tchanda et al. 2024). Students can analyze trends, explore concepts, and enhance assignments efficiently using digital tools, promoting a creative education. Innovation depends on the capacity to critically assess facts, as it aids in differentiating between credible and non-credible knowledge while fostering an evidence-based approach to development. Additionally, digital literacy encourages experimentation, which is crucial for innovation (Wei 2023). This perspective advocates for adaptability and resilience, essential qualities in a constantly changing environment. Digital literacy enables students to disseminate ideas and participate globally, augmenting creativity and amplifying its impact.

SkillFusionLab

SkillFusionLab was founded in 2014 at the University of Molise (Italy) as a workshop under the Organizational Design course. This is an innovative program aimed at university students wanting to improve their soft skills (Das et al. 2024; Di Virgilio 2024).

The SkillFusionLab aims to prepare students to achieve success as managers in both public administration and private enterprises and to evolve into future entrepreneurs proficient in navigating a continuously dynamic work environment, enhancing employability skills. The digital era has improved educational opportunities by allowing students to access information and resources immediately (González-Rico and Lluch Sintes 2024). Thus, the lab focuses on team building and teamwork: students must collaborate to develop interdisciplinary solutions, integrate their knowledge, and solve complex problems. SkillFusionLab allows for combining individual tasks with collaborative dynamics, raising comparisons, the sharing of ideas, and collective growth—critical elements for the success of the project and essential preparation for the professional world. Students engaged in team projects in higher education institutions significantly increase their collaboration abilities, irrespective of their academic backgrounds (Di Virgilio 2024; Johnsen et al. 2024).

The project is intended for third-year undergraduates and graduates in Business Administration, Management, and Business Consulting. These students, having already acquired specialized skills during the initial years of their studies—commonly known as hard skills—now could further develop the transversal skills needed to tackle global challenges. In this way, SkillFusionLab fills the gap between theoretical knowledge and soft skills, preparing participants to succeed in complex and dynamic professional environments and facilitating their entry and success in the labor market while fostering a strong managerial and innovation culture (Das et al. 2024; Di Virgilio 2024). The challenge for students is that SkillFusionLab is part of curricular activities. Instead, extracurricular activities significantly enhance students' acquisition of soft skills (Feraco et al. 2023). In this way, students are encouraged to develop autonomous and strategic time management skills in daily activities and team projects. The digital collaboration during the lab is guaranteed using any online platform, project management software, and communication tools; all of these are powered by OpenAI tools. Thus, students can improve their organizational capabilities and efficiency. Additionally, students have the opportunity to participate in seminars with select guest experts, including managers and recruitment and assessment specialists, during the SkillFusionLab. These events provide students with the opportunity to observe the significant relevance of digital literacy and time management in modern work environments (Das et al. 2024; Di Virgilio 2024).

Every year, students study contemporary and pertinent management subjects, which enables them to investigate topics such as sustainability, management design, and organizational dynamics through real-world case studies related to the year's lab topic. This integration relates effortlessly with the objectives of SkillFusionLab, preparing students to become skilled professionals inside enterprises. The SkillFusionLab is built of various phases, each with different activities (Figure 2). There are three phases: (1) Kick-Off, (2) Action Stage, and (3) Final Audit. Each main phase consists of three steps.

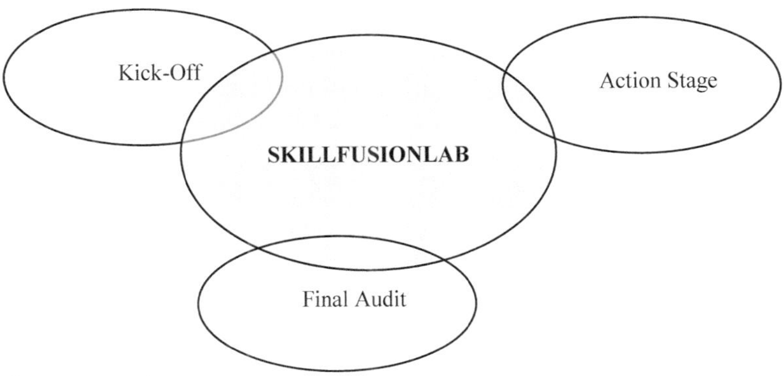

Figure 2. The SkillFusionLab structure. Source (s): Authors' own work.

Kick-Off

The Kick-off phase, the initial stage of the SkillFusionLab, provides students with the concept that will direct their project efforts. The project objectives are delineated, and the anticipated deliverables and dates are defined. From the outset, time management is emphasized to ensure that goals are accomplished within the designated timeframe. During the kick-off, the students who participated in the SkillFusionLab received all necessary information and details about the project topic and the project expectations, which were aligned among all participants and the criteria for project evaluation. This alignment is crucial for establishing a shared base to guide team members in their subsequent analysis, implementation, and collaboration phases.

In this phase, the roles and responsibilities of team members are defined, and the course's professor creates a climate of trust and, in general, a favorable environment for open communication. The professor's role includes guiding the project, providing necessary resources, and facilitating discussions. Thus, teams are well-equipped, and this environment will help address any challenges during the project.

The Kick-off phase offers the initial input and establishes a clear structure, allowing teams to start with a shared vision and a well-organized scheme for the upcoming phases. The Kick-Off phase includes (1.1) Instruction and tools, (1.2) Team building, and (1.3) Gathering online information. All these steps are completed in one week.

1.1 Instruction and tools: The leader (the professor of the course) provides all information about the topic of the project work, for example, "People first" and "Talent acquisition," and gives the "Best practices," supported by digital tools like AI to collect data for the chosen case study (other tools: AI, Google Sources, direct contacts, etc.).

1.2 Team building: Students are divided into teams, with the selection of team members being free (the teams include no more than five students). The objective is to establish efficient teams that can jointly and strategically tackle project work, ensuring an ideal allocation of roles and responsibilities to achieve the defined objectives. Specific responsibilities are assigned to each member. The leader encourages teams to start brainstorming sessions and share ideas and strategies. This collaborative class atmosphere promotes team cohesion and knowledge sharing. The structure of feedback sessions maximizes the contributions of all members and creates a solid foundation for successful project execution.

1.3 Gathering online data: Teams start developing initial ideas for the project. In this stage, students engage the initial digital strategy: teams may employ internet resources to gather pertinent information and investigate their selected subjects comprehensively. Furthermore, they begin utilizing digital planners, instruments that facilitate the efficient organization of incoming tasks, allocation of responsibilities, and monitoring of progress, as well as platforms for online collaboration. The final step in the Kick-Off enhances digital literacy competencies. It facilitates the development of other key skills, including time management and teamwork, and promotes engagement and cooperation among all team members. University students obtaining education-related degrees recognize the importance of training in OpenAI tools, which can augment motivation and positively impact the cultivation of generic abilities (Cebrián Cifuentes et al. 2024). OpenAI Tools may act as a virtual assistant, offering on-demand elucidations, responding to inquiries, and providing legal counsel on a variety of academic subjects (Farrokhnia et al. 2024). These tools have the potential to facilitate communication between educators and students, thereby promoting the development of innovative methods to enhance the teaching-learning process (Lozano and Blanco Fontao 2023).

Action Stage

During the operational phase, known as the Action Stage, the teams implement all the strategies they have devised in accordance with their project. Each team delineates distinct duties for its members, facilitating collaboration to attain the project's objectives. In this phase, the teams have to collaborate to implement the planned activities and to transform the idea and the strategies into concrete actions. Moreover, the team may need to modify the original plan and strategies in response to new information that is discovered online and/or unanticipated challenges. Teams must be adaptable in response to these requirements.

The project's success depends on how effectively the team senses challenges and achieves the established goals. This phase requires many skills, including collaboration (for the project work), time management (aligned with deadlines), decision-making (for any issue), and problem-solving activities (to achieve goals). Furthermore, self-management is vital for the project's success because it enables students to manage their time efficiently, organize their activities, and prioritize their tasks, ultimately boosting their teamwork's overall effectiveness.

The Action Stage is the heart of the lab experience and fills the gap between the theoretical plan and practical work. It is an opportunity to complete a project and a crucial phase for developing students' professional and personal skills, preparing them to tackle future challenges with greater boldness and competence.

The Action Stage represents the core phase of the entire lab, during which teams engage in (2.1) Project development, (2.2) Preparation of the presentation, and (2.3) the presentation of the project work. This phase utilizes the remaining time allocated over the two months.

2.1 Project development: The project is developed through collaboration among the teams, which capitalizes on concepts that arose during the kick-off phase. The topic initiative is typically based on the selection of local and non-local companies. Each member team must leverage their unique skills for the planning and organization of activities. Additionally, a set of digital tools is the base for enabling real-time collaboration and document sharing. Additionally, the quality of the final output is enhanced by the accessibility of constructive information, case studies, and resources through online research platforms. Teams may integrate data processing into their work, contingent upon the project's progression. This work necessitates the acquisition and refinement of skills in the use of software for data processing and the potential for statistical analysis. This will involve the use of digital tools such as Python, Excel, R, and OpenAI tools (such as ChatGPT and DeepSeek).

2.2 Presentation preparation: The required output is a video of up to seven minutes. Teams have to translate the developed ideas into both oral and visual formats. This stage involves utilizing presentation software, enabling students to learn how to synthesize information clearly and concisely while adhering to established time limits. Additionally, the official language is English. Thus, the video's audio must be in English, enabling students to improve their language skills and time management skills, which are essential in the job market, especially for those aspiring to managerial roles.

2.3 Presentation of the project work: The last step has significance in the acquisition of essential skills, such as the effective use of digital and OpenAI tools and communication. This is the most critical moment, during which teams are afforded the opportunity to present and exhibit their project work to a committee of project management professionals. The project must provide an organized overview of the work that is relevant to the subject matter, emphasizing the project's value and the skills that were acquired. Each team member is afforded the chance to contribute, which aids in the development of a shared comprehension of the subject matter. Students can further develop their digital skills by acquiring the ability to edit videos and employ specific software to produce a high-quality final product through the use of video technology.

Final Audit

The last week dedicated to the SkillFusionLab focuses on the Final Audit phase, which involves (3.1) the evaluation of the projects, (3.2) the identification of the winning team, and (3.3) the assessment of skills acquired throughout both the course and the SkillFusionLab. The Final Audit is a crucial phase of the SkillFusionLab, where the team's work is evaluated, and the achievement of the training objectives is measured. This phase marks the lab's conclusion and is partly connected to the presentation of the project works. Figure 3 provides an overview of the main phases of the SkillFusionLab framework.

3.1 Evaluation of the projects: As mentioned above, the committee analyzes the various videos in detail during the presentations. The Final Audit is not limited to judging the final project; the objective is to highlight the skills that students have developed during the course. This moment is fundamental for reviewing applied knowledge and skill development, such as digital tools, teamwork, problem-solving, and self-management.

3.2 Identification of the winning team: The evaluation committee (the Leader, PhD student, Researcher, and Expert in Project Management) analyzes every aspect of the project, considering not only the result but also the development process, originality of ideas, the digital tools used, and the quality of the presentation. During this step, the winning team is identified based on their ability to combine creativity, technical skills, and presentation abilities (clearly and persuasively communicating). The competition among the teams motivates students to perform at their best and engage constructively, preparing them to handle similar challenges in professional contexts.

3.3 Assessment of skills acquired throughout and the SkillFusionLab: The final step of the SkillFusionLab focuses on measuring the skills students have acquired throughout the lab using the direct observation method. This phase evaluates the final project results and the students' behaviors during the

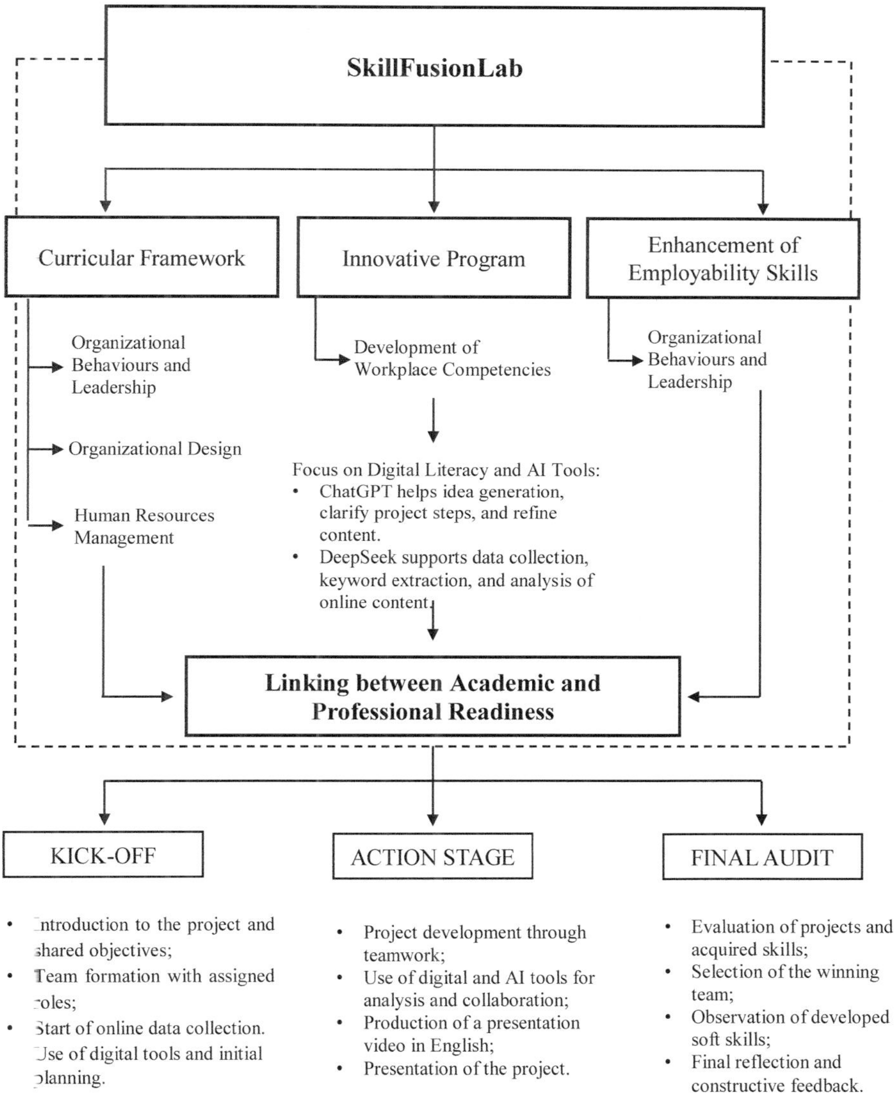

Figure 3. Resume of SkillFusionLab. Source (s): Authors' own work.

experience lab. Students are evaluated on many different skills that they acquire during the SkillFusionLab, such as their capacity to effectively collaborate in groups, manage time, solve problems, and utilize digital technologies. The work environment places a high value on soft skills, including adaptability, leadership, and communication, in addition to technical skills. The final skill assessment step allows students to have a clear vision: each student will know their strengths (in terms of soft skills) and the areas that, on the contrary, need greater attention and further development. Furthermore, this evaluation process encourages students to think critically about their performance. The constructive feedback received promotes personal improvement, contributing to growth in future employability in the world of work. Indeed, the Final Audit offers the students a valuable opportunity to reflect on their SkillFusionLab experience.

Theoretical and Practical Implications

The introduction of a university laboratory, such as the SkillFusionLab, focused on the development of digital literacy through AI tools and project work on organizational design issues, can yield both practical implications in HEIs.

The suggested methodology integrates SRL for enhancing employability skills and professional readiness (Rashidi et al. 2023). SkillFusionLab and other programs broaden the ideas of SRL beyond educational contexts, highlighting transversal abilities that link fundamental competences to professional achievement (Hussain et al. 2024). This methodology highlights the importance of digital literacy and OpenAI Tools for professional readiness, while simultaneously stressing the essential role of soft skills in HEIs.

SkillFusionLab enhances academic literature by demonstrating how experiential learning fosters employability skills and autonomy through practical, reflective exercises. It adapts SRL to career development, emphasizing AI tools as a mediator between digital literacy and career success. Key soft skills—adaptability, digital collaboration, and problem-solving—are shown to be essential for job market access.

The SkillFusionLab methodology can be used by HEIs to better match their curricula with labor market requirements. Focusing on modules like digital literacy allows targeted development of Adaptability, Digital Collaboration and Critical Thinking skills. HEIs can use the model to create tailored experiential learning programs, such as workshops, online courses, or simulations, to build job-relevant competencies. This hands-on learning approach enables students to manage projects, meet deadlines, and use digital tools—all critical skills for corporate environments. It cultivates expertise in work management, delegation, and productivity tools, hence improving digital literacy and reducing the gap between knowledge and skills.

Conclusion and Future Research

This chapter examined how SRL drives a SkillFusionLab framework that merges digital literacy and OpenAI technologies to enhance soft skills. Programs such as SkillFusionLab assist students in acquiring vital digital competencies required for success in the contemporary job market. HEIs can utilize this concept to develop educational trajectories that equip students for evolving professional landscapes. Future research should empirically validate the hypothesis by collecting longitudinal data on the impact of digital literacy on the enhancement of soft skills and employability. Future studies may examine the impact of flexibility and digital cooperation on personalized training programs. Understanding the most effective SRL components in digital contexts may lead to more accurately tailored interventions. Assessing digital literacy as an essential competency in the job market and examining its impact on career adaptability may yield insights into long-term career advancement and resilience, highlighting the importance of soft skills for enduring professional success amid the continuously changing labor market challenges.

References

Adiguzel, T., Kaya, M. and Cansu, F. 2023. Revolutionizing education with AI: exploring the transformative potential of ChatGPT. Contemp. Educ. Technol. 15(3).

Alneyadi, S., Abulibdeh, E. and Wardat, Y. 2023. The impact of digital environment vs. traditional method on literacy skills: reading and writing of Emirati fourth graders. Sustainability 15(4): 3418.

Aničić, K. P. and Bušelić, V. 2020. Importance of generic skills of ICT graduates—Employers, teaching staff, and students perspective. IEEE Trans Educ. 64(3): 245–252.

Antoniuk, L. and Zasiadivko, V. 2023. Digital literacy and technologies for education: Principles and tools. Grail Sci. 26: 249–252.

Ateş Akdeniz, A. 2023. Exploring the impact of self-regulated learning intervention on students' strategy use and performance in a design studio course. Int. J. Technol. Des. Educ. 33: 1923–1957.

Babashahi, L., Barbosa, C. E., Lima, Y., Lyra, A., Salazar, H., Argôlo, M. et al. 2024. AI in the workplace: A systematic review of skill transformation in the industry. Adm. Sci. 14(6): 127.

Beaunoyer, E., Dupéré, S. and Guitton, M. J. 2020. COVID-19 and digital inequalities: reciprocal impacts and mitigation strategies. Comput. Hum. Behav. 111: 106424.

Bhattacharya, K., Bhattacharya, A. S., Bhattacharya, N., Yagnik, V. D., Garg, P. and Kumar, S. 2023. ChatGPT in surgical practice—a new kid on the block. Indian J. Surg. 85(6): 1346–1349.

Boulahmel, A., Djelil, F., Smits, G. 2025. Investigating self-regulated learning measurement based on trace data: A systematic literature review. Technol. Knowl. Learn. 30: 119–156. https://doi.org/10.1007/s10758-025-09816-y.

Cebrián Cifuentes, S., Guerrero Valverde, E. and Checa Caballero, S. 2024. The vision of University students from the educational field in the integration of ChatGPT. Digital. 4(3): 648–659.

Chiu, T. K. 2024. A classification tool to foster self-regulated learning with generative artificial intelligence by applying self-determination theory: a case of ChatGPT. Educational Technology Research and Development 72: 2401–2416.

Chukwuere, J. E. and Handoko, B. L. 2024. The future of generative AI chatbots in higher education. J. Emerg. Technol. 4(1): 36–44.

Clarke, M. 2018. Rethinking graduate employability: The role of capital, individual attributes and context. Stud. High Educ. 43(11): 1923–1937.

Dai, Y., Lai, S., Lim, C. P. and Liu, A. 2023. ChatGPT and its impact on research supervision: Insights from Australian postgraduate research students. Australas J. Educ. Technol. 39(4): 74–88.

Das, S., Di Virgilio, F., Ianiro, G. and Puccio, A. 2024. Empowering entrepreneurial skills by Contamination Lab experience in higher education institutions. *In*: Gomes, O., Lins de Moraes, M. and Fagandini, P. (eds.). The Agent ID Model: A Multidisciplinary Framework of Evolutionary Human Behavior. Cham (CH): Springer Nature.

Deja M., Bobkowski, P., Huvila, I. and Mierzecka, A. 2024. Empowering through digital skills: a case of alumni in the business services sector. J. Assoc. Inf. Sci. Technol.

Dempere, J., Modugu, K., Hesham, A. and Ramasamy, L. K. 2023. The impact of ChatGPT on higher education. Front Educ. 8: 1206936.

Di Virgilio, F. 2024. Competence and soft skills in higher education – Innovation in evaluating the learning outcomes of university students: The TECO Project. pp. 215–220. *In*: de Bem Machado, A., Sousa, M. J., Dal Mas, F., Secinaro, S. and Calandra, D. (eds.). Digital Transformation in Higher Education Institutions. Cham (CH): Springer.

Drajati, N. A. and Putra, K. A. (eds.). 2022. Teacher education and teacher professional development in the COVID-19 turn: Proceedings of the International Conference on Teacher Training and Education (ICTTE 2021), Surakarta, Indonesia, August 25–26, 2021. Taylor & Francis.

Dumitru, D. and Halpern, D. F. 2023. Critical thinking: Creating job-proof skills for the future of work. J. Intell. 11: 194.

Esnaashari, S., Gardner, L. A., Arthanari, T. S. and Rehm, M. 2023. Unfolding self-regulated learning profiles of students: A longitudinal study. J. Comput. Assist. Learn. 39: 1116–1131.

Farrokhnia, M., Banihashem, S. K., Noroozi, O. and Wals, A. 2024. A SWOT analysis of ChatGPT: Implications for educational practice and research. Innov Educ Teach Int. 61(3): 460–474.

Faza, A. and Lestari, I. 2025. Self-regulated learning in the digital age: A systematic review of strategies, technologies, benefits, and challenges. Int. Rev. Res. Open Distrib. Learn. https://doi.org/10.19173/irrodl.v26i2.8119.

Feraco, T., Resnati, D., Fregonese, D., Spoto, A. and Meneghetti, C. 2023. An integrated model of school students' academic achievement and life satisfaction. Linking soft skills, extracurricular activities, self-regulated learning, motivation, and emotions. Eur. J. Psychol. Educ. 38(1): 109–130.

González-Rico, P. and Lluch Sintes, M. 2024. Empowering soft skills through artificial intelligence and personalised mentoring. Educ Sci. 14(7).

Healy, M., Hammer, S. and McIlveen, P. 2022. Mapping graduate employability and career development in higher education research: A citation network analysis. Stud High Educ. 47(4): 799–811.

Hussain, S., Soni, G. and Shah, F. A. 2024. Soft skills and interpersonal skills for tourism and hospitality industry. *In*: Sharma, A. (ed.). Int Handb Skill Educ Learn Res Dev Tour Hosp. Singapore: Springer.

Huzooree, G. and Soupramanien, L. D. B. 2025. Empowering students for the 21st century through digital literacy. pp. 161–200. *In*: Huzooree, A. and Chandan, H. (eds.). Revitalizing Student Skills for Workforce Preparation. IGI Global.

Imjai, N., Aujirapongpan, S. and Yaacob, Z. 2024. Impact of logical thinking skills and digital literacy on Thailand's Generation Z accounting students' internship effectiveness: Role of self-learning capability. Int. J. Educ. Res. Open. 6: 100329.

Jackson, D. and Bridgstock, R. 2021. What actually works to enhance graduate employability? The relative value of curricular, co-curricular, and extra-curricular learning and paid work. High Educ. 81(4): 723–739.

Johnsen, M. M. W., Sjølie, E. and Johansen, V. 2024. Learning to collaborate in a project-based graduate course: A multilevel study of student outcomes. Res. High Educ. 65(3): 439–462.

Kaputa, V., Loučanová, E. and Tejerina-Gaite, F. A. 2022. Digital transformation in higher education institutions as a driver of social-oriented innovations. Soc. Innov. High. Educ. 61: 81–85.

Kee, D..M..H., Anwar, A., Gwee, S. L. and Ijaz, M. F. 2023. Impact of acquisition of digital skills on perceived employability of youth: Mediating role of course quality. Information 14(42): 42.

Kharroubi, S. and ElMediouni, A. 2024. Conceptual review: Cultivating learner autonomy through self-directed learning & self-regulated learning: A socio-constructivist exploration. Int. J. Lang. Lit. Stud. 6: 276–296.

Lan, M. and Zhou, X. 2025. A qualitative systematic review on AI empowered self-regulated learning in higher education. npj Sci. Learn. 10(1): 21.

Lozano, A. and Blanco Fontao, C. 2023. Is the education system prepared for the irruption of artificial intelligence? A study on the perceptions of students of primary education degree from a dual perspective: Current pupils and future teachers. Educ. Sci. 13(7): 733.

Moore, T. and Morton, J. 2017. The myth of job readiness? Written communication, employability, and the "skills gap" in higher education. Stud. High Educ. 42(3): 591–609.

Mosly, I. 2024. Artificial intelligence's opportunities and challenges in engineering curricular design: a combined review and focus group study. Societies 14(6): 89.

Murtadho, M. I., Rohmah, R. Y., Jamilah, Z. and Furqon, M. 2023. The role of digital literacy in improving students' competence in digital era. Al-Wijdān J. Islam Educ. Stud. 8(2): 253–260.

Na, C., Jeong, S., Clarke-Midura, J. and Shin, Y. 2024. Linking self-regulated learning to community of inquiry in massive open online courses: A person-centered approach. Educ. Technol. Res. Dev.

Panduwinata, L. and Setiawati, F. 2024. Digital literacy's influence on critical thinking skills of office administration education students at UNESA. J. Simki Pedagogia.

Pegalajar Palomino, M. d. C. and Rodríguez Torres, Á. F. 2024. Digital literacy in university students of education degrees in Ecuador. Front. Educ. 8: 1299059.

Picco, E., Gragnano, A., Daghini, A. and Miglioretti, M. 2022. Systematic review of intervention studies to foster sustainable employability core components: Implications for workplace promotion. Sustainability 14(6): 3300.

Rashidi, S. N., Abd Majid, F. and Hashim, H. 2023. Exploring the mediating role of students' satisfaction towards personal record building in the influence of self-regulated learning strategies on employability skills. Asian J. Univ. Educ. 19(4): 676–689.

Reddy, P., Chaudhary, K. and Hussein, S. 2023. A digital literacy model to narrow the digital literacy skills gap. Heliyon 9: e14878.

Rizun, N., Ryzhkova, H., Pawlyszyn, I. and Alexopoulos, C. 2024. Employment of university graduates in the era of digitalization and artificial intelligence: Challenges and prospects. pp. 1037–1039. *In*: Proc 25th Annu Int. Conf. Digit. Gov. Res.

Römgens, I., Scoupe, R. and Beausaert, S. 2020. Unraveling the concept of employability: Bringing together research on employability in higher education and the workplace. Stud. High Educ. 45(12): 2588–2603.

Silva, L., Mendes, A., Gomes, A. and Fortes, G. 2024. What learning strategies are used by programming students? A qualitative study grounded on the self-regulation of learning theory. ACM Trans. Comput. Educ. 24: 1–36.

Small, L., Shacklock, K. and Marchant, T. 2018. Employability: A contemporary review for higher education stakeholders. J. Vocat. Educ. Train. 70(1): 148–166.

Soliman, M., Di Virgilio, F., Figueiredo, R. and Sousa, M. J. 2021. The impact of workplace spirituality on lecturers' attitudes in tourism and hospitality higher education institutions. Tour. Manag. Perspect. 38: 100826.

Soliman, M., Sinha, R., Di Virgilio, F., Sousa, M. J. and Figueiredo, R. 2023. Emotional intelligence outcomes in higher education institutions: Empirical evidence from a Western context. Psychol. Rep. 00332941231197165.

Spurava, S. and Kotilainen, S. 2023. Digital literacy as a pathway to professional development in the algorithm-driven world: A case study. Nord. J. Digit. Lit. 18: 47–60.

Tchanda, C. T., Zohaib, H. S., Mpolomoka, D. L., Akpan, W. M. and Mainde, D. 2024. Curriculum design for the digital age: strategies for effective technology integration in higher education. Int. J. Res. 11(7): 185–201.

Teng, W., Ma, C., Pahlevansharif, S. and Turner, J. J. 2019. Graduate readiness for the employment market of the 4th industrial revolution: The development of soft employability skills. Educ. Train. 61(5): 590–604.

Tian, X., Park, K. and Liu, Q. 2023. Deep learning influences on higher education students' digital literacy: the mediating role of higher-order thinking. Int. J. Eng. Pedagog. 13: 33–49. https://doi.org/10.3991/ijep.v13i6.38177.

Van Laar, E., Van Deursen, A. J. A. M., Van Dijk, J. A. G. M. and De Haan, J. 2017. The relation between 21st-century skills and digital skills: A systematic literature review. Comput. Hum. Behav. 72: 577–588.

Vedapradha, R., Hariharan, R., Sudha, E. and Divyashree, V. 2024. Artificial intelligence–talent acquisition in HEIs recruitments. Int. J. Inf. Learn Technol. [ahead-of-print].

Wang, K., Cui, W. and Yuan, X. 2025. Artificial intelligence in higher education: The impact of need satisfaction on artificial intelligence literacy mediated by self-regulated learning strategies. Behav Sci. 15(2): 165.

Wei, Z. 2023. Navigating digital learning landscapes: unveiling the interplay between learning behaviors, digital literacy, and educational outcomes. J. Knowl. Econ. 1–31.

Wolters, C. A. and Brady, A. C. 2021. College students' time management: a self-regulated learning perspective. Educ. Psychol. Rev. 33(4): 1319–1351.

Yun, H., Song, H. and Kim, Y. 2024. Identifying university students' online self-regulated learning profiles: predictors, outcomes, and differentiated instructional strategies. Eur. J. Psychol. Educ. https://doi.org/10.1007/s10212-024-00907-5.

Yupelmi, M., Giatman, M. and Syah, N. 2024. Transformation of students' career orientation in the era of artificial intelligence: A systematic literature review. Indones J. Comput. Sci. 13(3).

Zimmerman, B. J. 2002. Becoming a self-regulated learner: An overview. Theory Into Practice 41: 64–70.

Chapter 2

Exploring the Pathway towards Innovation

A Meta-Synthesis of Artificial Intelligence (AI) Adoption within the Public Sector

Simona Mormile,[1,*] *Roberta Romano,*[2] *Gabriella Piscopo*[3] and *Paola Adinolfi*[4]

Introduction

Artificial intelligence (AI) refers to the simulation of human intelligence in machines that are programmed to think, learn, and solve problems. AI involves the development of computer systems or algorithms that can perform tasks typically requiring human intelligence, such as understanding natural language, recognizing patterns, making decisions, and solving complex problems (Zhang and Lu 2021). AI systems are designed to analyze data, adapt to new information, and continuously improve their performance (Woschank et al. 2020). AI research has been ongoing for more than

[1] Research Fellow, Department of Business Studies – Management & Innovation Systems, University of Salerno, Fisciano, Italy.
[2] Ph.D. Student, Department of Business Studies – Management & Innovation Systems, University of Salerno, Fisciano, Italy.
[3] Associate Professor, Department of Business Studies – Management & Innovation Systems, University of Salerno, Fisciano, Italy.
[4] Full Professor, Department of Business Studies – Management & Innovation Systems, University of Salerno, Fisciano, Italy.
Emails: robromano@unisa.it, gpiscopo@unisa.it, padinolfi@unisa.it
* Corresponding author: smormile@unisa.it

DOI: 10.1201/9781003535393-2

65 years and has achieved significant milestones in both theoretical exploration and practical implementations (Jiang et al. 2022).

While there are different categorizations of AI systems based on their capabilities and functionalities, they all share some common features (Borges et al. 2021; Gupta et al. 2021): (i) learning (they can learn from data and improve their performance over time); (ii) adaptation (they can adapt to changing environments or new data); (iii) reasoning (they can use logic and rules to make informed decisions and solve complex problems); (iv) problem-solving (they can tackle complex problem-solving tasks, including optimization problems, planning, and decision-making in dynamic environment); (v) perception (they can sense and interpret their environment through, e.g., cameras, microphones, or other data sources); (vi) natural language processing (they can understand, interpret, and generate human language); (vii) autonomy (they can make decisions and take actions without human intervention); and (viii) decision-making (they can make decisions based on data and predefined rules or criteria).

AI technologies are applicable in a variety of fields, ranging from finance (Goodell et al. 2021; Milana and Ashta 2021) and manufacturing (Arinez et al. 2020; Lee et al. 2018) to agriculture (Eli-Chukwu 2019; Jha et al. 2019) and education (Chen et al. 2020). AI's adaptability and capacity to process vast amounts of data make it a transformative force across these different sectors, offering the potential for increased productivity, cost savings, and improved decision-making. Given these extraordinary potential advantages, there has been a significant surge in AI advancement driven by large investments by technology giants like Amazon, Google, Facebook, and Microsoft (Horvitz 2016; Kejriwal 2022).

However, although AI technology has received considerable interest in some subject areas, the same cannot be said with respect to the public sector (Aoki 2020; Wirtz et al. 2019). A common definition of AI in science remains lacking (Scherer 2015), and few studies analyze which aspects of this technology can be applied to the public sector. Although there are interesting contributions to this topic, the public sector currently shows little theoretical propensity with reference to AI (Mergel et al. 2023). The literature is largely silent on the challenges of AI associated with the public sector, and a consensus on how to address these challenges in the future has not been reached (Wirtz et al. 2020). Furthermore, an area requiring further research is that of understanding the factors influencing AI adoption in the public sector (Zhang et al. 2021). Another gap in the AI literature concerns research on qualitative approaches (Tangi et al. 2023), which are needed because AI is still in an early stage and thus requires further study on the underlying processes (Wirtz et al. 2021). Therefore, it is critical to promote new empirical research, especially qualitative research, to create a virtuous collaboration between academics and practitioners (van Noordt and Misuraca 2022).

Our study aims at understanding the multiple facets involved in public organizations' adoption of AI technologies. Using a meta-synthesis of qualitative research, we selected 24 qualitative studies with the aim of exploring the impact of artificial intelligence (AI) adoption in public sector organizations by focusing on the factors and challenges that influence its utilization. This meta-synthesis contributes to the existing literature in at least three ways. First, since there are not many studies investigating the topic of AI adoption within the public sector, despite the perceived need for such work (Sun and Medaglia 2019; Wirtz et al. 2019), this study seeks to emphasize the importance of this emerging technology for public organizations, so as to get a more complete view of the phenomenon. Moreover, it may be extremely interesting to increase the number of studies that map the challenges of AI within the public sector (Mutawa and Rashid 2020; Susar and Aquaro 2019), as well as the main barriers that could limit its adoption and usage (Zuiderwijk et al. 2021). Finally, it is critically important to provide an overview of the AI phenomenon, addressing the questions of why and how AI is (or is not) adopted by public organizations (Gesk and Leyer 2022), to shed light on this critical issue that remains to be explored in the public sector. In sum, this study supplements the knowledge generated by the quantitative meta-analysis of AI and enriches the literature with a process view on AI adoption in public sector organizations.

Literature Review

The concept of employing computers to replicate intelligent behavior and critical thinking was first proposed by Alan Turing in 1950 in his work titled "Computing Machinery and Intelligence" (Ramesh et al. 2004). Turing introduced a simple test, subsequently recognized as the "Turing test", designed to assess the potential of computers to exhibit human-like intelligence (Kaul et al. 2020). Six years later, John McCarty first coined the term "artificial intelligence", defining it as "the science and engineering of creating intelligent machines" (Haenlein and Kaplan 2019). McCarty proposed the concept during an academic conference held at Dartmouth University, giving birth to the AI scientific field (Zhang and Lu 2021). From 1956 to today, AI has evolved to encompass a broad range of applications and has attracted increasing attention from researchers and practitioners from various fields and countries.

Although originally conceived as the simple theory of human intelligence being exhibited by machines (Helm et al. 2020), AI is now recognized as a multidisciplinary form of technology with the capability of integrating cognition, machine learning, emotion recognition, human–computer interaction, data storage, and decision-making (Lu 2019; Wirtz et al. 2021). Today, AI is making an increasingly profound impact on human life and is considered the cornerstone of technology in the contemporary era and beyond (Jiang et al. 2022).

The rapid evolution of AI in recent years has significantly impacted various fields, including the public sector (Zhang and Lu 2021). Therefore, to obtain benefits in the provision of public services, public organizations have significantly increased their adoption of AI-based systems (de Sousa et al. 2019; Vatamanu and Tofan 2025). Indeed, the adoption of AI within the public sector, traditionally characterized by its bureaucratic procedures and hierarchical structures, is likely to enhance government effectiveness and efficiency as well as citizens' satisfaction. Moreover, AI-driven innovations have the potential to facilitate connectivity and interactivity while simultaneously reducing administrative burdens (Moon 2002). Therefore, this unprecedented revolution underscores the importance of understanding the factors driving the adoption of AI within the public sector, as well as the challenges and opportunities that lie ahead (Alhosan and Alhashmi 2024).

A growing number of scholars have recently focused on the application of AI in the public sector (Criado et al. 2025; Mergel et al. 2023; Tangi et al. 2023; Wirtz et al. 2019). For instance, AI has been recognized as a strategic tool for supporting public organizations and for reducing processing time, as well as for minimizing workload and improving workflow (Wirtz et al. 2020). AI also has the potential to provide substantial benefits to public organizations and public value to citizens, in terms of efficiency and effectiveness in service delivery and policymaking (Medaglia and Tang 2022). Mehr (2017) emphasized benefits arising from task automation and employee empowerment through the recommendations of AI systems. Madan and Ashok (2023) provided a systematic literature review to identify factors influencing AI adoption and diffusion within the public sector. Regarding public policy issues related to AI technology, Tang and Wen (2009) highlight how AI systems can support predictive models to minimize damage and casualties from natural disasters. Despite these significant benefits, however, Wirtz et al. (2020) pointed out the risk associated with AI implementation in the public sector in terms of data privacy and security, workforce replacement, and ethical problems.

In this growing body of literature, research on AI adoption in the public sector using qualitative methods is underrepresented (Hogg et al. 2023), despite the fact that early studies were primarily qualitative. The complexity surrounding the AI implementation within the public sector requires a better understanding of the interactions between public organizations, social processes, and contextual conditions that shape implementation. Therefore, qualitative research offers a valuable approach to studying this topic, because it allows research communities to investigate the relationship between social processes and the contextual factors that shape the implementation of change (Febiri and Hub 2021), and it allows for greater variety compared to quantitative research (Cheek et al. 2004). For instance, qualitative research may center on evaluating the emotional and behavioral consequences of AI on employees, whereas quantitative investigations might concentrate on quantifiable factors associated with particular AI adoption scenarios.

In other words, qualitative studies aim to investigate the motivations, reasons, viewpoints, and behaviors of individuals, whereas quantitative studies examine predetermined variables for empirical testing (Neuman 2006). As these distinct methodologies aim to address distinct research inquiries, both types are needed to gain a full picture of the scope and impact of AI, as well as the extent of its potential with respect to the public sector (Wirtz et al. 2019), regarding which there seems to be a discrepancy between literature and practice (Tangi et al. 2023).

To address these gaps in the literature while responding to calls from scholars (Veale et al. 2018), this study aims at expanding the knowledge about AI through a meta-synthesis of 24 qualitative studies analyzing the factors influencing AI adoption in the public sector.

Method

To understand and describe key and recurring insights and topics about the implementation of AI within the public sector, we conducted a meta-synthesis of qualitative evidence (Hoon 2013; Walsh and Downe 2005). Similar to a meta-analysis, a meta-synthesis involves systematically analyzing and combining results from multiple studies to identify common themes, patterns, or concepts across a body of research (Finfgeld-Connett 2018). However, unlike a meta-analysis, which combines data from different studies to evaluate an overall effect, a meta-synthesis develops and expands the results by evaluating the uniqueness of a study within a comprehensive and interpretive whole (Clemmens 2003). It is a valuable approach for integrating diverse qualitative research findings and can be particularly useful in fields where a comprehensive understanding of complex phenomena is necessary. It helps to uncover deeper insights, identify gaps in existing research, and inform future research directions (Zimmer 2006). Our methodological approach was based on five sequential steps explained in detail in the following subsections.

Formulating the Research Question

Based on the reference literature on AI adoption in the public sector, we set up a meta-synthesis of the qualitative research that could provide insights into the factors influencing public organizations' AI adoption. We therefore guided the meta-synthesis using the following research question: How do public sector organizations navigate the challenges and opportunities of AI adoption, and what factors determine its successful implementation?

Locating Relevant Research

The second step involved identifying studies that may be considered relevant to our meta-synthesis through a computerized search using Scopus, one of the largest and most widely used databases among researchers (Singh et al. 2021). This study was conducted using specific search terms and considered all publications on AI in the public sector from the beginning of research in the field up to February 24, 2025, when the data search was carried out.

In particular, compound concepts consisting of two words were enclosed in quotation marks to preserve the combined meaning of the terms. To refine the search, we used Boolean operators: the "AND" operator was used between two words, fields, or values to retrieve documents containing both terms or values, rather than just one. Similarly, the "OR" operator was applied to capture any of the given concepts.

To improve the completeness of the query, we incorporated several synonyms, ensuring the retrieval of documents dealing with the same topic but using different terminology. This approach was essential to avoid the risk of excluding relevant content due to overly specific search parameters. In the field of titles, abstracts, and keywords on Scopus, we employed the following search string: ("Artificial intelligence" OR "AI") AND ("Public sector" OR "Public administration" OR "Government organization" OR "Public service" OR "Public organization" OR "E-Government" OR "Electronic government" OR "Smart government") AND ("Qualitative study" OR "Case study" OR "Interview" OR "Focus group" OR "Literature review" OR "Ethnography"). This query yielded 48.736 documents.

Determining Inclusion/Exclusion Criteria

Although a meta-synthesis should be comprehensive and include as many studies as possible (Kisamore and Brannick 2008), we planned to focus only on open access published articles in English. This choice provides scientific rigor, as peer-reviewed publication processes provide at least one benchmark to which to adhere when selecting articles (Hoon 2013). In addition, we excluded categories unrelated to the objective of this study, such as mathematics, medicine, and energy. Instead, we included the following subject areas: business, management and accounting; social sciences; economics, econometrics and finance; decision sciences; psychology; and multidisciplinary studies. Also on Scopus, we limited the search to the following keywords: "Artificial Intelligence", "Digital Transformation", "Public Sector", "Public Health", "Public Administration", "Digital Government", "Government", "E-government", "Digitization", "Human Resource Management", "Management Practice", "Theoretical Study", "Case Studies".
Application of these criteria returned 2.246 documents.

Then, we applied the following inclusion criteria to ensure that the sample of articles used for the analysis was appropriate: (i) the main theme of the study related to AI adoption within the public sector, and the study included (ii) a qualitative research design with data collected from focus groups, interviews, observations, or narrative approaches; (iii) a clear description of the method of analysis; (iv) the use of primary data; (v) an appropriate and justified qualitative approach; (vi) clearly stated research questions; (vii) a clear description of the study context; and (viii) a clear description of the sampling method and the data collection. After an initial screening of titles and abstracts, we found 1649 studies to be false positives, since AI was not their main topic of investigation (e.g., AI was used to explain results). Next, after obtaining the studies' full-text versions, all authors independently reviewed all the papers and together reached a final agreement on the dataset for this study, excluding studies if they were quantitative (n = 324); failed to state the research method or the theoretical framework (n = 90); were not focused on the public sector (n = 77); did not provide an adequate description of the research question (n = 32), the appropriateness of the qualitative methodology (n = 19), or the role of the researcher (n = 5); or did not use purposefully collected data (instead using, e.g., existing data that functioned as an illustrative example) (n = 26). After all the studies were read in their entirety, 24 of them met all the inclusion criteria and were ultimately incorporated into the meta-synthesis (Table 1).

Table 1. Details of studies selected for meta-synthesis.

Authors	Year of Publication	Title	Journal/Book	Doi
Alakash, M. A. N., Abuirmilah, B. M. A., Al-Zubaidi, K., Alkhawaldeh, A., & Al Daraiseh, A. K. M. S	2024	The Strategy Of Establishing E-Government And Developing The Performance Of Public Administration	*Pakistan Journal of Criminology*	10.62271/pjc.16.3.385.402
Alanazi, A.	2023	Clinicians' Views on Using Artificial Intelligence in Healthcare: Opportunities, Challenges, and Beyond	*Cureus*	10.7759/cureus.45255
Alshahrani, A., Dennehy, D., & Mäntymäki, M.	2022	An attention-based view of AI assimilation in public sector organizations: The case of Saudi Arabia	*Government Information Quarterly*	10.1016/j.giq.2021.101617
AlSukhayri, A. M., Aslam, M. A., Saeedi, K., & Malik, M. S. A.	2020	A linked open data-oriented sustainable system for transparency and open access to government data: A case study of the public's response to women's driving in Saudi Arabia	*Sustainability*	10.3390/su12208608
Bitonti, A.	2024	Tools of digital innovation in public affairs management: A practice-oriented analysis	*Journal of public affairs*	10.1002/pa.2888
Campion, A., Gasco Hernandez, M., Jankin Mikhaylov, S., Esteve, M.	2022	Overcoming the challenges of collaboratively adopting artificial intelligence in the public sector	*Social Science Computer Review*	10.1177/0894439320979953
Chen, Y. C., Ahn, M. J., & Wang, Y. F.	2023	Artificial intelligence and public values: value impacts and governance in the public sector.	*Sustainability*	10.3390/su15064796
Corvo, L., Pastore, L., Mastrodascio, M., & Tricarico, L.	2022	The impact of COVID-19 on Public/Third-Sector collaboration in the Italian contex	*Sustainability*	10.3390/su14042228
De Classe, T. M., De Araujo, R. M., Xexéo, G. B., & Siqueira, S. W. M.	2021	Public processes are open for play	*Digital Government: Research and Practice*	10.1145/3474879

Fest, I., Schäfer, M., van Dijck, J., Meijer, A.	2023	Understanding Data Professionals in the Police: A Qualitative Study of System-Level Bureaucrats	*Public Management Review*	10.1080/14719037.2023.2222734
Fest, I., Wieringa, M., & Wagner, B.	2022	Paper vs. practice: How legal and ethical frameworks influence public sector data professionals in the Netherlands	*Patterns*	10.1016/j.patter.2022.100604
Ismail, A., Thakkar, D., Madhiwalla, N., & Kumar, N.	2023	Public health calls for/with AI: an ethnographic perspective	*Proceedings of the ACM on Human-Computer Interaction*	https://doi.org/10.1145/3610203
Juell-Skielse, G., Balasuriya, P., Güner, E. O., & Han, S.	2022	Cognitive robotic process automation: concept and impact on dynamic IT capabilities in public organizations	*Service Automation in the Public Sector: Concepts, Empirical Examples and Challenges*	10.1007/978-3-030-92644-1_4
Leikas, J., Johri, A., Latvanen, M., Wessberg, N., Hahto, A.	2022	Governing Ethical AI Transformation: A Case Study of AuroraAI	*Frontiers in Artificial Intelligence*	10.3389/frai.2022.836557
Lopes, K. M. G., Macadar, M. A., Luciano, E. M.	2019	Key drivers for public value creation enhancing the adoption of electronic public services by citizens	*International Journal of Public Sector Management*	10.1108/IJPSM-03-2018-0081
Maragno, G., Tangi, L., Gastaldi, L., Benedetti, M.	2023	Exploring the factors, affordances and constraints outlining the implementation of Artificial Intelligence in public sector organizations	*International Journal of Information Management*	10.1016/j.ijinfomgt.2023.102686

Table 1 contd. ...

...Table 1 contd.

Authors	Year of Publication	Title	Journal/Book	Doi
Morgenstern, J. D., Rosella, L. C., Daley, M. J., Goel, V., Schünemann, H. J., Piggott, T.	2021	AI's gonna have an impact on everything in society, so it has to have an impact on public health: a fundamental qualitative descriptive study of the implications of artificial intelligence for public health	*BMC Public Health*	10.1186/ s12889-020-10030-x
Neumann, O., Guirguis, K., Steiner, R.	2023	Exploring artificial intelligence adoption in public organizations: a comparative case study	*Public Management Review*	10.1080/ 14719037.2022.2048685
Salam, R., Sinurat, M., Yasin, A., Sacipto, R.	2023	Implementation of Artificial Intelligence in Governance: Potentials and Challenges	*Influence: International Journal of Science Review*	10.54783/ influencejournal.v5i1
Sciberras, M., Dingli, A	2023	Investigating AI Readiness in the Maltese Public Administration	*Investigating AI Readiness in the Maltese Public Administration*	10.1007/978-3-031-19900-4
Selten, F., Klievink, B.	2024	Organizing public sector AI adoption: Navigating between separation and integration	*Government Information Quarterly*	10.1016/ j.giq.2023.101885
Simmler, M., Brunner, S., Canova, G., Schedler, K.	2023	Smart criminal justice: exploring the use of algorithms in the Swiss criminal justice system	*Artificial Intelligence and Law*	10.1007/s10506-022-09310-1
Sobrino-García, I.	2021	Artificial intelligence risks and challenges in the Spanish public administration: An exploratory analysis through expert judgements	*Administrative Science*	10.3390/ admsci11030102
van Noordt, C., Tangi, L.	2023	The dynamics of AI capability and its influence on public value creation of AI within public administration	*Government Information Quarterly*	10.1016/ j.giq.2023.101860

Source: Author's elaboration.

Extracting and Coding Data

The fourth step in the meta-synthesis approach was to extract, code, and classify evidence from the selected studies (Noblit and Hare 1988). We used an open-coding approach (Denzin and Lincoln 2011; Strauss and Corbin 1998) to classify the insights generated by the researchers of the primary studies, especially focusing on the Results and Discussion sections (Hoon 2013). During this step, we were mindful of the different settings in which the primary studies were conducted, and we initially coded each primary study for its descriptive characteristics (e.g., setting, sample, data sources; see Supplementary Online Material) and then developed a list of open codes. All the coauthors read through the same three randomly selected studies to identify relevant codes. Then, two researchers independently coded the remaining articles according to the defined criteria. Working with two coders reduces mistakes in data recording and avoids omitting relevant constructs (Miles and Huberman 1994). We followed an iterative approach (Locke 2001), continuously iterating between our data and the emerging conceptualizations and comparing codes by engaging in discussions when disagreements emerged. We used Cohen's kappa coefficient (κ; Cohen 1972) to estimate the level of agreement between the coders. Initially, when all the coauthors codified the first three studies, a fair level of agreement was reached: $\kappa = 0.34$ (Landis and Koch 1977). By discussing the reasons for disagreements, particularly regarding terminological differences, we were able to identify and correct differences in the encoding process. Following this phase, in the final coding process, the observed agreement—that is, the percentage of agreement between the judgments of two raters when they independently coded the same data—reached a value of $\kappa = 0.86$, reflecting excellent agreement between the raters (Artstein and Poesio 2008).

Analyzing Different Conceptualizations and Synthesizing Findings

In the next step, we related the previously identified concepts and themes into theoretical categories so that the emerging constructs, based on the extant literature, were grounded in our data. In doing so, we lifted the data to a more theoretical level and moved from a case-specific to a cross-study level of analysis. Moreover, to obtain an outsider perspective and thereby verify our ideas, we engaged in informal meetings (e.g., internal seminars with fellow department members) and formal meetings (e.g., conference sessions) with other researchers not involved in the study to discuss emerging patterns and solicit critical questions regarding the data collection and analytical procedure. Thus, after settling on a set of theoretical categories, we identified key aggregate theoretical dimensions. The last phase involved synthesizing the concepts that had emerged to systematize findings related to qualitative AI research within the public sector. The findings are explained in detail in the following subsections.

Results

The results of the analysis clearly demonstrate that the adoption of AI and AI-based solutions in public organizations is shaped by both challenges and opportunities, making it a crucial and relevant phenomenon today. Based on the selected articles, this meta-synthesis examines how public sector organizations navigate the complexities of AI adoption, identifying the key factors that influence its successful implementation.

The Need for Organizational Change in the Public Sector

The first point that emerges from the findings concerns the organizational factors influencing AI utilization within public administration, as organizations are trying to balance the need for innovation and flexibility in adopting AI with existing formal structures and operational processes. Indeed, a hierarchical organizational structure implies that it is difficult for organizations to involve the various hierarchical levels of the organization (Campion et al. 2022).

AI is dealt with by data professionals, who may or may not be integrated with other business functions (Fest et al. 2023). According to Selten and Klievink (2024), there are two main approaches to business structures. The first of these is structural separation, in which the data science team is separated from the rest of the business teams. This approach encourages exploration and innovation in AI. Structurally separated data science teams have more freedom, time, and support to experiment, collaborate with knowledge institutes, and tackle complex technical issues.

These data professionals can focus on the implementation and ethical and legal compliance of AI in a coherent and centralized manner (Leikas et al. 2022). On the other hand, this separation can create innovation silos, hindering interconnection with other functional departments. Furthermore, integration problems may arise with existing operational processes in the absence of necessary support from leadership and operational employees. The second approach is the contextual approach, wherein the data team is integrated into the operational departments. This approach facilitates better alignment between AI and the day-to-day operations of the organization. Integrated data scientists have a deeper understanding of operational processes and strategic objectives, allowing for a more effective integration of AI solutions. This approach, however, can lead to a dispersion of data scientists among various departments, making it difficult to share knowledge and realize the full potential of AI throughout the organization.

In addition, the need for strong leadership support emerged from the data. Specifically, leadership support, change management, and an organizational culture of innovation and flexibility were highlighted as key elements for the success of AI adoption in the public sector (Neumann et al. 2023).

Furthermore, AI-driven public affairs platforms have revolutionized decision-making processes in government relations. According to Bitonti (2023), tools such as FiscalNote and Quorum provide public officials with real-time data analytics, allowing them to anticipate political trends, understand stakeholder dynamics, and optimize communication strategies. This shift towards data-driven decision-making necessitates organizational changes to integrate AI-based insights into traditional hierarchical structures.

Technological, Social, and Environmental Factors

The adoption of AI is driven both by top-down strategic initiatives and by bottom-up technological necessity. Usually, AI technologies are chosen because conventional technologies are not suited to solve existing problems. In some cases (Neumann et al. 2023), public organizations actively prepare for a future enhanced by AI technologies (e.g., by hiring specialists and aligning data infrastructure and strategy toward this goal), representing a top-down approach. In this process, AI algorithms must be effectively designed in terms of key features like computer systems, learning, and autonomy (Sobrino-Garcìa 2021); moreover, an ethical approach must be followed in the design in order to incorporate the organization's values into the technology.

A characteristic of AI that influences its development is its ability to interact, learn, and evolve through continuous relationships both with the environment and with humans. Unlike other technologies, AI requires not only technical maintenance but also human resources to engage with it and provide it with specific knowledge. Therefore, AI must be continuously trained in order to adequately support its evolutionary process (Maragno et al. 2023). Clearly, there are multiple risks in using AI algorithms, such as issues regarding access, the public or private nature of algorithms, biases transferred from humans to algorithms, and privacy-related risks (Morgenstern et al. 2021). Similarly, in the context of e-government, cybersecurity risks and data protection concerns are major challenges, requiring legal frameworks and strong governance mechanisms to ensure trust and transparency in digital services (Alakash et al. 2024; Alshahrani et al. 2022).

Moreover, AI governance must address public trust issues, as government employees often express concerns about algorithmic bias and decision opacity (Chen et al. 2023). Transparency and participatory AI governance are essential to ensuring fair and accountable AI adoption.

Another relevant finding that emerged from the analysis of the articles concerns environmental and social factors. The implementation of AI is not only linked to its technological components and its relationship with organizational agents but also to phenomena and issues beyond organizational boundaries (Sciberras and Dingli 2023). First and foremost, systems cannot be implemented independently of policies, national strategies, and frameworks that regulate data management and sharing. The presence or absence of laws and political frameworks governing the implementation of AI could have a positive or negative effect. Developing regulations is crucial to harnessing the features of AI, especially in public contexts (Maragno et al. 2023).

Thus, there are significant motivations driving the use of AI in the public sector, including political pressures, a demand for greater government and service efficiency, and a need for optimization of available resources (Simmler et al. 2023).

In this regard, AI can enhance many sectors, such as healthcare, education, and security. For instance, in education, AI can support adaptive learning and objective student assessments. According to Ismail et al. (2023), in public health interventions,

AI functions not only as a predictive tool but also as a mediator that reconfigures workflows and prioritizes resources.

However, greater attention is required due to the associated challenges, such as data privacy issues and the potential for unfair decisions (Salam et al. 2023).

In the AI adoption process, it's essential to involve citizens in the delivery of public services through a collaborative approach to ensure the creation of public value. The integration of AI into public services relies on factors such as usability, trust, and collaboration. These elements are crucial for enhancing the social dynamics that influence the successful AI adoption within the public sector. Lopes et al. (2019) highlight the importance of these factors, suggesting that a focus on improving them can significantly impact the acceptance and effectiveness of AI technologies in public service delivery.

Neumann et al. (2023) emphasize that there is not necessarily competitive pressure for public organizations, but there is pressure driven by unclear regulations and human resource management. Both accessing existing IT personnel and recruiting new employees are challenging. Recruitment can be difficult because public organizations have a reputation for not being particularly innovative. Existing resources are often not available long-term and cannot be utilized for unplanned artificial intelligence projects.

Barriers to and Drivers of AI Adoption in the Public Sector

Public organizations face significant challenges in adopting AI, including integration with existing operational processes and resistance from employees unfamiliar with AI technologies (Selten and Klievink 2024). In fact, the effectiveness of AI in public services depends on human-AI collaboration rather than AI acting independently (Ismail et al. 2023).

The study of AI-driven public health interventions also revealed that although AI can improve efficiency, it requires continuous human oversight to mitigate bias, improve transparency, and align technological capabilities with public sector goals (Ismail et al. 2023). Failure to adequately train human stakeholders or involve them in AI design can lead to misaligned AI applications that do not achieve their intended outcomes. Even after implementation, organizations often struggle with maintaining AI systems and effectively disseminating the knowledge developed.

To successfully support data scientists within their departments, operational leaders must possess both domain expertise and technical skills. However, despite the existence of legal and ethical frameworks for AI governance, their application remains inconsistent. For instance, Fest et al. (2022) found that in the Netherlands, public sector data professionals tend to apply ethical and legal guidelines implicitly rather than explicitly. This gap between regulation and practice underscores the need for continuous training and policy adjustments to ensure responsible AI implementation.

To address these challenges, public organizations should invest in targeted training programs for managers, equipping them with the necessary skills to oversee AI projects effectively and develop leadership competencies in this field. Furthermore, the lack of digital skills remains a key barrier to AI adoption in the public sector, as highlighted by Lopes et al. (2019). Strengthening digital literacy and fostering a culture of continuous learning will be essential for enabling a smoother and more effective integration of AI technologies. Indeed, limitations in the interpretation and interpretability of AI results and issues related to insufficient skills, low-quality data, and privacy concerns represent major barriers to AI adoption by public organizations (Morgenstern et al. 2021). The need for training and upskilling public employees is crucial, as highlighted by the case of e-government transformation where governments have had to invest significantly in digital literacy programs for their workforce (Alakash et al. 2024). AI adoption is often hindered by a misalignment between decision-making at the management level and AI-driven decision-making, as found in the case of Saudi Arabian public organizations (Alshahrani et al. 2022). Many managers expect AI to provide instant solutions without properly understanding its implementation challenges, requiring additional efforts in awareness-building and training.

A further critical challenge, as evidenced in Saudi Arabia, is data integrity and sharing (Alshahrani et al. 2022). Many public organizations lack unified databases, leading to fragmented data systems and difficulties in implementing AI-driven solutions. Data ownership disputes further complicate the situation, as different departments are reluctant to share information due to legal concerns or lack of awareness about AI's potential benefits.

A further issue lies in citizens' preference for in-person services and the associated lack of public awareness and sensitization to the use of AI. The government can play a key role in mitigating this barrier, as citizens' trust in the government increases their willingness to cooperate. If the government disseminates information on the use of AI, it can establish a collaborative process with citizens, fostering innovation and trust (Sobrino-García 2021). Overall, strategies must be implemented to address these challenges and thereby maximize public value (Lopes et al. 2019). Moreover, digital serious games have been proposed as an innovative way to enhance public service transparency and citizens' engagement.

Research by De Classe et al. (2021) demonstrated that game-based learning can help citizens understand complex bureaucratic processes, fostering greater trust and participation. This highlights the potential of AI-driven educational tools to support organizational change in public administration.

Challenges and Opportunities

The adoption of AI in the public sector has proven to be very complex, highlighting the need to balance innovation with adaptation to existing processes in order to overcome the barriers and risks highlighted.

For example, the structure of the organization can bring specific advantages and challenges. We have seen that the most frequently adopted models are structural separation and integration.

According to Selten and Klievink (2024), structural separation promotes innovation in AI, as data science teams have more freedom to experiment, collaborate with knowledge institutes, and address technical issues. However, this scenario can create innovation silos and hinder interconnection with other departments. On the other hand, integrating teams into operational departments facilitates better alignment between AI and day-to-day operations but disperses data scientists and makes knowledge sharing difficult.

Common barriers to AI adoption include problems integrating with existing operational processes and lack of support from leadership. Organizations are addressing these challenges by creating data science hubs, linking data scientists in various departments, and establishing central ethics committees.

Another opportunity for public organizations concerns interoperability: public organizations need to move towards an inter-organizational approach. Being able to manage co-creation and collaboration is a strong component of AI capability. Thus, internal collaboration between IT and business departments is necessary to ensure the quality of AI in the organization, while external collaboration enables the sharing of data and the summation of computational resources (Juell-Skielse et al. 2022). To achieve this, public organizations must share a common understanding of the problem with other public organizations in a unified and non-segmented view of administration to avoid digital silos. Moreover, it is also important to remember that there is always an initial phase of systems integration and training required for all public organizations (van Noordt and Tangi 2023).

Other challenges relate to the fact that AI offers the potential to improve the efficiency of public services, facilitate more informed decision-making, and increase government transparency and accountability (Salam et al. 2023; Ismail et al. 2023). In the health sector, for example, it can speed up diagnosis and optimize resources (Alanazi 2023; Morgenstern et al. 2021; AlSukhayri et al. 2020). In this regard, several critical issues have emerged, including privacy and data security concerns and the fear of unfair decisions (Sobrino-Garcìa 2021). If left unchecked, AI could allow for discriminatory or unauthorized access to sensitive data. Possible solutions to address these challenges include ad-hoc legislative and administrative instruments, as well as the implementation of stricter data security standards, independent supervision and regulation of AI systems used for decision-making, and high transparency in AI decision-making procedures (Salam et al. 2023).

Further, regarding the problem of data privacy and security, one possible solution involves organizational routines: for instance, assigning formal roles to align project interests or directing attention differently to organizational problems can allow for a better definition of data needs and encourage data sharing even across multiple organizations (Campion et al. 2022; Corvo et al. 2022).

Finally, at the decision-making level, AI can support more objective decision-making. While experts agree that algorithms will not completely replace human judgment, they can present guidelines for making better decisions (Simmler et al. 2023).

Discussion and Conclusion

The aim of this study was to explore how public sector organizations navigate the challenges and opportunities of AI adoption and identify the key factors that determine its successful implementation. This is an understudied area with respect to innovation and technology that deserves further attention, as it could reveal several benefits and opportunities to public organizations and practitioners (Kejriwal 2022).

Through a meta-synthesis of qualitative literature, our findings suggest that AI adoption in public sector organizations is influenced by various factors, including organizational, technological, environmental, and social factors. Organizations must balance innovation and flexibility in AI adoption with existing formal structures and operational processes, considering key AI algorithm features, ethical design, and continuous learning management (Selten and Klievink 2024). Implementation is linked to external phenomena like policies, national strategies, and regulatory frameworks (Maragno et al. 2023).

The success of AI in public administration depends on how well organizations align their internal structures, invest in digital infrastructure, and develop an AI-ready workforce.

A key finding of this study is that citizen engagement is crucial for creating public value (Lopes et al. 2019). AI-driven public services must be designed with usability, trust, and collaboration in mind to ensure public legitimacy and broad acceptance. However, significant barriers remain, such as integration challenges, lack of digital skills, public resistance, and concerns over data security and transparency (Sobrino-Garcia 2021). These challenges highlight the importance of responsible AI governance, particularly regarding privacy protection, algorithmic fairness, and ethical decision-making.

Although there is a lack of clarity regarding the adoption, usage, and application of AI technologies within the public sector (Wirtz et al. 2021; Zuiderwijk et al. 2021) this study recognizes its relevance and offers some key contributions to theory and research. First, we address the issue of AI adoption within the public sector, which is a topic that has been little addressed in the literature (Aoki 2020; Mergel et al. 2023). AI provides several features and benefits to the public sector, including the potential to enhance the efficiency of public services, facilitate more informed decision-making, and increase government transparency.

Second, because we used a qualitative approach, which offers more varied and broader findings than a quantitative approach (Johnson et al. 2007), our findings enable us to offer in-depth knowledge of the process of AI technology adoption and to generate useful insights for the public sector. Drawing from 24 systematically selected qualitative studies, our findings highlight the factors influencing AI adoption within public sector organizations (Zhang et al. 2021). More specifically, our findings offer useful insights for academics and practitioners regarding the main reasons public organizations choose to adopt or not adopt AI technologies. These findings open up a variety of opportunities for public sector organizations, which can use AI technologies to enhance the efficiency, transparency, and overall effectiveness of public services.

It is also important to acknowledge the practical implications of the findings. Understanding the factors influencing AI adoption is critical to define effective strategies for integrating AI technologies within public sector organizations. By recognizing the multifaceted nature of AI adoption, decision makers can better allocate resources and design policies that meet the specific needs and challenges of their respective public sector organizations, thereby enabling more informed and focused decision-making processes. Thus, knowledge of the factors influencing AI adoption enables more efficient allocation of resources. Public sector organizations can direct funding and training efforts to areas that are most likely to be successful in implementing AI, thereby maximizing their return on investment. As a result, identifying barriers and facilitators to AI adoption can help tailor capacity-building programs. Training and skills development initiatives can be tailored to address the specific challenges public sector employees may face during AI integration. As such, policymakers can use the insights from this study to establish regulatory frameworks that balance innovation with responsible AI deployment fostering a more enabling environment for AI adoption while ensuring ethical and legal compliance. In summary, the practical implications of this study provide a roadmap for public sector organizations seeking to navigate the complexities of AI adoption. By understanding the influential factors and taking a strategic, informed approach, the public sector can harness the potential of AI technologies to improve governance, enhance services, and meet the evolving needs of the modern digital age.

Despite the theoretical contributions, this study is not without limitations. First, the scope of the meta-synthesis is limited to the included studies, and, despite the methodological rigor with which the articles were selected, some relevant studies may have been omitted due to language restrictions, database limitations, or other criteria. Therefore, this meta-synthesis may not provide a complete overview of the topic. Another limitation is related to the rapidly evolving nature of AI. Indeed, as AI is a very current topic and has been widely covered in the literature, this study may not capture the most recent developments in AI adoption in the public sector, thus limiting the relevance of the results. Moreover, while AI offers numerous benefits and represents a transformative force for the public sector (Sun and Medaglia 2019), it also presents challenges, including those related to data privacy, ethical issues, and job displacement. Therefore, future research should further investigate the potential risks related to AI technology. Finally, it would be interesting to conduct in-depth qualitative research to provide a comprehensive exploration of individuals' attitudes and behaviors toward AI technologies.

References

Alakash, M. A. N., Abuirmilah, B. M. A., Al-Zubaidi, K., Alkhawaldeh, A. and Al Daraiseh, A. K. M. S. 2024. The strategy of establishing E-government and developing the performance of public administration. Pakistan Journal of Criminology 16(3): 385–402.

Alhosani, K. and Alhashmi, S. M. 2024. Opportunities, challenges, and benefits of AI innovation in government services: a review. Discover Artificial Intelligence 4(1): 18.

Alshahrani, A., Dennehy, D. and Mäntymäki, M. 2022. An attention-based view of AI assimilation in public sector organizations: The case of Saudi Arabia. Government Information Quarterly 39(4).

AlSukhayri, A. M., Aslam, M. A., Saeedi, K. and Malik, M. S. A. 2020. A linked open data-oriented sustainable system for transparency and open access to government data: A case study of the public's response to women's driving in Saudi Arabia. Sustainability 12(20): 8608.

Alanazi, A. 2023. Clinicians' views on using artificial intelligence in healthcare: opportunities, challenges, and beyond. Cureus 15(9).

Aoki, N. 2020. An experimental study of public trust in AI chatbots in the public sector. Government Information Quarterly 37(4): 101490.

Arinez, J. F., Chang, Q., Gao, R. X., Xu, C. and Zhang, J. 2020. Artificial intelligence in advanced manufacturing: Current status and future outlook. Journal of Manufacturing Science and Engineering 142(11): 110804.

Artstein, R. and Poesio, M. 2008. Inter-coder agreement for computational linguistics. Computational Linguistics 34(4): 555–596.

Bitonti, A. 2024. Tools of digital innovation in public affairs management: A practice-oriented analysis. Journal of Public Affairs 24(1): 2888.

Borges, A. F., Laurindo, F. J., Spínola, M. M., Gonçalves, R. F. and Mattos, C. A. 2021. The strategic use of artificial intelligence in the digital era: Systematic literature review and future research directions. International Journal of Information Management 57: 102225.

Campion, A., Gasco-Hernandez, M., Jankin Mikhaylov, S. and Esteve, M. 2022. Overcoming the challenges of collaboratively adopting artificial intelligence in the public sector. Social Science Computer Review 40(2): 462–477.

Cheek, J., Onslow, M. and Cream, A. 2004. Beyond the divide: Comparing and contrasting aspects of qualitative and quantitative research approaches. Advances in Speech Language Pathology 6(3): 147–152.

Chen, X., Xie, H., Zou, D. and Hwang, G. J. 2020. Application and theory gaps during the rise of artificial intelligence in education. Computers and Education: Artificial Intelligence 1: 100002.

Chen, Y. C., Ahn, M. J. and Wang, Y. F. 2023. Artificial intelligence and public values: value impacts and governance in the public sector. Sustainability 15(2): 4796.

Clemmens, D. 2003. Adolescent motherhood: A meta-synthesis of qualitative studies. The American Journal of Maternal/Child Nursing 28(2): 93–99.

Cohen, J. 1972. Weighted chi square: An extension of the kappa method. Educational and Psychological Measurement 32(1): 61–74.

Corvo, L., Pastore, L., Mastrodascio, M. and Tricarico, L. 2022. The impact of COVID-19 on Public/Third-Sector collaboration in the Italian context. Sustainability 14(4): 2228.

Criado, J. I., Sandoval-Almazán, R. and Gil-Garcia, J. R. 2025. Artificial intelligence and public administration: Understanding actors, governance, and policy from micro, meso, and macro perspectives. Public Policy and Administration 40(2): 173–184.

De Classe, T. M., De Araujo, R. M., Xexéo, G. B. and Siqueira, S. W. M. 2021. Public processes are open for play. Digital Government: Research and Practice 2(4): 1–18.

de Sousa, W. G., de Melo, E. R. P., Bermejo, P. H. D. S., Farias, R. A. S. and Gomes, A. O. 2019. How and where is artificial intelligence in the public sector going? A literature review and research agenda. Government Information Quarterly 36(4): 101392.

Denzin, N. K. and Lincoln, Y. S. 2011. The Sage Handbook of Qualitative Research, Sage.

Eli-Chukwu, N. C. 2019. Applications of artificial intelligence in agriculture: A review. Engineering, Technology & Applied Science Research 9(4): 4377–4383.

Febiri, F. and Hub, M. 2021. Digitalization of global economy: a qualitative study exploring key indicators use to measure digital progress in the Public sector. SHS Web of Conferences 92.

Fest, I., Schäfer, M., van Dijck, J. and Meijer, A. 2023. Understanding data professionals in the police: a qualitative study of system-level bureaucrats. Public Management Review 1–21.

Fest, I., Wieringa, M. and Wagner, B. 2022. Paper vs. practice: How legal and ethical frameworks influence public sector data professionals in the Netherlands. Patterns 3(10).

Finfgeld-Connett, D. 2018. A Guide to Qualitative Meta-Synthesis, Routledge.

Gesk, T. S. and Leyer, M. 2022. Artificial intelligence in public services: When and why citizens accept its usage. Government Information Quarterly 39(3): 101704.

Goodell, J. W., Kumar, S., Lim, W. M. and Pattnaik, D. 2021. Artificial intelligence and machine learning in finance: Identifying foundations, themes, and research clusters from bibliometric analysis. Journal of Behavioral and Experimental Finance 32: 100577.

Gupta, R., Srivastava, D., Sahu, M., Tiwari, S., Ambasta, R. K. and Kumar, P. 2021. Artificial intelligence to deep learning: machine intelligence approach for drug discovery. Molecular Diversity 25: 1315–1360.

Haenlein, M. and Kaplan, A. 2019. A brief history of artificial intelligence: On the past, present, and future of artificial intelligence. California Management Review 61(4): 5–14.

Helm, J. M., Swiergosz, A. M., Haeberle, H. S., Karnuta, J. M., Schaffer, J. L., Krebs, V. E. et al. 2020. Machine learning and artificial intelligence: definitions, applications, and future directions. Current Reviews in Musculoskeletal Medicine 13: 69–76.

Hogg, H. D. J., Sendak, M. P., Denniston, A. K., Keane, P. A. and Maniatopoulos, G. 2023. Unlocking the potential of qualitative research for the implementation of artificial intelligence-enabled healthcare. Journal of Medical Artificial Intelligence 6.

Hoon, C. 2013. Meta-synthesis of qualitative case studies: An approach to theory building. Organizational Research Methods 16(4): 552–556.

Horvitz, E. 2016. One-hundred-year study on artificial intelligence. Available at: https://ai100.stanford.edu. (accessed December 2016).

Ismail, A., Thakkar, D., Madhiwalla, N. and Kumar, N. 2023. Public health calls for/with AI: an ethnographic perspective. Proceedings of the ACM on Human-Computer Interaction 7: 1–26.

Jha, K., Doshi, A., Patel, P. and Shah, M. 2019. A comprehensive review on automation in agriculture using artificial intelligence. Artificial Intelligence in Agriculture 2: 1–12.

Jiang, Y., Li, X., Luo, H., Yin, S. and Kaynak, O. 2022. Quo vadis artificial intelligence? Discover Artificial Intelligence 2(1): 4.

Juell-Skielse, G., Balasuriya, P., Güner, E. O. and Han, S. 2022. Cognitive robotic process automation: concept and impact on dynamic IT capabilities in public organizations. pp. 65–88. In Service Automation in the Public Sector: Concepts, Empirical Examples and Challenges. Cham, Springer International Publishing.

Kaul, V., Enslin, S. and Gross, S. A. 2020. History of artificial intelligence in medicine. Gastrointestinal Endoscopy 92(4): 807–812.

Kejriwal, M. 2022. Artificial Intelligence for Industries of the Future: Beyond Facebook, Amazon, Microsoft and Google, Springer International Publishing.

Kisamore, J. L. and Brannick, M. T. 2008. An illustration of the consequences of meta-analysis model choice. Organizational Research Methods 11(1): 35–53.

Landis, J. R. and Koch, G. G. 1977. The measurement of observer agreement for categorical data. Biometrics 33(1): 159–174.

Lee, J., Davari, H., Singh, J. and Pandhare, V. 2018. Industrial Artificial Intelligence for industry 4.0-based manufacturing systems. Manufacturing Letters 18: 20–23.

Leikas, J., Johri, A., Latvanen, M., Wessberg, N. and Hahto, A. 2022. Governing ethical AI transformation: A case study of AuroraAI. Frontiers in Artificial Intelligence 5(13).

Locke, K. 2001. Grounded Theory in Management Research. London, UK, Sage.

Lopes, K. M. G., Macadar, M. A. and Luciano, E. M. 2019. Key drivers for public value creation enhancing the adoption of electronic public services by citizens. International Journal of Public Sector Management 32(5): 546–561.

Lu, Y. 2019. Artificial intelligence: a survey on evolution, models, applications and future trends. Journal of Management Analytics 6(1): 1–29.

Madan, R. and Ashok, M. 2023. AI adoption and diffusion in public administration: A systematic literature review and future research agenda. Government Information Quarterly 40(1): 101774.

Maragno, G., Tangi, L., Gastaldi, L. and Benedetti, M. 2023. Exploring the factors, affordances and constraints outlining the implementation of Artificial Intelligence in public sector organizations. International Journal of Information Management 73: 102686.

Medaglia, R. and Tangi, L. 2022. The adoption of Artificial Intelligence in the public sector in Europe: drivers, features, and impacts. pp. 10–18. *In*: Amaran, L., Soares, D., Zheng, L., Peixoto, M. and Braga, C. (eds.). Proceedings of the 15th International Conference on Theory and Practice of Electronic Governance, Association for Computing Machinery, New York, NY.

Mehr, H. 2017. Artificial intelligence for citizen services and government.

Mergel, I., Dickinson, H., Stenvall, J. and Gasco, M. 2023. Implementing AI in the public sector. Public Management Review 1–13.

Milana, C. and Ashta, A. 2021. Artificial intelligence techniques in finance and financial markets: a survey of the literature. Strategic Change 30(3): 189–209.

Miles, M. B. and Huberman, A. M. 1994. Qualitative Data Analysis: An Expanded Sourcebook. Thousand Oaks, CA, Sage.

Moon, M. J. 2002. The evolution of e-government among municipalities: rhetoric or reality? Public Administration Review 62(4): 424–433.

Morgenstern, J. D., Rosella, L. C., Daley, M. J., Goel, V., Schünemann, H. J. and Piggott, T. 2021. AI's gonna have an impact on everything in society, so it has to have an impact on public health: a fundamental qualitative descriptive study of the implications of artificial intelligence for public health. BMC Public Health 21: 1–14.

Mutawa, M. A. and Rashid, H. 2020. Comprehensive review on the challenges that impact artificial intelligence applications in the public sector. Paper presented at the 5th NA International Conference on Industrial Engineering and Operations Management, 10–14 August, Detroit, Michigan, USA.

Neuman, W. L. 2006. Social Research Methods: Qualitative and Quantitative Approaches, 6th ed.; Allyn and Bacon, Boston, MA, USA.

Neumann, O., Guirguis, K. and Steiner, R. 2023. Exploring artificial intelligence adoption in public organizations: a comparative case study. Public Management Review: 1–28.

Noblit, G. W., and Hare, R. D. 1988. Meta-ethnography: Synthesizing qualitative studies, 11. Sage.

Ramesh, A. N., Kambhampati, C., Monson, J. R. and Drew, P. J. 2004. Artificial intelligence in medicine. Annals of the Royal College of Surgeons of England 86(5): 334.

Salam, R., Sinurat, M., Yasin, A. and Sacipto, R. 2023. Implementation of artificial intelligence in governance: potentials and challenges. Influence: International Journal of Science Review 5(1): 243–255.

Scherer, M. U. 2015. Regulating artificial intelligence systems: Risks, challenges, competencies, and strategies. Harvard Journal of Law & Technology 29: 353, available at: https://heinonline.org/HOL/LandingPage?handle=hein.journals/hjlt29&div=15&id=&page=.

Sciberras, M. and Dingli, A. 2023. Investigating AI Readiness in the Maltese Public Administration Vol. 568, Springer Nature.

Selten, F. and Klievink, B. 2024. Organizing public sector AI adoption: Navigating between separation and integration. Government Information Quarterly 41(1): 101885.

Simmler, M., Brunner, S., Canova, G. and Schedler, K. 2023. Smart criminal justice: exploring the use of algorithms in the Swiss criminal justice system. Artificial Intelligence and Law 31(2): 213–237.

Singh, V. K., Singh, P., Karmakar, M., Leta, J. and Mayr, P. 2021. The journal coverage of Web of Science, Scopus and Dimensions: A comparative analysis. Scientometrics 126: 5113–5142.

Sobrino-García, I. 2021. Artificial intelligence risks and challenges in the Spanish public administration: An exploratory analysis through expert judgements. Administrative Sciences 11(3): 102.

Strauss, A. and Corbin, J. 1998. Basics of Qualitative Research Techniques. Sage.

Susar, D. and Aquaro, V. 2019. Artificial intelligence: Opportunities and challenges for the public sector. pp. 418–426. *In*: Dhau, S., Carter, L. and Gregory, M. (eds.). Proceedings of the 12th International Conference on Theory and Practice of Electronic Governance, Association for Computing Machinery, New York, NY.

Tang, A. and Wen, A. 2009. An intelligent simulation system for earthquake disaster assessment. Computers & Geosciences 35(5): 871–879.

Tangi, L., van Noordt, C. and Rodriguez Müller, A. P. 2023. The challenges of AI implementation in the public sector. An in-depth case studies analysis. pp. 414–422. *In*: Duenas Cid, D., Sabatini, N., Hagen, L. and Liao, H. (eds.). Proceedings of the 24th Annual International Conference on Digital Government Research, Association for Computing Machinery, New York, NY.

van Noordt, C. and Misuraca, G. 2022. Exploratory insights on artificial intelligence for government in Europe. Social Science Computer Review 40(2): 426–444.

van Noordt, C. and Tangi, L. 2023. The dynamics of AI capability and its influence on public value creation of AI within public administration. Government Information Quarterly 101860.

Vatamanu, A. F. and Tofan, M. 2025. Integrating artificial intelligence into public administration: Challenges and vulnerabilities. Administrative Sciences 15(4): 49.

Veale, M., Van Kleek, M. and Binns, R. 2018. Fairness and accountability design needs for algorithmic support in high-stakes public sector decision-making. pp. 1–14. In Proceedings of the 2018 CHI Conference on Human Factors in Computing Systems.

Walsh, D. and Downe, S. 2005. Meta-synthesis method for qualitative research: a literature review. Journal of Advanced Nursing 50(2): 204–211.

Wirtz, B. W., Langer, P. F. and Fenner, C. 2021. Artificial intelligence in the public sector-a research agenda. International Journal of Public Administration 44(13): 1103–1128.

Wirtz, B. W., Weyerer, J. C. and Geyer, C. 2019. Artificial intelligence and the public sector-applications and challenges. International Journal of Public Administration 42(7): 596–615.

Wirtz, B. W., Weyerer, J. C. and Sturm, B. J. 2020. The dark sides of artificial intelligence: An integrated AI governance framework for public administration. International Journal of Public Administration 43(9): 818–829.

Woschank, M., Rauch, E. and Zsifkovits, H. 2020. A review of further directions for artificial intelligence, machine learning, and deep learning in smart logistics. Sustainability 12(9): 3760.

Zhang, C. and Lu, Y. 2021. Study on artificial intelligence: The state of the art and future prospects. Journal of Industrial Information Integration 23: 100224.

Zhang, W., Zuo, N., He, W., Li, S. and Yu, L. 2021. Factors influencing the use of artificial intelligence in government: Evidence from China. Technology in Society 66: 101675.

Zimmer, L. 2006. Qualitative meta-synthesis: a question of dialoguing with texts. Journal of Advanced Nursing 53(3): 311–318.

Zuiderwijk, A., Chen, Y. C. and Salem, F. 2021. Implications of the use of artificial intelligence in public governance: A systematic literature review and a research agenda. Government Information Quarterly 38(3): 101577.

Chapter 3

Digital Evolution and Information Systems to Support Decision-Making Processes in Sport

Marzia Ventura,[1,*] *Concetta Lucia Cristofaro,*[2] *Walter Vesperi*[3] and *Anna Maria Melina*[4]

Introduction

In today's digital age, organizations are presented with and exploit the explosion of emerging technologies (Gavrilova et al. 2017; Samoilă et al. 2023) that now pervades every aspect of organizational life (Bailey et al. 2019). The benefits of these technologies reach well beyond improved efficiency and decision-making, strengthening organizational culture (Ransbotham et al. 2021). Technology has long been part of sports and recently football (also known as 'soccer') has also started to modernize. In 2018, the video assistant referee (VAR) was launched to correct clear and obvious errors and serious missed incidents. Football refereeing is a difficult task that requires the analysis of challenging and fast in-game situations in a matter of seconds. These situations can involve several players, and many times referees have very limited visibility (Lex et al. 2015). Controversial referee decisions can severely

[1] University of Catanzaro.
[2] University E-campus.
[3] University of Palermo.
[4] University of Messina.
Emails: concettalucia.cristofaro@uniecampus.it, walter.vesperi@unipa.it, amelina@unime.it
* Corresponding author: marziaventura@unicz.it

DOI 10.1201/9781003535393-3

affect the outcome of a match and as a result, football authorities have finally started to modernize the game to improve quality and fairness. These changes, encompassing the use of new technologies, were long overdue when compared with the digital transformation already present in other sports and seeing the rapid development of the Internet of Things (IoT) and artificial intelligence (AI). VAR watches the games from a video operation room (VOR) and automatically checks every decision being made on the pitch related to the four established reviewable calls – goal or no goal, penalty or no penalty, direct red card, and in the case of mistaken identity when the referee cautions or sends off the wrong player (International Football Association Board, 2020). VAR is a technological system that includes a human factor (i.e., the video referee and assistant referee, the operator), a technological factor (the video system, the audio system), a human–technology interface (Sánchez Cid and García García 2020), and a social–ethical factor (e.g., referee team dynamics, perceptions of fairness and justice) (de Dios Crespo 2020). As such, its introduction has presented major modifications in the way referees train, prepare for and officiate matches (Armenteros and Webb 2020; Fernández Ruiz et al. 2020), as well as in refereeing psychology (de la Vega and Fuentes 2020). Nowadays, people are becoming ever more involved in adopting technology, which provides them with new ways to communicate, investigate and support decisions. The required harmonization of technologies with operational decision-making demands a new alignment of software techniques. The subject of using technology as a decision support has become an interesting topic for many researchers in organizational studies (Ali et al. 2017). The aim of this chapter is to explore how the implementation of the VAR system has influenced decision-making processes and contributed to technological change within professional football, with a specific focus on the Italian Serie A context. Through this lens, the study addresses the following research questions:

RQ1: How has the introduction of VAR impacted referees' decision-making processes during matches?
RQ2: In what ways has the diffusion of VAR contributed to technological transformation within the football system?

To address these questions, the study adopts a qualitative case study approach, focusing on the Italian Serie A league. Data collection involves a combination of document analysis, including official reports, refereeing guidelines, and institutional sources (e.g., the International Football Association Board (IFAB)), as well as a review of relevant academic literature. The analysis is guided by themes related to technological integration, organizational change and decision-making processes in professional sports officiating. The choice of a case study is justified by the exploratory nature of the research and the unique institutional and cultural characteristics of Italian football, which has been among the early adopters of VAR technology at the league level.

Theoretical Background

Organizations undergoing technology-driven change must understand that technology is one of several interrelated components that drive organizational performance. The implementation of technologies has a significant impact (Haake 2009; Balmer et al. 2011; Foster et al. 2012; Stefani 2012; Dyer 2015) on performance and requires adequate information management with excellent decision-making. Scott and Bruce (1995) defined decision-making style as the habitual, learned response pattern an individual exhibits when tackling a problem or situation. Decisions are the result of a complex decision-making process, including several subsequent yet logically connected phases. Some authors focus on how to implement decision-making in the sports world. In this regard, the main objective of Tur-Porcar et al. (2020) is to create a hierarchy of emotional and motivational factors that sports organizations can use to increase commitment to athletes. The analysis in this study was performed using the analytic hierarchy process (AHP). This structured decision-making process has made it possible to demonstrate that motivation and the regulation of emotions are the most important criteria for generating this commitment within sports organizations. Calder and Durbach (2015) focus their studies on how to adopt decision support tools, including technological ones, within the various sports organizations like rugby. The method considers the players' performance with regard to a number of attributes and resolves uncertainty in both performance evaluation and preferences for some aspects of the game over others. It emerged from the study that the model aims to support the decisional process by helping coaches better understand the players available to them and the preferences that each player favours. In contrast, the research by Marquez et al. (2020) provides information on consumer behaviour with regard to the use of technology that can assist the decision-making process of sports managers. The main focus of the study by Samuel et al. (2019) was to test the usefulness of a new decision simulator designed for qualified soccer referees. The challenge was to create a simulator that simulated the referee's task (i.e., numerous sequential episodes of decision-making under physical effort) and could be easily applied by referees on a regular basis. The results support the use of a simulator as a potentially innovative method for referee training in sequential decision-making. Finally, Schnyder et al. (2017) aim to reconstruct subjective theories on the decision-making process of football referees in offside situations. Winand et al. (2021) found that referees prefer decision-aid technology because it reduces the pressure on them.

Their increased use and potential have led to the development of emerging technologies that will create new opportunities in the sports sector and that are at the forefront of technological innovation and research (Petrović et al. 2015). The term 'emerging technology' (ET) has often been used by information technology professionals and academics. Stahl (2011) notes that Cloud computing, artificial intelligence, virtual reality and social networking websites are labelled as emerging technologies (ET). However, according to Halaweh (2013), there are few studies that have shed light on this term and that have specified its characteristics and meaning.

Indeed, there is no widely accepted definition of 'emerging technologies. Technology is defined as emerging when it causes a radical change in business, industry or society.

According to Turner et al. (2010), emerging technology, globalization and social change are creating a background in which sporting organizations must seek to quickly adapt to manage their ongoing activities and operations.

Jordaan and Surujlal (2013) argued that technology has always played a significant role in sports, enhancing the experience of players, referees and other stakeholders. According to Catteeuw et al. (2009), in sports, a referee is often blamed for a team's poor outcome, receiving condemnation for bias in applying the rules accurately.

Therefore, using technology has been proposed to improve sports officials' decision-making. The implementation of VAR in association football is one example of how technology can be used to assist decision-making.

Literature Review and Specific Contribution

VAR was introduced into the laws of the game in 2018 to support match officials by reviewing their decisions and monitoring how well they follow the rules through screening video footage for three game situations (goals, red card incidents and penalties) and one administrative incident (mistaken identity). In these cases, if a referee makes a clear and obvious error of assessment VAR intervenes to increase (objective) fairness and to assist in correct decision-making (Fédération Internationale de Football Association 2019; Lago-Peñas et al. 2019). In practice, once VAR has reviewed the video material, the head referee is informed via headset about the content of the specific video sequence, and appropriate decisions or actions can then be taken. The VAR team is in a centralized video operation room (VOR) and can access all relevant broadcast cameras and two dedicated offside cameras. As a result, the introduction of VAR can be used to examine whether it can help support referees' decision-making. The general impact of VAR on the game was analysed by Lago-Peñas et al. (2019). They concluded that the VAR system does not substantially modify the game in professional football but only leads to a decrease in the number of offside violations, fouls and yellow cards, and an increase in the number of minutes added to the regular playing time at the end of the first half, but not at the end of the second. In particular, Bryson et al. (2021) found that, across 17 countries, significantly fewer yellow cards were issued to the away teams. Considering that the football business has developed rapidly and has become faster and more athletic (i.e., Matheson 2003; Frick 2007), the challenges referees face have increased, as have their overall responsibility and physical and mental requirements. To become an official in professional football, referees have undergo a long training and reviewing process.

A football match lasts 90 minutes and is equally divided into two 45-minute periods separated by a 15-minute half-time recovery after which both competing teams change ends. At the end of each half, the referee can allow extra time to recover any time lost during the play. The referee represents the maximum authority on the field, and their main objective is to guarantee that the laws of the game are respected (Mallo et al. 2008). In making decisions, the referee is supported by VAR technology (Sabag et al. 2020). The VAR follows the progress of the action on a series of screens, and when he realizes that the referee on the pitch has made a wrong decision, he communicates via radio so that the referee can correct it. VAR can only intervene in four categories defined as game-changing situations (Mather and Breivik 2020), which are:

1. To establish the regularity of a goal
2. To award a penalty kick
3. For sending off players, which requires the direct showing of the red card
4. For identity error (exchanging the player to be warned or sent off with another).

Analysing the literature concerning VAR, it has been noted that the experiments conducted on video technologies have led to several advantages for the decision-making process of referees:

- videos from different angles provide a record of physical and tactical information of different players (Meng et al. 2020).
- the use of instant replay enables the referees to make more accurate decisions (Salomon et al. 2011). VAR provides access to a replay of the videos in real time and slow motion. The impact of the video speed on the referees' decision-making indicated that the slow-motion footage increases the accuracy of the referees' technical decisions (no foul, indirect free kick, direct free kick or penalty kick), particularly for corner situations.

When VAR was officially introduced into the rules of the game in 2018 (Federation International Football Association 2019), it sparked widespread interest and debate among stakeholders across various sports (Zhekambayeva et al. 2024). This interest was largely concerned with possible disruptions to the flow of the game (Winand et al. 2021). Spitz et al. (2020) showed that in the main national leagues in the world, the VAR check has a median duration of 22 seconds with an increasing rate of accuracy for the initial referee's decision of 92.1%–98.3%. Another study by Lago-Peñas et al. (2019) found a decrease in the number of offsides, fouls and yellow cards after the implementation of VAR in the German Bundesliga and the Italian Serie A, and an increase in the number of minutes added to the playing time in the first half and the full game, but not in the second half. Similar results were found for the Spanish LaLiga (Lago-Peñas et al. 2021) and the Chinese Super League (Han et al. 2020), namely a decrease in the number of offsides and a slight increase in the number of minutes added to the playing time. Studies concluded that VAR does not substantially modify the game in elite soccer; however, Lago-Peñas et al. (2021) suggest reducing the number of on-field reviews to retain the flow of the game. In their study, Carlos et al. (2019) showed how the introduction of the VAR system influenced the play in football. In a study by Mather and Breivik (2022), 80 Premier League (English league) professional football referees watched 60 videos of players (faults, yellow cards and red cards) with variations in playback speed, and were asked to give their opinion on the assisted move. Other studies look at the fans' perspective of VAR in football. Scanlon et al. (2022) studied the perception of VAR of the Premier League football fans who were physically present at matches in the 2019/2020 season, with the data being collected from different areas of the stadiums. Bouzas-Rico et al. (2022) carried out a systematic literature review of field tests to evaluate the aptitude of referees, considering databases up to May 2020. The authors found a total of 13 studies that analysed the psychometric properties of aptitude tests, while 7 investigations focused on field physical aptitude tests specifically designed to evaluate aerobic endurance. Aragão and Pina et al. (2022) carried out a literature review on football refereeing. Frandsen and Landgrebe (2022) using the Danish Superliga as a case, explore how football's implementation of VAR instigates complex processes of change, which imply not only a further decrease in football's institutional autonomy but also intensifies inequality. In terms of the refereeing decision-making sequence, VAR intervention appears at the end of the process, when the on-field referee has already made a decision and receives external feedback from the refereeing team. They are then faced with a subsequent decision – namely, to keep or change the original decision (Samuel et al. 2020). The study exposes the complexities between VAR and the experience of fans on match days. They found that there was a significant decrease in the number of offsides, fouls and yellow cards after the implementation of VAR, and there was an increase in the number of minutes added to the playing time in the first half and the full game. VAR plays an important role in enhancing the quality of the refereeing, and there is no doubt that video technology assists referees in their decision-making process with regard to decisions such as establishing whether a goal has been scored or which player has in fact committed a foul. It was introduced for this reason, providing more objective information and helping to avoid wrong decisions being made. Several studies have shown that referees' decisions can be influenced by several factors such as crowd noise, social pressure, match status or the strength of the teams (Garicano et al. 2005; Boyko et al. 2007; Dohmen 2008; Unkelbach and Memmert 2010; Riedl et al. 2015). The study by Işın and Yi (2024) analysed the effect of VAR on home advantages and referee bias in football in the Turkish Super League. The findings of the study showed that, with or without VAR, home teams had an advantage over away teams in points and goals.

Methodology

The International Federation of Football approved the use of video to provide support for football refereeing. The federation claimed that this technology is an effective aid in decision-making. The use of video technologies in football refereeing and other sports analyses the capacity of audio-visual technology from different perspectives to help understand the best implementation of the VAR system in football. The purpose of this chapter is twofold: firstly, to analyse the state of the art of the diffusion of VAR in the Italian Serie A football system; secondly, to examine whether the introduction of VAR has modified the decision-making process of referees and whether its application has led to significant changes, particularly on a technological level.

This research has been divided into two phases (Figure 1):

1. In the first phase we propose a literature review, starting with the online database (Scopus) through specific keywords to establish the current state of analysis.
2. In the second phase we present an implementation of a VAR project in Italian Football – Serie A.

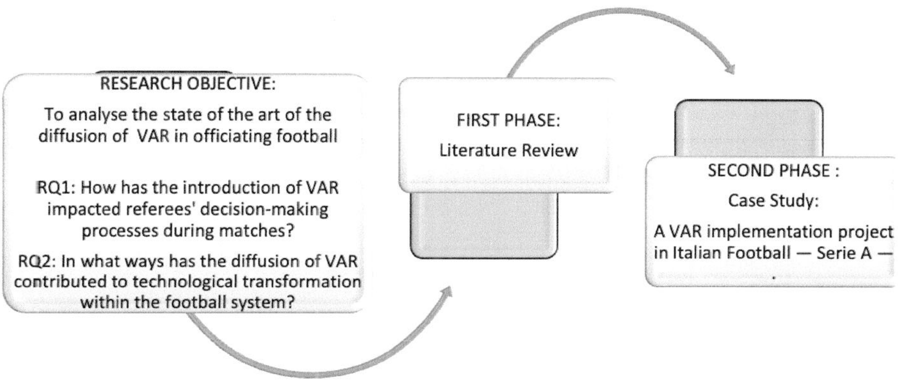

Figure 1. Methodological design. Source: authors' elaboration.

Results and Discussion

Systematic Literature Review

A systematic literature review was conducted in January 2025 by the authors in accordance with the Preferred Reporting Items for Systematic Review and Meta-Analyses (PRISMA) guidelines (Moher 2009). However, this protocol was modified by incorporating the article screening process as each article was identified, rather than as a single solitary stage later in the process. The search strategy used a series of specific keywords. Specific keywords namely Video Assistant Referee "AND" Decision Making "AND" Football "OR" Italy. The chapter examined the system of football, specifically the Italian Serie A. One relevant bibliographic database – Scopus – was used for this purpose. Furthermore, as per the PRISMA protocol, additional records were identified through other sources. These sources included the use of article reference lists identified through the primary search stage and the use of Google Scholar. The search strings included:

1. Date of the search – 2024.
2. Publication periods: 2018–2024. The Italian Football Association introduced the VAR system to their highest leagues during the 2017/2018 season.
3. Publication in English language.

The inclusion and exclusion criteria can be based on research design and methodology (Okoli and Schabram 2010; Xiao and Watson 2019). For instance, studies may be restricted to those carried out in certain geographic areas (Italy) of certain units of analysis (Serie A).

The process:

1. The articles for inclusion are based on the review of abstracts.
2. The second step is followed by a refined quality assessment based on a full-text review.

The purpose of this early screening is to weed out articles with content that is inapplicable to the research question(s) and/or established criteria. At this stage, reviewers should be inclusive; that is to say, if in doubt, the articles should be included (Okoli and Schabram 2010). The overall methodology for screening is the same across different types of literature reviews (Figure 2).

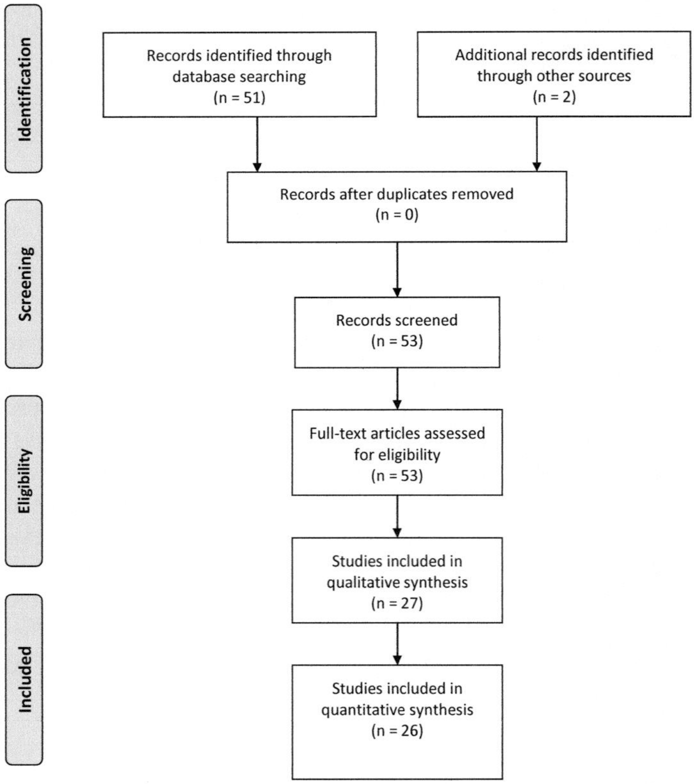

Figure 2. Literature search and evaluation for inclusion. Source: authors' elaboration.

Subsequently, 53 publications met these conditions and were included in this review (Table 1 and Table 2 are reported in the Appendix. Table 1 reports a selection of publications from the Scopus database and Table 2 reports supplementary literature obtained from the Scholar database).

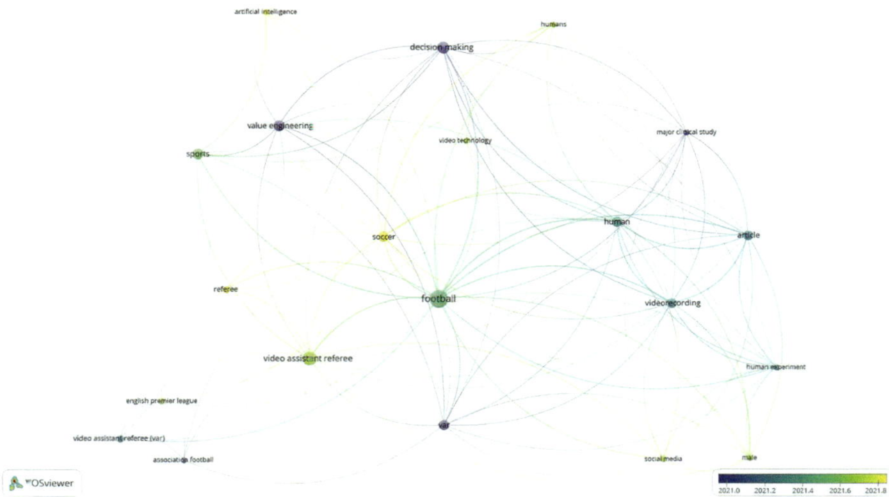

Figure 3. Keywords map. Source: elaboration between VOSviewer - www.vosviewer.com.

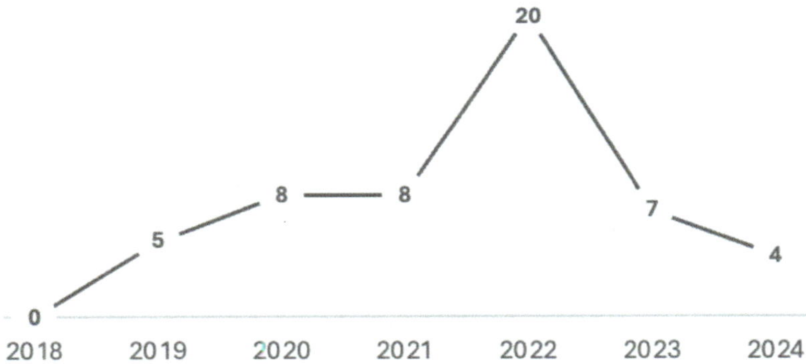

Figure 4. Documents by year.

Of the 53 papers that met the criteria, 51 were extrapolate from the Scopus database, and the remaining 2 from the Scholar database. Of the 53 papers analysed, 27 present a qualitative and 26 a quantitative methodology. Only 5 papers have analysed and studied the phenomenon with the use of a literature review.

From the keywords of the various articles examined, it was possible to create the visualization of similarities (VOS) map. In this research, the VOSviewer is used to create maps of authors' publications and to create maps of keywords based on a co-occurrence network.

Figure 3 shows the analysis performed with regard to the article keywords.

In the figure, items (keywords) are indicated by a small coloured circle. The scatter view can be useful for an overview of the general theme.

From the analysis of the literature, it emerged that the year in which the most studies on the subject of VAR and decision-making support were produced was 2022 (Figure 4).

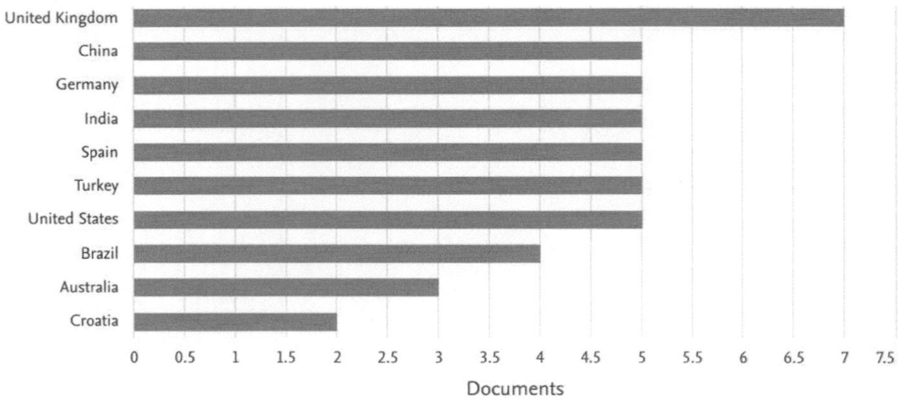

Figure 5. Documents by country.

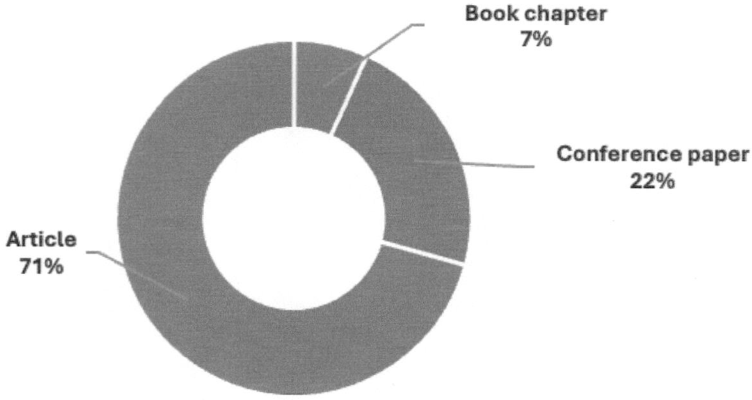

Figure 6. Documents by type.

The country in which the literary production on this topic was most relevant was the UK (Figure 5).

The majority of documents produced were in the form of journal articles (70.8%) compared to book chapters (6.7%) and conference articles (22.5%) (Figure 6).

The following figure shows the authors who have been most interested in the topic of VAR in the period 2018 to 2024 (Figure 7).

The area of greatest interest that has seen the greatest number of publications on the phenomenon of VAR and the decision-making process is that relating to the social sciences with a percentage of scientific production equal to 16.3% (Figure 8).

In view of the literature review carried out, it is possible to state that, although it is certain that there have been some changes, there are currently doubts about how and to what extent the introduction of the new technological system has influenced football referees' decision-making.

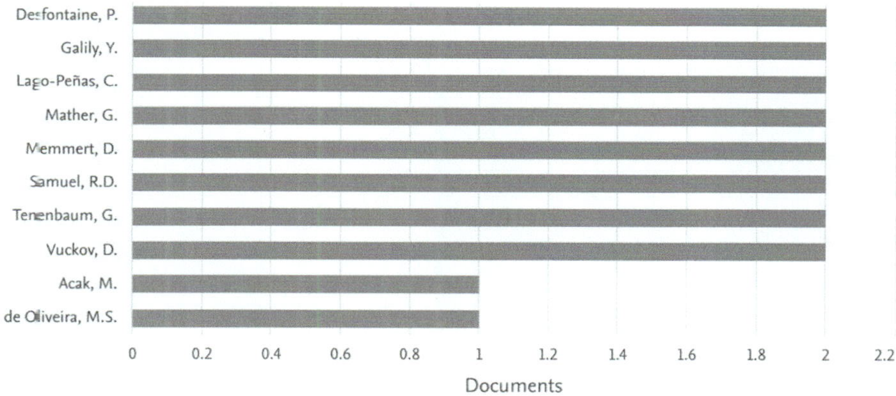

Figure 7. Documents by authors.

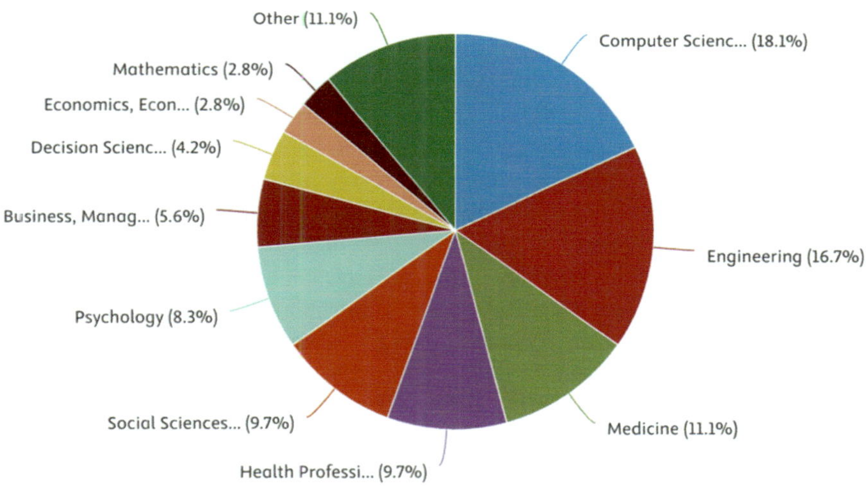

Figure 8. Documents by subject area.

Case Study: Video Assistant Referee Project

The second phase of this work is the application and implementation of VAR in the Italian Serie A matches.

Following the IFAB's decision to implement VAR in various federations, starting in 2018, and its successful use in the 2018 World Cup, the major European countries integrated VAR into their regular leagues. Italy is affiliated to the Union of European Football Associations (UEFA) and the Italian Football Association, together with the Italy Professional Football Leagues Directory, therefore began considering the implementation of a VAR project in Italy. Italy was somewhat of a pioneer in the context of implementing such a complex project. In 2018, a public announcement was made that the VAR would already be integrated into the same season's Serie A matches (Figures 9 and 10).

Figure 9 and Figure 10. The VAR team is in a centralized VOR. Source: Final Report 'Video Assistant Referee Project', 2018.

This created a very tight schedule – 9 months – for such a complex implementation project, resulting in high pressure and a very focused process. The project team was in charge of setting up the technological infrastructure as well as the professional instruction and certification. As the VAR project was novel, the professional manager had to individually strategize the implementation process, including the designing of an instruction programme to align with the IFAB's strict certification demands. Furthermore, a training area was required to be modified to include two simulator rooms and an instruction classroom for the theoretical and practical instruction of the referees. There was a strict learning protocol that each referee had to undergo, including: (a) theoretical knowledge of the VAR system and protocol; (b) an offline simulator of clips and then full matches; and (c) live simulations. For the final step, the referees experienced offline performance in real matches. In total, the referees engaged in 210 hours of instruction.

Next, a pilot phase was initiated in the Serie A of the 2017–2018 season. As part of the ongoing instruction, they gave feedback to support the operator.

- Video Assistant Referee Project: Participants

  The participants were 22 professional male referees from the Italian Serie A (Table 3).

Table 3. Project Numbers.

22	Referees have received the necessary training
60	Hours of theory and applicability of the IFAB protocol in Sportilia and Coverciano
90	Hours of training on the use of technology and VAR/operator communication processes
60	Hours of training for Hawk-eye operators
17	Stadiums tested and approved
60	Serie A Championship offline matches
70	Friendly online matches organized specifically for practice
1047	Accidents analysed
35	Referee decisions changed

Source: Final Report 'Video Assistant Referee Project', 2018

Excerpts from interviews released by referees.

Italy is the first country in the world to have a unique VAR room. It's impossible not to make a mistake but now we are in the best position to avoid making more mistakes" (Alfredo Trentalange 2021– Referee).

The new structure will make it possible to directly coordinate the work of the referee commission with a supervisor present on site; in this way, we avoid dispersion and give immediate feedback (Gianluca Rocchi 2021– Referee Designator).

This unique VAR room will connect all 17 Serie A stadiums with the 8 VAR rooms dedicated to referees for Serie A matches.

The VAR system does not make any decisions; it supports the referee in the decision-making process and the final decision can only be taken by the referee.

The VAR was introduced to help make football a fairer sport. The present study provides new information about how the implementation of VAR has changed referee decisions and the phenomenon of Italian football (Serie A). To do so, we compared the difference between the season in which VAR was implemented (2017/2018) and the season before (2016/2017) (Table 4). The results were mainly retrieved from the institutional website of Italian Association Referees (AIA-FiGC).

Table 4. Statistics.

	2016/17	2017/18	VARIATION	%
TOTAL YELLOWS	1719	1508	– 211	– 12,3%
PROTESTS	137	113	– 24	– 17,5%
SIMULATIONS	34	22	– 12	– 35,3%
UNSPORTSMANLIKE CONDUCT	114	107	– 7	– 6,1%
TOTAL REDS	97	91	– 6	– 7,1%
AGGRESSIVE BEHAVIOR	28	33	5	+ 17,8%

Source: Final Report "Video Assistant Referee Project", 2018

With the use of the VAR system, the percentage of referee errors dropped to 0.89%. The officiating error rate would have been 5.78% without VAR. The following were evaluated: 397 games, 2023 checks, 117 referee corrections.

There was one intervention every 3.39 games and the average time for the VAR DECISION in Serie A was 31' 5".

There was minimum interference for maximum benefit as desired at the beginning of the project (Tables 5 and 6).

Table 5. VAR Statistics.

EPISODE CATEGORIES	TOTALS	%
GOALS	1060	53%
PENALTIES	538	27%
RED CARDS	407	20%

397 MATCHES:
380 SERIE A and 16 TIM CUP
2023 CHECK
(5,1 CK/MATCH)
117 OVERRULE

Source: Final Report "Video Assistant Referee Project", 2018

Table 6. VAR Statistics.

CATEGORIES CORRECTIONS	TOTALS	%
GOALS	42	36%
PENALTIES	59	50%
RED CARDS	16	14%

ON FIELD REVIEW (O.F.R.): **76**
NO O.F.R.: **41**
CONFIRMATIONS WITH O.F.R.: **18**

Source: Final Report "Video Assistant Referee Project", 2018

With the implementation of the VAR system, the rate of refereeing errors has decreased to 0.89%. Without VAR, the error rate would have been 5.78%. The analysis evaluated 397 matches, involving 2,023 checks and 117 referee corrections. Given the complexity of the project, which spanned multiple areas, a series of corrective measures would go on to be implemented, starting in the following season (2018/2019). These measures will include improvements to the technological area and communication system, training, and VAR intervention guidelines and times. Specifically, the corrective measures will aim to further optimize intervention times, eliminating overlap between VAR and referee review times (Figure 11). The implementation of the VAR system has been a game-changer in football, aiming to reduce critical errors in referees' decision-making and enhance the perception of

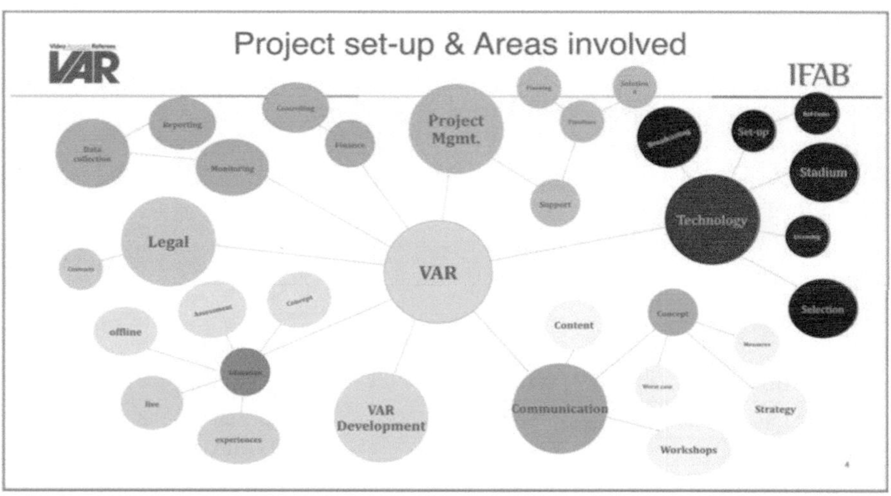

Figure 11. Corrective measures. Source: Final Report "Video Assistant Referee Project", 2018.

equity. On the one hand, the benefits of VAR are clear: it has significantly improved the accuracy of refereeing decisions, reducing controversy and increasing fairness in the game. However, there are also challenges and limitations to consider: technical limitations, standardization issues, and behavioural constraints of individuals, as well as organizational constraints, can hinder the effective implementation of VAR. Some of the key drawbacks include technical glitches, inconsistent application of VAR protocols, and the potential for VAR to disrupt the flow of the game. Despite these challenges, VAR can enhance the overall integrity of the game and improve the fan experience. Nevertheless, it is crucial to address the limitations and challenges associated with VAR to ensure its effective implementation and maximize its benefits.

Conclusions and Future Steps

By analysing the reference literature, an attempt was made to verify how scholars of this subject have addressed the contribution that VAR technology can make in supporting sports decisions in football matches. Football referees are required to keep up with play at all times to ensure optimal positioning in making key decisions, and VAR, intended to correct egregious mistakes, has taken close calls to a place beyond the abilities of humans to perceive them, a matter of centimetres measured by a computer. The introduction and implementation process of the VAR system within the Italian Serie A reflected a technical–technological change event in the work of referees, which introduced potential implications for training (Armenteros and Webb 2020; de la Vega and Fuentes 2020). Based on the taxonomy of Kolbinger and Lames (2017), some technologies are used to replace referees for a specific decision, and technological aids help the referee to enforce rules (i.e., the vanishing spray in soccer). The VAR system is designed to improve the decision-making of referees by offering additional viewing angles as well as video replays. However, it might also set conditions for replacing the referee with regard to certain basic decisions, such as offsides and goals. Furthermore, knowing that they are being watched and supervised by the VAR, players are committing fewer fouls (Lago-Peñas et al. 2019). The official data on the implementation of the VAR system in the Italian Serie indicated that the initial use of the system was far from perfect. In the Italian implementation phase, the reported level of error was 1%, with 1,708 decisions being reviewed over 210 matches, which led to 60 decisions being corrected, 11 of those being incorrect, including seven that influenced the outcome of the game. The Italian Serie A referees perceived the implementation of VAR as a change event. This change event had mainly influenced the technical–technological aspect of their performance, with moderate effects on pre-match preparation, players' management and communication, public perception and decision-making. VAR was designed to reduce critical errors in the decision-making of football referee, thereby increasing the social perceptions of justice.

From the referees' perspective, the implementation of VAR represents a technical–technological career change event. The effects were experienced in pre-match preparation, players' management, public perception and decision-making. The referees felt that their perceived pressure during the matches decreased. This change event produced off-field demands mostly related to the educational process and on-field demands mainly related to developing proficiency in VAR. The referees also experienced off-field (e.g., rewards system) and on-field barriers (e.g., errors made by the VARs). To effectively cope with these new demands and barriers, most of them initially consulted with others and then made a decision to apply all necessary adjustments in response to the new situation. The referees showed some professional improvements; nevertheless, they experienced scrutiny from the clubs, the media and the Referee Union. Thus, the 22 referees in this study perceived the outcome of this change process favourably.

The discussion presents reflections on these findings in light of the recently emerging literature on technological officiating aids in sports. The inclusion of video referee technology can lead to various stressors pertaining to training, decision-making, media, coaches and players and communication issues (Baldwin 2014). These changes resulted in significant challenges in terms of the referees' coping and motivation. Yet, currently, there is a scarcity of scientific publications concerning its potential influence on the motivation, performance and career development of referees (Samuel et al. 2020b).

These findings may help coaches, players and managers to better understand the effects of the VAR system on professional football and to identify strategies to improve refereeing during matches. However, as Benz and Lopez (2021) pointed out, generalization based on findings from a single league may not be possible. Future studies should thus examine the effects found in other football leagues. The future step in this research will be interviews with the professionals in order to understand the role of VAR in decision-making, trying to understand if VAR is a decision support tool or a tool that they have to become accustomed to because it is envisaged at the governance level. This current work leads us to some implications: the introduction of technologies leads to an organizational imbalance. To successfully assimilate technology requires that the other elements considered for the adequacy of the organizational set-up (objectives, strategies, structure…) can be adapted to a new equilibrium (Burton et al. 2020). For the successful adoption of technologies, they will need to be used or made available by the right people, in the right way, at the right time. Finally, adopting these technologies will enable existing decision-making procedures and policies to be questioned, thus forcing changes in work activities.

References

Abubakar, A. M., Elrehail, H., Alatailat, M. A. and Elçi, A. 2019. Knowledge management, decision-making style and organizational performance. Journal of Innovation & Knowledge 4(2): 104–114.

Associazione Italiana arbitri. 2018. Report Finale Video Assistant Referee Project. Available https://www.aia-figc.it/news.

Aleza, M. E. and Vetrithangam, D. 2023, April. Use of artificial intelligence to avoid errors in referring a football match. pp. 1–6. *In*: 2023 International Conference on Artificial Intelligence and Applications (ICAIA) Alliance Technology Conference (ATCON-1). IEEE.

Ali, M. H., Zolkipli, M. F., Mohammed, M. A. and Jaber, M. M. 2017. Enhance of extreme learning machine-genetic algorithm hybrid based on intrusion detection system. J. Eng. Appl. Sci. 12(16): 4180–4185.

Aragão e Pina, A., Passos, D. and Araújo, M. T. 2018. Maynard, Football refereeing: An integrative review. Psychol. Sport Exerc. 35: 10–26.

Ariyo, E. S., Faniyi, O. and Turcott, R. 2021. Utterly ashamed of their behavior: Examining the media coverage of Cameroon versus England in the 2019 FIFA Women's World Cup. pp. 27–51. 2019 FIFA Women's World Cup: Media, Fandom, and Soccer's Biggest Stage.

Armenteros, M., Benitez, A. J. and Betancor, M. 2020. The Use of Video Technologies in Refereeing and Football and Other Sports. New York, NY: Routledge.

Aycan, H. and Onağ, Z. 2022. Views of Turkish football stakeholders on video assistant referee technology. International Sports Studies 44(2).

Bailey, D., Faraj, S., Hinds, P., von Krogh, G. and Leonardi, P. 2019. Special issue of organization science: emerging technologies and organizing. Organization Science 30(3): 642–646.

Bae, R. and Han, B. 2023. The influence of the video assistance referee (VAR) on the english premier league. Int. J. Perform Anal. Sport. 24(3): 241–50.

Bonazzi, G. 1999. Dire fare pensare: decisioni e creazione di senso nelle organizzazioni (Vol. 36). FrancoAngeli.

Bouzas-Rico, S., De Dios-Álvarez, V., Suárez-Iglesias, D. and Ayán-Pérez, C. 2022. Field-based tests for assessing fitness in referees: A systematic review. Res. Sports Med. 30(4): 439–457.

Boyko, R. H., Boyko, A. R. and Boyko, M. G. 2007. Referee bias contributes to home advantage in English Premiership football. Journal of Sports Sciences 25(11): 1185–1194.

Brunnström, K., Djupsjöbacka, A., Ozolins, O., Billingham, J., Wistel, K. and Evans, N. 2023. Quality measurement methods for video assisting refereeing systems. Sports Engineering 26(1): 17.

Bryson, A., Dolton, P., Reade, J. J., Schreyer, D. and Singleton, C. 2021. Causal effects of an absent crowd on performances and refereeing decisions during Covid-19. Economics Letters 198: 109664.

Buyukcelebi, H., Duz, S., Acak, M., Nalbant, U., Svatora, K., Gabrys, T. et al. 2022. Development of the effect of video assistant referee application on football parameters. Applied Sciences 12(12): 6088.

Calder, J. M. and Durbach, I. N. 2015. Decision support for evaluating player performance in rugby union. International Journal of Sports Science & Coaching 10(1): 21–37.

Carlos, L. P., Ezequiel, R. and Anton, K. 2019. How does Video Assistant Referee (VAR) modify the game in elite soccer? International Journal of Performance Analysis in Sport 19(4): 646–653.

Catteeuw, P., Helsen, W. F., Gilis, B. and Wagemans, J. 2009. Decision-making skills, role specificity, and deliberate practice in association football refereeing. Journal of Sports Sciences 27(11): 1125–1136.

Collins, H., Evans, R. and Higgins, C. 2016. Bad Call: Technology's Attack on Referees and Umpires and How to Fix it. MIT Press.

Collins, L. and Collins, D. 2019. Managing the cognitive loads associated with judgment and decision-making in a group of adventure sports coaches: a mixed-method investigation. Journal of Adventure Education and Outdoor Learning 1–16.

D'Andréa, C. and Stauff, M. 2022. Mediatized engagements with technologies: "Reviewing" the video assistant referee at the 2018 world cup. Communication & Sport 10(5): 830–853.

Dawson, P., Massey, P. and Downward, P. 2019. Television match officials, referees, and home advantage: Evidence from the European Rugby Cup. Sport Management Review.

De Dios Crespo, J. 2020. The contributions of VARs to fairness in sport. pp. 23–35. *In*: Armenteros, M., Benítez, A. J. and Betancor, A. M. (eds.). The Use of Video Technologies in Refereeing Football and Other Sports (New York, NY: Routledge).

De la Vega, R. and Fuentes, J. P. 2020. Psychological response of the referee to the introduction of VAR. pp. 339–350. *In*: Armenteros, M., Benítez, A. J. and Betancor, A. M. (eds.). The Use of Video Technologies in Refereeing Football and Other Sports (New York, NY: Routledge).

De Oliveira, M. S., Steffen, V. and Trojan, F. 2023. A systematic review of the literature on video assistant referees in soccer: Challenges and opportunities in sports analytics. Decision Analytics Journal 100232.

Defruyt, S., Wylleman, P., Kegelaers, J. and De Brandt, K. 2020. Factors influencing Flemish elite athletes' decision to initiate a dual career path at higher education. Sport in Society 23(4): 660–677.

Desfontaine, P., Borel-Hänni, F. and Wille, F. 2022. Sports media and the use of audiovisual technology in soccer: Media coverage of video assistant referee use during the 2018 and 2019 FIFA World Cups. Staps 137(3): 121–142.

Dohmen, T. J. 2008. The influence of social forces: Evidence from the behavior of football referees. Economic Inquiry 46(3): 411–424.

Eppler, M. J. and Platts, K. W. 2009. Visual strategizing: The systematic use of visualization in the strategic-planning process. Long Range Planning 42(1): 42–74.

Fernández Ruiz, M., Betancor, M. Á. and Armenteros, M. 2020. Didactic teaching strategies for the VAR: an approach to gamification and 21st-Century skills. pp. 328–338. *In*: Armenteros, M., Benítez, A. J. and Betancor, A. M. (eds.). The Use of Video Technologies in Refereeing Football and Other Sports (New York, NY: Routledge).

FIFA. VAR at the. 2018 FIFA World Cup 2018 [22, 06, 2024]. Available from: https://inside.fifa.com/innovation/standards/video-assistant-referee/var-at-the-2018-fifa-world-cup.

FIFA. Inside look into the VAR review process 2018b [10-09-2024]. Available from: h t t p s : / / w w w.fifa. c o m / n e w s / i n s i d e - l o o k - i n t o- t h e- v a r-r e v i e w-p r o c e s s.

Fişne, M., Bardakçi, S. and Hasaan, A. 2021. Analysis of perceptions of turkish fans of video-assistant-referees in elite soccer. South African Journal for Research in Sport, Physical Education and Recreation 43(2): 29–46.

Frandsen, K. and Landgrebe, K. 2022. Video assistant referee in a small-nation context: intensified mediatization. Communication & Sport 10(5): 811–829.

Frick, B. 2007. The football players'labor market: empirical evidence from the major european leagues. Scottish Journal of Political Economy 54(3): 422–446.

Garicano, L., Palacios-Huerta, I. and Prendergast, C. 2005. Favoritism under social pressure. Review of Economics and Statistics 87(2): 208–216.

Gavrilova, T., Alsufyev, A., Grinberg, E. and Mailov, E. 2017. Knowledge visualization as a new discipline: Swiss Bias. In ECKM 2017 18th European Conference on Knowledge Management (Vol. 1). Academic Conferences and Publishing Limited.

Ghosh, S., Sasmal, S., Bhui, S., Dutta, S., Mukherjee, S., Majumder, A. et al. 2019, March. Radio frequency identification based goal line technology for quick decision making in a football match. pp. 441–445. In 2019 Devices for Integrated Circuit (DevIC). IEEE.

Hafeez, A., Hafeez, U., Amin, A. and Hasan, S. 2022. VAR technology in English football; Implications of intervening in a fast-moving game. International Sports Studies (1).

Halaweh, M. 2013. Emerging technology: What is it. Journal of Technology Management & Innovation 8(3): 108–115.

Hamsund, T. and Scelles, N. 2021. Fans' perceptions towards video assistant referee (VAR) in the english premier league. Journal of Risk and Financial Management 14(12): 573.

Han, B., Chen, Q., Lago-Peñas, C., Wang, C. and Liu, T. 2020. The influence of the video assistant referee on the Chinese Super League. International Journal of Sports Science & Coaching 15(5-6): 662–668.

Harding, J., Lock, D. and Toohey, K. 2016. A social identity analysis of technological innovation in an action sport: Judging elite half-pipe snowboarding. European Sport Management Quarterly 16(2): 214–232.

Harrison, E. F. 1995. The Managerial Decision-Making Process (Vol. 4, pp. 1–39). Boston, MA: Houghton Mifflin.

Hedelin, L. and Allwood, C. M. 2002. IT and strategic decision making. Industrial Management & Data Systems 102(3): 125–139.

Hoang, H. T. T., Ha, C. N., Nguyen, D. T., Nguyen, T. N., Huynh, T. N., Phan, T. T. et al. 2022, November. Poses Classification in a Taekwondo lesson using skeleton data extracted from videos with shallow and deep learning architectures. pp. 447–461. In International Conference on Future Data and Security Engineering. Singapore: Springer Nature Singapore.

Holder, U., Ehrmann, T. and König, A. 2022. Monitoring experts: insights from the introduction of video assistant referee (VAR) in elite football. Journal of Business Economics 92(2): 285–308.

Işın, A. and Yi, Q. 2024. Does video assistant referee technology change the magnitude and direction of home advantages and referee bias? A proof-of-concept study. BMC Sports Science, Medicine and Rehabilitation 16(1): 21.

İspa, M., Yarışan, U. and Kaya, T. 2022. Clustering English premier league referees using unsupervised machine learning techniques. pp. 230–237. In Intelligent and Fuzzy Techniques for Emerging Conditions and Digital Transformation: Proceedings of the INFUS 2021 Conference, held August 24–26, 2021. Volume 2. Springer International Publishing.

Joly, A. and Desfontaine, P. 2022. La technologisation des arbitres de l'élite dans le football français: entre arbitrage humain et rationalité numérique (1980–2021). Movement & Sport Sciences (3): 15–24.

Kiuchi, Y. 2022. Football Fan Reactions to Video Assistant Referee. Routledge Handbook of Sport Fans and Fandom (1st ed).

Kostuk, K. J. and Willoughby, K. A. 2012. A decision support system for scheduling the Canadian Football League. Interfaces 42(3): 286–295.

Kubayi, A., Larkin, P. and Toriola, A. 2022. The impact of video assistant referee (VAR) on match performance variables at men's FIFA World Cup tournaments. Proceedings of the Institution of Mechanical Engineers, Part P: Journal of Sports Engineering and Technology 236(3): 187–191.

Lago-Peñas, C., Gómez, M. A. and Pollard, R. 2021. The effect of the Video Assistant Referee on referee's decisions in the Spanish LaLiga. International Journal of Sports Science & Coaching 16(3): 824–829.

Lago-Peñas, C., Rey, E. and Kalén, A. 2019. How does video assistant Referee (VAR) modify the game in elite soccer? Int. J. Perform. Anal. Sport 19: 646–653.

Leveaux, R. 2010. Facilitating referee's decision making in sport via the application of technology. Communications of the IBIMA 2010: 1–8.

Lombardi, R., Trequattrini, R. and Battista, M. 2014. Systematic errors in decision making processes: the case of the Italian Serie A football championship. International Journal of Applied Decision Sciences 7(3): 239.

Lucić, I., Babić, S. and Vučkov, D. 2020, September. Perception of using VAR technology in football after completion of training and education and experiences of Croatian video assistant referees (VARs) and assistant VARs (AVARs). pp. 905–911. In 2020 43rd International Convention on Information, Communication and Electronic Technology (MIPRO). IEEE.

Mallo, J., Navarro, E., García-Aranda, J. M., Gilis, B. and Helsen, W. 2008. Analysis of the kinematical demands imposed on top-class assistant referees during competitive soccer matches. The Journal of Strength & Conditioning Research 22(1): 235–242.

Marquez, A., Cianfrone, B. A. and Kellison, T. 2020. Factors affecting spectators' adoption of digital ticketing: the case of interscholastic sports. International Journal of Sports Marketing and Sponsorship.

Märtins, J., Westmattelmann, D. and Schewe, G. 2022. Affected but not involved: Two-scenario based investigation of individuals' attitude towards decision support systems based on the example of the video assistant referee. Journal of Decision Systems 1–25.

Mather, G. 2020. A step to VAR: the vision science of offside calls by Video Assistant Referees. Perception 49(12): 1371–1374.

Mather, G. and Breivik, S. 2020. Is the perception of intent by association football officials influenced by video playback speed?. Royal Society Open Science 7(6): 192026.

Matheson, V. A. 2003. European Football: A Survey of the Literature. Williamstown, MA: Williams College, Department of Economics.

Meneguite, Y. N. F., Leite, L. B., Da Silva, D. C., De Moura, A. G. and Lavorato, V. N. 2022. Influence of the video assistant referee (VAR) on the Brazilian Men's Soccer Championship. Journal of Physical Education and Sport 22(4): 858–862.

Meng, X., Li, Z., Wang, S., Karambakhsh, A., Sheng, B., Yang, P. et al. 2020. A video information driven football recommendation system. Computers & Electrical Engineering 85: 106699.

Moshayedi, A. J., Chen, Z., Liao, L. and Li, S. 2019, December. Kinect based virtual referee for table tennis game: TTV (Table Tennis Var System). pp. 354–359. In 2019 6th International Conference on Information Science and Control Engineering (ICISCE). IEEE.

Nasiri, M. M., Ranjbar, M., Tavana, M., Santos Arteaga, F. J. and Yazdanparast, R. 2019. A novel hybrid method for selecting soccer players during the transfer season. Expert Systems 36(1): e12342.

Navaneeth, M. M. and Nimkar, N. 2020. Fan perception towards the usage of technology in football. Annals of Tropical Medicine–Public Health 23(S17): SP231731.

Nuhrat, Y. 2023. Challenging ocularcentric fairness assumptions of the video assistant referee (VAR) system in football. The Senses and Society 1–15.

Oliver, R. 2002. The role of ICT in higher education for the 21st century: ICT as a change agent for education. Retrieved April 14, 2007.

Panchuk, M., Panchuk, T. and Panchuk, A. 2022, March. Peculiarities of application of information technologies in Footbal and Futsal. pp. 702–708. In 2022 International Conference on Decision Aid Sciences and Applications (DASA). IEEE.

Panse, N. and Mahabaleshwarkar, A. 2020, October. A dataset & methodology for computer vision based offside detection in soccer. pp. 19–26. In Proceedings of the 3rd International Workshop on Multimedia Content Analysis in Sports.

Petersen-Wagner, R. and Lee Ludvigsen, J. A. 2023. The video assistant referee (VAR) as neo-coloniality of power? Fan negative reactions to VAR in the 2018 FIFA Men's World Cup. Sport in Society 26(5): 869–883.

Petrović, L. T., Milovanović, D. and Desbordes, M. 2015. Emerging technologies and sports events. Sport, Business and Management: An International Journal 5(2): 175–190. doi:10.1108/sbm-06-2012-0021.

Pina, J. A., Passos, A., Araújo, D. and Maynard, M. T. 2018. Football refereeing: An integrative review. Psychology of Sport and Exercise 35: 10–26.

Pizzera, A., Marrable, J. and Raab, M. 2022. The video review system in association football: Implementation and effectiveness for match officials and referee education. Managing Sport and Leisure 1–17.

Ponce-Bordón, J. C., Lobo-Triviño, D., Rubio-Morales, A., López del Campo, R., Resta, R. and López-Gajardo, M. A. 2022. The effect of the video assistant referee system implementation on match physical demands in the Spanish LaLiga. International Journal of Environmental Research and Public Health 19(9): 5125.

Qiao, J. 2022. The application of artificial intelligence in football risk prediction. Computational Intelligence and Neuroscience 2022.

Quanshu, S., Kotaro, H., Samad, K. M. A. and Kou, Y. 2023. Algorithm Research of Human Recognition and Their Application to Conjecture.

Ransbotham, S., Candelon, F., Kiron, D., LaFountain, B. and Khodabandeh, S. 2021. The Cultural Benefits of Artificial Intelligence in the Enterprise. MIT Sloan Management Review. https://sloanreview.mit.edu/projects/thecultural-benefits-of-artificial-intelligence-in-the-enterprise/.

Rantapuska, T. and Ihanainen, O. 2008. Knowledge use in ICT investment decision making of SMEs. Journal of Enterprise Information Management 21(6): 585–596.

Riedl, D., Strauss, B., Heuer, A. and Rubner, O. 2015. Finale furioso: referee-biased injury times and their effects on home advantage in football. Journal of Sports Sciences 33(4): 327–336.

Rintala, J. 1995. Sport and technology: human questions in a world of machines. Journal of Sport and Social Issues 19(1): 62–75.

Robinson, J 2019. Video Assistant Referee Technology Grinds the Women's World Cup to a Halt; The tournament isn't even through the round of 16 and has already seen more VAR stoppages than the entire men's tournament in 2018. Wall Street Journal (Online); New York, N.Y. [New York, N.Y] 25 June 2019.

Sabag, E., Lidor, R., Morgulev, E., Arnon, M., Azar, O. and Bar-Eli, M. 2020. To dive or not to dive in the penalty area? The questionable art of deception in soccer. International Journal of Sport and Exercise Psychology 18(3): 296–307.

Samoilă, C., Ursuțiu, D., Modran, H. A. and Chamunorwa, T. 2023. New challenges for remote experiment design in the digitalization era (Industry 4.0). pp. 957–966. In International Conference on Interactive Collaborative Learning. Cham: Springer International Publishing.

Samuel, R. D., Galily, Y., Filho, E. and Tenenbaum, G. 2020. Implementation of the video assistant referee (VAR) as a career change-event: The Israeli premier league case study. Frontiers in Psychology 11: 564855.

Samuel, R. D., Galily, Y., Guy, O., Sharoni, E. and Tenenbaum, G. 2019. A decision-making simulator for soccer referees. International Journal of Sports Science & Coaching 14(4): 480–489.

Sánchez Cid, M. and García García, A. L. 2020. The interaction between audio and the video assistant referee in football. pp. 70–85. *In*: Armenteros, M., Benítez, A. J. and Betancor, A. M. (eds.). The Use of Video Technologies in Refereeing Football and Other Sports (New York, NY: Routledge).

Scanlon, C., Griggs, G. and McGillick, C. 2022. 'It's not football anymore': perceptions of the video assistant referee by english premier league football fans. Soccer & Society 23(8): 1084–1096.

Schnyder, U., Schmid, D., Lippens, V. and Hossner, E. J. 2017. Offside decision-making by assistant referees in football: a reconstruction of subjective theories. Zeitschrift Fur Sportpsychologie 24(1): 3–16.

Shollo, A. and Xiao, X. 2019. Back to the Future: De-sequencing Time with Video Assistant Referee Technology.

Silver, M. S. and Silver, M. S. 1991. Systems that Support Decision Makers: Description and Analysis (p. 272). New York: Wiley.

Spitz, J., Wagemans, J., Memmert, D., Williams, A. M. and Helsen, W. F. 2021. Video assistant referees (VAR): The impact of technology on decision making in association football referees. Journal of Sports Sciences 39(2): 147–153.

Stahl, B. C. 2011. What does the Future Hold? A critical view of emerging information and communication technologies and their social consequences. pp. 59–76. *In*: Chiasson, M., Henfridsson, O., Karsten, H. and DeGross, J. I. (eds.). Researching the Future in Information Systems: IFIP WG 8.2 Working Conference, Future IS 2011, Turku, Finland, June 6–8, 2011, Proceedings (lst ed.). Heidelberg: Springer.

Surujlal, J. and Jordaan, D. B. 2013. Goal line technology in soccer: are referees ready for technology in decision making?: Technology and innovation. African Journal for Physical Health Education, Recreation and Dance 19(2): 245–257.

Svantesson, D. J. B. 2014. The extraterritoriality of EU data privacy law-its theoretical justification and its practical effect on US businesses. Stan. J. Int'l L. 50: 53.

Tur-Porcar, A. and Ribeiro-Soriano, D. 2020. The role of emotions and motivations in sport organizations. Frontiers in Psychology 11.

Turner, P. and Shilbury, D. 2010. The impact of emerging technology in sport broadcasting on the preconditions for interorganizational relationship (IOR) formation in professional football. Journal of Sport Management 24(1): 10–44.

Unkelbach, C. and Memmert, D. 2010. Crowd noise as a cue in referee decisions contributes to the home advantage. Journal of Sport and Exercise Psychology 32(4): 483–498.

Van Quaquebeke, N. and Giessner, S. R. 2010. How embodied cognitions affect judgments: Height-related attribution bias in football foul calls. Journal of Sport and Exercise Psychology 32(1): 3–22.

Vučkov, D. and Babić, S. 2021, September. VARs/AVARs in Croatian Top Division (1. HNL) and Major League Soccer: Experiences with VAR System. pp. 820–825. In 2021 44th International Convention on Information, Communication and Electronic Technology (MIPRO). IEEE.

Winand, M., Schneiders, C., Merten, S. and Marlier, M. 2021. Sports fans and innovation: An analysis of football fans' satisfaction with video assistant refereeing through social identity and argumentative theories. Journal of Business Research 136: 99–109.

Yu, L., Ling, P. and Zhang, H. 2010, December. Study on the decision support system of techniques and tactics in net sports and the application in beijing Olympic games. pp. 170–174. In 2010 Second WRI Global Congress on Intelligent Systems (Vol. 1). IEEE.

Zglinski, J. 2022. Rules, standards, and the video assistant referee in football. Sport, Ethics and Philosophy 16(1): 3–19.

Zhang, Y., Li, D., Gómez-Ruano, M. Á., Memmert, D., Li, C. and Fu, M. 2022. The effect of the video assistant referee (VAR) on referees' decisions at FIFA Women's World Cups. Frontiers in Psychology 13: 984367.

Zhiliang, J. 2021. A Study on the Application of Video Assistant Referee (VAR) technology in chinese football professional league. In E3S Web of Conferences (Vol. 292, p. 02009). EDP Sciences.

Zhang, L. and Liu, Z. 2024. Designing an event management system for campus football using 3D images and machine vision. Signal, Image and Video Processing 18(3): 2965–2974.

Zhekambayeva, M., Yerekesheva, M., Ramashov, N., Seidakhmetov, Y. and Kulambayev, B. 2024. Designing an artificial intelligence-powered video assistant referee system for team sports using computer vision. Retos: nuevas tendencias en educación física, deporte y recreación (61): 1162–1170.

Appendix

Table 1. Selection of publications from the Scopus database.

Authors	Title	Purpose	Methodology
Ghosh S.; Sasmal S.; Bhui S.; Dutta S.; Mukherjee S.; Majumder A.; Ganguly B. (2019)	Radio Frequency Identification based Goal Line Technology for Quick Decision Making in a Football Match	This study aims to design an automatic goal-line detection system with the help of radio frequency identification (RFID) - Arduino interfacing.	Quantitative
Moshayedi A.J.; Chen Z.; Liao L.; Li S. (2019)	Kinect Based Virtual Referee for Table Tennis Game: TTV (Table Tennis Var System)	In this research paper, a novel VAR system (TTV system) based on Kinect and Raspberry pi has been presented. The main aspect of this design is to have a portable system which can be used for any type of LCD system and help the referees to count the ball better during the game to have a more qualified game.	Quantitative
Shollo A.; Xiao X. (2019)	Back to the future: De-sequencing Time with Video Assistant Referee Technology	This short paper investigates how digital technology influences different aspects of time and related experiences. The research was inspired by a specific incident that occurred in the sports setting involving the use of Video Assistance Referee (VAR) technology in a live football match, which served as a revelatory case.	Qualitative
Samuel R.D.; Galily Y.; Guy O.; Sharoni E.; Tenenbaum G. (2019)	A decision-making simulator for soccer referees	The purpose of this study is the use of the simulator as a potentially innovative method for training referees in sequential decision-making.	Quantitative
Carlos L.-P.; Ezequiel R.; Anton K. (2019)	How does Video Assistant Referee (VAR) modify the game in elite soccer?	The aim of this study was to examine how the introduction of the VAR system influenced the play in elite soccer. The sample consists of 1024 matches played in the Italian Serie A and the German Bundesliga league during the seasons before and after the implementation of the VAR system.	Qualitative
Mather G. (2020)	A Step to VAR: The Vision Science of Offside Calls by Video Assistant Referees	This study proposes suggestions on how to compensate for the different problems that arise during the decision-making process.	Qualitative

Table 1 contd. ...

...Table 1 contd.

Authors	Title	Purpose	Methodology
Samuel R.D.; Galily Y.; Filho E.; Tenenbaum G. (2020)	Implementation of the Video Assistant Referee (VAR) as a Career Change-Event: The Israeli Premier League Case Study	This study investigates the implementation of the VAR system within the Israeli Premier League context. The results indicate that the initial VAR performance rates of the Israeli referees were not high compared with data from other countries (e.g., Italy). The Israeli referees perceived the VAR implementation as a moderate change-event in their careers.	Qualitative
Mm N.; Nimkar N. (2020)	Fan perception towards the usage of technology in football	The objective of this study was to understand the perception fans had regarding the usage of technology in football. The study looks into major refereeing decisions and how technology could have changed the outcome of these events, how technology in the field of e-sports was important in popularising the sport, the pros and cons of Goal-Line technology and VAR, how technology was important in improving fan engagement through social media and how fans perceive the usage of technology in football. The result of the study indicates that both the human element and technology should go hand in hand for the improvement of the game	Qualitative
Mather G.; Breivik S. (2020)	Is the perception of intent by association football officials influenced by video playback speed?	This study tests whether the decisions of referees are subject to a bias of slow-motion replays. Eighty elite English professional football officials made decisions about 60 incidents recorded in professional European leagues (recorded as fouls, yellow-card offences or red-card offences by the on-field referee).	Quantitative
Panse N.; Mahabaleshwarkar A. (2020)	A Dataset & Methodology for Computer Vision based Offside Detection in Soccer	This paper presents a computational offside decision algorithm for soccer match images.	Quantitative
Han B.; Chen Q.; Lago-Peñas C.; Wang C.; Liu T. (2020)	The influence of the video assistant referee on the Chinese Super League	The purpose of this study is to explore the impact of the introduction of VAR on football matches and referees' performance.	Quantitative

Table 1 contd. ...

...Table 1 contd.

Authors	Title	Purpose	Methodology
Lucic I.; Babic S.; Vuckov D. (2020)	Perception of Using VAR Technology in Football after Completion of Training and Education and Experiences of Croatian Video Assistant Referees (VARs) and Assistant VARs (AVARs)	This paper shows the results of the research on the perception(s) of using VAR technology in football of Croatian Video Assistant Referees (VARs) and Assistant VARs (AVARs) that received training and education regarding the use of VAR technology on the football field.	Qualitative
Fişne M.; Bardakçi S.; Hasaan A. (2021)	Analysis of perceptions of Turkish fans of video-assistant-referees in elite soccer	The purpose of this study was to investigate the fans' opinions of VAR. The results indicated that VAR increases the competitiveness between teams, helps referees feel less pressured due to the assistance of VAR and reduces the effect of human error. Fans believe that VAR has brought justice and fair play to football, as VAR decision-making does not discriminate.	Qualitative
Hamsund T.; Scelles N. (2021)	Fans' Perceptions towards Video Assistant Referee (VAR) in the English Premier League	This article aims to investigate fans' perceptions towards VAR in the EPL.	Qualitative
Lago-Peñas C.; Gómez M.A.; Pollard R. (2021)	The effect of the Video Assistant Referee on referee's decisions in the Spanish LaLiga	The aim of this study was to examine how the implementation of this technology has modified the play in elite soccer.	Quantitative
Ariyo E.S.; Faniyi O.; Turcott R. (2021)	"Utterly ashamed of their behavior": Examining the media coverage of Cameroon versus England in the 2019 FIFA women's world cup	This paper examines the dominant media frames emerging from international media regarding the dispute and examines differences between coverage from major newspapers and football-specific news websites.	Qualitative
Giglio S.S.; Weishaupt Proni M. (2021)	The Controversy Over the Introduction of the VAR in Brazil	This chapter's objective is to recover the debate on the use of VAR in Brazilian football with a focus on the opinions published in the national sports press until 2019, which was marked by dichotomous analyses.	Qualitative

Table 1 contd. ...

...*Table 1 contd.*

Authors	**Title**	**Purpose**	**Methodology**
Spitz J.; Wagemans J.; Memmert D.; Williams A.M.; Helsen W.F. (2021)	Video assistant referees (VAR): The impact of technology on decision making in association football referees	This study reports that the predictive odds for making the correct decision after VAR intervention were significantly higher than for the initial referee's decision, with accuracy increasing from 92.1% to 98.3%. Findings have implications for the current debate about the introduction of technology in association football and may help set guidelines regarding the use of technology across other sports and professional domains.	Quantitative
Jia Z. (2021)	A Study on the Application of Video Assistant Referee (VAR) Technology in Chinese Football Professional League	By using the methods of literature review, video, video analysis and mathematical statistics, this paper studied the application of VAR technology in 30 rounds and 240 matches in the Chinese super league in 2019 and compared it with the Super League and 2018 FIFA world cup in 2018.	Quantitative
Vuckov D.; Babic S. (2021)	VARs/AVARs in Croatian Top Division (1. HNL) and Major League Soccer: Experiences with VAR System	This paper explores the similarities and differences between VARs/AVARs' experiences in the Croatian Top Division (1. HNL) and Major League Soccer (MLS) in relation to the efficiency, possible limitations and improvements of the VAR system.	Quantitative
Zglinski J. (2022)	Rules, Standards, and the Video Assistant Referee in Football	This article investigates the problems that have become apparent with the system. It argues that the success of technological aids like the VAR depends on the nature of the norms on which they adjudicate.	Quantitative
Aycan H.; Onağ Z. (2022)	Views of Turkish football stakeholders on video assistant referee technology	The purpose of this study was to carry out an in-depth examination of the views of Turkish football stakeholders on VAR technology. The participants' opinion about the future of VAR Technology was that the use of this technology will continue developing in the coming years and should be supported.	Qualitative

Table 1 contd. ...

...Table 1 contd.

Authors	**Title**	**Purpose**	**Methodology**
Qiao J. (2022)	The Application of Artificial Intelligence in Football Risk Prediction	This study analyses the utilisation of smart technologies for data acquisition using sensor networks and an intelligent data analysis. The proposed algorithm is compared with the fuzzy logic model (FLM) and found that it is 7.2% of higher risk predication by the proposed model than the existing.	Quantitative
Hafeez A.; Hafeez U.; Amin A.; Hasan S. (2022)	VAR technology in English football; Implications of intervening in a fast-moving game	This paper studies the impact of introducing VAR technology to one of Europe's top five leagues. Its focus is on how incidents that fall under the dual jurisdiction, i.e., the on-field referee and the VAR technology have evolved in the English Premier League (EPL).	Qualitative
Kiuchi Y. (2022)	Football Fan Reactions to Video Assistant Referee: No More Hand of God	Fan tweets show that a general lack of knowledge about the Laws of the Game and unfamiliarity with officiating procedures, as well as fans' emotional investment in their favorite team, make it nearly impossible for the VAR to convince fans about the accuracy of a call.	Qualitative
Buyukcelebi H.; Duz S.; Acak M.; Nalbant U.; Svatora K.; Gabrys T.; Karayigit R. (2022)	Development of the Effect of Video Assistant Referee Application on Football Parameters	The study aimed to determine the effect of the VAR system in international football organisations on the game over the years.	Quantitative
Kubayi A.; Larkin P.; Toriola A. (2022)	The impact of video assistant referee (VAR) on match performance variables at men's FIFA World Cup tournaments	This study explored how VAR has influenced match performance variables at Fédération Internationale de Football Association (FIFA) World Cup tournaments.	Quantitative
Frandsen K.; Landgrebe K. (2022)	Video Assistant Referee in a Small-Nation Context: Intensified Mediatization	Using the Danish Superliga as a case, this article explores how football's implementation of a VAR instigates complex processes of change which imply not only a further decrease in football's institutional autonomy, but also intensifies inequality.	Qualitative

Table 1 contd. ...

...Table 1 contd.

Authors	**Title**	**Purpose**	**Methodology**
Panchuk M.; Panchuk T.; Panchuk A. (2022)	Peculiarities of Application of Information Technologies in Footbal and Futsal	The paper investigates and systematises materials on the application of information technologies in the sphere of football and futsal. It is established that, as of today, a number of information technologies are in operation, which help in decision-making for the successful organisation of sports competitions, the effective performance of training process and the prevention of sports injuries.	Quantitative
Meneguite Y.N.F.; Leite L.B.; Da Silva D.C.; De Moura A.G.; Lavorato V.N. (2022)	Influence of the video assistant referee (VAR) on the Brazilian Men's Soccer Championship	The objective of this study was to analyse the influence of VAR in the 2019 Men's First Division Brazilian Football Championship, compared to the 2018 edition, in which VAR was not present.	Qualitative
Scanlon C.; Griggs G.; McGillick C. (2022)	'It's not football anymore': perceptions of the video assistant referee by english premier league football fans	This article draws on the responses of one hundred English Premier League Football fans and their perceptions of the VAR during the 2019/2020 season.	Qualitative
Zhang Y.; Li D.; Gómez-Ruano M.-Á.; Memmert D.; Li C.; Fu M (2022)	The effect of the video assistant referee (VAR) on referees' decisions at FIFA Women's World Cups	This study intended to explore how the VAR affects refereeing decisions at Fédération Internationale de Football Association (FIFA) Women's World Cup competitions.	Qualitative
d Andréa C.; Stauff M. (2022)	Mediatized Engagements with Technologies: "Reviewing" the Video Assistant Referee at the 2018 World Cup	This article presents the implementation of the VAR as an example of the increasingly layered mediatization of sports.	Qualitative

Table 1 contd. ...

...Table 1 contd.

Authors	**Title**	**Purpose**	**Methodology**
Desfontaine P.; Borel-Hänni F.; Wille F. (2022)	Sports media and the use of audiovisual technology in soccer: media coverage of video assistant referee use during the 2018 and 2019 fifa world cups; [le traitement médiatique du recours à la technique audiovisuelle dans le football: la couverture de l'assistance vidéo à l'arbitrage lors des coupes du monde 2018 et 2019]	This article looks at how the French Printed Press covers the use of audiovisual technology by soccer referees. More precisely, it analyzed journalists' social responsibility by examining the newspaper L'Équipe's (France's main sports daily paper) coverage of the use of VAR during the two most recent FIFA World Cups, Russia 2018 (men) and France 2019 (women), the first in which VAR was allowed.	Qualitative
Hoang H.T.T.; Ha C.N.; Nguyen D.T.; Nguyen T.N.; Huynh T.N.; Phan T.T.; Nguyen H.T. (2022)	Poses Classification in a Taekwondo Lesson Using Skeleton Data Extracted from Videos with Shallow and Deep Learning Architectures	This study uses Fast Forward Moving Picture Experts Group (FFMPEG) technique to extract images from the video of Taekwondo and generate skeleton data from extracted frames with MoveNet.	Quantitative
Pizzera A.; Marrable J.; Raab M. (2022)	The video review system in association football: implementation and effectiveness for match officials and referee education	The aim of this study was to investigate the influence and effectiveness of a video review system for match officials and their education in association football.	Qualitative
Holder U.; Ehrmann T.; König A. (2022)	Monitoring experts: insights from the introduction of video assistant referee (VAR) in elite football	Considering the monitoring of experts, this study evaluated the introduction of the most recent monitoring technology in football, the virtual assistant referee (VAR). Focusing on the German Bundesliga and the Italian Serie A, it analysed whether VAR has changed referees' decision-making behaviour and, in particular, whether this led to changes in referees' well-documented preferential treatment of home teams.	Qualitative

Table 1 contd. ...

...Table 1 contd.

Authors	**Title**	**Purpose**	**Methodology**
Joly A.; Desfontaine P. (2022)	The technologisation of elite referees in French football: between human refereeing and digital rationality (1980–2021); [La technologisation des arbitres de l'élite dans le football français: entre arbitrage humain et rationalité numérique (1980–2021)]	This socio-historical research aims to study the introduction of digital techniques in football refereeing from 1980 until now. This paper relies on literature in increasing development on this topic, as well as sources composed by institutional archives, interviews and the print press (L'Équipe, France Football, Les Cahiers du Football)	Quantitative
Ponce-Bordón J.C.; Lobo-Triviño D.; Rubio-Morales A.; Del Campo R.L.; Resta R.; López-Gajardo M.A. (2022)	The Effect of the Video Assistant Referee System Implementation on Match Physical Demands in the Spanish LaLiga	This study aimed to analyse the influence of the Video Assistant Referee (VAR) on the physical demands of matches in the top Spanish professional football league.	Qualitative
İsoa M.; Yarışan U.; Kaya T. (2022)	Clustering English Premier League Referees Using Unsupervised Machine Learning Techniques	In this research, as a different approach to the referees' objectivity problem, referees are classified based on the statistical outcome of the matches using unsupervised machine learning techniques. Meaningful clusters should not be found to be able to state the referees are objective. This study was conducted in a 10-year period with the English Premier League between 2009–2018 data.	Quantitative
Brunnström K.; Djupsjöbacka A.; Ozolins O.; Billingham J.; Wistel K.; Evans N. (2023)	Quality measurement methods for video assisting refereeing systems	This article describes the development of the test methods and illustrates some initial results from a test event on Video Assistant Referees system candidates.	Quantitative
Petersen-Wagner R.; Lee Ludvigsen J.A. (2023)	The video assistant referee (VAR) as neo-coloniality of power? Fan negative reactions to VAR in the 2018 FIFA Men's World Cup	The analysis of the technologisation of sports shows how it was experienced by both supporters as a power implementing artefact and also how it provided a place for loosely defined anti-systemic movements to emerge.	Qualitative

Table 1 contd. ...

...Table 1 contd.

Authors	Title	Purpose	Methodology
Nuhrat Y. (2023)	Challenging ocularcentric fairness assumptions of the video assistant referee (VAR) system in football	The purpose of this study is the VAR system's ocularcentrism, which, as foreshadowed by televisation, creates an ocular mode separate from that of the field by muting it and visually dissecting its plays.	Qualitative
Märtins J.; Westmattelmann D.; Schewe G. (2023)	Affected but not involved: Two-scenario based investigation of individuals' attitude towards decision support systems based on the example of the video assistant referee	Drawing on transparency and justice research, the study examined the role of transparency, procedural justice and social influence on individuals' attitudes towards the VAR.	Qualitative
Song Q.; Hashikura K.; Kamal M.A.S.; Yamada K. (2023)	Algorithm research of human recognition and their application to conjecture	This paper proposes a specific algorithm for multi-target recognition in simple scenes using human recognition technology.	Quantitative
de Oliveira M.S.; Steffen V.; Trojan F. (2023)	A systematic review of the literature on video assistant referees in soccer: Challenges and opportunities in sports analytics	This study reviews the literature on VAR in football using the Methodi Ordinatio. Methodi Ordinatio is a methodology used to select and rank relevant scientific papers, combining the impact factor, number of citations and year of publication.	Quantitative
Aleza M.E.; Vetrithangam D. (2023)	Use of Artificial Intelligence to Avoid Errors in Referring a Football Match	This research proposes the creation of an AI assisted referee system that makes judgments during a match using information from an AI agent. The AI agent may detect mistakes such as penalties, card punishments or any other miscalculations that may occur throughout a game.	Quantitative
Işın, A., Yi, Q. (2024)	Does video assistant referee technology change the magnitude and direction of home advantages and referee bias? A proof-of-concept study	This study analyzed how Video Assistant Referee (VAR), introduced to improve the accuracy of referee decisions in football, changes the magnitude and direction of home advantage and referee bias in the Turkish Super League. The findings revealed that the only variable that changed significantly after VAR was implemented was fouls, which decreased for both home ($p < .001$; $d = 0.56$, medium effect) and away teams ($p < .001$; $d = 0.69$, medium effect).	Quantitative

Table 1 contd. ...

...Table 1 contd.

Authors	Title	Purpose	Methodology
Zhekambayeva M.; Yerekesheva M.; Ramashov N.; Seidakhmetov Y.; Kulambayev B. (2024)	Designing an artificial intelligence-powered video assistant referee system for team sports using computer vision	This paper investigates the efficacy of an AI-powered Video Assistant Referee (VAR) system in enhancing officiating accuracy, efficiency, and consistency in team sports. Employing a combination of artificial intelligence and computer vision, the system was tested in a local championship in Almaty, involving eight football teams. Results indicated that the AI-powered VAR system significantly increased the accuracy of decisions and reduced the decision-making time, thereby maintaining the fluidity of gameplay.	Quantitative
Zhang L.; Liu Z. (2024)	Designing an event management system for campus football using 3D images and machine vision	This paper focuses on the event management system for campus football by analyzing the administration system and suggests a machine vision approach by using an underlying neural network. Images of three different regions, A, B, and C were used as the experimental objects in this work. This paper analyzes machine vision, a discrete Hopfield neural network, to establish a Hopfield model for recognizing cross-line types.	Quantitative
Bao R.; Han B. (2024)	The influence of the video assistance referee (VAR) on the English Premier League	The Video Assistant Referee (VAR) was introduced into football in order to assist referees in their decision making during the match. The English Premier League (EPL) introduced VAR in the 2019–2020 season. The aim of this study was to explore the influence of the introduction of VAR on the English Premier League. The results demonstrated that after the introduction of VAR, the first half time, second half time, total time and fouls increased significantly ($p < 0.01$). In contrast, a significant decrease ($p < 0.01$) was found in the number of offsides after the implementation of VAR.	Quantitative

Source: our elaboration, 2025

Table 2. Selection of publications from the Scholar database.

Authors	**Title**	**Purpose**	**Methodology**
Sabag, E., Lidor, R., Morgulev, E., Arnon, M., Azar, O., & Bar-Eli, M. (2020).	To dive or not to dive in the penalty area? The questionable art of deception in soccer	This study aimed to examine the questionable use of the diving act in the penalty area in soccer.	Qualitative
Winand, M., Schneiders, C., Merten, S., & Marlier, M. (2021).	Sports fans and innovation: An analysis of football fans' satisfaction with video assistant refereeing through social identity and argumentative theories.	This study investigates football fans' satisfaction with video assistant refereeing (VAR).	Qualitative

Source: our elaboration, 2025

Chapter 4

A Decision Model for Aligning AI Adoption with Organizational Models and Operational Complexity

Francesco Bolici,[1] *Alberto Varone*[2,*] and *Gabriele Diana*[1]

Introduction

Artificial intelligence (AI) is currently reshaping the anatomy of work and organizations, influencing daily operations, managerial routines, and structural design (Chui et al. 2023; Eloundou et al. 2023; Handa et al. 2025; Mayer et al. 2025). This transformation extends beyond routine automation to encompass creativity-intensive roles (Ritala et al. 2024), high-level decision-making (Trunk et al. 2020), and promotes the emergence of new forms of human–machine collaboration (Brynjolfsson et al. 2019; Crowston and Bolici 2019; Noy and Zhang 2023; Handa et al. 2025).

Yet, despite heavy financial commitments to AI systems, only a small fraction of organizations consider themselves at a mature stage of AI adoption, where AI is fully integrated into workflows and drives substantial business outcomes (Mayer et al. 2025). Scholars attribute this implementation gap to three organizational failures: failure to reconfigure work practices in a way that is consistent with AI's features (Benbya et al. 2020; Agrawal et al. 2024), insufficient workforce reskilling

[1] University of Cassino and Southern Lazio.
[2] University of Cassino and Southern Lazio; Syracuse University - School of Information Studies.
Emails: f.bolici@unicas.it, gabriele.diana@unicas.it
* Corresponding author: alberto.varone@unicas.it

DOI: 10.1201/9781003535393-4

(Brynjolfsson et al. 2023; Crowston and Bolici 2025), and poor adaptation of established structural organizational elements (Valentine et al. 2024). These failures reflect a fundamental conceptual fallacy: organizations view AI adoption as a technological challenge rather than a socio-technical transformation, preventing them from realizing the financial benefits of their investments (Benbya et al. 2020).

This perspective is also visible in the literature on AI's impacts on work, where a strong focus is placed on both the micro-level (i.e., focus on individual tasks) (Brynjolfsson et al. 2023; Dell'Acqua et al. 2023; Noy and Zhang 2023) and the macro-level impacts (i.e., industries, occupations, and economies) (Eloundou et al. 2023; Handa et al. 2025). While both perspectives offer valuable insights, they neglect a critical third dimension: the meso-level organizational analysis. This research gap mirrors the implementation failures observed in practice, where organizations struggle precisely because AI adoption occurs within complex organizational systems that cannot be understood through individual task studies or industry-wide impact assessments. Consequently, organizations lack practical frameworks for navigating AI adoption complexities and diagnostic tools for selecting context-appropriate implementation strategies based on their specific organizational characteristics.

This conceptual study adopts a meso-level organizational perspective to address this gap. It develops a decision-support framework that helps answer the following research question: *What is the appropriate alignment between organizational characteristics and AI adoption modes (replace, reinforce, reveal) to maximize implementation success?*

Adopting a theory-building approach that integrates established theoretical foundations with emerging AI implementation practices, this chapter develops a framework through four steps (see Figure 1).

1. *Conceptual grounding*: it synthesizes literature on Socio-technical Systems Theory (Trist and Bamforth 1951; Pasmore et al. 2019) and Organizational Design Theory (Perrow 1967; Burns and Stalker 1994) to establish conceptual foundations for understanding how organizational characteristics should align with technology adoption patterns.
2. *Dimension identification*: Within the body of theories previously identified, it pinpoints a set of relevant variables for framework construction (Figure 2). These are organizational structures (mechanistic, hybrid, organic), operational complexity (routine, engineering/craft, non-routine), and AI adoption modes (replace, reinforce, reveal) (Gama and Magistretti 2023).
3. *Framework construction*: It constructs a decision matrix by systematically mapping the intersections between organizational structures and operational complexity levels to identify context-appropriate AI adoption strategies. This mapping process creates nine distinct organizational configurations, each requiring different AI adoption approaches based on their structural and operational characteristics.
4. *Practical synthesis*: It translates the theoretical framework into practical implementation guidance by developing a decision model with supporting diagnostic tools for managerial application. This includes specific

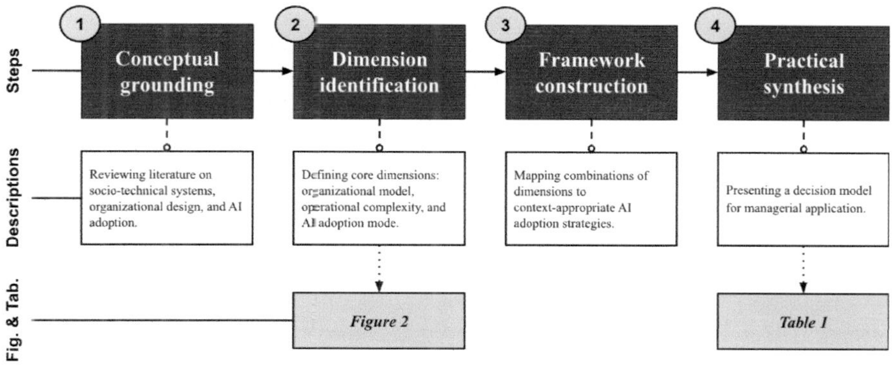

Figure 1. Theory-building approach adopted, steps, descriptions, and associated Figure and Table.

recommendations for each organizational configuration while incorporating moderating variables such as organizational culture, digital maturity, and strategic objectives that may influence implementation success (Table 1).

By following this process, this chapter makes theoretical and practical contributions to AI implementation strategies. Theoretically, it bridges the disconnect between organizational design theory and AI implementation strategy by adopting a socio-technical perspective that recognizes organizations as complex adaptive systems where AI success depends on alignment with existing structures and processes. Practically, the proposed framework provides decision-makers with a diagnostic tool to assess organizational characteristics, identify aligned AI applications, anticipate necessary adaptations, and avoid implementation pitfalls that affect the majority of organizations struggling with AI maturity.

The remainder of this paper proceeds as follows. Section 2 establishes theoretical foundations by examining organizations as socio-technical systems and reviewing current AI adoption challenges. Section 3 presents framework development, detailing the three core dimensions and their interactions. Section 4 discusses the framework's application across different organizational configurations with practical examples. Section 5 discusses implications for theory and practice. Section 6 states this chapter's conclusions and directions for future research.

Theoretical Background

Organizations as Socio-Technical Systems

Sociotechnical Systems (STS) Theory emerged from the seminal work of Trist and Bamforth (1951), who observed that technological changes in coal mining operations required corresponding adaptations in social structures to maintain productivity. Cherns (1976) later formalized STS principles to emphasize work autonomy, minimal critical specification, and continuous adaptation. These principles—revisited and extended in a number of works—remain the cornerstone of technological implementations, including AI, in a manner that safeguards both efficiency and human well-being. Socio-technical approaches gained traction in the design of information systems through studies like Bostrom and Heinen (1977), who argued that many management of information systems failures result from neglecting the "social" facets of technology deployment. More recently, Sawyer and Jarrahi (2014) show how STS frameworks can bridge technology-driven organizational change with collective behavior, while Davis et al. (2014) call for applications of STS in broader societal and predictive contexts—going beyond post-hoc system analyses to proactively design for emergent complexities.

When viewed through a sociotechnical lens, organizations represent complex systems where technical and social elements continuously interact (Bostrom and Heinen 1977; Sawyer and Jarrahi 2014). Technical elements include not only technology but also tasks, processes, and physical arrangements, while social elements encompass people, relationships, reward systems, and authority structures. These elements form a network of interdependencies to be managed (Malone and Crowston 1990; Crowston et al. 2004), where changes in one domain necessitate adjustments in others to maintain system effectiveness. Accordingly, STS Theory highlights the importance of joint optimization: designing technical and social systems in concert rather than optimizing one at the expense of (or in isolation with respect to) the other (Trist and Bamforth 1951). Research by Pasmore et al. (2019) demonstrates that technological implementations that neglect social dimensions often fail to deliver expected benefits, regardless of the sophistication of the technology itself.

AI adoption has profound implications from the perspective of STS Theory. It suggests that introducing AI solutions inevitably disturbs existing socio-technical equilibria, requiring careful consideration of how these technologies will interact with established social systems (Bresnahan 2021). Successful AI implementation thus requires attention to both the technical capabilities being introduced and the social systems with which they interact, including work practices, roles, skills, and cultural dimensions. In the face of AI's rapid advancements, scholars such as Herrmann (2024) advocate revising STS heuristics to reflect AI's opacity, continuous evolution, and autonomous decision-making capabilities. Similarly, Kudina and van de Poel (2024) emphasize that AI must be analyzed not only as a technological artifact but as embedded in social, cultural, and institutional processes—a truly socio-technical system. Hence, the synergy between AI and STS Theory underpins contemporary frameworks for AI governance, ethics, and alignment with organizational design.

The socio-technical perspective helps explain why technologically sophisticated AI solutions may fail to deliver expected benefits. These include: i. neglecting organizational context and user involvement (Bostrom and Heinen 1977; Murphy and Largacha-Martinez 2024), which leads to resistance and underutilization; ii. overemphasizing technical automation, which can induce deskilling and fail to leverage human skills (Chuang 2022; Rinta-Kahila et al. 2023); and iii. poorly aligned structures, roles, and task interdependencies, creating disjointed workflows (Agrawal et al. 2024; Valentine et al. 2024; Wulff and Finnestrand 2024). Furthermore, a lack of continuous adaptation and governance can result in stagnant projects and overlooked ethical and regulatory concerns (Cherns 1976; Davis et al. 2014; Benbya et al. 2020; Olan et al. 2022; Yu et al. 2022). Finally, unlike earlier technologies, AI systems often exhibit agency-like qualities, making the sociotechnical interaction particularly complex. Failure to acknowledge this aspect is associated with the loss of human agency and misapplication of AI in strategic decisions (Trunk et al. 2020; Kudina and van de Poel 2024; Ruissalo 2024).

By recognizing organizations as STS, the proposed model moves beyond narrow, task-based approaches to AI adoption toward a more holistic perspective that considers how AI technologies interact with organizational structures, processes, and social dynamics. This approach acknowledges that effective AI adoption is not merely about implementing technology but about reconfiguring STS to leverage both technological capabilities and human expertise.

AI is "Nothing" Without Orchestration (and Task Coordination)

Bresnahan (2021) emphasizes that AI is an information technology, and traditionally, such technologies have required organizational redesign to be fully adopted. Yet, the bulk of AI studies have concentrated either on task-level impacts (Brynjolfsson et al. 2023; Dell'Acqua et al. 2023; Noy and Zhang 2023; Cui et al. 2025) or on industry-wide effects (Eloundou et al. 2023; Handa et al. 2025), rather than on comprehensive transformations within organizations.

Under a theoretical perspective, the dominant frameworks guiding AI adoption research are the Technology Acceptance Model (TAM) (Davis 1989; Venkatesh and Davis 2000; Venkatesh and Bala 2008) and the Unified Theory of Acceptance and Use of Technology (UTAUT) (Venkatesh et al. 2003). While these approaches provide valuable insights into factors influencing individual AI adoption, they fail to account for the complex interplay between AI technologies and organizational structures, processes, and interdependencies (Robertson et al. 2025).

More holistic frameworks exist, but are relatively underemphasized. An example is TOE (Technology-Organization-Environment) (Tornatzky and Fleischer 1990), positing that new technologies are adopted by an organization based on environmental and organizational context (Baker 2012). While TOE effectively captures the external pressures and organizational conditions that drive innovation uptake, it tends to treat technology as something that organizations adopt, rather than one that reshapes the inner workings of roles, tasks, and social structures. By contrast, in STS Theory, technology is embedded within social structures and must be co-designed with work processes. Thus, STS Theory provides a nuanced view of how AI alters work, decision-making processes, and organizational routines, making it a more suitable theoretical foundation for this chapter. This view is appropriate for filling the identified literature gap in understanding how organizations should adapt to AI technologies holistically, beyond task-specific implementations (Agrawal et al. 2024; Ritala et al. 2024).

Transitioning from individual tasks to system-level analysis, Valentine et al. (2024) show that algorithmic decision-making often conflicts with hierarchical organizational structures—especially where established "org charts" fix responsibilities within rigid departments. AI, by contrast, may optimize decisions across roles and teams without regard to official boundaries, creating tension between "algorithmic logic" and the traditional divisions of labor. Agrawal et al. (2024)

formalize this tension in an economic model, arguing that AI heightens decision variation and thus demands new coordination mechanisms when organizational tasks are highly interdependent. In particular, more modular (less interdependent) structures can facilitate AI adoption but reduce potential synergies among tasks, whereas coordinated mechanisms (e.g., cross-functional teams) can harness AI's benefits if leadership invests in system-wide integration. Moreover, Park et al. (2025) categorize AI-driven organization development interventions—from human process to techno-structural changes—and caution that each domain poses unique ethical and adoption challenges. For example, adopting AI for strategic change (e.g., advanced analytics for new business models) inevitably disrupts employees' roles, calling for robust communication strategies, re-skilling programs, and explicit AI governance. Thus, if organizations adopt AI into some of their tasks, this tends to be adopted in isolation, which may generate gains in the context of the specific task accomplished, but not result in overall organizational improvement, as organizations are complex systems: coordination needs, integration, variability, and dynamism. A comprehensive approach to AI adoption must recognize that organizations are more than the sum of their tasks—they are complex adaptive systems where changes in one area affect the entire system. Accordingly, this chapter proposes that appropriately adopting AI requires the alignment of organization design characteristics, operational complexity, and the appropriate typology of AI mode of use.

Framework Development

The framework presented in this chapter classifies organizations based on operational complexity and organizational models, mapping them to AI adoption strategies that maximize impact. This approach recognizes that effective AI implementation requires alignment between technological capabilities and organizational characteristics rather than following universal best practices. By identifying the intersection of organizational structure and task complexity, leaders can select AI adoption modes that complement their specific operational contexts. Thus, the proposed framework focuses on three core dimensions:

1. Organizational Model (mechanistic, hybrid, and organic)
2. Operational Complexity (routine, engineering/craft, non-routine)
3. AI Mode of Adoption (replace, reinforce, reveal)

Figure 2 illustrates these three core dimensions and a sample of relevant moderating variables that influence AI implementation outcomes. This visualization emphasizes the interconnected nature of these dimensions and highlights the socio-technical perspective that informs this chapter.

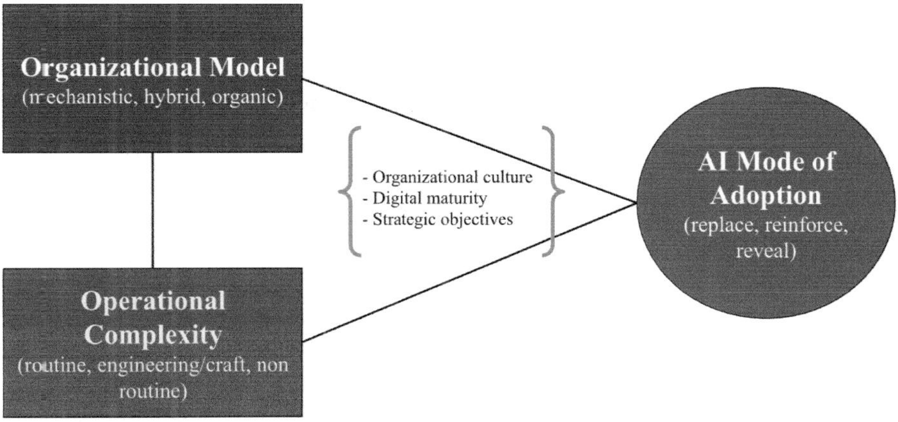

Figure 2. The three core dimensions of the decision model (Organizational Model, Operational Complexity, and AI mode of Adoption) and a sample of moderating variables (organizational culture, digital maturity, and strategic objectives).

Organizational Model

Burns and Stalker (1994) distinguish between mechanistic and organic structures in their seminal work on organizational innovation. Mechanistic organizations are characterized by hierarchical structures, centralized decision-making, standardized procedures, and formalized communication channels. These organizations optimize efficiency in stable environments by emphasizing specialization, vertical information flows, and clearly defined responsibilities. Examples include traditional manufacturing firms, large financial institutions with established processes, and government bureaucracies.

In contrast, organic structures feature decentralized authority, flexible role definitions, lateral communication patterns, and distributed expertise. These organizations prioritize adaptability over efficiency, enabling rapid response to changing environments through collaborative problem-solving and informal networks. Examples include innovative technology firms, creative agencies, and research organizations operating in dynamic, uncertain environments.

Most modern organizations adopt hybrid models that balance efficiency and adaptability needs, as articulated by O'Reilly and Tushman (2013) in their work on organizational ambidexterity. These hybrid structures may maintain mechanistic characteristics in some functions (like manufacturing or accounting) while adopting organic approaches in others (like research and development or customer experience). They may also employ structural differentiation, with some units organized mechanistically and others organically, connected through integration mechanisms that facilitate coordination across different structural types.

The structural configuration of an organization profoundly influences its information processing capabilities, coordination mechanisms, and adaptability—all factors that determine how effectively it can integrate AI technologies. Mechanistic organizations with their standardized processes may readily benefit from AI automation of routine tasks, but struggle to leverage AI for innovation. Conversely, organic organizations may effectively use AI to enhance creative processes but face challenges in standardizing AI applications across fluid structures. Hybrid organizations must navigate the complexity of implementing AI across diverse structural arrangements, requiring differentiated adoption strategies.

Operational Complexity

Perrow (1967) developed an influential framework for understanding task complexity based on two dimensions: task analyzability and task variety. Task analyzability refers to the degree to which work can be reduced to programmable procedures with established solutions. Highly analyzable tasks follow logical, sequential processes with clear cause-and-effect relationships. Task variety concerns the frequency of unexpected or novel events that require different approaches or responses. Together, these dimensions create a four-quadrant model of operational complexity:

- Routine tasks exhibit high analyzability and low variety, following standardized procedures with few exceptions. Examples include transaction processing, standardized manufacturing, and repetitive service operations. These tasks are characterized by stability, predictability, and clearly defined inputs and outputs.
- Engineering tasks combine high analyzability with high variety, involving established methodologies applied to diverse problems. Examples include software development following established methodologies, customized manufacturing, and consulting services with standardized frameworks. While these tasks involve variability, they remain analyzable through systematic approaches.
- Craft tasks feature low analyzability but low variety, requiring tacit knowledge and experience-based judgment applied to relatively stable problem domains. Examples include skilled trades, artistic production, and specialized professional services. These tasks rely heavily on practitioner expertise and intuition rather than explicit procedures.
- Non-routine tasks exhibit both low analyzability and high variety, demanding creative problem-solving in unpredictable environments. Examples include scientific research, strategic planning, and crisis management. These tasks involve complex, ambiguous situations where cause-and-effect relationships are unclear and standardized approaches are insufficient.

This classification of operational complexity has significant implications for AI adoption. Different types of AI technologies align with different complexity categories: rule-based systems and robotic process automation excel at routine tasks; machine learning algorithms can handle engineering tasks by applying learned patterns to varied situations; while advanced generative AI might assist with craft and non-routine tasks by augmenting human expertise and creativity. Understanding the complexity profile of organizational operations is therefore essential for selecting appropriate AI implementation approaches.

AI Modes of Adoption

Contrary to initial beliefs that AI would simply have a substitution effect over human labor (i.e., tasks accomplished by humans are automated through AI systems), AI's impact has been found to be more heterogeneous. Raisch and Krakowski (2021) propose the "automation–augmentation paradox", suggesting that automation (AI substituting human tasks) and augmentation (AI enhancing human tasks) are interdependent rather than mutually exclusive, creating organizational tensions if overemphasized in either direction. Ritala et al. (2024) further elaborate on this distinction through a 2 × 2 algorithmic assistance matrix, classifying tasks according to routine versus creative nature and the degree of AI usefulness, resulting in distinct configurations such as "Human Vulnerable," "Human Augmented," "Human Ingenious," and "Human Mastery." Ruissalo (2024) highlights how professional roles can shift from augmentation to automation unintentionally over time, demonstrating the fluidity of boundaries between these configurations. Finally, empirical evidence from Handa et al. (2025), analyzing millions of Claude AI conversations, quantitatively validates the coexistence of augmentation and automation patterns, illustrating that real-world applications of AI frequently fall within a hybrid spectrum rather than purely automating or augmenting human labor.

In this chapter, the perspective of Gama and Magistretti (2023) is adopted, identifying three distinct ways organizations can implement AI technologies: Replace, Reinforce, and Reveal.

Replace mode involves substituting human labor with AI systems in structured, repetitive tasks where efficiency and consistency are paramount. This approach automates routine processes through technologies like robotic process automation (RPA), rule-based expert systems, and template-driven AI applications. The replace mode is most effective for well-defined, standardized tasks with clear success criteria and minimal need for contextual judgment or creativity.

Reinforce mode focuses on augmenting human expertise in semi-structured environments, creating human-AI partnerships where each contributes complementary capabilities. This approach leverages AI to handle data-intensive aspects of work while preserving human judgment for contextual understanding, ethical considerations, and stakeholder management. Technologies in this mode include decision support systems, predictive analytics platforms, and AI-enhanced productivity tools that amplify rather than replace human capabilities.

Reveal mode employs AI to generate new insights in complex, unstructured settings where pattern recognition, scenario exploration, and innovation are critical. Rather than automating existing processes, this approach uses AI to discover previously unrecognized opportunities, identify emerging trends, and explore creative possibilities. Technologies in this mode include unsupervised learning algorithms and simulation platforms that extend the boundaries of human imagination and analytical capacity.

This mode-based classification aligns with Crowston and Bolici's (2019) distinction between Decision Support, Blended Decision-Making, and Complete Automation as key AI adoption patterns. Their work underscores that AI implementation is rarely a binary choice between full automation and human-led processes but rather exists on a continuum where technology and workers interact dynamically. The proposed model expands on this by explicitly integrating organizational structure and task complexity, offering a more tailored approach for organizations to strategically position AI within their workflows.

Moderating Variables

Beyond the core dimensions of organizational models, operational complexity, and AI adoption modes, several moderating variables influence the effectiveness of AI implementation.

Organizational culture can significantly impact AI adoption through its influence on technology acceptance, risk tolerance, and collaborative practices. Indeed, according to Murphy and Largacha-Martinez (2024), organizational culture acts not as an abstract entity but as a mediating force that shapes how AI technologies are perceived and integrated. They distinguish between authoritarian organizations that view AI primarily as a control mechanism versus democratic organizations where AI serves as a collaborative tool for empowerment. This cultural orientation fundamentally determines adoption success, as Park et al. (2025) confirm that organizations with open, innovative cultures are more likely to embrace AI-driven transformation. The trust dimension of culture proves particularly critical; Yu et al. (2022) found that employee trust in AI systems significantly predicts adoption rates, while cultural resistance remains a primary barrier to implementation. Their SST perspective reveals that personnel factors, including psychosocial aspects like fear of automation and perceived job security, directly influence AI acceptance. Robertson et al. (2025) extend this understanding by identifying resistance to change as a key cultural challenge in AI integration, noting that employee attitudes toward AI are shaped by organizational values around innovation and risk-taking. Beyond acceptance, culture also determines how ethically AI is deployed. Park et al. (2025) emphasize that organizational cultures prioritizing transparency and accountability are better positioned to address AI bias and discrimination concerns. Leadership plays a crucial role in this cultural alignment. Chuang (2022) suggests that organizations must cultivate cultures that balance technical efficiency with human-centered values to make workers "robot-proof" while fostering an environment where AI augments rather than threatens human capabilities.

Digital maturity influences an organization's readiness to implement AI technologies effectively. Trunk et al. (2020) identify technological readiness as a critical factor in successful AI implementation, emphasizing that organizations with advanced IT infrastructure adopt AI more effectively and experience fewer integration challenges. This finding is reinforced by Yu et al. (2022), who categorize technical subsystem factors as essential antecedents for AI adoption, noting that legacy systems and outdated technology stacks significantly hinder AI initiatives. (Robertson et al. 2025) highlight specific technical barriers, including poor data quality and inadequate infrastructure, as fundamental limitations preventing retailers from scaling AI solutions across their operations. These challenges reflect Valentine et al.'s (2024) observation that AI implementation often conflicts with existing organizational structures and technical architecture, particularly when algorithms require data access across traditionally siloed departments. Storey et al. (2025) further note that AI readiness requires specific technical capabilities like data governance frameworks and robust privacy protections. Thus, organizations with low digital maturity may need to invest in foundational capabilities before pursuing advanced AI applications, whereas digitally sophisticated organizations can focus on optimizing AI integration with existing systems.

Strategic objectives also shape AI adoption by determining which capabilities and outcomes organizations prioritize. For instance, organizations pursuing cost leadership strategies may emphasize efficiency-focused AI applications that reduce operational expenses, while those pursuing differentiation may invest in AI-powered innovation and customer experience enhancement (Porter 1998). Similarly, organizations focused on exploration (discovering new opportunities) may adopt different AI applications than those prioritizing exploitation (optimizing existing processes) (Miles et al. 1978). Strategic alignment ensures that AI investments support organizational goals rather than creating technological sophistication without business value.

Additional moderating factors include leadership commitment (Mayer et al. 2025), regulatory context (Viskova-Robertson 2023), and workforce capabilities (Chuang 2022; Crowston and Bolici 2025). Altogether, these variables create a complex contingency landscape where optimal AI adoption approaches depend not only on core organizational and operational characteristics but also on a constellation of contextual factors that shape implementation possibilities and constraints.

Framework Discussion

The proposed decision model implies the existence of multiple configurations aligning organizational models, operational complexity, and AI modes of adoption. Table 1 concisely presents them, and they are further discussed in this section, providing a practical decision model for organizations seeking to effectively implement AI solutions. This framework offers guidance for matching AI adoption modes to specific combinations of organizational structure and operational complexity, ensuring that AI implementations complement rather than contradict organizational characteristics. While the framework presents structured recommendations, AI adoption remains context-dependent—meaning operational complexity within the same organization may vary across functions. For example, a mechanistic organization may still have non-routine tasks, requiring a more flexible approach to AI adoption that accommodates structural and operational diversity.

Mechanistic Organizations and AI Adoption

Mechanistic organizations with routine tasks gain the most from process automation (Replace mode), improving efficiency through ERP, RPA, and automated workflows. These organizations, characterized by hierarchical structures and standardized processes, naturally align with AI applications that codify and automate established procedures. For instance, a large insurance company might implement automated claims processing to handle standard cases, reducing processing time and error rates

Table 1. A decision model for aligning AI with organizational models and operational complexity.

Org. Model	**Operational Complexity**	**AI Mode**	**Use Cases (examples)**
Mechanistic	Routine	Replace (Automation)	Back-office automation, ERP systems, RPA (robotic process automation)
Mechanistic	Engineering/Craft	Replace/Reinforce (AI supporting semi-structured activities)	AI-Assisted Predictive Maintenance, AI-Assisted Compliance Audits, AI-Powered Supply Chain Optimization
Mechanistic	Non-Routine	Reinforce (AI proposing new insights)	AI for Risk Assessment & Fraud Detection, AI-Powered Medical Diagnostics for Complex Cases
Hybrid	Routine	Replace/Reinforce (Automation in stable functions, augmentation elsewhere)	AI-driven reporting automation, AI-supported customer service bots
Hybrid	Engineering/Craft	Reinforce (AI supporting decision-making)	AI-enhanced Market Analysis, AI-Powered Personalized Customer Experiences
Hybrid	Non-Routine	Reinforce/Reveal (AI uncovering patterns and aiding innovation)	AI-driven Research Assistance, AI-powered Strategic Forecasting
Organic	Routine	Reinforce (AI assisting humans in complex but structured tasks)	AI-powered Process Optimization, AI-supported Content Curation
Organic	Engineering/Craft	Reveal (AI generating novel insights)	AI-powered Trend Analysis, AI-Assisted Product Design
Organic	Non-Routine	Reveal (AI driving innovation and knowledge discovery)	AI-driven Innovation Labs, AI-Augmented Scientific Discovery

while freeing human employees for exception handling and customer interaction. The clear decision rules and stable processes in mechanistic organizations provide ideal conditions for AI automation of routine work.

When mechanistic organizations encounter engineering or craft tasks—those with either higher variety or lower analyzability—they benefit from a hybrid Replace/Reinforce approach. For engineering tasks with high variety but clear procedures, AI can handle rule-based components while supporting human decision-making for variable elements. Examples include AI-assisted predictive maintenance systems that analyze equipment data but involve maintenance technicians in final decision-making, or AI-powered compliance audits that flag potential issues for human reviewers. This approach preserves the efficiency orientation of mechanistic structures while accommodating task variability.

Even mechanistic organizations face non-routine tasks in areas like risk management, strategic planning. For these complex activities, the Reinforce mode provides the most effective approach, with AI systems generating insights and recommendations that inform human decision-making. Applications such as AI for risk assessment and fraud detection exemplify this approach, where algorithms identify patterns and anomalies, but human experts make final determinations based on contextual understanding and professional judgment. This human-AI collaboration maintains hierarchical decision structures while enhancing analytical capabilities.

Hybrid Organizations and AI Adoption

Hybrid organizations—those balancing mechanistic and organic elements—require differentiated AI adoption strategies across their varying structural components. For routine functions organized mechanistically, hybrid organizations can implement Replace/Reinforce approaches similar to fully mechanistic organizations. However, they must ensure these implementations integrate effectively with more organic functions through appropriate interfaces and coordination mechanisms. For example, AI-driven reporting automation might serve standardized reporting needs while feeding insights to more flexible strategic teams.

For engineering and craft tasks, which predominate in many hybrid organizations, the Reinforce mode offers optimal alignment by supporting human expertise with AI capabilities. Applications such as AI-enhanced market analysis tools that process vast data sets but preserve human interpretation of results, or AI-powered personalized customer experience platforms that suggest interventions for human approval, exemplify this approach. These implementations respect the semi-structured nature of many tasks in hybrid organizations while enhancing productivity and decision quality.

In addressing non-routine tasks, hybrid organizations benefit from combined Reinforce/Reveal approaches that balance enhancement of existing capabilities with exploration of new possibilities. AI-driven research assistance tools that both augment current analytical approaches and suggest novel research directions, or AI-powered strategic forecasting systems that enhance traditional planning while revealing unexpected scenario possibilities, represent this dual approach. This combination supports the ambidexterity that defines hybrid organizations, facilitating both exploitation of current knowledge and exploration of new opportunities.

Organic Organizations and AI Adoption

Organic organizations, with their flexible structures and emphasis on adaptation, approach AI adoption differently than their mechanistic counterparts. Even for routine tasks, organic organizations typically favor the Reinforce mode over full automation, using AI to assist humans in complex but structured tasks rather than replacing them entirely. This approach maintains the adaptability and contextual sensitivity that characterize organic structures while enhancing efficiency in routine operations. AI-powered process optimization tools that suggest improvements rather than impose standardization exemplify this approach.

For engineering and craft tasks, organic organizations benefit most from the Reveal mode, using AI to generate novel insights that fuel innovation and adaptation. AI-powered trend analysis systems that identify emerging patterns in unstructured data, or AI-assisted product design tools that suggest creative alternatives beyond conventional solutions, demonstrate this approach. These applications leverage AI's pattern recognition and generative capabilities to extend human creativity and analytical capacity without constraining the flexibility that defines organic structures.

Non-routine tasks, which often predominate in organic organizations operating in dynamic environments, are best supported through the Reveal mode focused on driving innovation and knowledge discovery. AI-driven innovation labs that explore unconventional combinations of ideas, or AI-augmented scientific discovery platforms that identify non-obvious relationships in complex phenomena, represent this approach. These implementations position AI as a catalyst for human creativity rather than a replacement for human judgment, maintaining the core advantages of organic organization while enhancing exploratory capabilities.

Contributions and Implications

The work proposed in this chapter has important implications for theory and practice.

Contribution 1: Bridging Organizational Design and AI Strategies

This chapter addresses a key gap by showing how AI can align with specific organizational structures, rather than operate in isolation. As Valentine et al. (2024) highlight, AI often conflicts with established boundaries because it optimizes decisions across silos, while traditional org charts keep tasks neatly segmented. The proposed framework extends this understanding by providing a structured approach for aligning AI initiatives with existing organizational models. This integration is particularly important as AI adoption frequently requires system-wide change rather than isolated implementation, affecting interdependent decision processes throughout the organization (Agrawal et al. 2024). The proposed framework acknowledges this perspective by recognizing that successful AI implementation must be compatible and aligned with existing socio-technical subsystem characteristics. The implications are significant for organizational designers who must consider how AI reshapes coordination mechanisms and decision rights. As von Krogh (2018) suggests, AI introduces new organizational phenomena that cannot be explained by existing theories, requiring novel theoretical frameworks like the one here proposed. Murphy and Largacha-Martinez (2024) reinforce this point by noting that organizations are not abstract vessels where AI is simply "dumped" but complex socio-technical systems that mediate technological implementation. Implication: designers gain a practical guide to align AI projects with existing organizational structures and dynamics, reducing friction and boosting adoption success.

Contribution 2: Advancing a Contingency Perspective on AI Adoption

Rather than pushing a one-size-fits-all method, the framework presented describes context-specific adoption pathways, drawing on each organization's unique mix of goals, tasks, and structure. This addresses the "automation–augmentation paradox" (Raisch and Krakowski 2021), in which AI can simultaneously replace and empower human work. Moreover, the proposed decision model has important implications for long-term AI strategy. The proposed framework helps organizations make AI investments more profitable, in line with the findings of Mayer et al. (2025), pointing out that only 1% of organizations consider themselves at full AI maturity, and highlighting the need for tailored approaches based on organizational readiness and characteristics. Implication: leaders can move beyond trial-and-error, adopting tailored AI solutions that match their current readiness level and strategic ambitions, thus maximizing both efficiency and innovation.

Conclusion and Future Research

This chapter addressed the critical challenge of aligning AI adoption strategies with organizational characteristics. By integrating organizational design theory with AI implementation practices, it has developed a decision model that helps organizations identify appropriate AI applications based on their structural characteristics. This tool provides a practical approach to assessing AI appropriateness for specific organizational contexts, moving beyond a one-size-fits-all approach. Specifically, rather than viewing AI as a universal solution, the proposed framework enables organizations to select AI applications that complement organizational characteristics, whether to replace routine tasks, reinforce existing capabilities, or reveal new insights. This approach promises more successful AI implementations by ensuring alignment between technological capabilities and organizational realities.

Future research is needed to empirically validate the model, strengthen its applicability, and eventually refine its components. Moreover, longitudinal studies examining how organizations evolve as they implement AI would provide valuable insights into the dynamic relationship between organizational characteristics and AI adoption over time.

References

Agrawal, A., Gans, J. S. and Goldfarb, A. 2024. Artificial intelligence adoption and system-wide change. Journal of Economics & Management Strategy 33: 327–337.

Baker J. 2012. The Technology–organization–environment framework. pp. 231–245. *In*: Dwivedi, Y. K., Wade, M. R. and Schneberger, S. L. (eds.). Information Systems Theory New York, NY: Springer New York.

Benbya, H., Davenport, T. and Pachidi, S. 2020. Special Issue Editorial. Artificial Intelligence in Organizations: Current State and Future Opportunities. MIS Quarterly Executive 19.

Bostrom, R. P. and Heinen, J. S. 1977. MIS problems and failures: a socio-technical perspective. Part I: The Causes. MIS Quarterly 1: 17–32.

Bresnahan, T. 2021. Artificial intelligence technologies and aggregate growth prospects. pp. 132–170. *In*: Diamond, J. W. and Zodrow, G. R. (eds.). Prospects for Economic Growth in the United States Cambridge University Press.

Brynjolfsson, E., Li, D. and Raymond, L. (2023). Generative AI at Work. w31161.

Brynjolfsson, E., Rock, D. and Syverson, C. 2019. Artificial intelligence and the modern productivity paradox: a clash of expectations and statistics. pp. 23–60. *In*: Agrawal, A., Gans, J. and Goldfarb, A. (eds.). The Economics of Artificial Intelligence: An Agenda University of Chicago Press.

Burns, T. and Stalker, G. M. 1994. The Management of Innovation. Oxford University Press, Oxford.

Cherns, A. 1976. The principles of sociotechnical design. Human Relations 29: 783–792.

Chuang, S. 2022. Indispensable skills for human employees in the age of robots and AI. European Journal of Training and Development 48: 179–195.

Chui, M., Hazan, E., Roberts, R., Singla, A., Smaje, K., Sukharevsky, A. et al. 2023. The economic potential of generative AI: The next productivity frontier.

Crowston, K. and Bolici, F. 2019. Impacts of Machine Learning on Work.

Crowston, K. and Bolici, F. 2025. Deskilling and Upskilling with Generative AI Systems. iConference.

Crowston, K., Rubleske, J. and Howison, J. 2004. Coordination theory: A ten-year retrospective. Human-Computer Interaction in Management Information Systems.

Cui, Z. (Kevin), Demirer, M., Jaffe, S., Musolff, L., Peng, S. and Salz, T. 2025. The effects of generative ai on high-skilled work: evidence from three field experiments with software developers.

Davis, F. D. 1989. Perceived usefulness, perceived ease of use, and user acceptance of information technology. MIS Quarterly 13: 319.

Davis, M. C., Challenger, R., Jayewardene, D. N. W. and Clegg, C. W. 2014. Advancing socio-technical systems thinking: A call for bravery. Applied Ergonomics 45: 171–180.

Dell'Acqua, F., McFowland, E., Mollick, E. R., Lifshitz-Assaf, H., Kellogg, K., Rajendran, S. et al. 2023. Navigating the jagged technological frontier: field experimental evidence of the effects of AI on knowledge worker productivity and quality. SSRN Electronic Journal.

Eloundou, T., Manning, S., Mishkin, P. and Rock, D. 2023. GPTs are GPTs: An early look at the labor market impact potential of large language models.

Gama, F. and Magistretti, S. 2023. Artificial intelligence in innovation management: A review of innovation capabilities and a taxonomy of AI applications. Journal of Product Innovation Management 42: 76–111.

Handa, K., Tamkin, A., McCain, M., Huang, S., Durmus, E., Heck, S. et al. 2025. Which economic tasks are performed with AI? Evidence from Millions of Claude Conversations.

Herrmann, T. 2024. Comparing Socio-technical Design Principles with Guidelines for Human-Centered AI. p. 60–74.

von Krogh, G. 2018. Artificial intelligence in organizations: new opportunities for phenomenon-based theorizing. Academy of Management Discoveries 4: 404–409.

Kudina, O. and van de Poel, I. 2024. A sociotechnical system perspective on AI. Minds and Machines 34: 21.

Malone, T. W. and Crowston, K. 1990. What is Coordination Theory and How Can It Help Design Cooperative Work Systems.

Mayer, H., Yee, L., Chui, M. and Roberts, R. 2025. AI in the workplace: A report for 2025.

Miles, R. E., Snow, C. C., Meyer, A. D. and Coleman, H. J. 1978. Organizational strategy, structure, and process. The Academy of Management Review 3: 546–562.

Murphy, J. W. and Largacha-Martinez, C. 2024. Introducing AI-artificial intelligence into organizations that actually exist. pp. 347–367. *In*: Pava, M. L. and Dion, M. (eds.). Justifying Next Stage Capitalism: Exploring a Hopeful Future Cham: Springer International Publishing.

Noy, S. and Zhang, W. 2023. Experimental evidence on the productivity effects of generative artificial intelligence. Science 381: 187–192.

Olan, F., Ogiemwonyi Arakpogun, E., Suklan, J., Nakpodia, F., Damij, N. and Jayawickrama, U. 2022. Artificial intelligence and knowledge sharing: Contributing factors to organizational performance. Journal of Business Research 145: 605–615.

O'Reilly, C. A. and Tushman, M. 2013. Organizational Ambidexterity: Past, Present and Future.

Park, S., Chai, D. S., Park, J. J. and Oh, J. 2025. Exploring opportunities for artificial intelligence in organization development. Human Resource Development Review 24: 3–36.

Pasmore, W., Winby, S., Mohrman, S. A. and Vanasse, R. 2019. Reflections: Sociotechnical systems design and organization change. Journal of Change Management 19: 67–85.

Perrow, C. 1967. A framework for the comparative analysis of organizations. American Sociological Review 32: 194.

Porter, M. E. 1998. Competitive Advantage: Creating and Sustaining Superior Performance: With A New Introduction. New York: Free Press.

Raisch, S. and Krakowski, S. 2021. Artificial intelligence and management: the automation–augmentation paradox. Academy of Management Review 46: 192–210.

Rinta-Kahila, T., Penttinen, E., Salovaara, A., Soliman, W. and Ruissalo, J. 2023. The vicious circles of skill erosion: a case study of cognitive automation. Journal of the Association for Information Systems 24: 1378–1412.

Ritala, P., Ruokonen, M. and Ramaul, L. 2024. Transforming boundaries: how does ChatGPT change knowledge work? Journal of Business Strategy 45: 214–220.

Robertson, J., Botha, E., Oosthuizen, K. and Montecchi, M. 2025. Managing change when integrating artificial intelligence (AI) into the retail value chain: The AI implementation compass. Journal of Business Research 189: 115198.

Ruissalo, J. 2024. Transition to Human-AI Work: Shifts in routines' dynamics and the implications for roles in knowledge-intensive work. Annual Hawaii International Conference on System Sciences pp. 5806–5815.

Sawyer, S. and Jarrahi, M. H. 2014. Sociotechnical Approaches to the Study of Information Systems. Computing Handbook Chapman and Hall/CRC.

Storey, V. C., Yue, W. T., Zhao, J. L. and Lukyanenko, R. 2025. Generative artificial intelligence: evolving technology, growing societal impact, and opportunities for information systems research. Information Systems Frontiers.

Tornatzky, L. G. and Fleischer, M. 1990. The Processes of Technological Innovation. Lexington (Mass.) Toronto: Lexington books.

Trist, E. L. and Bamforth, K. W. 1951. Some social and psychological consequences of the longwall method of coal-getting: an examination of the psychological situation and defences of a work group in relation to the social structure and technological content of the work system. Human Relations 4: 3–38.

Trunk, A., Birkel, H. and Hartmann, E. 2020. On the current state of combining human and artificial intelligence for strategic organizational decision making. Business Research 13: 875–919.

Valentine, M. A., Pratt, A. L., Hinds, R. and Bernstein, M. S. 2024. The algorithm and the Org Chart: How algorithms can conflict with organizational structures. Proc. ACM Hum.-Comput. Interact. 8: 364:1–364:31.

Venkatesh, V., Morris, M.G., Davis, G.B. and Davis, F.D. 2003. User acceptance of information technology: toward a unified view. MIS Quarterly 27: 425–478. https://doi.org/10.2307/30036540.

Venkatesh, V. and Bala, H. 2008. Technology acceptance model 3 and a research agenda on interventions. Decision Sciences 39: 273–315.

Venkatesh, V. and Davis, F. D. 2000. A theoretical extension of the technology acceptance model: four longitudinal field studies. Management Science 46: 186–204.

Viskova-Robertson, A. 2023. Socio-technical system and organizational AI integration: An integrative literature review. Academy of Management Proceedings 2023: 14029.

Wulff, K. and Finnestrand, H. 2024. Creating meaningful work in the age of AI: explainable AI, explainability, and why it matters to organizational designers. AI & SOCIETY 39: 1843–1856.

Yu, X., Xu, S. and Ashton, M. 2022. Antecedents and outcomes of artificial intelligence adoption and application in the workplace: the socio-technical system theory perspective. Information Technology & People 36: 454–474.

Chapter 5

From Mechanical Calculation to Intelligent Machines

The Evolution of Artificial Intelligence from Management and Organization Perspective

Kamran Khan[1,*] and *Daniela Mancini*[2]

Introduction

The evolution of AI represents one of the most profound technological transformations in human history, fundamentally reshaping organizational structures, managerial practices, and strategic decision-making processes across industries (Brynjolfsson and McAfee 2014; Jordan and Mitchell 2015). From the early mechanical computation devices of Charles Babbage in the 1830s to today's sophisticated deep learning systems, this technological progression has continuously redefined the relationship between human intelligence and machine capabilities within organizational contexts (Ceruzzi 2003; LeCun et al. 2015). Understanding this evolution from an organizational and managerial perspective is crucial for comprehending how contemporary businesses leverage AI technologies and for anticipating future transformations in workplace dynamics and strategic management (Kaplan 2016; Mikalef and Gupta 2021).

The intersection of AI development and organizational transformation has received considerable attention from scholars across multiple disciplines, yet a

[1] University of Padova, Italy.
[2] University of Teramo, Italy.
Email: dmancini@unite.it
* Corresponding author: kamran.khan@unipd.it

DOI: 10.1201/9781003535393-5

comprehensive historical analysis examining this co-evolution from a managerial perspective remains limited (Laudon and Laudon 2004; Floridi et al. 2018). While existing literature extensively covers either technological aspects of AI development (Sheikh et al. 2023; Sarker 2021) or organizational implications of specific AI applications (Black and van Esch 2020; Wedel and Kannan 2016), few studies provide an integrated historical perspective that traces the simultaneous evolution of AI technologies and organizational management practices. This gap is particularly significant given that technological innovations do not occur in isolation but rather emerge from and subsequently transform the organizational contexts in which they are developed and implemented (Rogers 1962; Christensen 2015). Second, understanding this historical co-evolution is crucial for contemporary managers who must navigate AI implementation while anticipating future organizational transformations. Third, current AI adoption frameworks often lack the historical depth necessary to understand why certain organizational patterns emerge and how they might evolve.

This chapter addresses this research gap by providing a comprehensive theoretical examination of AI evolution from an organizational and managerial perspective. The study adopts a historical-analytical approach, tracing the development of computing and AI technologies across six distinct periods, from mechanical calculation systems to modern intelligent machines. This is a conceptual and theoretical study that synthesizes existing literature to understand the co-evolutionary relationship between AI technologies and organizational management practices. The research does not involve primary empirical data collection but rather employs a narrative literature review strategy and historical analysis methodologies to examine how each phase of AI development has influenced and been influenced by organizational structures, managerial roles, and business operations (Randell 2013; Haigh et al. 2016). The chapter is guided by the research questions (RQs); How has the evolution of technology, from mechanical calculation to intelligent machines, shaped organizational and managerial transformations? In what ways can the historical trajectory of AI provide a conceptual framework to understand current and future challenges in organizations? How do different technological eras (mechanical, electronic, AI birth, PC revolution, internet, ML/cloud, and deep learning) correspond to distinct phases of organizational change?

The study's analytical approach examines six chronological phases of AI evolution: (1) Early Ideas of Computing and Organizational Implications (1830s–1940s), focusing on mechanical calculation systems and their impact on data processing practices (Babbage 1982; Austrian 1982); (2) The Dawn of Electronic Computers and Business Automation (1940s–1950s), examining the transition from mechanical to electronic systems and their organizational applications (Haigh et al. 2016; Ceruzzi 1997); (3) The Birth of AI and Early Organizational Applications (1950s–1970s), analyzing the emergence of AI as a field and its initial business implementations (McCarthy et al. 2006; Buchanan and Feigenbaum 1981); (4) The Personal Computing Revolution and Organizational Transformation (1970s–1990s), investigating the democratization of computing and its impact on organizational structures (Elliott and Kraemer 2008); (5) Networking, Internet Era, and Digital

Business Strategies (1990s–2000s), exploring the rise of networked organizations and digital transformation (Leiner et al. 1997; Bharadwaj et al. 2013); and (6) Machine Learning Era and Organizational Decision-Making (2000s–present), examining contemporary AI applications in strategic management (LeCun et al. 2015; Brynjolfsson and McAfee 2014).

Figure 1 presents a comprehensive timeline of AI evolution and its organizational implications, illustrating the progression from mechanical calculation to intelligent automation and highlighting key technological milestones alongside their corresponding organizational impacts. This visual representation synthesizes the complex relationship between technological advancement and organizational change, offering a clear framework for understanding the co-evolutionary process examined throughout this study.

This theoretical investigation contributes to the literature by providing an integrated historical perspective on AI-organizational co-evolution, bridging technology history with management theory. The analysis offers valuable insights for contemporary managers and organizational leaders seeking to understand the historical foundations of current AI applications and anticipate future developments in AI-driven organizational transformation (Jordan and Mitchell 2015; Kaplan 2016). By examining this evolution through an organizational lens, the study provides a comprehensive framework for understanding AI's transformative impact on modern business practices and strategic decision-making processes (Mikalef and Gupta 2021; Floridi et al. 2018).

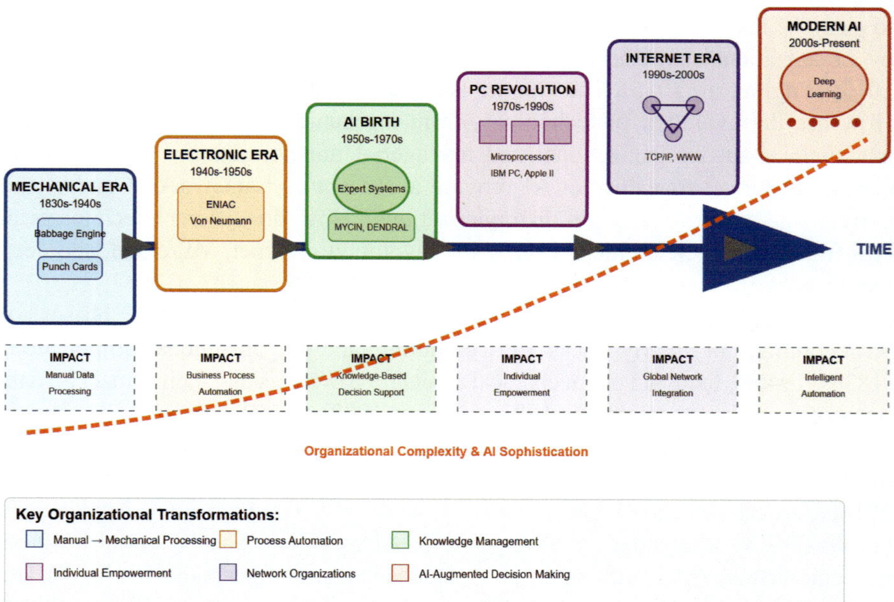

Figure 1. AI evolution and organizational impact (Source: Authors).

Early Ideas of Computing and their Organizational Implications

The concept of automation and computation has roots in the mechanical era, particularly with Charles Babbage's Analytical Engine in the 1830s (Randell 2013). One of the earliest pioneers, Charles Babbage, a British mathematician, mechanical engineer, and philosopher, conceived the idea of a programmable computer (Hyman 1985). His design for the Analytical Engine is considered one of the first concepts for a general-purpose computer, that was ahead of its time. Babbage's Analytical Engine was designed to be powered by steam and capable of being programmed using punched cards (Ceruzzi 2003, p. 15), was intended to perform a variety of calculations automatically (Babbage 1982). The machine could perform any mathematical calculation automatically and was intended to have a memory unit and a central processing unit, which are fundamental components of today's computers.

Several decades later, Herman Hollerith furthered the use of automation in data processing, with his invention of the punched card system (Heide 1997). In the late 19th century, encountered with the challenge of managing vast amounts of data for the U.S. Census (Anderson 2015), Hollerith devised a system that encoded information onto punched cards, which could then be read by mechanical tabulators. This system marked a significant leap in data handling capabilities, supporting large datasets to be processed instantly and accurately—a predecessor to modern data processing tools (Austrian 1982). It became a standard technology for data input and storage in computers until the mid-20th century. Hollerith's work laid the basis for modern information processing and led to the founding of his Tabulating Machine Company in 1896, which was one of four companies that merged to form the Computing-Tabulating-Recording Company (CTR) in 1911, which later became IBM in 1924, a company that played a pivotal role in the development of computing (O'Regan 2018). The use of punched cards and mechanical tabulation became a bridge for programmable computing. The transition from mechanical to automated data processing laid the groundwork for modern organizational management practices. This early consolidation highlights the interplay between technological innovation and organizational strategy, where mergers and acquisitions (M&As) became critical tools for scaling capabilities. For instance, the 1911 merger that created CTR, combining Hollerith's firm with the International Time Recording Company, Bundy Manufacturing Company, and Computing Scale Corporation, demonstrated how firms leveraged M&As to integrate complementary technologies and market access, aligning with later theories like the resource-based view (Barney et al. 2001) and dynamic capabilities (Teece et al. 1997). Such horizontal and vertical integrations became foundational to industrial consolidation strategies (Chandler 1962), enabling firms like IBM to dominate markets through combined technical and operational synergies (Eichner 1978).

The Dawn of Electronic Computers and the Rise of Business Automation

As the 20th century progressed, the next significant theoretical leap occurred with Alan Turing, whose work on programmability laid the mathematical foundations for digital computing (Hromkovič 2015). In 1937, Turing initiated the concept of a "Universal Machine", now known as the Turing Machine, which established the idea that a machine could simulate any algorithmic process. This theoretical model provided the foundation for the concept of a general-purpose computer, a machine capable of executing any computable function. During World War II, Turing's ideas were materialized through his work on the Bombe, an electromechanical tool used for breaking the Enigma cipher, which the German military used to encode communications (Negnevitsky 2005). It demonstrated the practical application of machines in solving complex challenges. This demonstrated an early example of machines being used for automated reasoning, a keystone of modern AI. Turing's advancements in theoretical computation stimulated the shift from mechanical computing models to more sophisticated and flexible electronic models (Muggleton 2014).

The following decades saw the creation of electromechanical computers like the Z3 by Konrad Zuse (a German engineer), recognized as one of the earliest functioning computers. In contrast to Babbage's theoretical designs, the Z3, built in 1941, was a significant advancement and is considered the world's first fully functional and programmable computer (Ceruzzi 1981; Rojas 1997). It was mainly used for aircraft design calculations during WWII, demonstrating the practical application of computing technology to solve complex engineering problems (Rojas 2023). These pioneering technologies evolved from theoretical designs to practical tools that initiated to resemble today's computers, revolutionizing data processing and calculation methods across different sectors. Both machines featured programmability, a vital aspect that conceded them to execute a range of tasks based on commands fed into them via punched cards. This concept of programmability was foundational, as it introduced the flexibility needed for general-purpose computing (Randell 2013; Rojas 1997).

Concurrently, the development of the ENIAC (Electronic Numerical Integrator and Computer) in 1945 marked the transition from mechanical to electronic computing. The ENIAC built on previous advancements in programmability and automation but represented a major leap in speed and efficiency. Unlike its mechanical predecessors, ENIAC was fully electronic and could process 5,000 additions per second, about 1,000 times faster than any other machine at the time (Haigh et al. 2016). In less than three years after its development began, the ENIAC dramatically impacted the scientific, military, and industrial communities (Haigh et al. 2016). The adoption of ENIAC by military and industrial entities underscores the role of institutional stakeholders in driving technological diffusion, a concept later explored in innovation adoption frameworks (Rogers 1962). Its high operational costs also reflect early challenges in cost-benefit analysis for large-scale IT investments, a topic central to IT governance literature (Weill and Ross 2004).

The next significant advancement came with John von Neumann's development of the stored-program architecture in 1945. Von Neumann's architecture allowed both data and instructions to be stored within the same memory system, dramatically improving the flexibility and efficiency of computers (Ceruzzi 1997). John von Neumann, considered the third founder of modern AI, introduced the principle of storing instructions electronically within the computer's memory alongside data. Unlike former machines, which required physical rewiring to perform various tasks, von Neumann's architecture allowed instructions to be stored electronically in the machine's memory, just like data (Haigh et al. 2013). This architecture enabled computers to dynamically adjust their programs in response to new information, thereby embodying the initial steps towards adaptive learning. This capacity for modification and self-improvement in programming was instrumental in transitioning from static computational models to ones capable of evolution and learning, aligning closely with the intelligent behaviors seen in contemporary AI technologies (Steunebrink et al. 2016). This paradigm shifts not only enhanced computational efficiency and flexibility but also laid the foundational framework for more complex programming capabilities. The invention of electronic computers significantly enhanced organizational capabilities in information management, operational efficiency, and decision-making processes. This development directly influenced the evolution of management information systems (MIS), enabling complex calculations and data-driven decisions to be performed swiftly, while revolutionizing managerial roles and the organizational structures that support them (Laudon and Laudon 2004).

The Birth of Artificial Intelligence and its Early Applications in Organizations

The era of 1950s and 1960s marked a turning point for the unanswered questions "whether machine can be intelligent, or it can think?" where the convergence of digital technology development and early AI research began to take shape (Kaplan 2016). The initial years of AI are characterized by enormous enthusiasm, great idea, and with very constrained success. The Dartmouth Conference in 1956 is considered the official birth of AI as an academic field. In this summit various researchers coined the term "Artificial Intelligence" argued the possibility of building machines proficient of performing tasks that would be clever of human-like intelligence (McCarthy et al. 2006). The meeting stressed how machines could take on tasks that normally require human intelligence. This became possible thanks to the digital technology of the time, mainly with the advance of stored-program architecture, which permitted machines to use symbolic reasoning and follow rule-based processes. Significant developments in AI were revealed through the growth of primitive programs, i.e., the Logic Theorist (Gugerty 2006), and the General Problem Solver (Newell et al. 1959). These programs demonstrated the capability of digital computers to execute symbolic manipulations and resolve complex logical puzzles, taking gain of the evolving computational power and mounting memory capabilities. During this period, the field of AI not only attracted notable scientists but also fostered the development of pioneering ideas across multiple domains, including knowledge representation, learning algorithms, neural computing, and computing with words. The computational power available at the time was insufficient to fully implement these concepts. However, by the 1980s, improvements in computing facilities made it possible to transform these theoretical frameworks into practical applications. This showed the significant and persistent impact of these early innovations in AI (Dean 2022; Grimson and Patel 1987).

The formal establishment of AI research at Dartmouth also signified a pivotal shift for businesses. Companies began recognizing AI's potential in automating decision-making and optimizing organizational processes. Early AI applications, such as heuristic programs and symbolic reasoning, allowed firms to automate complex analytical tasks, resulting in improved decision accuracy and productivity. For instance, **MYCIN**, an early expert system, used heuristic rules for medical diagnosis, enabling faster and more accurate decision-making in healthcare (Lipscombe 1989). Similarly, **DENDRAL**, another heuristic-based expert system, applied to chemical analysis, demonstrated how AI could automate complex tasks in industries like product formulation and quality control (Buchanan and Feigenbaum 1981). Moreover, the **General Problem Solver (GPS)**, developed in the 1950s, utilized symbolic reasoning to automate logical problem-solving, laying the foundation for decision-support systems in business operations (Newell et al. 1959). One of the most notable business applications was **XCON**, an expert system developed by Digital Equipment Corporation (DEC) to automate the configuration of their VAX computers, which greatly increased productivity by reducing errors in the configuration process (Buchanan and Feigenbaum 1981). In management, expert systems enabled firms to improve efficiency in domain such as logistics, healthcare, and finance. This period also marked the emergence of high-level programming languages such as FORTRAN in 1957 (Backus 1978) and COBOL (Sammet 1978), which significantly enlarged the approachability of computers from dedicated technicians to business organizations and scientific communities.

The 1970s witnessed a breakthrough in AI with the emergence of expert systems, which utilized domain-specific knowledge to tackle complex problems by replicating the decision-making processes of human specialists (Buchanan and Feigenbaum 1981). The success of these expert systems demonstrated the practicality of AI in specific fields, such as medicine, geology, and business (Bramer 1988; Tzafestas et al. 1993).

Despite their successes, expert systems faced notable limitations. Knowledge acquisition, a critical challenge, required substantial human effort and extensive computational resources, making maintenance complex and costly (Partridge 1987). Nonetheless, the commercialization of expert systems in the 1980s marked a significant milestone in AI's transition from academic research to real-world implementation (Bonarini and Maniezzo 1991; Yoon et al. 1995). Organizations seeking to integrate expert systems encountered structural and operational challenges, necessitating investments in workforce reskilling, organizational adaptability, and knowledge management (Partridge 1987). These challenges underscored the broader implications of AI adoption in business and management, highlighting the necessity of aligning technological capabilities with organizational structures to fully harness AI's potential.

The Personal Computing Revolution and its Organizational Transformation

At the same time, the evolution of digital technology was progressing rapidly. The 1970s and 1980s marked the democratization of computing, shifting from large, centralized mainframes to Personal Computers (PCs) accessible to individuals and small businesses (Elliot and Kraemer 2008). This transition aligns with disruptive innovation theory (Christensen 2015), which explains how new technologies, initially perceived as inferior, gradually displace established technologies by offering greater accessibility and affordability. The emergence of personal computing reshaped competitive landscapes and organizational workflows, necessitating new digital integration strategies. One response to this transformation was the development of enterprise resource planning (ERP) systems, which enabled businesses to streamline operations, integrate data management, and enhance efficiency (Davenport 1998).

A pivotal moment in this transition was the introduction of the microprocessor, which significantly reduced the size, cost, and power consumption of computers, making computing widely available (Ceruzzi 2003; O'Regan 2016). The release of the Apple II in 1977 (Stein 2011) and the IBM PC in 1981 (O'Regan 2016) marked a turning point, fundamentally altering how businesses and individuals interacted with technology. As hardware capabilities advanced, software innovations became equally instrumental in shaping digital transformation (Mens et al. 2005). Operating systems like Microsoft DOS (O'Regan 2021) and graphical user interfaces (GUIs), such as the Macintosh OS (Martinez 2011), made computing more intuitive, accessible, and commercially viable (Carpenter 2011). The proliferation of productivity software, including spreadsheets, word processors, and database management systems, solidified personal computers as essential business tools (Schneider 2005).

As personal computing became widespread, technology adoption theories emerged to explain how organizations and individuals integrated these innovations into their workflows. The Technology Acceptance Model (TAM) (Davis 1989) introduced two fundamental factors influencing technology adoption: perceived usefulness, or the extent to which a technology improves job performance, and perceived ease of use, or how effortless it is to interact with the system. The rise of GUIs and user-friendly software significantly enhanced ease of use, thereby accelerating the adoption of personal computers in businesses (O'Regan 2021). Complementing this, the Task-Technology Fit (TTF) model (Goodhue and Thompson 1995) emphasized that technology adoption was most effective when the system's capabilities aligned with user tasks. The increasing availability of task-specific applications, such as Lotus 1-2-3 for financial modeling and database management tools for enterprise data storage, demonstrated how well-integrated technology improved business operations and efficiency (Weaver 1985).

Building upon these models, the Unified Theory of Acceptance and Use of Technology (UTAUT) (Venkatesh et al. 2003) further expanded adoption theories by incorporating performance expectancy, effort expectancy, social influence, and facilitating conditions as determinants of adoption. The spread of personal computing in organizations was heavily influenced by workplace norms, managerial strategies, and the availability of training and technical support, aligning with UTAUT's social and organizational determinants. The varying pace of technology adoption across industries reflected these models; large enterprises with ERP systems and formal IT support structures were often early adopters, while smaller firms followed once the technology was proven cost-effective and accessible.

Thus, the rise of personal computing was not merely a technological shift but a fundamental transformation in organizational structures and strategic management. The democratization of computing technology significantly reshaped organizational structures and business operations. Personal computers allowed small businesses and departments within larger organizations to independently manage and analyze data, thereby decentralizing decision-making processes and flattening organizational hierarchies (Elliott and Kraemer 2008). The rise of user-friendly software also increased organizational productivity and efficiency. Theoretical models such as TAM, TTF, and UTAUT provided valuable insights into why and how organizations adopted computing technologies, influencing modern technology adoption strategies.

Networking and the Internet Era: AI's in Digital Business Strategies

As personal computing matured, the next significant phase in the evolution of digital technology was the development of networks that could connect these computers (Peterson and Davie 2007). The ARPANET, the predecessor to the today internet (Paloque-Berges and Schafer 2019), initially envisioned for military and research purposes, demonstrated the feasibility of packet-switching technology (Hunter and Andonovic 2000), which allowed data to be broken into packets and transmitted across a network. During the 1980s, ARPANET expanded to include more academic and research institutions. This expansion paved the way for the commercialization of the internet (Leiner et al. 1997). A breakthrough came in 1983 with the introduction of the Transmission Control Protocol/Internet Protocol (TCP/IP), which became the standard networking protocol (Meinel and Sack 2013). TCP/IP enabled different networks to connect, forming a global network of networks, the internet as we know it today (Goralski 2017). The growth of high-speed connectivity and distributed computing altered digital technology and significantly motivated AI research. These developments made it possible to take-up data-driven approaches that depend on large datasets and large computational power. In addition, the advance of the internet permitted remote access to both data and computing resources, further speeding up advancement in AI. The internet dramatically altered organizational management by enabling global collaboration, real-time communication, and distributed work practices. Businesses transformed their operational strategies by adopting network-based platforms for collaboration, knowledge sharing, and remote management. This facilitated the emergence of networked and virtual organizational forms, reshaping managerial practices and business models (Leiner et al. 1997). The internet's emergence catalysed network-based business models, such as virtual organizations (Malone and Malone 1992) and platform ecosystems (Gawer and Cusumano 2002). These models redefined value creation, emphasizing scalability and collaboration, principles now central to digital transformation strategies (Bharadwaj et al. 2013).

The Machine Learning Era: Neural Network Resurgence and Organizational Decision Making

By the mid-1980s, dissatisfaction with expert systems, particularly their inability to learn, adapt, and scale efficiently, led AI researchers to revisit neural networks, a concept that had been largely abandoned following Minsky and Papert's (1969) critique. However, with advances in computational power and a more refined understanding of biological neural networks, researchers revived this approach, enabling machines to recognize complex patterns without explicit rule-based programming (Sheikh et al. 2023). The introduction of the backpropagation algorithm (Rumelhart et al. 2013) significantly improved training efficiency, allowing multilayer neural networks to learn from vast datasets. This breakthrough marked a paradigm shift in AI development, emphasizing machine learning and adaptive intelligence over static rule-based systems (Chauvin and Rumelhart 2013; Baldi et al. 2013).

The revival of neural networks coincided with the rise of data-driven decision-making in organizations, fundamentally altering how firms manage uncertainty, optimize operations, and develop competitive advantages (McAfee and Brynjolfsson 2012). As businesses accumulated vast amounts of data, traditional heuristic and expert systems proved inadequate in handling dynamic, complex, and high-dimensional datasets. Neural networks enabled companies to leverage predictive analytics, automate strategic forecasting, and improve operational efficiency (Zhang et al. 2023).

For example, in the financial sector, JP Morgan and Goldman Sachs adopted neural networks for credit risk modeling and algorithmic trading, reducing exposure to market volatility and improving portfolio management. Similarly, in supply chain management, firms like Amazon and Walmart leveraged neural networks to forecast demand fluctuations, optimize inventory distribution, and improve logistics efficiency (Nguyen et al. 2018). These applications illustrate how AI's computational advancements directly influence strategic decision-making and organizational performance.

Alongside the resurgence of neural networks, evolutionary computation emerged as another powerful AI paradigm. Inspired by Darwinian evolution, evolutionary computation techniques, including genetic algorithms, evolutionary strategies, and genetic programming, offered a new approach to solving complex optimization problems (Back et al. 1997). Unlike traditional optimization methods, genetic algorithms, first introduced by John Holland (1975), simulate natural selection mechanisms to identify optimal solutions without explicitly predefined heuristics (Sivanandam and Deepa 2008).

The business implications of evolutionary computation became particularly evident in domains where traditional problem-solving approaches struggled. In workforce scheduling and operations management, companies like British Airways and Lufthansa applied genetic algorithms to optimize crew scheduling, minimizing labor costs and regulatory compliance issues.

In manufacturing, firms such as Siemens and General Electric integrated evolutionary computation to enhance production line scheduling, leading to significant improvements in efficiency, throughput, and cost reduction. In financial modeling, firms leveraged genetic algorithms for portfolio optimization, risk assessment, and fraud detection, adapting real-time strategies to market fluctuations (Mitchell 1998).

By the late 1980s, AI research increasingly moved toward hybrid systems, integrating symbolic reasoning, neural networks, and fuzzy logic, to create more robust, adaptable decision-making models (Garcez and Lamb 2023; Castillo and Melin 2023). These hybrid AI models provided organizational leaders with enhanced tools for managing uncertainty, improving real-time data interpretation, and adapting to shifting market conditions.

The rise of machine learning (ML) and deep learning (DL) has profoundly transformed organizational decision-making, strategic management, and workforce dynamics. The transition from rule-based AI systems to data-driven learning algorithms has allowed organizations to leverage predictive analytics, automate complex tasks, and enhance competitive advantage (Jordan and Mitchell 2015). This evolution has been driven by the explosion of digital data, advancements in cloud computing, and increased computational power, enabling firms to integrate AI into strategic planning, customer insights, supply chain management, and human resource optimization (Brynjolfsson and McAfee 2014).

Unlike symbolic AI, which relied on manually encoded rules, machine learning enabled systems to recognize patterns and improve performance over time, making it highly applicable to organizational decision-making and strategic management. In business and management, machine learning quickly became a strategic asset, allowing firms to leverage data-driven insights for competitive advantage. Supervised learning became integral to customer relationship management (CRM), enabling firms to personalize marketing campaigns and optimize customer segmentation (Wedel and Kannan 2016). For instance, Amazon's recommendation system, powered by collaborative filtering algorithms, increased conversion rates by providing highly personalized product suggestions, reinforcing customer engagement and loyalty (Smith and Linden 2017). Meanwhile, unsupervised learning facilitated supply chain optimization, as companies used clustering algorithms to detect inefficiencies and streamline logistics (Simchi-Levi et al. 2015). Walmart, for example, applied machine learning models to anticipate inventory demand fluctuations across thousands of stores, leading to better stock management and cost reduction (Boylan and Syntetos 2015). Reinforcement learning also found its way into finance and operations, where firms used self-learning algorithms to optimize investment portfolios and dynamic pricing models (Kaelbling et al. 1996; Caruana and Niculescu-Mizil 2006).

The advent of cloud computing in the 2000s, exemplified by Amazon Web Services (AWS), Microsoft Azure, and Google Cloud, revolutionized AI by democratizing access to large-scale computational resources (Hashemipour and Ali 2020; Buyya et al. 2009). This cloud-based infrastructure significantly reduced barriers to AI adoption, allowing organizations to train complex deep learning models without investing in expensive in-house hardware (Saiyeda and Mir 2017).

Deep learning, a subset of machine learning based on artificial neural networks with multiple layers, rapidly gained traction as the dominant paradigm in AI (LeCun et al. 2015). By the 2010s, companies like Google, Facebook, and Tesla leveraged deep learning to develop state-of-the-art applications in image recognition, speech processing, natural language understanding, and self-driving cars (Najafabadi et al. 2015; Sarker 2021).

From an organizational perspective, deep learning played a transformative role in corporate strategy, operational efficiency, and workforce management. In finance, firms like JP Morgan Chase implemented deep learning algorithms for fraud detection, reducing false positives in transaction monitoring and enhancing security (Provost and Fawcett 2013). In human resource management, AI-driven applicant tracking systems (ATS) used deep learning to analyze resumes and predict candidate success rates, streamlining the recruitment process (Black and van Esch 2020). However, the integration of deep learning also presented managerial challenges. Firms had to redesign job roles, invest in reskilling initiatives, and navigate ethical concerns related to algorithmic biases (Martin and Pear 2019). Companies that successfully navigated these challenges through ethical AI governance frameworks (Floridi et al. 2018) achieved greater trust, regulatory compliance, and long-term sustainability.

The convergence of machine learning, neural networks, and evolutionary computation has revolutionized organizational decision-making, shifting it from reactive practices to proactive, data-driven strategies. By harnessing AI-powered models, organizations enable continuous learning (Senge 1990), empowering them to anticipate trends, optimize performance, and secure enduring competitive advantages. The evolution from traditional machine learning to advanced deep learning systems has further redefined organizational structures, strategic priorities, and decision-making frameworks. Firms now leverage data-centric insights to enhance operational efficiency, customer experiences, and workforce productivity, embedding these technologies into management practices to foster resilience and sustained growth (Brynjolfsson and McAfee 2017).

Theories such as technology adoption, organizational ambidexterity, and modularity provide critical lenses for understanding how businesses integrate AI within complex ecosystems. Yet, as deep learning reshapes industries, organizations face the challenge of balancing technological innovation with human-centric governance. Ensuring AI deployment aligns with core values, ethical principles, and long-term strategic goals is imperative (Mikalef and Gupta 2021). Moreover, scaling AI adoption demands careful alignment with organizational objectives, regulatory frameworks, and societal expectations. Companies that successfully navigate these dynamics, harmonizing technological capabilities with adaptive governance, will not only lead the next wave of digital transformation but also dominate innovation and competitive advantage in the 21st-century business landscape.

Conclusion

The historical and continuing evolution of technology, from early mechanical devices to modern AI, reveals a clear track toward increasingly advanced, autonomous, and integrated systems. The evolution of AI and digital technology manifest a vigorous interaction between advancements in computational approaches and the raising capabilities of digital infrastructure. From the rise of expert systems in the 1970s to the deep learning innovation of the 2010s, every phase of AI advancement was deeply influenced by high-tech innovations such as personal computing, networking, and cloud computing. Today's AI environment, built on machine learning and fuelled by big data, raises as a testimony to the constant convergence of these two key disciplines in shaping the future of technology. As these disciplines continue to develop and merge, we can imagine further innovation across industries, from healthcare and business to autonomous systems, modeling the future of technology. From a management perspective, AI's evolution mirrors the transition from closed innovation to open innovation paradigms (Chesbrough 2003), where collaboration across ecosystems drives progress. Future research should explore AI's role in organizational agility (Atienza-Barba et al. 2024) and ethical governance (Martin and Pear 2019), ensuring alignment with stakeholder expectations. This historical evolution emphasizes not only technological advancement but also critical organizational and managerial transformations. Effective AI integration into organizational structures requires strategic leadership, employee engagement, and adaptive organizational cultures to manage the challenges associated with workforce dynamics, ethical considerations, and regulatory compliance (Jordan and Mitchell 2015; Kaplan 2016). Organizations must embrace continuous learning, agility, and proactive governance strategies to fully exploit AI's transformative potential and sustain competitive advantage.

References

Anderson, M. J. 2015. The American Census: A Social History. Yale University Press.

Atienza-Barba, M., del Río, M. D. L. C., Meseguer-Martínez, Á. and Barba-Sánchez, V. 2024. Artificial intelligence and organizational agility: An analysis of scientific production and future trends. European Research on Management and Business Economics 30(2): 100253.

Austrian, G. D. 1982. Herman Hollerith: Forgotten Giant of Information Processing. Columbia University Press.

Babbage, H. P. 1982. Babbage's analytical engine. *In*: Randell, B. (ed.). The Origins of Digital Computers.

Babbage, H. P. 1982. Babbage's analytical engine. pp. 67–70. In The Origins of Digital Computers: Selected Papers. Berlin, Heidelberg: Springer Berlin Heidelberg.

Back, T., Hammel, U. and Schwefel, H. P. 1997. Evolutionary computation: Comments on the history and current state. IEEE Transactions on Evolutionary Computation 1(1): 3–17.

Backus, J. 1978. The history of Fortran I, II, and III. ACM Sigplan Notices 13(8): 165–180.

Baldi, P., Chauvin, Y. and Hornik, K. 2013. Backpropagation and unsupervised learning in linear networks. pp. 389–432. In Backpropagation. Psychology Press.

Barney, J., Wright, M. and Ketchen Jr, D. J. 2001. The resource-based view of the firm: Ten years after 1991. Journal of Management 27(6): 625–641.

Bharadwaj, A., El Sawy, O. A., Pavlou, P. A. and Venkatraman, N. V. 2013. Digital business strategy: toward a next generation of insights. MIS Quarterly 471–482.

Black, J. S. and van Esch, P. 2020. AI-enabled recruiting: What is it and how should a manager use it?. Business Horizons 63(2): 215–226.

Bonarini, A. and Maniezzo, V. 1991. Integrating expert systems and decision-support systems: principles and practice. Knowledge-Based Systems 4(3): 172–176.

Boylan, J. E. and Syntetos, A. A. 2015. Supply chain forecasting: the customer dimension. pp. 12–15. In Conference Proceedings. 27th European Conference on Operational Research EURO.

Bramer, M. A. 1988. Expert systems in business: a British perspective. Expert Systems 5(2): 104–117.

Brynjolfsson, E. and McAfee, A. 2014. The Second Machine Age: Work, Progress, and Prosperity in a Time of Brilliant Technologies. WW Norton & Company.

Buchanan, B. G. and Feigenbaum, E. A. 1981. DENDRAL and Meta-DENDRAL: Their applications dimension. pp. 313–322. In Readings in Artificial Intelligence. Morgan Kaufmann.

Buyya, R., Yeo, C. S., Venugopal, S., Broberg, J. and Brandic, I. 2009. Cloud computing and emerging IT platforms: Vision, hype, and reality for delivering computing as the 5th utility. Future Generation Computer Systems 25(6): 599–616.

Carpenter, T. 2011. Microsoft Windows Operating System Essentials. John Wiley & Sons.

Caruana, R. and Niculescu-Mizil, A. 2006, June. An empirical comparison of supervised learning algorithms. pp. 161–168. In Proceedings of the 23rd International Conference on Machine Learning.

Castillo, O. and Melin, P. (eds.). 2023. Fuzzy Logic and Neural Networks for Hybrid Intelligent System Design. Springer.

Ceruzzi, P. E. 1981. The early computers of Konrad Zuse, 1935 to 1945. Annals of the History of Computing 3(3): 241–262.

Ceruzzi, P. 1997. Crossing the divide: architectural issues and the emergence of the stored program computer, 1935–1955. IEEE Annals of the History of Computing 19(1): 5–12.

Ceruzzi, P. E. 2003. A History of Modern Computing. MIT Press.

Chandler, A. D. 1962. Strategy and Structure: Chapters in the History of the Industrial Empire. Cambridge Mass 5(1): 12–48.

Chauvin, Y. and Rumelhart, D. E. 2013. Backpropagation: Theory, Architectures, and Applications. Psychology Press.

Chesbrough, H. W. 2003. Open Innovation: The New Imperative for Creating and Profiting from Technology. Harvard Business Press.

Christensen, C. M. 2015. The Innovator's Dilemma: When New Technologies Cause Great Firms to Fail. Harvard Business Review Press.

Davenport, T. H. 1998. Putting the enterprise into the enterprise system. Harvard Business Review 76(4): 121–131.

Davis, F. D. 1989. Technology acceptance model: TAM. Al-Suqri, MN, Al-Aufi, AS: Information Seeking Behavior and Technology Adoption 205(219): 5.

Dean, J. 2022. A golden decade of deep learning: Computing systems & applications. Daedalus 151(2): 58–74. https://doi.org/10.1162/daed_a_01900.

Eichner, A. S. 1978. The Visible Hand. The Managerial Revolution in American Business. By Alfred D. ChandlerJr., Cambridge, Mass., Harvard University Press, 1977. Pp. xvi+ 608. $18.50. Business History Review 52(1): 98–101.

Elliott, M. S. and Kraemer, K. L. (eds.). 2008. Computerization Movements and Technology Diffusion: From Mainframes to Ubiquitous Computing. Information Today, Inc..

Floridi, L., Cowls, J., Beltrametti, M., Chatila, R., Chazerand, P., Dignum, V. et al. 2018. AI4People—an ethical framework for a good AI society: opportunities, risks, principles, and recommendations. Minds and Machines 28: 689–707.

Garcez, A. d. and Lamb, L. C. 2023. Neurosymbolic AI: the 3rd wave. Artif. Intell. Rev. 56: 12387–12406. https://doi.org/10.1007/s10462-023-10448-w.

Gawer, A. and Cusumano, M. A. 2002. Platform Leadership: How Intel, Microsoft, and Cisco Drive Industry Innovation (Vol. 5, pp. 29–30). Boston: Harvard Business School Press.

Goodhue, D. L. and Thompson, R. L. 1995. Task-technology fit and individual performance. MIS Quarterly 213–236.

Goralski, W. 2017. The Illustrated Network: How TCP/IP Works in a Modern Network. Morgan Kaufmann.

Grimson, W. E. and Patil, R. S. 1987. AI in the 1980s and Beyond. DOI: https://doi.org/10.7551/mitpress/1166.001.0001.

Gugerty, L. 2006. Newell and Simon's Logic Theorist: Historical background and impact on cognitive modeling. Proceedings of the Human Factors and Ergonomics Society Annual Meeting 50(9): 880–884. https://doi.org/10.1177/154193120605000904.

Haigh, T., Priestley, M. and Rope, C. 2013. Reconsidering the stored-program concept. IEEE Annals of the History of Computing 36(1): 4–17.

Haigh, T., Priestley, P. M. and Rope, C. 2016. ENIAC in Action: Making and Remaking the Modern Computer. MIT Press.

Haigh, Thomas, Mark Priestley and Crispin Rope. 2016. 'ENIAC Arrives at the Ballistic Research Lab', Eniac in Action: Making and Remaking the Modern Computer (Cambridge, MA, 2016; online edn, MIT Press Scholarship Online, 18 May 2017), https://doi.org/10.7551/mitpress/9780262033985.003.0006,

Hashemipour, S. and Ali, M. 2020. Amazon Web Services (AWS) – An overview of the on-demand cloud computing platform. *In*: Miraz, M. H., Excell, P. S., Ware, A., Soomro, S. and Ali, M. (eds.). Emerging Technologies in Computing. iCETiC 2020. Lecture Notes of the Institute for Computer Sciences, Social Informatics and Telecommunications Engineering, vol 332. Springer, Cham. https://doi.org/10.1007/978-3-030-60036-5_3.

Heide, L. 1997. Shaping a technology: American punched card systems 1880–1914. IEEE Annals of the History of Computing 19(4): 28–41.

Hromkovič, J. 2015. Alan Turing and the foundation of computer science. Turing's Revolution: The Impact of His Ideas about Computability 273–281.

Hunter, D. K. and Andonovic, I. 2000. Approaches to optical Internet packet switching. IEEE Communications Magazine 38(9): 116–122.

Hyman, A. 1985. Charles Babbage: Pioneer of the Computer. Princeton University Press.

Jordan, M. I. and Mitchell, T. M. 2015. Machine learning: Trends, perspectives, and prospects. Science 349(6245): 255–260.

Kaelbling, L. P., Littman, M. L. and Moore, A. W. 1996. Reinforcement learning: A survey. Journal of Artificial Intelligence Research 4: 237–285.

Kaplan, J. 2016. Artificial Intelligence: What Everyone Needs to knowR. Oxford University Press.

Laudon, K. C. and Laudon, J. P. 2004. Management Information Systems: Managing the Digital Firm. Pearson Educación.

LeCun, Y., Bengio, Y. and Hinton, G. 2015. Deep learning. Nature 521(7553): 436–444.

Leiner, B. M., Cerf, V. G., Clark, D. D., Kahn, R. E., Kleinrock, L., Lynch, D. C. et al. 1997. The past and future history of the Internet. Communications of the ACM 40(2): 102–108.

Lipscombe, B. 1989. Expert systems and computer-controlled decision making in medicine. AI & Society 3: 184–197.

Malone, M. S. and Malone, M. S. 1992. The Virtual Corporation: Structuring and Revitalizing the Corporation for the 21st Century:[lessons from the World's Most Advanced Companies]. E. Burlingame Books.

Martin, G. and Pear, J. J. 2019. Behavior Modification: What it is and How to Do It. Routledge.

Martinez, W. L. 2011. Graphical user interfaces. Wiley Interdisciplinary Reviews: Computational Statistics 3(2): 119–133. https://doi.org/10.1002/wics.150.

McAfee, A. and Brynjolfsson, E. 2012. Big Data. The management revolution. Harvard Business Review 90(10): 61–68.

McCarthy, J., Minsky, M. L., Rochester, N. and Shannon, C. E. 2006. A proposal for the dartmouth summer research project on artificial intelligence, august 31, 1955. AI Magazine 27(4): 12–12.

Meinel, C. and Sack, H. 2013. Internetworking: Technological Foundations and Applications. Springer Science & Business Media.

Mens, T., Wermelinger, M., Ducasse, S., Demeyer, S., Hirschfeld, R. and Jazayeri, M. 2005, September. Challenges in software evolution. pp. 13–22. In Eighth International Workshop on Principles of Software Evolution (IWPSE'05). IEEE.

Mikalef, P. and Gupta, M. 2021. Artificial intelligence capability: Conceptualization, measurement calibration, and empirical study on its impact on organizational creativity and firm performance. Information & Management 58(3): 103434.

Minsky, M. and Papert, S. 1969. Perceptrons. MIT Press, Cambridge, MA. USA.

Mitchell, M. 1998. An Introduction to Genetic Algorithms. MIT Press.

Muggleton, S. 2014. Alan Turing and the development of Artificial Intelligence. AI Communications 27(1): 3–10.

Najafabadi, M. M., Villanustre, F., Khoshgoftaar, T. M., Seliya, N., Wald, R. and Muharemagic, E. 2015. Deep learning applications and challenges in big data analytics. Journal of Big Data 2: 1–21. DOIhttps://doi.org/10.1186/s40537-014-0007-7.

Negnevitsky, M. 2005. Artificial Intelligence: A Guide to Intelligent Systems. Pearson Education.

Newell, A., Shaw, J. C. and Simon, H. A. 1959, June. Report on a general problem-solving program. In IFIP Congress (Vol. 256, p. 64).

Nguyen, T., Li, Z. H. O. U., Spiegler, V., Ieromonachou, P. and Lin, Y. 2018. Big data analytics in supply chain management: A state-of-the-art literature review. Computers & Operations Research 98: 254–264.

O'Regan, G. 2016. The IBM Personal Computer. *In*: Introduction to the History of Computing. Undergraduate Topics in Computer Science. Springer, Cham. https://doi.org/10.1007/978-3-319-33138-6_12.

O'Regan, G. 2016. The Microprocessor Revolution. *In*: Introduction to the History of Computing. Undergraduate Topics in Computer Science. Springer, Cham. https://doi.org/10.1007/978-3-319-33138-6_10.

O'Regan, G. 2018. Hollerith's Tabulating Machines and the Birth of IBM. *In*: The Innovation in Computing Companion. Springer, Cham. https://doi.org/10.1007/978-3-030-02619-6_31.

O'Regan, G. 2018. Transistor. *In*: The Innovation in Computing Companion. Springer, Cham. https://doi.org/10.1007/978-3-030-02619-6_52.

O'Regan, G. 2021. History of operating systems. *In*: A Brief History of Computing. Springer, Cham. https://doi.org/10.1007/978-3-030-66599-9_13.

Paloque-Bergès, C. and Schafer, V. 2019. Arpanet (1969–2019). Internet Histories 3(1): 1–14.

Partridge, D. 1987. The scope and limitations of first-generation expert systems. Future Generation Computer Systems 3(1): 1–10.

Peterson, L. L. and Davie, B. S. 2007. Computer Networks: A Systems Approach. Morgan Kaufmann.

Provost, F. and Fawcett, T. 2013. Data Science for Business: What You Need to Know About Data Mining and Data-Analytic Thinking. " O'Reilly Media, Inc.".

Randell, B. (ed.). 2013. The Origins of Digital Computers: Selected Papers. Springer.

Rogers, E. M. 1962. Diffusion of Innovations. 1st Edition. New York. Free Press of Glen-coe.

Rojas, R. 1997. Konrad Zuse's legacy: the architecture of the Z1 and Z3. IEEE Annals of the History of Computing 19(2): 5–16.

Rojas, R. 2023. The Architecture of the Z3. *In*: Konrad Zuse's Early Computers. History of Computing. Springer, Cham. https://doi.org/10.1007/978-3-031-39876-6_5.

Rojas, R. 2023. The S1 and S2: Zuse's Work for the German Military 1941–1945. pp. 119–133. In Konrad Zuse's Early Computers: The Quest for the Computer in Germany. Cham: Springer Nature Switzerland.

Rumelhart, D. E., Durbin, R., Golden, R. and Chauvin, Y. 2013. Backpropagation: The basic theory. pp. 1–34. In Backpropagation. Psychology Press.

Saiyeda, A. and Mir, M. A. 2017. Cloud computing for deep learning analytics: A survey of current trends and challenges. International Journal of Advanced Research in Computer Science 8(2).

Sammet, J. E. 1978. The early history of COBOL. pp. 199–243. In History of Programming Languages.

Sarker, I. H. 2021. Deep learning: a comprehensive overview on techniques, taxonomy, applications and research directions. SN Computer Science 2(6): 420.

Schneider, S. 2005. Essential software: databases, spreadsheets, word processing, and presentation software. pp. 183–193. In Informatics for the Clinical Laboratory: A Practical Guide. New York, NY: Springer New York.

Sheikh, H., Prins, C. and Schrijvers, E. 2023. Artificial Intelligence: Definition and Background. *In*: Mission AI. Research for Policy. Springer, Cham. https://doi.org/10.1007/978-3-031-21448-6_2.

Simchi-Levi, D., Wang, H. and Wei, Y. 2018. Increasing supply chain robustness through process flexibility and inventory. Production and Operations Management 27(8): 1476–1491.

Sivanandam, S. and Deepa, S. 2008. Genetic algorithms. *In*: Introduction to Genetic Algorithms. Springer, Berlin, Heidelberg. https://doi.org/10.1007/978-3-540-73190-0_2.

Smith, B. and Linden, G. 2017. Two decades of recommender systems at Amazon. com. IEEE Internet Computing 21(3): 12–18.

Stein, J. A. 2011. Domesticity, gender and the 1977 Apple II personal computer. Design and Culture 3(2): 193–216.

Steunebrink, B. R., Thórisson, K. R. and Schmidhuber, J. 2016, June. Growing recursive self-improvers. pp. 129–139. In International Conference on Artificial General Intelligence. Cham: Springer International Publishing.

Teece, D. J., Pisano, G. and Shuen, A. 1997. Dynamic capabilities and strategic management. Strategic Management Journal 18(7): 509–533.

Tzafestas, S. G., Kokkinaki, A. I. and Valavanis, K. P. 1993. An overview of expert systems. *In*: Tzafestas, S. (eds.). Expert Systems in Engineering Applications. Springer, Berlin, Heidelberg. https://doi.org/10.1007/978-3-642-84048-7_1.

Venkatesh, V., Morris, M. G., Davis, G. B. and Davis, F. D. 2003. User acceptance of information technology: Toward a unified view. MIS Quarterly 425–478.

Weaver, K. R. 1985, May. Lotus 1-2-3 for mainframes (bringing a product to market). pp. 207–214. In Proceedings of the International Conference on APL: APL and the Future.

Wedel, M. and Kannan, P. K. 2016. Marketing analytics for data-rich environments. Journal of Marketing 80(6): 97–121.

Weill, P. and Ross, J. W. 2004. IT Governance: How Top Performers Manage IT Decision Rights for Superior Results. Harvard Business Press.

Yoon, Y., Guimaraes, T. and O'Neal, Q. 1995. Exploring the factors associated with expert systems success. MIS Quarterly 83–106.

Zhang, B., Zhu, J. and Su, H. 2023. Toward the third-generation artificial intelligence. Sci. China Inf. Sci. 66: 121101. https://doi.org/10.1007/s11432-021-3449-x.

Chapter 6

The Algorithmic Workplace

Artificial Intelligence and the Future of Organizational Behavior

Filomena Buonocore,[1] *Davide de Gennaro,*[1,*] *Ludovica Del Barone*[2] and *Viviana Colombi Evangelista*[1]

Introduction

Artificial Intelligence (AI) is no longer a distant prospect or a futuristic tool confined to specific industries or technical fields. It has become a pervasive and transformative force that is reshaping the core dynamics of organizational life—impacting decision-making processes, task distribution, leadership, communication, and employee engagement (Canbul Yaroğlu 2024; Csaszar and Steinberger 2022; Von Krogh 2018). In this shifting landscape, organizations increasingly rely on AI systems to carry out a broad spectrum of functions, including predictive analytics, performance assessment, autonomous decision-making, and human resource management (Bankins 2021; Vrontis et al. 2023). Once integrated into daily routines, AI does more than improve existing practices; it introduces new logics of action, alters power relations, and reshapes expectations around work and behavior (Anthony et al. 2023; Boyd and Holton 2018).

This transformation compels scholars and practitioners alike to revisit foundational questions within the field of organizational behavior. What are the consequences for motivation and job satisfaction when decisions are made by

[1] University of Naples "Parthenope", Naples, Italy.
[2] University of Salento, Lecce, Italy.
* Corresponding author: davide.degennaro@uniparthenope.it

DOI: 10.1201/9781003535393-6

algorithms instead of human supervisors (e.g., Langer and Landers 2021)? How do employees relate to their work when AI tools mediate—or even replace—their everyday tasks (e.g., Bhargava et al. 2021)? How does AI influence the psychological contract between workers and organizations, and what implications does this have for leadership, trust, and organizational citizenship behaviors (e.g., Bankins and Formosa 2020)?

The adoption of AI technologies poses a significant challenge to long-standing organizational theories, many of which are built on assumptions of human rationality, bounded decision-making, hierarchical control, and clearly delineated role structures. In contrast, AI introduces dynamic, data-driven processes that operate across various levels of the organization, often bypassing formal hierarchies and redistributing decision-making authority (Clough and Wu 2022; Dunleavy and Margetts 2025). The rise of algorithmic management illustrates this shift, as tasks such as scheduling, performance monitoring, and workload distribution are increasingly overseen by opaque algorithmic systems rather than direct human supervision (Kim et al. 2025). While this may enhance operational efficiency, it simultaneously raises pressing concerns around autonomy, surveillance, fairness, and transparency (Akinrinola et al. 2024; Felzmann et al. 2020).

The organizational impact of AI is far from homogeneous. Its consequences depend on a range of contextual factors, including organizational culture, sector-specific characteristics, digital maturity, and leadership approaches (Rajagopal et al. 2022). In some contexts, AI serves as a tool for employee empowerment—relieving them of repetitive tasks and providing real-time insights that improve decision quality (Qudus 2025). In others, it restricts discretion, diminishes agency, and fosters work environments marked by continuous monitoring (Novelli et al. 2024). These divergent outcomes underscore the importance of developing a more refined understanding of how AI is reshaping the relational and emotional fabric of organizational life.

Furthermore, AI technologies are not neutral instruments. They embody particular values, assumptions, and biases embedded in their design and use (Ntoutsi et al. 2020; Oyeniran et al. 2022). As such, they influence whether existing organizational norms and practices are reinforced or disrupted. The introduction of AI systems often magnifies inequalities, shaping who benefits from technological innovation and who bears its burdens (Ernst et al. 2019). Workers in highly routinized roles may face greater risks of deskilling or redundancy, whereas those involved in strategic or data-driven functions may gain new avenues for growth. At the same time, the growing reliance on AI calls into question the traditional competencies expected of leaders and managers, prompting the need for skills in digital literacy, ethical reasoning, and adaptive change management (Babashahi et al. 2024; Bobitan et al. 2024; Rezaei et al. 2024).

This chapter seeks to contribute to ongoing debates regarding the organizational implications of AI (Bankins et al. 2024; Shrestha et al. 2019), focusing on its effects on key dimensions of organizational behavior, including motivation, engagement, autonomy, leadership, trust, and resistance to change. Drawing on both established and emerging theoretical perspectives—such as psychological contract theory

(Cullinane and Dundon 2006), socio-technical systems theory (Appelbaum 1997), and current debates on algorithmic governance (Katzenbach and Ulbricht 2019)—it proposes an integrative framework for understanding how AI is redefining work roles, interpersonal relationships, and managerial responsibilities.

Viewed through this lens, AI is more than a means of enhancing operational efficiency. It functions as a socio-organizational actor that helps to shape expectations, influence relationships, and reconfigure organizational identities (Hanelt et al. 2021; Kemal and Shah 2024). This conceptualization allows us to move beyond deterministic narratives and focus on the organizational and human conditions under which AI can support empowerment, foster participation, and contribute to meaningful work.

In pursuing this line of inquiry, the chapter also engages with broader questions of ethics and power in organizational life. Who decides how AI is implemented and governed within the workplace? Which stakeholders are granted a voice in these decisions, and which are excluded? What are the long-term implications for employee voice, job quality, and perceptions of justice? These questions have become increasingly urgent with the widespread adoption of generative AI technologies, such as large language models, which are already transforming the nature of knowledge work and professional identity (Malik et al. 2021; Morandini et al. 2023; Tortorella et al. 2025).

Ultimately, this chapter aims to deepen theoretical insight into the relationship between AI and organizational behavior through a critical and constructive lens. It argues that the consequences of AI integration are not determined by the technology itself, but rather by the choices, values, and governance arrangements that shape its use (De Almeida et al. 2021; Wirtz et al. 2022). A central challenge for scholars and practitioners is to move beyond questions of technical capability and ask instead what kind of organizational future AI should help bring about.

The New Organizational Context Enabled by AI

AI is reshaping the organizational landscape in ways that are both subtle and far-reaching. What is unfolding is not merely a change in tools or procedures, but a deeper transformation in the logic through which organizations function, make decisions, and engage with their members (Jarrahi 2018; Trunk et al. 2020). AI systems—especially those based on machine learning and generative models—are now embedded in core organizational functions, ranging from strategic decision-making and coordination to performance management and internal communication (Chukwuka and Dibie 2024). These systems do more than support human processes; they actively shape them, introducing new forms of control, visibility, and power that challenge long-standing assumptions within organizational theory (Feldstein 2019; Liu 2018).

In this evolving context, traditional hierarchical structures are gradually giving way to more fluid and adaptive configurations (Magistretti and Trabucchi 2025; Tominc et al. 2023). Authority, once concentrated in managerial roles, is increasingly delegated to algorithmic systems (Candrian and Scherer 2022). This shift—commonly referred to as algorithmic management—redefines organizational control (Busuioc 2021; Fügener et al. 2022). Rather than being exercised exclusively through interpersonal relationships, control now takes the form of data-driven mechanisms that monitor behavior, allocate tasks, and assess performance in real time (Lazaroiu et al. 2022). These mechanisms do not merely automate prior practices; they reconfigure them. They alter how managerial oversight is exercised and how employees experience accountability, often without the transparency that once accompanied human supervision (Yanamala 2023).

One compelling example of these dynamics is offered by Uber. The company does not function as a conventional hierarchical organization but as a digitally mediated coordination system, where key managerial tasks—such as assigning work, monitoring performance, and determining pay—are governed by algorithms. Drivers interact with the platform through a mobile application that uses predictive analytics to allocate rides, implement dynamic pricing, and evaluate performance based on customer ratings and behavioral data. In this environment, there is no direct supervisor; coordination is continuous, automated, and largely opaque. Drivers often lack insight into why they are assigned certain tasks, how performance thresholds are established, or how their evaluations impact future opportunities. Autonomy becomes paradoxical: drivers are formally independent yet operationally constrained by systems they cannot easily understand or influence. Uber's model exemplifies how authority becomes embedded in technological systems rather than in roles, and how organizational boundaries blur in the process. It also reflects broader concerns around fairness, explainability, and trust—issues that increasingly affect not only platform-based companies but also traditional organizations experimenting with AI-driven models of management.

Beyond control, AI intensifies the datafication of work (Cole et al. 2021). Employees now operate in environments where their actions, interactions, and even emotional states may be captured and analyzed (Lavazza and Farina 2023; Saifer and Dacin 2022). The workplace becomes a space of continuous data extraction, where each digital trace contributes to predictive modeling (Zirar et al. 2023). While such systems may offer benefits in terms of personalization and optimization, they also raise serious concerns related to surveillance, trust, and personal autonomy (Wilkens 2020). The psychological contract between employees and employers risks being transformed by these invisible infrastructures of control, with work increasingly experienced as transactional, shaped by systems that appear objective yet remain opaque (He et al. 2025; Huang and Gursoy 2024).

This reconfiguration also alters how expertise is recognized and distributed. AI systems are often prized for their ability to process volumes of data that exceed human capacity, thereby shifting organizational authority from experiential knowledge to algorithmic output (Raisch and Krakowski 2021). Where once judgment, intuition, and relational intelligence guided decision-making, organizations now turn to models that identify patterns and generate probabilistic forecasts. This change can create friction, particularly when algorithmic outputs contradict professional insights or when employees are expected to implement decisions without having participated in their formation (Miracchi 2019). As a result, many individuals find themselves transitioning from being sources of knowledge to becoming interpreters, monitors, or executors of machine-generated recommendations (Selenko et al. 2022).

Organizational culture is not immune to these transformations. The diffusion of AI requires not only technical adjustments but also cultural change (Murire 2024). Organizations are increasingly called upon to cultivate environments that encourage experimentation, digital curiosity, and continuous learning (Benvenuti et al. 2023). AI systems do not conform to existing routines; rather, they demand that those routines evolve to become more flexible, iterative, and informed by data (Agarwal 2024). Employees are expected to adapt alongside intelligent systems—learning to engage with new interfaces, feedback loops, and modes of collaboration that involve non-human agents (Anthony et al. 2023; Gladden et al. 2022). However, this adaptive capacity is unevenly distributed. Digital divides—whether generational, functional, or cognitive—can exacerbate pre-existing inequalities and generate new fractures within the workforce (Carter et al. 2020; Morandini et al. 2023).

Simultaneously, organizational boundaries are becoming more permeable. AI technologies are frequently developed by external vendors, trained on datasets that originate beyond the organization, and updated through processes outside direct managerial control (Steimers and Schneider 2022). This reliance complicates issues of governance and accountability, while blurring the distinction between internal and external knowledge, and between organizational actors and their technological environment (Raisch and Krakowski 2021). Increasingly, the effectiveness of decision-making hinges on how well externally developed systems align with internal values, operational practices, and strategic objectives (Rajagopal et al. 2022; Trunk et al. 2020).

Despite the aspirational narratives that often accompany AI adoption, many organizations face a significant gap between vision and execution (Ransbotham et al. 2017). While leaders may anticipate transformative outcomes, implementation efforts frequently falter due to infrastructural deficiencies, workforce resistance, skill shortages, or misalignment between technological solutions and organizational readiness (Bukartaite and Hooper 2023; Sidhu et al. 2024). These barriers reveal that AI integration does not occur in a vacuum. It interacts with entrenched cultures, institutional legacies, and existing distributions of power (Bareis and Katzenbach 2022). In some instances, AI reinforces centralization and managerial authority; in others, it enables more distributed forms of intelligence and collaborative decision-making (Pietronudo et al. 2022). The outcomes remain highly contingent on context.

What emerges is a complex and often ambiguous organizational context. AI creates opportunities for greater agility, insight, and responsiveness (Popa et al. 2025), yet it also introduces ethical challenges, demands new capabilities, and destabilizes core assumptions about work, authority, and autonomy. Making sense of this evolving environment requires more than tracking technological advancements. It calls for deep analysis of how structures, practices, and relationships are being reconfigured by a form of intelligence that is non-human yet increasingly central to organizational life.

This chapter argues that AI cannot be meaningfully examined without considering the organizational forms and behaviors it both influences and is influenced by. Rather than treating AI as an external force acting upon static systems, it should be understood as a constitutive element of contemporary organizations—one that co-produces meaning, structure, and agency. The sections that follow explore how this new organizational context affects critical aspects of behavior at work, including motivation, engagement, leadership, and resistance, offering a reflection on the human consequences of intelligent technologies in the workplace.

Methodological Positioning

This chapter adopts a conceptual and interpretive approach, aiming to critically examine the interplay between AI and organizational behavior through the integration of diverse theoretical perspectives and empirical insights from existing literature. Rather than presenting original empirical data, the chapter develops a framework that synthesizes findings from multiple disciplines—including organizational theory, psychology, management studies, and information systems—offering a reflective lens through which the socio-organizational implications of AI can be understood.

The analysis is grounded in a selective but systematic review of recent academic contributions published between 2018 and 2025. These sources were identified through targeted searches in scholarly databases (e.g., Scopus, Web of Science, JSTOR) using keywords such as “AI and work,” “algorithmic management,” “organizational behavior,” “digital transformation,” and “psychological contract.” Priority was given to peer-reviewed articles that investigate the impact of AI on workplace dynamics, leadership practices, motivation, engagement, and resistance, as well as conceptual pieces proposing new interpretive frameworks.

The chapter follows an interpretive and configurational epistemology, focusing on how meaning, power, and identity are co-constructed at the intersection of human and algorithmic agency. In doing so, it embraces a post-positivist stance, acknowledging the socially embedded and context-dependent nature of organizational phenomena. This methodological orientation allows for a nuanced exploration of both enabling and constraining dynamics associated with AI adoption, moving beyond linear cause-effect logics toward a more relational and situated understanding of change.

Additionally, the chapter engages with illustrative cases—such as the transformation of coordination and control mechanisms in platform-based companies like Uber—to exemplify how AI-driven systems alter traditional organizational roles and structures. These cases are not presented as exhaustive or generalizable, but rather as heuristic devices that help surface tensions, paradoxes, and critical questions that extend across sectors and institutional forms.

The goal is to offer a theoretical contribution that is both analytically robust and practically resonant, supporting future research and managerial reflection. By mapping how AI challenges established models of organizational behavior and reshapes key constructs—such as trust, autonomy, leadership, and the psychological contract—the chapter lays the groundwork for empirical inquiry and interdisciplinary dialogue in the years ahead.

Implications of AI for Organizational Behavior

Behavioral Implications

One of the most salient areas where the influence of AI emerges is employee motivation (see Vinichenko et al. 2020). Classical theories of motivation emphasize the importance of intrinsic drivers such as autonomy, mastery, and purpose (Ryan et al. 2019). AI systems have the potential to reshape how these motivational elements are accessed and experienced in the workplace. When AI tools structure tasks, define priorities, or deliver performance feedback, they may enhance employees' clarity and sense of direction. Yet, these same systems can also undermine autonomy by limiting the discretion individuals have over their work (Langer and Landers 2021). In environments where employees feel they are "managed by machines," the consequences can go beyond disengagement and lead to more profound forms of alienation. In such cases, work risks losing its subjective meaning and becoming a mechanical activity, externally imposed and disconnected from personal agency.

This risk intensifies when AI is implemented without adequate transparency. When employees do not understand how decisions are made or which data underpin performance evaluations, confusion, distrust, and emotional detachment can emerge (Hartyándi 2025; Uygungil-Erdogan et al. 2025). Motivation may deteriorate not only due to reduced control, but also because the psychological contract between the individual and the organization is disrupted (Braganza et al. 2021). When workers feel they are being evaluated by opaque systems without opportunities for input or contextualization, the relational fabric of work weakens. Even high-performing employees may become demotivated if measured against metrics that fail to reflect the complexity of their roles.

Employee engagement is also redefined in AI-enabled environments. Intelligent systems can contribute positively by aligning individual strengths with assigned tasks (Gabriel 2020), offering personalized workflows, targeted learning suggestions, or real-time coaching. Such tools can foster a culture of continuous development and flow. At the same time, these systems may contribute to over-surveillance, emotional fatigue, or a growing sense of pressure, particularly when feedback mechanisms are constant and intrusive (Marabelli and Lirio 2024). The impact of AI on engagement depends not only on what the technology enables, but also on how it is introduced, communicated, and integrated within the organizational culture.

Closely related to motivation and engagement is the issue of job autonomy. AI can reduce routine work and free employees to focus on creative or interpersonal aspects of their roles. Yet in other instances, it fragments work into narrowly defined micro-tasks controlled by algorithms, diminishing space for initiative and judgment. The way AI is designed and implemented becomes decisive: does it augment human capacity or constrain it? Research on job design and job crafting suggests that when employees have some influence over how they interact with AI, they are more likely to retain a sense of agency and ownership. Conversely, top-down implementations that exclude workers from design processes tend to provoke resistance and detachment (Cheng et al. 2023).

These tensions inevitably extend to leadership and authority. The rise of AI challenges traditional models of leadership by introducing non-human agents that issue instructions, provide feedback, and even trigger disciplinary mechanisms (Hossain et al. 2025). Managers, once the exclusive custodians of performance data and evaluative criteria, now share this space with algorithmic systems that produce assessments of their own (Sposato 2024). This redistribution of authority prompts important questions: who is ultimately accountable for decisions influenced by AI? How can employees maintain trust in leadership when their leaders themselves defer to systems they may not fully understand? In this context, the managerial role shifts toward one of mediation—translating technical outputs, contextualizing algorithmic judgments, and guiding employees through complex human-machine interactions. This calls for new competencies that combine digital fluency with emotional intelligence and the ability to sustain open dialogue about the place of AI in organizational life.

Trust—both in leadership and in technological systems—emerges as a central concern (Braganza et al. 2021; Hartyándi 2025). Employees must learn to engage with tools that may appear impersonal, unpredictable, or inscrutable. Organizations, in turn, must foster environments where AI is framed not as a threat but as a support for human development. Much depends on cultural framing: is AI introduced as a pathway to growth, or as a mechanism of control? Are employees invited to shape its application, or are they merely expected to adapt? These dynamics significantly influence whether individuals feel respected, empowered, and valued during the transition to AI-mediated work.

A concrete illustration of these dynamics can be seen in IBM's recent adoption of AI to support performance evaluation and talent development. The company implemented an AI-driven system that offered tailored feedback, recommended personalized learning trajectories, and predicted future performance based on employees' digital activity—such as email usage, calendar data, and collaboration tools. Some employees welcomed these insights, appreciating the immediacy and personalization of the feedback. Others expressed concern about being constantly monitored, questioned the fairness of algorithmic assessments, and felt uneasy about how contextual and relational aspects of their work were being interpreted by a machine. In cases where algorithmic recommendations clashed with human judgment, trust in the evaluation system declined. This case exemplifies the broader ambiguity of AI's impact: the same technology can be perceived as developmental or invasive, depending on the way it is communicated, governed, and embedded in organizational routines.

The introduction of AI often elicits resistance, which should not be dismissed as mere inertia or opposition to innovation (Amin et al. 2025). Resistance may reveal a misalignment between the logic of AI systems and the values embedded within the organization. It can signal valid concerns regarding fairness, depersonalization, and the erosion of professional discretion. Employees' behavioral responses to AI—ranging from skepticism and withdrawal to creative adaptation—are strongly influenced by how the technology is introduced, who participates in its implementation, and whether individuals are treated as active contributors or passive recipients of change.

Finally, AI affects the emotional tone of organizational life. Anxiety, confusion, and ambivalence are common in workplaces undergoing digital transition (Li and Huang 2020). Employees may fear being replaced, constantly judged, or misunderstood by systems that lack empathy. These emotions are not irrational but rooted in real uncertainties surrounding the evolving nature of work and human agency in automated environments. Addressing such concerns requires more than technical training. It calls for emotional support, the cultivation of psychological safety, and mechanisms that allow for honest expression of doubts and discomfort without fear of stigma.

The growing role of AI also invites a reconsideration of what makes work meaningful (Bankins and Formosa 2023). When tasks are shaped—or even defined—by algorithmic logics, the traditional sources of meaning at work may shift. For some, AI may unlock new opportunities for purpose and creativity. For others, it may reduce work to the execution of externally generated decisions, weakening the sense of contribution and identity. Organizations that wish to sustain or enhance meaningfulness must introduce AI thoughtfully, ensuring it aligns with human values, reinforces inclusion, and supports rather than substitutes human strengths. To synthesize these dynamics, Table 1 summarizes the key areas in which AI is reshaping organizational behavior, highlighting the associated changes and their behavioral implications.

Table 1. Key areas of AI impact on organizational behavior.

Area	AI-Driven Change	Implications for Organizational Behavior
Decision-making	Predictive analytics and AI-assisted decision support systems	Redefinition of human roles; blurred responsibility and accountability boundaries
Monitoring and coordination	Real-time performance tracking and automated feedback loops	Rise of "invisible" or soft control mechanisms
Motivation and job design	Automation of repetitive tasks; personalized workflows	Potential for alienation or empowerment, depending on implementation context
Leadership	AI integration in supervision and performance evaluation	Demand for hybrid leadership skills and narrative competence
Work identity and meaning	Mediation of communication and value assessment through AI	Reconfiguration of professional identity and perceived agency

Theoretical Implications

The growing integration of AI into organizational life transforms not just practices, but also questions the foundational theories that underpin our understanding of how organizations function. In its algorithmic, adaptive, and increasingly autonomous forms, AI invites scholars to revisit long-held assumptions about decision-making, control, motivation, leadership, and the very nature of organizational behavior. Theoretical frameworks that once offered stable interpretive lenses for understanding human action within structured environments must now evolve to account for the presence of non-human agents that contribute to the construction of meaning, authority, and outcomes.

A first area of theoretical tension concerns the process of decision-making. Classical models place the human actor at the center, typically constrained by bounded rationality and incomplete information. AI unsettles this assumption by dramatically expanding the capacity to process data, detect patterns, and simulate potential outcomes at a scale well beyond human capability. Yet this expansion does not eliminate the boundaries of rationality—it redistributes them. Algorithms are limited by the data they are trained on, the design assumptions they embed, and the unintended consequences that emerge from their application. In this light, AI does not resolve bounded rationality but reframes it in algorithmic and institutional terms. Organizational decision-making theories must therefore extend their scope to include hybrid constellations of human and machine judgment, examining how discretion, trust, and accountability are negotiated in distributed and data-driven contexts.

Control and coordination—central concepts in classical theories of bureaucracy, systems, and cybernetics—also require re-examination. In traditional models, control is exercised through hierarchy, procedures, and managerial oversight. The logic introduced by AI differs markedly: it enables continuous, data-driven, and often subtle forms of control. Performance is no longer reviewed periodically but monitored constantly. Influence is exerted not through direct human supervision but through algorithmic signals embedded in digital platforms and workflows. This evolution suggests a shift from control as a managerial act to control as an environmental feature, diffused across the organization's technological infrastructure. These emerging forms of "soft control" may prompt employees to internalize algorithmic expectations even in the absence of explicit managerial oversight. Theoretical models must adapt to account for the psychological, behavioral, and normative implications of automated feedback, predictive analytics, and real-time surveillance.

In the domain of motivation and work design, AI also introduces new complexities. Established models of motivation emphasize intrinsic drivers such as task significance, autonomy, and meaningful feedback. AI complicates these dimensions by simultaneously enhancing and constraining them. While some systems may relieve employees of repetitive tasks and suggest personalized development paths, others fragment work into narrowly defined, automated tasks that limit creativity and discretion. Theoretical efforts must move beyond binary oppositions such as empowerment versus alienation, and instead focus on the specific conditions under which AI fosters engagement, sustainability, and purpose. This may require bridging job design theory with socio-technical systems thinking and exploring how people, algorithms, and organizational structures interact in dynamic and reciprocal ways.

The psychological contract also merits reconsideration. Traditionally understood as the unwritten set of expectations between employees and employers, it has relied on principles of trust, fairness, and mutual commitment. AI can destabilize these expectations—particularly when key decisions regarding development, task assignment, or performance evaluation are delegated to systems that appear impersonal, opaque, or resistant to human input. The fundamental question of "who decides" increasingly becomes "what decides," raising issues of legitimacy and perceived agency. Theories of the psychological contract must now include the influence of non-human agents—systems that shape work experience but are not held to human standards of ethics or reciprocity. This calls for attention to concepts such as algorithmic fairness, explainability, and the perception of voice and participation in technology-mediated environments.

Leadership theory, too, is confronted with significant challenges. Most traditional leadership models—from transformational to servant leadership—are rooted in assumptions of emotional resonance, symbolic communication, and human connection. In AI-mediated workplaces, however, many leadership functions are delegated to intelligent systems. Algorithms may now set goals, deliver feedback, and monitor performance—functions that once required personal presence and interpersonal judgment. This shift raises fundamental questions: what remains distinctively human in leadership when authority is shared with machines? How can leaders maintain credibility and trust when they themselves rely on systems whose logic they may not fully grasp? Theoretical models must begin to conceptualize hybrid leadership roles, in which leaders function as interpreters of algorithmic output, facilitators of collective sensemaking, and stewards of ethical engagement. This transformation requires a renewed focus on the symbolic and emotional labor of leadership in technologically mediated environments.

More broadly, AI invites organizational scholars to engage with post-humanist perspectives that challenge the anthropocentric foundations of much traditional theory. From this standpoint, organizations are not solely composed of human actors, but of assemblages in which people, technologies, and material infrastructures co-evolve. Agency is seen as distributed—emerging from the interactions among actors rather than residing within individuals. This ontological shift positions algorithms, data systems, and digital platforms as organizational agents, capable of influencing routines, shaping meanings, and reinforcing institutional logics. Embracing such perspectives opens new avenues for understanding how power, identity, and structure are negotiated in contexts where human and non-human actors are increasingly interdependent.

Finally, AI raises urgent ethical questions that compel a rethinking of long-standing assumptions about alignment between organizational goals and employee interests. Classical theories often presumed that such alignment could be achieved through participatory processes and shared values. AI complicates this premise. Systems designed for efficiency may overlook context, disregard ethical nuance, or unintentionally perpetuate bias. As decision-making becomes more automated, processes of exclusion and marginalization may be harder to detect, yet more deeply embedded in organizational life. Theories of justice, voice, and participation must evolve to address these challenges. Scholars must consider how power is exercised through technological design, how dissent is expressed and received in digital environments, and how organizations can cultivate a culture of algorithmic responsibility grounded in transparency, equity, and human dignity.

Practical Implications

The integration of AI into organizational systems presents a multifaceted challenge for management. While attention often gravitates toward technical aspects such as infrastructure, data governance, and system reliability, the more enduring and complex issues are organizational in nature. Managers are increasingly called upon to do more than implement new technologies; they are expected to shape the social, cultural, and interpretive conditions under which AI is introduced and assimilated. Their task is to ensure that AI is not only operationally effective but also aligned with the organization's values and with employees' expectations and experiences.

One of the most critical responsibilities for managers in this context is enabling sensemaking. As AI systems become more widespread—and often less transparent—employees may struggle to understand how decisions are made, what types of data are collected and interpreted, and how their roles are being redefined. Managers must therefore act as translators and communicators: not just of strategic direction, but of the technological logics and ethical boundaries that inform AI implementation. This role requires more than technical competence; it demands narrative skill—the ability to articulate complexity in accessible ways, to frame change coherently, and to anticipate questions and concerns before they manifest as resistance.

Equally important is the need to protect and strengthen employee autonomy and agency. AI is frequently introduced with the promise of increased efficiency and optimization, yet in practice, it can reduce the discretionary space that makes work meaningful. Managers must carefully evaluate how AI systems affect decision rights, task structures, and professional identities. The goal should be to augment human judgment rather than displace it—positioning AI as a supportive resource, not a directive authority. This involves engaging employees in the design and refinement of AI applications, ensuring that systems reinforce their expertise rather than constrain it, and preserving areas where human intuition and ethical reasoning remain indispensable.

In parallel, managers must cultivate the capacity to lead hybrid teams—composed of individuals with diverse roles and skills, working alongside algorithmic agents embedded in organizational workflows. Leading such teams requires a departure from hierarchical command-and-control models in favor of participatory, relational, and adaptive leadership styles. Managers must facilitate collaboration across different levels of intelligence, integrating algorithmic insights with human perspectives and organizational values. At the same time, they must remain attentive to the risks of over-reliance on automated outputs, misunderstandings of system logic, and the gradual erosion of critical thinking when algorithmic authority is left unquestioned.

Trust and psychological safety emerge as central concerns in AI-mediated work environments. Intelligent systems can make employees feel observed, measured, or exposed in ways they find intrusive or unsettling. In such contexts, trust cannot be presumed; it must be intentionally cultivated. Managers have a key role in creating safe spaces where employees feel empowered to raise concerns, ask difficult questions, and challenge AI-influenced decisions without fear of negative repercussions. Building trust involves clarifying how systems function, explaining how human and machine judgments interact, and acknowledging the emotional dimensions of technological transformation. Recognizing that confusion, doubt, or discomfort are legitimate responses to rapid change is a necessary step in safeguarding employee well-being.

Managers must also address the structural risks of exclusion and inequality in AI-enhanced organizations. Digital literacy is unevenly distributed, and not all roles benefit equally from the introduction of intelligent systems. Without deliberate attention, AI may amplify existing divides—between high-skilled and low-skilled workers, or between those empowered by data and those whose roles become increasingly monitored and routinized. Inclusive approaches to digital transformation are therefore essential. This means ensuring fair access to training and reskilling opportunities, involving a wide range of stakeholders in decision-making, and promoting a culture in which every employee is seen as capable of contributing meaningfully to the organization's evolution, regardless of their initial familiarity with technology.

At a strategic level, managers must establish clear and accountable frameworks for the ethical governance of AI. This includes defining who is responsible for algorithmic decisions, determining how data is collected and used, and setting up mechanisms for oversight, review, and appeal. Ethical governance cannot be reduced to compliance protocols. It is foundational to organizational legitimacy and long-term trust. Managers should advocate for principles such as explainability, fairness, and proportionality, embedding them in the design and deployment of AI. Moreover, they must encourage ethical reflexivity—both individually and collectively—by fostering critical reflection on the assumptions embedded in AI systems and adapting practices in light of emerging values, dilemmas, and responsibilities.

Effective leadership in the age of AI requires adopting a long-term, adaptive mindset. AI implementation is not a discrete event, but an ongoing process characterized by experimentation, learning, and recalibration. Managers must learn to navigate ambiguity, respond constructively to feedback, and lead with humility in environments where clear answers are often lacking. This entails shifting from a logic of control to a logic of stewardship—guiding change with care and responsibility, listening actively to employees, and remaining accountable not only for performance outcomes but also for the relational and ethical processes through which those outcomes are achieved.

Navigating Resistance to Change

The introduction of AI into organizational contexts frequently triggers resistance—manifesting in forms that range from subtle hesitation to overt contestation, and from individual discomfort to collective dissent. While resistance to change has long been studied within organizational theory, the character of AI as a disruptive, opaque, and identity-shaping technology reconfigures its nature and significance. Resistance in this setting is not merely a reaction to unfamiliar tools; it often signals a deeper sense of threat to core dimensions of work, including autonomy, meaning, recognition, and control.

Unlike previous technological innovations that modified procedures or augmented tasks, AI tends to challenge the foundational dynamics of work—who performs it, how it is assessed, and what it ultimately signifies within the broader institutional order. This creates a form of resistance that cannot be reduced to simple reluctance. Employees may experience unease not only about being replaced or monitored, but also about being subjected to systems that lack contextual sensitivity, interpretive nuance, or emotional resonance. These reactions are rarely irrational. They express fundamental concerns about fairness, legitimacy, and agency in environments where decisions are increasingly shaped by systems that are difficult to question or influence.

A central source of this tension lies in the interpretability—or lack thereof—of AI systems. Unlike traditional tools whose functions can be observed and gradually mastered, many AI applications operate as opaque mechanisms. Machine learning models, in particular, may produce outcomes without offering intelligible explanations, even to their designers. In such cases, resistance does not emerge from opposition to innovation per se, but from a perceived absence of transparency and accountability. When employees do not understand how decisions are made or feel excluded from influencing them, they may disengage, contest, or devise informal workarounds to reassert human discretion.

The deployment of AI also subtly reconfigures organizational power. As decisions about task allocation, performance evaluation, or communication flows become increasingly automated, employees may perceive a diminishing control over their professional lives. This shift can be disorienting, especially when AI is introduced without adequate dialogue, framing, or opportunities for participation. Resistance, in these circumstances, often targets the process through which AI is implemented rather than the technology itself. The issue becomes one of governance: who decides, on what basis, and with what consequences.

The organizational culture in which AI is introduced significantly shapes how resistance unfolds. In environments characterized by open communication, mutual trust, and a tolerance for experimentation, employees are more likely to voice concerns constructively and engage critically with the new systems. Conversely, in settings where dissent is discouraged or innovation is driven top-down without consultation, resistance tends to be less visible but more corrosive. It may manifest as quiet disengagement, passive non-compliance, or covert sabotage. These forms of resistance are difficult to detect and can undermine the legitimacy of AI initiatives over time, particularly when employees feel alienated from the processes that redefine their roles and identities.

Attention must also be paid to the emotional landscape of resistance. Technological transitions—especially when rapid and framed in terms of efficiency or disruption—can provoke anxiety, fear, or resentment. When change is introduced without acknowledging its affective impact, employees may experience a rupture in their sense of stability and belonging. In these cases, resistance becomes a form of emotional defense, a way to preserve continuity and protect one's professional identity. Treating such responses as signals, rather than symptoms to be managed, allows organizations to engage with the emotional undercurrents of change in a more ethical and effective manner.

Resistance may also carry generative potential. Employees sometimes challenge AI systems not because they reject innovation, but because they wish to uphold standards of care, discretion, or ethical responsibility that they believe are compromised. In these moments, resistance becomes a form of professional advocacy—a defense of practices and values that technologies alone cannot reproduce. Organizations that recognize this dynamic can reframe resistance as constructive feedback, using it to refine AI design, implementation, and alignment with the institutional mission.

This perspective aligns with the emerging discourse on AI readiness. Successful implementation rarely depends on technical preparedness alone. It also requires cultural alignment, emotional awareness, and a participatory approach to change. Organizations that manage resistance effectively tend to invest in skills development, cultivate psychological safety, and invite employees into the design and evaluation of AI applications. Readiness, in this sense, reflects a collective mindset—a willingness to engage in dialogue, to address concerns, and to share responsibility for shaping the future of work.

Viewing resistance as a dialogue rather than a dysfunction offers valuable insight into how employees interpret technological change. It reveals whether they feel seen, heard, and respected in the process. Addressing resistance thoughtfully allows organizations to deepen their ethical engagement with AI, creating conditions for more sustainable and meaningful forms of transformation—ones in which human judgment, emotion, and agency continue to matter. Table 2 summarizes the main forms of resistance to AI observed in organizational contexts and outlines corresponding managerial responses.

Table 2. Forms of resistance to AI and managerial responses.

Type of Resistance	Description	Managerial Strategy
Cognitive resistance	Difficulty understanding AI systems ("black box" effect); perceived opacity	Enhance explainability; offer training and transparent communication
Emotional resistance	Anxiety, fear, or loss of identity linked to automation and surveillance	Acknowledge emotions; foster psychological safety; human-centered storytelling
Behavioral resistance	Passive disengagement, workaround strategies, or active challenge	Encourage participation in design; create feedback loops; adapt implementation
Cultural resistance	Mismatch between AI-driven practices and organizational norms or values	Align AI use with shared values; promote cultural sensemaking
Ethical resistance	Concerns over fairness, accountability, and human judgment	Establish ethical oversight mechanisms; clarify human-in-the-loop processes
Political resistance	Perceived shifts in power/control; fear of exclusion or deskilling	Promote inclusive governance; support reskilling and equitable participation

AI Applications in the Field of Organizational Behavior

The real-world application of AI in organizational behavior is no longer a speculative domain. Across industries and sectors, AI is actively shaping how people interact with their work, with each other, and with the structures that govern organizational life. These applications span recruitment and selection, employee engagement, performance management, learning and development, well-being monitoring, and even leadership decision support. They not only illustrate the potential of AI to support human behavior at work, but also expose the tensions, risks, and opportunities inherent in algorithmic intervention.

In the domain of recruitment and selection, tools like HireVue and Pymetrics have fundamentally altered how candidates are assessed. HireVue employs AI-driven video interview analysis, using natural language processing and facial recognition to evaluate tone of voice, micro-expressions, and verbal fluency, comparing candidate performance to successful profiles. Pymetrics applies neuroscience-based games combined with machine learning to assess cognitive and emotional traits, matching candidates to roles where they are predicted to thrive. While these tools claim to increase objectivity and efficiency, they raise important questions about fairness, transparency, and the opacity of algorithmic decision-making. Organizations such as Unilever have widely adopted these platforms in graduate recruitment campaigns, significantly reducing time-to-hire and expanding the diversity of candidate pools. Yet this success is not without scrutiny, particularly regarding the explainability of results and the risk of reinforcing biases embedded in training data.

In employee engagement and sentiment analysis, AI is also playing an increasingly active role. Platforms such as Culture Amp and Glint (now integrated within Microsoft Viva) gather continuous feedback from employees through pulse surveys and open-text responses, which are then analyzed using natural language processing to detect themes, sentiments, and emotional trends over time. This enables HR leaders and managers to receive early warnings about disengagement, burnout, or emerging cultural tensions. These systems aim to provide more dynamic and responsive ways of managing morale compared to traditional annual surveys. However, they also raise concerns around surveillance, trust, and the fine line between support and control—particularly when feedback is automatically flagged for managerial attention.

In performance management, the integration of AI has redefined how objectives are set, monitored, and reviewed. Salesforce's "Einstein" and SAP's SuccessFactors incorporate predictive analytics and real-time performance dashboards to provide individualized performance insights, detect productivity trends, and even recommend development actions. These systems claim to reduce manager bias and improve objectivity in evaluations. At IBM, for example, AI has been used to predict which employees are likely to leave and why, enabling proactive interventions. However, when employees feel constantly monitored and evaluated by opaque systems, the psychological consequences—ranging from pressure to anxiety—can become counterproductive. AI does not eliminate subjectivity; it displaces it into the algorithm, often without offering mechanisms for dialogue or contestation.

AI also plays a key role in learning and development, enabling adaptive, personalized training. Platforms like Coursera for Business, LinkedIn Learning, and Fuse Universal use recommendation engines similar to those of Netflix or Spotify, suggesting training paths based on an employee's role, past behavior, and career interests. At companies like Schneider Electric, AI-powered learning systems offer real-time skills assessments and development recommendations aligned with strategic talent planning. These tools support continuous learning and empower employees to navigate evolving job requirements. Still, the personalization logic behind such systems is rarely transparent, and it may reinforce existing gaps if the algorithm's assumptions about an individual's trajectory are biased or limited.

In the realm of workforce well-being, some organizations have begun experimenting with AI tools that monitor indicators of stress and burnout. For example, the software company Humanyze offers AI-driven organizational network analysis, capturing data from communication tools (like email, calendar, and chat platforms) to infer collaboration patterns, responsiveness, and overload risks. Microsoft's Workplace Analytics provides similar capabilities, generating insights on work-life balance, focus time, and meeting overload. These applications promise to support well-being at scale, but their effectiveness depends heavily on how transparently they are introduced and how respectfully they are interpreted. Employees may perceive them as intrusive or paternalistic unless clear boundaries are established.

AI is also being leveraged in leadership support and decision-making. Tools like Crystal provide personality insights based on online data, helping leaders tailor communication styles to individual preferences. AI-enabled dashboards help leaders synthesize complex information rapidly and model different scenarios. At Ericsson, for instance, AI is used to support leadership decisions around team structure and project allocation, integrating data on performance, skillsets, and collaboration networks. While such tools can enhance strategic alignment, they may also increase dependence on data-driven outputs at the expense of human intuition and interpersonal nuance.

Finally, AI is being used to support diversity, equity, and inclusion (DEI) initiatives. Tools such as Textio assist recruiters and managers in crafting job descriptions that are more inclusive by flagging gendered or biased language. Platforms like Syndio analyze pay equity across organizational units and recommend adjustments based on role, tenure, and performance. These applications offer actionable insights into systemic disparities, enabling organizations to monitor and correct them more systematically. However, such systems do not automatically generate equity—they must be accompanied by cultural change, institutional commitment, and meaningful employee participation.

Collectively, these examples illustrate how AI is reshaping not only the mechanics of organizational behavior, but also its meanings and moral contours. Each application offers potential benefits—efficiency, fairness, personalization—but also carries risks related to opacity, bias, exclusion, and emotional disengagement. The challenge lies not in the technology itself, but in how it is framed, governed, and integrated into existing organizational realities.

These cases underscore a broader insight: AI does not function in a vacuum. It interacts with cultural norms, power relations, professional identities, and human expectations. As such, the adoption of AI in organizational behavior is not simply a technical implementation—it is a social and ethical project, one that must be navigated with reflection, openness, and humility. Table 3 illustrates how these

Table 3. Real-world applications of AI in organizational behavior.

Organization	AI Technology Used	Application Area	Observed Effects
IBM	IBM Watson	Leadership coaching and support	Enhanced managerial development and distributed leadership functions
Accenture	AI chatbot for onboarding	Employee experience and training	Faster onboarding processes and increased newcomer engagement
Google	People analytics algorithms	Turnover prediction and team dynamics	Improved predictive accuracy; more informed HR decision-making
Unilever	HireVue (video interview AI)	Candidate selection and assessment	Greater efficiency in recruitment; raised concerns over algorithmic bias
SAP	Joule (AI employee assistant)	Daily support and HR self-service	Improved responsiveness and employee autonomy; reduction of routine HR queries

dynamics unfold in practice by presenting selected real-world applications of AI in organizational behavior across different organizational functions.

Conclusion

The integration of AI into organizational life marks a profound transformation in the way work is conceived, practiced, and regulated. Far from being a mere technological enhancement, this shift redefines foundational dimensions of organizational behavior. As intelligent systems assume roles in coordination, evaluation, and communication, they actively reshape the environment in which individuals interpret their tasks, interact with leadership, and find meaning in their professional identity. These changes do not follow a linear or uniform path. Their outcomes depend on how AI is framed, how it is introduced into workflows, and how it resonates with or disrupts existing values, institutional logics, and relational dynamics.

Throughout this chapter, it has been argued that examining AI within organizational contexts requires moving beyond efficiency or productivity concerns. AI must be approached as a phenomenon that engages behavioral, emotional, and normative dimensions simultaneously. It functions as more than a set of tools—it assumes the role of a novel agent, intervening in patterns of authority, influencing organizational sensemaking, and altering the distribution of power and trust. This calls for a renewal of organizational theory, one that incorporates technological agency while safeguarding the centrality of human experience, discretion, and dignity.

In this landscape, managerial responsibility becomes increasingly complex. Leaders are no longer asked to simply implement technological systems; they must guide their integration in ways that respect human values and foster constructive engagement. Navigating this terrain requires fluency not only in systems and data, but also in empathy, ethical judgment, and cultural sensitivity. AI holds the potential to enable more personalized and adaptive forms of work, to stimulate learning, and to strengthen resilience. Yet these outcomes are not guaranteed. They depend on whether AI is deployed within frameworks that ensure clarity, accountability, and care.

The trajectory of work remains open. While AI will undoubtedly play a significant role in shaping organizational futures, it will do so in ways that reflect the human choices that surround its design and use. These choices include how transparency is ensured, how governance structures are defined, and how workers are included in conversations about purpose and change. There is a pressing need for dialogue and cooperation among scholars, professionals, and institutions to ensure that technological innovation advances alongside social responsibility and democratic participation.

The fundamental question is not how to tame AI, but how to coexist with it in organizational environments that promote growth, integrity, and mutual respect. This entails envisioning workplaces as adaptive communities—places where human and machine intelligence co-evolve through shared learning and critical reflection. The aim is to cultivate organizations that are not merely efficient in form, but wise in intention, and deeply anchored in the values that sustain human flourishing.

References

Agarwal, G. 2024. Robust data pipelines for AI Workloads: Architectures, challenges, and future directions. International Journal of Advanced Research in Science, Communication and Technology 5(2): 622–632. https://dx.doi.org/10.48175/IJARSCT-23391.

Akinrinola, O., Okoye, C. C., Ofodile, O. C. and Ugochukwu, C. E. 2024. Navigating and reviewing ethical dilemmas in AI development: Strategies for transparency, fairness, and accountability. GSC Advanced Research and Reviews 18(3): 50–58. https://doi.org/10.30574/gscarr.2024.18.3.0088.

Amin, S. M., El-Gazar, H. E., Zoromba, M. A., El-Sayed, M. M. and Atta, M. H. R. 2025. Sentiment of nurses towards artificial intelligence and resistance to change in healthcare organisations: A mixed-method study. Journal of Advanced Nursing 81(4): 2087–2098. https://doi.org/10.1111/jan.16435.

Anthony, C., Bechky, B. A. and Fayard, A. L. 2023. Collaborating with AI: Taking a system view to explore the future of work. Organization Science 34(5): 1672–1694. https://doi.org/10.1287/orsc.2022.1651.

Appelbaum, S. H. 1997. Socio-technical systems theory: An intervention strategy for organizational development. Management Decision 35(6): 452–463. https://doi.org/10.1108/00251749710173823.

Babashahi, L., Barbosa, C. E., Lima, Y., Lyra, A., Salazar, H., Argôlo, M. A. et al. 2024. AI in the workplace: A systematic review of skill transformation in the industry. Administrative Sciences 14(6): 1–28. https://doi.org/10.3390/admsci14060127.

Bankins, S. 2021. The ethical use of artificial intelligence in human resource management: A decision-making framework. Ethics and Information Technology 23(4): 841–854. https://doi.org/10.1007/s10676-021-09619-6.

Bankins, S. and Formosa, P. 2020. When AI meets PC: Exploring the implications of workplace social robots and a human-robot psychological contract. European Journal of Work and Organizational Psychology 29(2): 215–229. https://doi.org/10.1080/1359432X.2019.1620328.

Bankins, S. and Formosa, P. 2023. The ethical implications of artificial intelligence (AI) for meaningful work. Journal of Business Ethics 185(4): 725–740. https://doi.org/10.1007/s10551-023-05339-7.

Bankins, S., Ocampo, A. C., Marrone, M., Restubog, S. L. D. and Woo, S. E. 2024. A multilevel review of artificial intelligence in organizations: Implications for organizational behavior research and practice. Journal of Organizational Behavior 45(2): 159–182. https://doi.org/10.1002/job.2735.

Bareis, J. and Katzenbach, C. 2022. Talking AI into being: The narratives and imaginaries of national AI strategies and their performative politics. Science, Technology, & Human Values 47(5): 855–881. https://doi.org/10.1177/01622439211030007.

Benvenuti, M., Cangelosi, A., Weinberger, A., Mazzoni, E., Benassi, M., Barbaresi, M. et al. 2023. Artificial intelligence and human behavioral development: A perspective on new skills and competences acquisition for the educational context. Computers in Human Behavior 148: 1–8. https://doi.org/10.1016/j.chb.2023.107903.

Bhargava, A., Bester, M. and Bolton, L. 2021. Employees' perceptions of the implementation of robotics, artificial intelligence, and automation (RAIA) on job satisfaction, job security, and employability. Journal of Technology in Behavioral Science 6(1): 106–113. https://doi.org/10.1007/s41347-020-00153-8.

Bobitan, N., Dumitrescu, D., Popa, A. F., Sahlian, D. N. and Turlea, I. C. 2024. Shaping tomorrow: Anticipating skills requirements based on the integration of artificial intelligence in business organizations—a foresight analysis using the scenario method. Electronics 13(11): 1–17. https://doi.org/10.3390/electronics13112198.

Boyd, R. and Holton, R. J. 2018. Technology, innovation, employment and power: Does robotics and artificial intelligence really mean social transformation? Journal of Sociology 54(3): 331–345. https://doi.org/10.1177/1440783317726591.

Braganza, A., Chen, W., Canhoto, A. and Sap, S. 2021. Productive employment and decent work: The impact of AI adoption on psychological contracts, job engagement and employee trust. Journal of Business Research 131: 485–494. https://doi.org/10.1016/j.jbusres.2020.08.018.

Bukartaite, R. and Hooper, D. 2023. Automation, artificial intelligence and future skills needs: An Irish perspective. European Journal of Training and Development 47(10): 163–185. https://doi.org/10.1108/EJTD-03-2023-0045.

Busuioc, M. 2021. Accountable artificial intelligence: Holding algorithms to account. Public Administration Review 81(5): 825–836. https://doi.org/10.1111/puar.13293.

Canbul Yaroğlu, A. 2024. The effects of artificial intelligence on organizational culture in the perspective of the hermeneutic cycle: The intersection of mental processes. Systems Research and Behavioral Science 1–13. https://doi.org/10.1002/sres.3037.

Candrian, C. and Scherer, A. 2022. Rise of the machines: Delegating decisions to autonomous AI. Computers in Human Behavior 134: 1–16. https://doi.org/10.1016/j.chb.2022.107308.

Carter, L., Liu, D. and Cantrell, C. 2020. Exploring the intersection of the digital divide and artificial intelligence: A hermeneutic literature review. AIS Transactions on Human-Computer Interaction 12(4): 253–275. https://doi.org/10.17705/1thci.00138.

Cheng, B., Lin, H. and Kong, Y. 2023. Challenge or hindrance? How and when organizational artificial intelligence adoption influences employee job crafting. Journal of Business Research 164: 1–10. https://doi.org/10.1016/j.jbusres.2023.113987.

Chukwuka, E. J. and Dibie, K. E. 2024. Strategic role of artificial intelligence (AI) on human resource management (HR) employee performance evaluation function. International Journal of Entrepreneurship and Business Innovation 7(2): 269–282. https://doi.org/10.52589/IJEBI-HET5STYK.

Clough, D. R. and Wu, A. 2022. Artificial intelligence, data-driven learning, and the decentralized structure of platform ecosystems. Academy of Management Review 47(1): 184–189. https://doi.org/10.5465/amr.2020.0222.

Cole, M., Radice, H. and Umney, C. 2021. The political economy of datafication and work: A new digital taylorism? Socialist Register 23: 78–99.

Csaszar, F. A. and Steinberger, T. 2022. Organizations as artificial intelligences: The use of artificial intelligence analogies in organization theory. Academy of Management Annals 16(1): 1–37. https://doi.org/10.5465/annals.2020.0192.

Cullinane, N. and Dundon, T. 2006. The psychological contract: A critical review. International Journal of Management Reviews 8(2): 113–129. https://doi.org/10.1111/j.1468-2370.2006.00123.x.

De Almeida, P. G. R., dos Santos, C. D. and Farias, J. S. 2021. Artificial intelligence regulation: A framework for governance. Ethics and Information Technology 23(3): 505–525. https://doi.org/10.1007/s10676-021-09593-z.

Dunleavy, P. and Margetts, H. 2025. Data science, artificial intelligence and the third wave of digital era governance. Public Policy and Administration 40(2): 185–214. https://doi.org/10.1177/09520767231198737.

Ernst, E., Merola, R. and Samaan, D. 2019. Economics of artificial intelligence: Implications for the future of work. IZA Journal of Labor Policy 9(1): 1–35. https://doi.org/10.2478/izajolp-2019-0004.

Feldstein, S. 2019. The road to digital unfreedom: How artificial intelligence is reshaping repression. Journal of Democracy 30(1): 40–52. https://doi.org/10.1353/jod.2019.0003.

Felzmann, H., Fosch-Villaronga, E., Lutz, C. and Tamò-Larrieux, A. 2020. Towards transparency by design for artificial intelligence. Science and Engineering Ethics 26(6): 3333–3361. https://doi.org/10.1007/s11948-020-00276-4.

Gladden, M., Fortuna, P. and Modliński, A. 2022. The empowerment of artificial intelligence in post-digital organizations: Exploring human interactions with supervisory AI. Human Technology 18(2): 98–121. https://doi.org/10.14254/1795-6889.2022.18-2.2.

Hanelt, A., Bohnsack, R., Marz, D. and Antunes Marante, C. 2021. A systematic review of the literature on digital transformation: Insights and implications for strategy and organizational change. Journal of Management Studies 58(5): 1159–1197. https://doi.org/10.1111/joms.12639.

Hartyándi, M. J. 2025. Distrust and disillusionment toward generative artificial intelligence: Psychodramatic exploration of employee trust in organizational technology acceptance. Society and Economy 1–21. https://doi.org/10.1556/204.2025.00002.

He, C., Xiong, H., Cai, W. and Song, J. 2025. How does AI awareness affect employees' voice behavior in the service industry? A transactional theory of stress perspective. International Journal of Contemporary Hospitality Management 1–19. https://doi.org/10.1108/IJCHM-04-2024-0618.

Hossain, S., Fernando, M. and Akter, S. 2025. Digital leadership: Towards a dynamic managerial capability perspective of artificial intelligence-driven leader capabilities. Journal of Leadership & Organizational Studies 1–20. https://doi.org/10.1177/15480518251319624.

Huang, Y. and Gursoy, D. 2024. How does AI technology integration affect employees' proactive service behaviors? A transactional theory of stress perspective. Journal of Retailing and Consumer Services 77: 1–9. https://doi.org/10.1016/j.jretconser.2023.103700.

Jarrahi, M. H. 2018. Artificial intelligence and the future of work: Human-AI symbiosis in organizational decision making. Business Horizons 61(4): 577–586. https://doi.org/10.1016/j.bushor.2018.03.007.

Katzenbach, C. and Ulbricht, L. 2019. Algorithmic governance. Internet Policy Review 8(4): 1–18. https://doi.org/10.14763/2019.4.1424.

Kemal, A. A. and Shah, M. H. 2024. Digital innovation in social cash organizations–the effects of the institutional interactions for transforming organizational practices. Information Technology & People 37(5): 2092–2126. https://doi.org/10.1108/ITP-02-2023-0176.

Kim, S., Khoreva, V. and Vaiman, V. 2025. Strategic human resource management in the era of algorithmic technologies: Key insights and future research agenda. Human Resource Management 64(2): 447–464. https://doi.org/10.1002/hrm.22268.

Langer, M. and Landers, R. N. 2021. The future of artificial intelligence at work: A review on effects of decision automation and augmentation on workers targeted by algorithms and third-party observers. Computers in Human Behavior 123: 1–20. https://doi.org/10.1016/j.chb.2021.106878.

Lavazza, A. and Farina, M. 2023. Infosphere, datafication, and decision-making processes in the AI era. Topoi 42(3): 843–856. https://doi.org/10.1007/s11245-023-09919-0.

Lazaroiu, G., Androniceanu, A., Grecu, I., Grecu, G. and Neguriță, O. 2022. Artificial intelligence-based decision-making algorithms, Internet of Things sensing networks, and sustainable cyber-physical management systems in big data-driven cognitive manufacturing. Oeconomia Copernicana 13(4): 1047–1080. https://doi.org/10.24136/oc.2022.030.

Li, J and Huang, J. S. 2020. Dimensions of artificial intelligence anxiety based on the integrated fear acquisition theory. Technology in Society 63: 1–10. https://doi.org/10.1016/j.techsoc.2020.101410.

Liu, H. Y. 2018. The power structure of artificial intelligence. Law, Innovation and Technology 10(2): 197–229. https://doi.org/10.1080/17579961.2018.1527480.

Magistretti, S. and Trabucchi, D. 2025. Agile-as-a-tool and agile-as-a-culture: A comprehensive review of agile approaches adopting contingency and configuration theories. Review of Managerial Science 19(1): 223–253. https://doi.org/10.1007/s11846-024-00745-1.

Malik, N., Tripathi, S. N., Kar, A. K. and Gupta, S. 2021. Impact of artificial intelligence on employees working in industry 4.0 led organizations. International Journal of Manpower 43(2): 334–354. https://doi.org/10.1108/IJM-03-2021-0173.

Marabelli, M. and Lirio, P. 2024. AI and the metaverse in the workplace: DEI opportunities and challenges. Personnel Review 53(3): 844–853. https://doi.org/10.1108/PR-04-2023-0300.

Miracchi, L. 2019. A competence framework for artificial intelligence research. Philosophical Psychology 32(5): 588–633. https://doi.org/10.1080/09515089.2019.1607692.

Morandini, S., Brambilla, M., Gualtieri, A. and Cattaneo, A. 2023. The impact of artificial intelligence on workers' skills: Upskilling and reskilling in organisations. Informing Science 26: 39–68. https://dx.doi.org/10.28945/5078.

Oyeniran, C. O., Smith, J. D., Taylor, R. W. and Wong, M. L. 2022. Ethical AI: Addressing bias in machine learning models and software applications. Computer Science & IT Research Journal 3(3): 115–126. https://doi.org/10.51594/csitrj.v3i3.1559.

Pietronudo, M. C., Croidieu, G. and Schiavone, F. 2022. A solution looking for problems? A systematic literature review of the rationalizing influence of artificial intelligence on decision-making in innovation management. Technological Forecasting and Social Change 182: 1–19. https://doi.org/10.1016/j.techfore.2022.121828.

Popa, I., Ştefan, S. C., Josan, A., Mircioiu, C. E. and Căruceru, N. 2025. Artificial Intelligence as a catalyst for management system adaptability, agility and resilience: Mapping the research agenda. Systems 13(1): 1–23. https://doi.org/10.3390/systems13010047.

Qudus, L. 2025. Leveraging Artificial Intelligence to enhance process control and improve efficiency in manufacturing industries. International Journal of Computer Applications Technology and Research 14(2): 18–38. https://doi.org/10.7753/IJCATR1402.1002.

Raisch, S. and Krakowski, S. 2021. Artificial intelligence and management: The automation–augmentation paradox. Academy of Management Review 46(1): 192–210. https://doi.org/10.5465/amr.2018.0072.

Rajagopal, N. K., Qureshi, N. I., Durga, S., Ramirez Asis, E. H., Huerta Soto, R. M., Gupta, S. K. et al. 2022. Future of business culture: An artificial intelligence-driven digital framework for organization decision-making process. Complexity 2022(1): 1–14. https://doi.org/10.1155/2022/7796507.

Ransbotham, S., Kiron, D., Gerbert, P. and Reeves, M. 2017. Reshaping business with artificial intelligence: Closing the gap between ambition and action. MIT Sloan Management Review 59(1).

Rezaei, M., Pironti, M. and Quaglia, R. 2024. AI in knowledge sharing, which ethical challenges are raised in decision-making processes for organisations?. Management Decision 1–20. https://doi.org/10.1108/MD-10-2023-2023.

Ryan, R. M., Bradshaw, E., Deci, E. L., Sternberg, R. and Pickren, W. 2019. A history of human motivation theories. pp. 391–411. *In*: Sternberg, B. and Pickren, W. (eds.). The Cambridge Handbook of the Intellectual History of Psychology. Cambridge, UK: University Press.

Saifer, A. and Dacin, M. T. 2022. Data and organization studies: Aesthetics, emotions, discourse and our everyday encounters with data. Organization Studies 43(4): 623–636. https://doi.org/10.1177/01708406211006250.

Selenko, E., Bankins, S., Shoss, M., Warburton, J. and Restubog, S. L. D. 2022. Artificial intelligence and the future of work: A functional-identity perspective. Current Directions in Psychological Science 31(3): 272–279. https://doi.org/10.1177/09637214221091823.

Shrestha, Y. R., Ben-Menahem, S. M. and Von Krogh, G. 2019. Organizational decision-making structures in the age of artificial intelligence. California Management Review 61(4): 66–83. https://doi.org/10.1177/0008125619862257.

Sidhu, G. S., Sayem, M. A., Taslima, N., Anwar, A. S., Chowdhury, F. and Rowshon, M. 2024. AI and workforce development: A comparative analysis of skill gaps and training needs in emerging economies. International Journal of Business and Management Sciences 4(8): 12–28. https://doi.org/10.55640/ijbms-04-08-03.

Sposato, M. 2024. Leadership training and development in the age of artificial intelligence. Development and Learning in Organizations: An International Journal 38(4): 4–7. https://doi.org/10.1108/DLO-12-2023-0256.

Steimers, A. and Schneider, M. 2022. Sources of risk of AI systems. International Journal of Environmental Research and Public Health 19(6): 1–32. https://doi.org/10.3390/ijerph19063641.

Tominc, P., Oreški, D. and Rožman, M. 2023. Artificial intelligence and agility-based model for successful project implementation and company competitiveness. Information 14(6): 1–26. https://doi.org/10.3390/info14060337.

Tortorella, G. L., Powell, D., Hines, P., Mac Cawley Vergara, A., Tlapa-Mendoza, D. and Vassolo, R. 2025. How does artificial intelligence impact employees' engagement in lean organisations? International Journal of Production Research 63(3): 1011–1027. https://doi.org/10.1080/00207543.2024.2368698.

Trunk, A., Birkel, H. and Hartmann, E. 2020. On the current state of combining human and artificial intelligence for strategic organizational decision making. Business Research 13(3): 875–919. https://doi.org/10.1007/s40685-020-00133-x.

Uygungil-Erdogan, S., Sahin, Y., Sökmen-Alaca, A. İ., Oktaysoy, O., Altıntaş, M. and Topçuoğlu, V. 2025. Assessing the effect of artificial intelligence anxiety on turnover intention: The mediating role of quiet quitting in Turkish small and medium enterprises. Behavioral Sciences 15(3): 1–21. https://doi.org/10.3390/bs15030249.

Vinichenko, M. V., Melnichuk, A. V. and Karácsony, P. 2020. Technologies of improving the university efficiency by using artificial intelligence: Motivational aspect. Entrepreneurship and Sustainability Issues 7(4): 1–19. https://doi.org/10.9770/jesi.2020.7.4(9).

Von Krogh, G. 2018. Artificial intelligence in organizations: New opportunities for phenomenon-based theorizing. Academy of Management Discoveries 4(4): 404–409. https://doi.org/10.5465/amd.2018.0084.

Vrontis, D., Christofi, M., Pereira, V., Tarba, S., Makrides, A. and Trichina, E. 2023. Artificial intelligence, robotics, advanced technologies and human resource management: A systematic review. Artificial Intelligence and International HRM 172–201. https://doi.org/10.1080/09585192.2020.1871398.

Wilkens, U. 2020. Artificial intelligence in the workplace–A double-edged sword. The International Journal of Information and Learning Technology 37(5): 253–265. https://doi.org/10.1108/IJILT-02-2020-0022.

Wirtz, B. W., Weyerer, J. C. and Kehl, I. 2022. Governance of artificial intelligence: A risk and guideline-based integrative framework. Government Information Quarterly 39(4): 1–17. https://doi.org/10.1016/j.giq.2022.101685.

Yanamala, K. K. R. 2023. Transparency, privacy, and accountability in AI-enhanced HR processes. Journal of Advanced Computing Systems 3(3): 10–18. https://doi.org/10.69987/JACS.2023.30302.

Zirar, A., Ali, S. I. and Islam, N. 2023. Worker and workplace Artificial Intelligence (AI) coexistence: Emerging themes and research agenda. Technovation 124: 1–17. https://doi.org/10.1016/j.technovation.2023.102747.

Chapter 7

Responsible Marketing

When Using AI in Customer-Bank Communication Relationships

Charlotte Van Hauwaert[1] and *Monica C. Scarano*[2,*]

Introduction

The evolution of marketing strategies in the banking sector has shifted significantly with the rise of digital technologies and artificial intelligence (AI). AI tools such as chatbots, predictive analytics, and automated decision-making systems now play a crucial role in enhancing customer engagement. While these innovations offer improved efficiency and customer support, they also risk diminishing trust and personal connection if not implemented responsibly. Banks must now balance the benefits of AI with the need to maintain personalized, human-centric customer relationships.

Indeed, in the digital age, we are now striving both to create a trustworthy and lasting relationship while using digital information and communication techniques. In this hybrid context, our research question is based on a line of inquiry expressed by Des Garets et al. (2009): "*Rather than promoting relationship marketing by creating a bond with the customer based on mutual engagement and trust, don't databases, digital tools, and communication technologies, due to the 'dehumanization of the relationship', call into question the components of relational exchange*?".

Based on a work-in-progress exploratory qualitative research, this chapter explores the integration of AI in customer-bank communication and emphasizes the importance of responsible marketing strategies which ethically balance the human

[1] Professional business manager, Banque Populaire du Nord.
[2] Associate professor, Université Catholique de Lille.
* Corresponding author: monica.scarano@univ-catholille.fr

DOI: 10.1201/9781003535393-7

contribution and the AI contribution in this service sector, in order to create value for customers. First, it analyzes theoretically the transition from transactional to relational marketing, the implications of digital tools in customer interactions, especially about the trust. After a presentation of the methodology used for this research, our first results are presented around some key aspects that will be discussed. Finally, we offer strategic recommendations for banks to improve the CRM balancing bank consultant and chatbots.

The Evolution of Relational Marketing in Banking

From the Transactional to the Relational Approach

Marketing in the banking sector has evolved significantly over the past few decades, transitioning from transactional marketing to relational marketing. This change reflects a growing focus on customer retention, personalized interactions, and the long-term value of customer relationships. Transactional marketing was dominant before the 1990s, focusing primarily on short-term sales objectives (Munzel 2021). This model emphasized the '4Ps' framework: Product, Price, Place, and Promotion and enabled businesses to focus on immediate sales targets and relied heavily on advertising, pricing strategies, and product-centric marketing efforts. The customer relationship was brief, often ending with the purchase. Customers were often viewed as isolated transactions rather than long-term relationships. For banks, transactional marketing is centered on promoting financial products such as savings accounts, loans, or credit cards. While this approach efficiently boosted short-term profits, it failed to secure customer loyalty.

In banking, the transition from transactional to relational marketing is linked to the deregulation of credit in 1984, which led to increased competition (Gatfaoui 2007). New players such as fintech companies and online banks emerged, while banking services became increasingly standardized. This context highlighted the need for customer retention strategies. Consequently, banks have recognized that focusing on customer relationship experience significantly improves business outcomes.

Relational marketing has evolved as a strategic approach that emphasizes building long-term customer relationships rather than focusing solely on individual transactions (Prim and Sabadie 2003). According to Berry (1983), relational marketing is defined as the creation, development, and maintenance of individualized customer relationships. This shift stems from companies recognizing that retaining existing customers is significantly more cost-effective than acquiring new ones, as retaining a customer is five times less expensive than gaining a new one (Pfeifer 2005). This model promotes loyalty through improved service, trust-building, and personalized engagement (Berry 1995). In the banking sector, this approach has evolved into what Cusin (2005) terms 'relational banking', which combines human interaction with trust-building efforts. Des Garets et al. (2009) explain that relationship marketing is crucial for banks to differentiate themselves in a competitive environment where customer choices are often driven by convenience or cost. Establishing trust and loyalty has become a priority in this sector.

Relational marketing is based on key principles such as customer satisfaction, retention, and continuous interaction. Banks recognized that nurturing customer relationships could lead to increased customer lifetime value (CLV) and reduce churn rates. Webster (1992) emphasized that relational marketing requires a customer-centric approach, highlighting the growing importance of creating trust through consistent, meaningful communication. Unlike transactional marketing, relational marketing relies heavily on customer feedback, tailored services, and proactive relationship-building strategies.

Rather than prioritizing immediate sales, it encourages organizations to develop sustained engagement with their clientele, because building a strong relational connection requires businesses to engage with their customers meaningfully. Lendrevie et al. (2006) outlines key practices for establishing this connection: knowing customers, listening to them, engaging in dialogue, rewarding their loyalty, and involving them in the co-creation process. This concept of involvement is further supported by Helfer and Orsoni (2005), who argue that businesses should view customers not only as consumers but also as partners who contribute to product and service creation. This collaborative approach can enhance satisfaction and ultimately foster loyalty.

Geoffroy and Koeberlé (2019) caution that marketing strategies combining both relational and transactional approaches may lead to conflicting objectives, causing relationship breakdowns. Balancing profit motives with trust-building efforts remains a key challenge for banks. However, Munzel (2021) offers a more nuanced perspective, arguing that the optimal marketing strategy should be adapted to the individual customer, some clients may appreciate a relational approach, while others may prefer a simpler transactional interaction.

The Role of Technology in Customer Relations

A successful customer relationship strategy hinges on satisfying and retaining clients who trust their bank and banks must adapt to changes in consumer behavior to maintain strong relationships (Lamarque 2021), also in the digital era. In fact, banks have implemented tools to build relationships with their customers, such as: (a) new communication technologies, which enable a new form of relationship to be built with customers; (b) database analysis, which enables customer segmentation strategies to be implemented and customers to be classified according to several criteria (Des Garets et al. 2009).

The adoption of multichannel strategies, which involves communicating and selling through several distinct channels, physicals and digitals, to contact the customer, has become essential. Banks have developed multichannel strategies that leverage customer data to improve communication and sales through various channels, including email, phone, mobile apps, and physical branches. A PWC study

(2020) founded that 15% of customers conduct their banking via mobile devices, reflecting a 34% annual growth rate. Despite 69% of French consumers now prefer that their advisors use digital tools to enhance service quality, up from 47% in 2017,[1] human interaction remains essential in banking services to avoid the psychological distance that can be caused by digital relationships (Dalla Pozza et al. 2017). Thus, 23% of customers would like their advisor to get to know them, 21% would like the advisor to be more attentive to their needs, and 15% of customers are looking for assistance with their projects.[2]

With the rise of digital tools, relational marketing evolved further to incorporate AI-driven solutions that enable personalized interactions at scale. AI tools are increasingly being adopted by banks to manage customer interactions. These tools leverage natural language processing (NLP) and machine learning algorithms to deliver automated yet customized responses. Key AI applications in banking communication include different tools and use such as chatbots and virtual assistants, predictive analytics, automated email and messaging systems. Many banks use AI-powered chatbots for handling routine inquiries such as account balances, payment statuses, and branch information. While these tools improve efficiency, they often fail to address complex issues that require human empathy and personalized advice. AI systems analyze customer transaction data to predict behaviors, such as identifying customers likely to seek a loan or require financial advice. These insights enable banks to deliver targeted marketing messages, enhancing customer experience. Banks also use AI-driven platforms to deliver automated yet personalized email campaigns. By analyzing customer behavior and transaction patterns, these systems ensure that messages are timely and relevant.

AI technologies such as chatbots, predictive analytics, and data-driven recommendations have emerged as key components in enhancing customer engagement. AI systems provide banks with powerful tools for analyzing customer data, predicting behaviors, and delivering targeted marketing campaigns. Predictive analytics, for instance, allows banks to identify customer preferences and proactively recommend financial products that align with individual needs. AI chatbots improve customer service by offering immediate responses to routine queries, improving accessibility for digitally active consumers.

Technological advancements have both improved customer relations and introduced new challenges. Digital tools strengthen client relationships but the overreliance on technology can depersonalize interactions and weaken collaboration (Leek et al. 2003). Customers accustomed to personalized service may find AI-driven communication impersonal or inadequate. As Des Garets et al. (2009) warn, the extensive use of AI can lead to 'dehumanization' in customer relationships, undermining trust and loyalty if not carefully implemented.

---

1 https://www.revue-banque.fr/archive/avenir-agence-bancaire-conseiller-CYRB19712.

2 https://www.revue-banque.fr/archive/avenir-agence-bancaire-conseiller-CYRB19712.

There is a paradox in the banking sector: while customers appreciate digital efficiency, they still value human connections for reassurance and trust-building (Mouillot 2019). Restoring customer trust requires combining efficient digital services with interpersonal relationships (Gatfaoui 2007).

Building Customer Trust Balancing AI and Human Interaction in Banking

Trust is the foundation of strong customer relationships, built on reliability, transparency, and personalized service (Morgan and Hunt 1994). It is essential for sustaining long-term customer relationships, especially in the banking sector where financial security is paramount. However, a Deloitte (2019) study found that only 43% of French consumers trust the banking system, reflecting concerns about impersonal services, hidden fees, and frequent advisor changes. Some researchers suggest using tools like Customer Relationship Management (CRM) to personalize customer experiences and rebuild trust (Des Garets et al. 2009).

AI systems must be designed to inspire confidence in customers. Banks can build trust by:

- Ensuring transparency in how AI systems operate and how customer data is utilized.
- Maintaining clear communication channels that enable customers to reach human advisors when needed.
- Implementing secure AI platforms that protect sensitive financial data.

While some customers are open to AI handling routine tasks, they often expect human support when facing significant financial concerns. The shift toward AI-driven communication presents a paradox for the banking sector. While automation offers speed and convenience, customers often value the emotional connection that human advisors provide. Dalla Pozza and Texier (2014) explained that while customers appreciate the convenience of digital banking tools, they often seek human advisors for significant financial decisions. For example, customers reported feeling disconnected when assigned rotating advisors, especially in commercial banks where frequent staff turnover is common. Younger generations often prefer digital self-service tools, while older clients place greater value on personalized, face-to-face interactions (Mouillot 2019). This highlights the need for financial institutions to tailor their communication strategies based on customer preferences.

Despite the relevance in integrating AI in the communication with bank customers and to balance the digital tools with the human relationship of the bank consultants, it is not clear how to create this balance, when use the AI and humans in the bank-customer relationship. What is the right degree of this mix, or the components of the relational exchange (Des Garets et al. 2009)? Our exploratory study would like to start considering it from the personal experience of bank customers.

Methodology

To explore customer perceptions of AI-driven communication in banking and evaluate its impact on relationship marketing strategies, a qualitative research approach was employed. This methodology allowed for an in-depth understanding of customer experiences and attitudes, particularly regarding the integration of digital tools in the banking sector.

Research Design and Sampling

A qualitative research design was chosen due to its ability to capture detailed insights and subjective customer experiences. This approach allowed for the collection of rich, nuanced data about how customers perceive the integration of AI in banking communication and its implications for trust and relationship marketing. The aim was not to generalize the findings but to understand the diversity of experiences and attitudes across different customer profiles.

To achieve this, semi-structured interviews were conducted, as this format provided both structure and flexibility. An interview guide ensured that key themes were consistently addressed, while the open-ended nature of questions allowed participants to freely express their experiences, perceptions, and emotions. This was especially valuable when discussing sensitive topics such as trust in financial institutions and the potential "dehumanization" of services through AI.

A purposive sampling method was used to select participants with varied backgrounds, banking preferences, and experiences. The sample included customers from three different banks to compare the experiences between mutual banks and commercial banks. The inclusion of clients from distinct banking models provided insights into differing relational marketing practices and customer expectations. Recruitment was conducted through personal networks and snowball sampling techniques, ensuring the inclusion of clients who had recent experiences interacting with their banks through both traditional and digital channels.

The final sample (see Table 1) included nine participants from three banks with distinct business models: BNP Paribas (a commercial bank), Banque Populaire du Nord (a mutual bank), and Banque Postale (another mutual bank). The group was intentionally diverse in terms of age (ranging from 23 to 76 years), profession (students, employees, retirees, self-employed), digital literacy, and banking history. Such variety ensured the inclusion of both digitally confident customers and those less familiar with online tools, providing a more holistic understanding of how AI-driven communication is perceived across different customer segments.

Table 1. Our sample.

Banks	**Participants**	**Age**	**Profession**
Banque Postale	Alexia	23	Financial auditor
	Bernard	53	IT project manager
	Lili	75	Retired sales consultant
Banque Populaire du Nord	Louis	26	Nurse
	Christine	53	Pastry cook
	Gilles	74	Retired executive
BNP Paribas	Théo	23	Student hairdresser
	Sandrine	51	Accounting assistant
	Anne-Marie	76	Retired butcher

Interview Structure and Data Collection

The interviews were conducted in person, ensuring participants felt comfortable and open to sharing their experiences. To maintain consistency, a standardized interview guide was employed. The guide included 15 questions divided into three key themes. The first was about practical experiences with questions focused on participants' preferred communication channels with their bank, their relationship with their advisor, and their satisfaction with digital tools such as chatbots and mobile apps. The second was about reactions to digitalization. Participants were asked to describe their reactions to the increasing use of AI tools in banking and the perceived impact on their relationship with their advisor. The third and final section was about motivations and barriers to explore what clients expect from their bank, what improvements they would like to see, and their concerns about AI in banking communication. The interview structure combined open-ended questions with targeted follow-ups to ensure responses covered both general experiences and specific AI-related concerns. This structure enabled participants to provide detailed feedback while allowing the researcher to probe deeper when necessary.

All interviews were recorded (with participants' consent) to ensure the accuracy of data collection. Notes were also taken to capture non-verbal cues and emphasize key themes during the conversation. Each interview lasted between 30 to 60 minutes, providing ample opportunity for participants to express their thoughts fully. Ethical principles were strictly followed throughout the research. Participants were informed about the study's purpose, their rights to withdraw at any time, and the confidentiality of their responses. Anonymity was maintained by assigning pseudonyms to all participants. Consent was obtained before recording the interviews to ensure participants felt comfortable sharing their experiences.

Data Analysis

The data analysis (see Figure 1) followed the thematic analysis approach (Braun and Clarke 2006), which is widely recognized for its suitability in qualitative research.

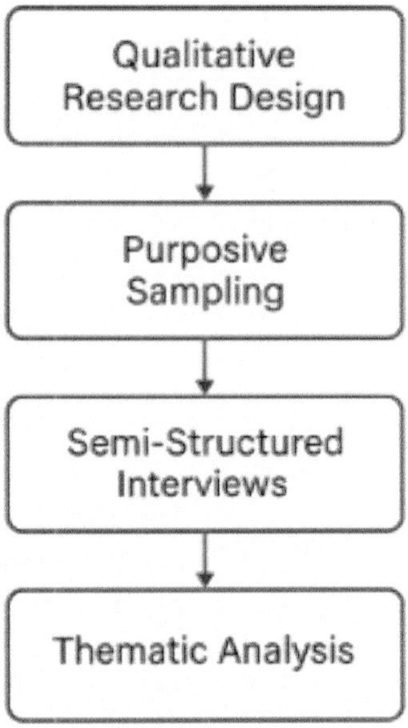

Figure 1. The steps of our research design.

Recorded interviews were fully transcribed verbatim to ensure accuracy. Transcripts were read multiple times to achieve data immersion before coding.

An inductive coding strategy was employed, meaning that codes emerged directly from the data rather than being imposed by pre-existing theories. Codes were then grouped into broader categories reflecting key themes such as: (a) Customer expectations of bank-advisor relationships; (b) Experiences with AI tools and digital platforms; (c) Perceptions of trust and depersonalization; (d) Digital literacy and training needs; (e) Balancing automation with human interaction.

Themes were compared across different banking models (mutual vs. commercial banks) to identify similarities and differences in experiences. Patterns were analyzed to understand how organizational practices and customer characteristics shape perceptions of AI-driven banking communication.

To enhance reliability and validity, preliminary findings were reviewed by a second researcher familiar with relationship marketing concepts, and discrepancies were resolved through discussion. This process helped ensure that the interpretations were grounded in the data and not biased by the primary researcher's perspective.

Results

The qualitative interviews provided valuable insights into customer perceptions of AI-driven communication in banking. The findings revealed key themes related to customer relationship with the bank advisor and AI's role in relationship management. Through participants' verbatim responses, this section explores these themes in detail, presented in Table 2.

Table 2. Some examples of verbatims, their explanation and effects or implications.

Verbatims	Explanation	Effects or implications
"My advisor always calls me back during the day if I have a question. She's always available and that reassures me." (Bernard)	Highlights the importance of advisor availability and personalized communication.	Builds trust and reassurance; strengthens loyalty to the bank.
"I used to know my advisor by heart, and he knew me too... Now I don't even know who's looking after me, and every time I ask a question, I get the same answer as any other customer." (Anne-Marie)	Reflects dissatisfaction with lack of continuity and impersonal service in commercial banks.	Leads to customer frustration and a sense of depersonalization, potentially reducing retention.
"I know that my advisor knows my situation well. She always gives me the right advice, and I feel confident." (Louis)	Shows the value customers place on advisors' knowledge of their personal circumstances.	Personalized advice fosters confidence and deepens trust in the bank.
"All I get is a letter telling me my advisor has changed. No one bothers to call me to introduce themselves." (Sandrine)	Illustrates negative impact of frequent staff turnover without proper communication.	Erodes trust and creates detachment from the bank, harming long-term relationships.
"When I needed my bank login, I came across a chatbot. It was impossible to get someone on the phone! In the end, I had to go to a branch to sort out what could have taken five minutes." (Théo)	Demonstrates frustration with lack of human assistance when AI tools are insufficient.	Reduces perceived efficiency and satisfaction with digital channels; may drive customers back to physical branches.
"The application is fast, but sometimes it takes someone to understand my request. A robot can't guess everything." (Christine)	Emphasizes limits of AI tools in understanding complex customer needs.	Reinforces the need for human intervention for nuanced issues.
"Nobody showed me how to use the app. I had to learn everything myself." (Louis)	Points out the lack of guidance for adopting digital tools.	Creates frustration and digital exclusion, especially for less tech-savvy customers.
"When the app doesn't work, I never know where to turn." (Christine)	Shows lack of support channels when digital tools fail.	Increases customer anxiety and dissatisfaction; highlights need for backup human support.
"It's fine for schedules or simple questions, but for serious things, I prefer to go to an agency." (Lili)	Recognizes the utility of AI for routine tasks but prefers human contact for complex issues.	Suggests the importance of hybrid models combining AI efficiency with human interaction.
"I find chatbots useless when you have a real question." (Bernard)	Criticizes the inability of AI to handle in-depth inquiries.	Risks lowering service quality perception if chatbots are overused.
"The chatbot is fast, but it lacks human reflection." (Alexia)	Acknowledges chatbot speed but notes lack of empathy and tailored advice.	Reinforces that AI should complement, not replace, human advisors.
"I feel like they want to replace advisors with robots, but robots can't understand our real needs." (Anne-Marie)	Expresses concern about AI replacing human advisors and the loss of empathy.	Creates fear and disengagement; highlights need for responsible AI integration prioritizing customer comfort.

The quotes highlight three main themes shaping customer experiences in modern banking about customer relationships, digitalization and perceptions.

Customer Relationships with the Bank Advisor: Between Frustration and Trust

Participants consistently emphasized their desire for availability, personalized advice, and clear communication with their advisors. The expectation of tailored service was particularly strong among clients from mutual banks. Conversely, clients of commercial banks frequently reported frustration due to inconsistent contact with their advisors. This contrast reflects differing relational marketing strategies. Mutual bank clients described a stronger sense of loyalty and trust, while commercial bank clients reported feeling overlooked and depersonalized. Trust emerged as a crucial factor in customer satisfaction. Several participants emphasized the importance of developing long-term relationships with a dedicated advisor to foster trust. Customers of mutual banks frequently reported more positive experiences in this regard. Conversely, clients from commercial banks, particularly BNP Paribas, often described feeling detached due to frequent staff turnover and inconsistent advisor contact. Sandrine shared her frustration. This revolving-door experience eroded trust and created a sense of detachment among commercial bank clients, further highlighting the importance of personalized communication in relational marketing.

Digitalization: Between Frustration and Efficiency

Participants acknowledged the convenience of digital tools but frequently cited negative experiences when using these systems. AI-driven chatbots, while fast, were often described as impersonal and frustrating when inquiries required human judgment. A recurring concern among participants was the lack of support in adopting digital platforms. Many customers reported feeling abandoned when attempting to navigate mobile apps or chatbots independently. This gap in support led to frustration, particularly for older clients who were less comfortable with digital tools. Participants consistently emphasized that banks should improve customer guidance and provide training to enhance digital literacy.

Despite these frustrations, some participants recognized the efficiency of AI tools for simple inquiries. These experiences demonstrate that while AI tools improve efficiency for routine tasks, customers expect human support for complex or emotionally significant inquiries.

Perceptions of AI as a Threat or Enhancement

Participants expressed mixed views on the role of AI in banking communication. While some saw AI tools as a helpful resource for simple tasks, others viewed them as a barrier to effective service. In contrast, some customers acknowledged the chatbot's speed but highlighted its inability to offer tailored advice. Participants indicated that responsible AI integration should ensure clear pathways to human support when automated tools fall short. The digital shift in banking often triggered emotional reactions such as frustration, anxiety, or disengagement. Customers frequently expressed concern that AI-driven systems would replace human advisors altogether. This emotional feeling highlights the need for responsible AI implementation that prioritizes customer comfort and confidence.

Discussion

The Coexistence of Transactional and Relational Strategies and their Tensions

The integration of AI tools in banking presents a fundamental tension: while digitalization enhances efficiency, it risks undermining the human relationships essential to customer trust and satisfaction. Although AI-driven solutions like chatbots effectively manage routine queries, they often fall short in addressing emotional and complex financial concerns. This gap is particularly evident in commercial banks, where frequent staff turnover and transactional interactions weaken relationship-building efforts. In contrast, mutual banks, with their emphasis on consistent advisor contact, demonstrate greater success in fostering customer loyalty and satisfaction.

This tension reflects core principles of relationship marketing, as defined by Berry (1983), which emphasizes customer loyalty through personalized communication. Mutual banks effectively apply this concept by blending human interaction with customer trust (Cusin 2004). Clients of mutual banks frequently report positive interactions and stable advisor relationships, reinforcing the benefits of this approach.

Conversely, commercial banks like BNP Paribas have faced customer dissatisfaction due to inconsistent advisor access. As Anne-Marie described, "*I don't even know who my advisor is anymore*", illustrating the disconnection that arises when banks prioritize automated systems without maintaining advisor continuity. Bank customers report feeling neglected when forced to rely heavily on digital tools, revealing a disconnect between relational marketing ideals and the reality of transactional practices. For example, Sandrine's case illustrates how her bank promised regular follow-ups when selling her a life insurance contract but failed to maintain contact afterward. This reflects a transactional approach focused more on short-term gains than sustained customer relationships.

While some scholars argue that transactional marketing has been replaced by relational strategies, others assert that both approaches can coexist. However, blending these models poses risks. Research by Geoffrey F. and Koeberlé (2019) highlights how combining strategies can erode customer trust, as seen in BNP Paribas' model where clients must pay to access a dedicated advisor. This system often leaves non-paying customers feeling overlooked, contradicting the personalized principles of relationship marketing.

Customer expectations further complicate the situation. Some customers, like Bernard, are content with digital services and prefer minimal human interaction, only reaching out to their advisor in times of difficulty. Conversely, clients like Anne-Marie and Alexia feel disappointed by the absence of personal contact. Despite these differing needs, banks often adopt a standardized approach that fails to address individual preferences. This uniform strategy appears inadequate in a context where customer expectations vary significantly. Munzel's (2021) perspective reinforces the importance of adapting marketing strategies to each client's profile. Tailoring interactions accordingly becomes even more crucial as banks increasingly digitalize their customer relationships. In contrast, Banque Populaire du Nord clients such as Louis described feeling more valued due to personalized service and consistent advisor relationships, reinforcing the effectiveness of relational marketing in banking. This confirms Webster's (1992) assertion that the shift from transactional to relational marketing is key to fostering long-term customer satisfaction.

The Use of Tools in Banking: Practical Aspects and Digital Literacy

Banks have increasingly adopted digital tools with the aim of reducing administrative workloads for advisors and offer faster and more efficient services. This shift is intended to enable advisors to focus on higher-value tasks, ultimately boosting the bank's revenue. However, this digital transformation must not compromise customer satisfaction. As illustrated by Théo's experience with BNP Paribas' chatbot, unresolved issues often require clients to visit branches in person, defeating the intended convenience of digital tools and creating anxiety, frustration, and distrust. This outcome aligns with Davis's (1989) Technology Acceptance Model, which stresses the importance of user-friendly technology that enhances, rather than complicates, customer interactions. Yet, technology could also generate customer dissatisfaction in some cases. Relationship marketing strategies emphasize customer satisfaction, and as prior research shows, these strategies must align with digitalization efforts. Digital tools can enhance relational strategies when used effectively, but their implementation is not always straightforward.

For instance, chatbots are designed to handle simple inquiries. However, as observed in interviews, they frequently fail to meet customer expectations. This issue transcends technological familiarity, age, or social background; rather, it reflects individual preferences and beliefs. For example, Bernard, an experienced IT project manager, expressed frustration with chatbots despite his technological competence. Conversely, Lili, a 76-year-old tech-savvy individual, values digital tools yet still maintain a strong connection with her bank advisor.

Digitalization has also exacerbated generational divides. Older clients, such as Christine and Louis, frequently expressed frustration with limited guidance in adopting digital tools. Without proper support, these clients risk feeling excluded, further straining their trust in banking services. This aligns with Dalla Pozza and Texier's (2014) observation that digital tools can create 'psychological distance', weakening customer trust when human support is lacking. Importantly, our qualitative study revealed that none of the interviewees had received guidance on using digital tools. Providing such support during onboarding could enhance customer satisfaction and reduce frustration. An informed client is more likely to adopt digital services confidently, reducing reliance on advisors for routine inquiries and allowing advisors to focus on higher-value tasks.

The Relevance to Balancing AI and Humans' Interactions

The paradox identified by Mouillot (2019) emphasizes customers' dual expectations: they seek both efficient self-service solutions and meaningful personal engagement. Digital innovations intended to enhance customer experience can undermine relational marketing principles if poorly executed. Therefore, balancing digital convenience with empathy is crucial. While AI tools can streamline operations, their success depends on complementing, rather than replacing, human advisors. This importance of balancing digital innovations with human interactions is also underlined by Lili who said: What role should digital tools play in the banking experience? Customers recognize the impact of digitalization on human relationships, making this a crucial consideration for banks.

The goal is not to passively endure digitalization but to control and direct its implementation. Digital tools can enhance customer-advisor interactions if clients continue to visit their advisor when needed. Digital tools should expedite routine transactions, freeing advisors to deliver value-added services, such as customized investment solutions. However, if customers feel forced into digital interactions without advisor support, the relationship risks becoming impersonal and unsatisfactory (Leek et al. 2003). Effectively, the primary customer dissatisfaction linked to digitalization stems from a perceived loss of human connection. According to Dalla Pozza and Texier (2014), the shift from traditional branch-based interactions to digital and direct sales strategies has disrupted the advisor-client relationship. While some customers appreciate the convenience of digital services, they also value direct communication with their advisor.

Some customers are indifferent to this shift, most customers interviewed stressed the need for personal connections. Lili, for example, maintains frequent contact with her advisor despite her comfort with digital tools. Anne-Marie finds it frustrating that she must book an appointment even for minor issues. As Bernard noted, "*A robot can't understand everything because it doesn't have a heart*". This sentiment warns about AI's inability to provide empathetic support could erode customer trust if deployed insensitively.

Customer trust in the banking system remains low, with only 43% of French clients expressing confidence in it (Deloitte 2019). However, recent trends suggest a renewed desire for personalized service. Clients increasingly value advisors who listen, understand their needs, and provide tailored guidance.[3] Contrary to common assumptions, younger customers also emphasize the importance of advisor relationships. This aligns with Tournois' (2017) argument that digital services can undermine relationships when they replace rather than support advisor interactions. Banks must balance the efficiency of digital services with opportunities for meaningful advisor engagement. The traditional image of bankers has suffered, though relationship marketing strategies are gradually improving this perception. Mutualist banks, in particular, have successfully shifted focus back to client

[3] https://www.revue-banque.fr/archive/avenir-agence-bancaire-conseiller-CYRB19712.

relationships. Conversely, clients of commercial banks often feel that their advisors prioritize sales targets over personal engagement.

Trust remains essential in maintaining strong advisor-client relationships. Banks increasingly promote digital self-service tools to encourage customer autonomy. However, building and sustaining trust requires maintaining consistent advisor relationships over time. Advisors play a pivotal role in fostering trust, especially regarding data privacy. Clients may feel uneasy providing personal information via banking apps. Advisors reassure clients that this data will enhance service quality rather than compromise their privacy. Furthermore, in their absence, advisors should ensure continuity by encouraging clients to contact trusted colleagues. Research shows that clients often avoid discussing sensitive matters with unfamiliar advisors, even when client service centers are available. This reinforces the need for advisors to actively build trust in digital tools. For example, BNP Paribas introduced 'Telmi', yet none of the interviewed clients were aware of its existence. Advisors must introduce and demonstrate these tools to ensure client confidence. Trust also depends on how banks manage customer interactions. For instance, La Banque Postale avoids call center intermediaries, preserving the advisor-client relationship. In contrast, BNP Paribas routes all customers' calls to platforms, frustrating clients who prefer direct contact.

To achieve responsible marketing, banks must strategically implement AI tools while preserving the relationship-driven principles that foster customer trust. Integrating digital solutions with personalized human support, investing in customer education, and ensuring continuity in advisor relationships are key strategies for ensuring AI supports—rather than undermines—relational marketing in banking. To ensure this balance, advisors must remain accessible. If customers visit their branch only to find their advisor unavailable or unwilling to engage, the benefits of digital tools will be lost. By embracing digital tools while prioritizing customer support, banks can create stronger, more satisfying relationships and restore trust in the advisor-client dynamic. Maintaining customer trust requires consistent advisor relationships and careful integration of digital tools.

Practical Implications

The study's findings carry significant practical implications for banking institutions aiming to balance efficiency and relationship marketing through AI adoption (see Table 3). Several key strategies emerge as essential to achieving responsible marketing outcomes.

Balancing AI and Human Support in Banking

The integration of artificial intelligence in banking presents a unique opportunity to enhance efficiency while maintaining high-quality customer service. However, achieving an effective balance between AI-driven automation and human interaction is crucial. AI tools are well-suited for handling routine inquiries, such as checking account balances, verifying branch hours, or providing transaction details. Yet,

Table 3. Summary table of practical implications.

Key strategy	Recommended actions
Balanced integration of AI and human support	Implement hybrid models, escalate complex queries to advisors, ensure proactive intervention when digital tools fail.
Enhanced customer education and digital literacy support	Develop tutorials, host onboarding sessions, and establish support helplines for guidance.
Building continuity in advisor relationships	Assign dedicated advisors, ensure smooth transitions during staff changes, and prioritize staff retention.
Transparent communication on AI usage and data Management	Communicate data usage clearly, offer clients control over data sharing, and design AI tools with explainable interfaces.
Strengthening emotional intelligence in AI systems	Develop chatbots with empathetic language capabilities and train staff to provide compassionate responses.
Developing AI for personalized financial advice	Build AI tools that analyze customer behavior for tailored recommendations, while empowering advisors with insights.
Maintaining multichannel accessibility	Continue investing in physical branches while expanding digital and phone service options.
Investing in AI ethics and governance	Establish governance teams, conduct regular bias audits, and ensure AI decisions align with ethical standards.

when it comes to more complex financial matters—such as investment planning or mortgage advice—customers should have seamless access to human advisors who can offer personalized guidance. A hybrid support model that combines automated assistance with human intervention is essential to maintaining customer satisfaction. For example, chatbots can initiate conversations and respond to basic queries before smoothly transferring clients to human advisors when necessary. Additionally, AI systems should be designed to recognize emotionally charged or complex conversations, escalating these cases to human advisors to prevent customer frustration. By strategically blending AI efficiency with human expertise, banks can ensure a supportive and responsive customer experience.

Enhancing Customer Education and Digital Literacy

One of the most significant challenges highlighted in this study is the lack of customer guidance when adopting digital banking tools. Many clients, particularly those unfamiliar with chatbots or mobile banking applications, reported experiencing anxiety and dissatisfaction due to insufficient support. The transition to digital banking should be accompanied by proactive measures to enhance digital literacy. Providing clear, step-by-step tutorials—through video guides or interactive demonstrations within banking apps—can empower customers to use digital tools with confidence. Additionally, integrating digital onboarding sessions at the time of account opening can help familiarize clients with the available banking technologies from the outset. To further support customers, banks should establish dedicated assistance channels, such as helplines or in-branch specialists, to provide real-time guidance when technical issues arise. By prioritizing customer education, banks can foster greater adoption of digital tools while reducing frustration.

Ensuring Continuity in Advisor Relationships

A recurring source of dissatisfaction among clients is the frequent turnover of bank advisors, particularly in commercial banking. Customers often express frustration when they are required to repeatedly build relationships with new advisors, as this disrupts trust and weakens long-term engagement. Stability in customer-advisor relationships is a critical factor in maintaining client loyalty. To address this issue, banks should assign dedicated advisors to clients, ensuring a consistent point of contact over time. Additionally, formalized transition protocols—where outgoing advisors introduce their replacements to clients—can help minimize disruption. Beyond individual relationships, banks must also invest in internal retention programs to reduce staff turnover. Strengthening these connections between clients and their advisors enhances trust, deepens financial engagement, and ultimately improves the overall customer experience.

Transparency in AI Usage and Data Management

For AI-driven banking solutions to be effective, they must be accompanied by clear and transparent communication regarding data usage. Many clients express discomfort with how their personal data is collected and utilized, particularly when AI is used to generate highly targeted marketing campaigns. Trust in AI depends on customers feeling informed and in control of their data. To address these concerns, banks should adopt transparent data usage policies, clearly explaining how customer information is used to inform financial recommendations and marketing strategies. Consent-based data collection should be prioritized, ensuring that clients have full awareness and control over their personal data preferences. Furthermore, AI-driven tools should be designed with clarity in mind, using user-friendly language to clarify decision-making processes. By prioritizing transparency, banks can foster greater customer trust and engagement with AI-driven services.

Strengthening Emotional Intelligence in AI Interactions

One of the limitations of current AI-driven banking tools is their inability to provide empathetic responses during emotionally sensitive situations. Financial matters often involve stress and uncertainty, and AI systems that lack emotional intelligence risk leaving customers feeling unheard or unsupported. To improve the customer experience, banks should develop AI tools that incorporate empathetic language and natural language processing (NLP) capabilities. Chatbots, for example, can be programmed to recognize emotional cues and respond with warmth and clarity. Additionally, human advisors should receive empathy training to ensure they are equipped to handle sensitive conversations when AI escalates complex or emotionally charged cases. By enhancing emotional intelligence in AI interactions, banks can create more human-like and reassuring digital experiences for their clients.

Advancing AI for Personalized Financial Advice

The ability of AI to provide tailored financial recommendations is a significant advantage for modern banking. However, many customers perceive these AI-driven suggestions as overly generic and impersonal, reducing their trust in automated financial advice. To maximize the potential of AI-driven personalization, banks must refine their approach. By incorporating behavioral analysis into AI models, financial institutions can develop systems that analyze customers' spending habits, life stages, and financial goals to deliver more relevant and meaningful advice. Furthermore, AI should not function in isolation but rather complement human expertise. Providing advisors with AI-generated insights can enhance the quality of personalized financial guidance while ensuring that human judgment remains central to the decision-making process. A thoughtful integration of AI and human expertise will enable banks to offer more precise and client-focused financial advice.

Maintaining Multichannel Accessibility

While digital banking tools offer undeniable convenience, customer preferences vary widely, and some individuals continue to value traditional communication methods. This study highlights that most of clients dealing with urgent or complex issues often prefer face-to-face interactions over digital channels. To accommodate diverse customer needs, banks must maintain a multichannel approach that allows clients to choose their preferred communication method. Preserving physical branch access remains essential for those who prefer in-person consultations, particularly for major financial decisions. Additionally, providing flexible communication options—such as phone consultations, chatbot interactions, in-branch visits, and video conferencing—ensures that customers have access to banking services in a way that aligns with their individual preferences. By maintaining this flexibility, banks can enhance customer satisfaction and engagement.

Ethical Considerations in AI Development

As the role of AI in banking continues to expand, ethical concerns surrounding algorithmic decision-making, data privacy, and potential biases must be proactively managed. Customers expect fairness, transparency, and accountability in AI-driven financial services. To uphold ethical standards, banks should establish dedicated AI governance teams responsible for overseeing AI development and ensuring compliance with ethical guidelines. Regular audits should be conducted to assess AI models for potential biases, ensuring fair treatment across diverse customer demographics. By committing to ethical AI practices, banks can build trust and reinforce their reputation as responsible financial institutions.

By implementing these strategies, banks can adopt AI responsibly without sacrificing the trust and personal relationships essential to customer loyalty. Combining automated systems with human support, ensuring transparency, and investing in customer education will enable banks to foster stronger, more resilient customer relationships in the digital age. This approach aligns with Berry's (1983) foundational work on relationship marketing, reaffirming that customer-centric strategies remain key to sustained success in financial services.

AI technologies have improved relational marketing by offering scalable solutions for customer engagement. However, to avoid the risks of impersonal interactions, banks must adopt responsible marketing practices that combine the efficiency of AI with the empathetic communication skills of human advisors. By integrating AI tools thoughtfully, ensuring transparency in data usage, and maintaining personalized relationships, banks can foster customer loyalty while leveraging digital innovations to enhance marketing strategies.

Conclusion

This study highlights the evolving role of AI in customer-bank relationships, emphasizing that while digital tools improve efficiency and accessibility, they risk diminishing trust and personal connection when poorly implemented. The findings reveal a critical need for banks to adopt responsible marketing practices that balance automation with human interaction. Mutual banks, which prioritize advisor continuity and personalized support, have successfully built stronger customer relationships, while commercial banks that rely heavily on digital tools have faced increased customer dissatisfaction.

AI-driven communication tools like chatbots offer practical benefits for routine inquiries, yet these tools alone cannot replace the empathy and judgment provided by human advisors. The study demonstrates that customers expect personalized interactions, particularly for complex or emotionally significant financial concerns. Moreover, inadequate digital literacy support and inconsistent advisor contact have led to frustration and reduced trust, underscoring the importance of thoughtful AI integration.

Responsible marketing in the AI era requires financial institutions to strategically combine digital tools with personalized service models. By doing so, banks can enhance customer experience, build trust, and improve long-term customer retention. To align digital tools with relationship marketing principles, banks should prioritize customer choice and autonomy. Providing guidance on digital tool adoption is essential to reducing frustration and improving customer satisfaction. By combining digital efficiency with accessible human support, banks can empower clients to engage confidently with digital services.

While the qualitative approach provided rich insights, several limitations were acknowledged. The sample size was relatively small, limiting the ability to generalize findings across the broader banking sector. This research is a work-in-progress which should be continued. Additionally, participants' perspectives may have been influenced by recent personal experiences, introducing potential bias. Future research could expand the sample size. Moreover, quantitative research could verify the impact of a really tailored relational marketing mixing AI and humans towards well-being and using a larger sample to provide broader generalizations. Despite these limitations, this study offers valuable insights into the role of AI in customer-bank relationships and provides actionable recommendations for responsible marketing strategies in the digital age.

References

Berry, L. L. 1983. Relationship marketing. pp. 25–28. *In*: Berry, L. L., Shostack, G. L. and Upah, G. D. (eds.). Emerging Perspectives on Services Marketing. Chicago, IL: American Marketing Association.

Berry, L. L. 1995. Relationship marketing of services—growing interest, emerging perspectives. Journal of the Academy of Marketing Science 23(4): 236–245.

Cusin, F. 2005. La relation bancaire en question. pp. 249–262. *In*: Gloukoviezoff, G. (ed.). Exclusion et liens financiers. Rapport du Centre Walras 2004. Paris: Economica.

Dalla Pozza, I. and Texier, L. 2014. Managing multichannel strategies in the service sector: the example of the French insurance industry. Journal of Applied Business Research 30(3): 863–868.

Dalla Pozza, I. and Texier, L. 2017. Vers un nouveau concept de proximité dans la relation conseiller-client: le cas de la banque et de l'assurance. Management & Prospective 34(1): 141–156.

Deloitte. 2019. Banking and capital markets outlook 2019. Retrieved from https://www2.deloitte.com/content/dam/Deloitte/global/Documents/Financial-ervices/gx-fsi-dcfs-2019-banking-cap-markets-outlook.pdf.

Des Garets, V., Paquerot, M. and Sueur, I. 2009. L'approche relationnelle dans les banques: Mythe ou réalité. Revue Française de Gestion 191(1): 123–138.

Gatfaoui, S. 2007. Comment développer une relation bancaire fondée sur la confiance. Décisions Marketing 46(2): 91–103.

Geoffroy, F. and Koeberlé, P. 2019. The dark side of relationship marketing in the banking industry. Recherches en Sciences de Gestion 131(2): 63–87.

Helfer, J. and Orsoni, J. 2005. Marketing. Paris: Vuibert.

Lamarque, E. 2021. L'évolution du comportement de la clientèle. pp. 109–129. *In*: Banques : stratégies et transformations. Paris: Dunod.

Leek, S., Turnbull, P. W. and Naude, P. 2003. How is information technology affecting business-to-business relationships? Results of a UK survey. Industrial Marketing Management 32: 119–126.

Lendrevie, J., Lévy, J. and Lindon, D. 2006. Mercator. Paris: DUNOD.

Morgan, R. M. and Hunt, S. D. 1994. The commitment-trust theory of relationship marketing. Journal of Marketing 58(July): 20–38.

Mouillot, P. 2019. La relation client à l'heure du numérique, le cas du marketing bancaire. Management & Avenir 108(2): 63–82.

Munzel, A. 2021. Le marketing relationnel. pp. 280–303. In Marketing. Paris: Dunod.

Pfeifer, P. E. 2005. The optimal ratio of acquisition and retention costs. Journal of Targeting, Measurement and Analysis for Marketing 13(2): 179–188.

Prim, I. and Sabadie, W. 2003. L'orientation relationnelle des clients: un nouvel outil de segmentation? *In*: 8th Journées de Recherche en Marketing de Bourgogne.

PwC. 2020. Retail banking 2020: Evolution or revolution? Retrieved from https://www.pwc.com/gx/en/bankingcapital-markets/banking-2020/assets/pwc-retail-banking-2020-evolution-or-revolution.pdf.

Tournois, N. 2017. Le marketing bancaire face aux nouvelles technologies. Paris: Elsevier Masson, Gestion Pratique Entreprise.

Webster, F. E. Jr. 1992. The changing role of marketing in the corporation. Journal of Marketing 56(4): 1–17.

Chapter 8

Exploring AI-Driven Solutions to Mitigate Burnout in Healthcare

A Systematic Literature Review

Laura Roma,[1,*] *Floriana Pollio,*[2] *Rocco Agrifoglio*[3] and *Concetta Metallo*[4]

Introduction

Burnout is a multifaceted concept characterized by emotional exhaustion, depersonalization and a diminished sense of personal accomplishment. As demonstrated in the research by Balch and Shanafelt (2011), individual traits such as perfectionism and idealism have been identified as contributing factors to burnout. This dynamic can give rise to behavioural changes, emotional fluctuations and unprofessional conduct have the potential to compromise team dynamics and, by extension, adversely impact the occupational atmosphere (West et al. 2006). The

[1] University of Naples "Parthenope", Department of Business and Economics, Via Generale Parisi, 13, 80133 Naples (NA) Italy.

[2] University of Salent, Department of Legal Sciences, Via per Arnesano, 73047, Monteroni di Lecce (LE) Italy.

[3] University of Naples "Parthenope", Department of Business and Economics, Via Generale Parisi, 13, 80133 Naples (NA) Italy.

[4] University of Naples "Parthenope", Interdepartmental School of Science, Engineering and Health Department of Science and Technology, Centro Direzionale, Isola C4, 80143 Naples (NA) Italy.

Emails: floriana.pollio@unisalento.it, rocco.agrifoglio@uniparthenope.it, concetta.metallo@uniparthenope.it

* Corresponding author: laura.roma001@studenti.uniparthenope.it

DOI: 10.1201/9781003535393-8

healthcare environment is particularly susceptible to the development of burnout, which can lead to a number of adverse outcomes, including a decline in quality of care indicators, an increase in medical errors, and high rates of turnover among healthcare personnel (Swensen et al. 2016; Dyrbye et al. 2017; Sinsky et al. 2017). The increased stress experienced by healthcare workers is attributable to numerous factors, including elevated workloads, diminished autonomy, inefficient workflows, and the transition to bureaucratic and technological systems (Linzer et al. 2001; Kristensen et al. 2005; Maslach and Leiter 2016).

Given the significant critical issues occurred in the workplace of various sectors, and in the healthcare in particular, several managerial scholars and practitioners have addressed their efforts to understand which factors help prevent burnout. One of the most critical factors to prevent (or reducing) burnout in the healthcare sector is communication. Indeed, research has shown that high-quality interactions among staff and clear communication from supervisors are essential to fostering a supportive work environment, which in turn mitigates emotional exhaustion and burnout symptoms (Mijakoski et al. 2018). Positive communication practices – such as participatory leadership and constructive feedback – strengthen the psychosocial climate (Toderi et al. 2015), enhance job satisfaction and reduce psychological distress (Lasalvia et al. 2009). Effective communication thus supports both care coordination, emotional resilience and professional engagement. However, communication leads to an increase in work demands, which, if not adequately supported, can lead to role stress. Exposure to large amounts of information through digital channels causes employees to experience cognitive fatigue, decreased performance, and increased emotional exhaustion (Karr-Wisniewski and Lu 2010). In the healthcare sector, the exponential rise of secure patient portals and internal messaging platforms has far exceeded the planned clinical capacity, creating a persistent gap between communication needs and attention resources. For this reason, transferring low-level, repetitive mental tasks to artificial intelligence is aimed at protecting cognitive capacity for higher-order relational work that requires active engagement and deep thinking, thus reducing emotional stress (Cavalier et al. 2025). Conversely, Mohammadi and Sebro (2024) and Fang et al. (2025) have observed that in specialties such as radiology, the deployment of AI systems can paradoxically lead to an escalation in the risk of burnout. This phenomenon arises from the generation of excess false positives, the imposition of heightened cognitive vigilance demands and the necessity for constant adaptation to the evolving software of these systems. As indicated by Gupta et al. (2021) and Liu et al. (2024), an additional benefit of artificial intelligence (AI) is its ability to facilitate the early detection of burnout by means of analysing communication patterns, response times and linguistic indicators of emotional stress. This approach enables the identification of attitudes or dynamics that may indicate symptoms of emotional or physical stress, thus facilitating the implementation of timely interventions. This integration of AI in the roles of workload filter and diagnostic aid serves to mitigate emotional exhaustion.

Apart from the different advantages and motivations that lead doctors, nurses and managers to use AI in healthcare, the latter was recognised by Information Systems (IS) and managerial literature as particularly suitable for augmenting the communication at different levels of analysis, like individual (workers) and organisational (within and without firms) levels (Dahmen et al. 2023). However, studies specifically linking AI-enabled communication to burnout prevention in healthcare remain sparse and fragmented. Given the vast spectrum of AI applications, this study specifically focuses on seeking AI solutions that improve communication – both between healthcare workers and between staff and management – as a pathway to mitigate burnout. Thus, we pose the following research question:

RQ How does AI improve communication to prevent burnout?

In what follows, we will discuss about the research methodology, with peculiar reference to the background (par. 2), the systematic literature review (par. 3), the research results (par. 4), and conclusions (par. 4).

Background

Burnout refers to a state of chronic stress that manifests physically, mentally and emotionally, usually in the workplace. It was first described by Herbert Freudenberger in the 1970s to characterise the emotional exhaustion some clinicians experience from overstress and their need to help patients. Further, Freudenberger suggested that the need to help others its accompanied by self-sacrificial behaviour is what puts these subjects at risk of emotional burnout. Using the term "burnout" gained wider popularity in Maslach's and Jackson's work (1986), who defined the syndrome as "emotional exhaustion along with increased negative feelings toward one's job and reduced feelings of personal accomplishment" (p. 630), which is now accepted in relational and social psychology. Over the years, research revealed three dominant themes that were later captured in the Maslach Burnout Inventory: (a) emotional exhaustion, (b) depersonalisation and (c) decline in personal accomplishment. Importantly, burnout is not an isolated event but a progressive process that begins with chronic stress, develops into feelings of helplessness and may ultimately result in clinical depression (Maslach et al. 1981). The syndrome is associated with a range of adverse outcomes, including substance abuse, interpersonal difficulties, relationship breakdowns and reduced quality of life. In extreme cases, burnout can lead to suicidal ideation or suicide (Shanafelt et al. 2010; Wallace et al. 2009), although the causal relationships remain debated (Maslach et al. 2001).

Healthcare professionals are susceptible to burnout, with its initial manifestations often being discerned by family members, friends, and colleagues. Alarming data underscores the gravity of the issue of burnout among healthcare professionals. Specifically, physicians exhibit a disproportionately higher risk compared to the general population. This risk is estimated at approximately 400 suicides per year in the United States (Center et al. 2003; Gold et al. 2013). The stigma of acknowledging one's mental health problems and seeking help must be addressed, as relapses are common in the absence of structured and sustainable stress management strategies (Maslach and Leiter 2016). Identifying factors that anticipate the symptoms observed in burnout syndrome, highlights the urgent need for systemic support strategies to enable proactive recognition (Shanafelt et al. 2012). In fact, among the factors contributing to burnout are individual traits such as perfectionism and idealism

(Balch and Shanafelt 2011), as well as organisational and systemic pressures within healthcare environments, which are becoming increasingly significant. Major factors contributing to increased stress among healthcare workers include high workloads, limited autonomy, inefficient workflows and the shift to bureaucratic and technological systems (Linzer et al. 2001; Kristensen et al. 2005; Maslach and Leiter 2016). Emotional dissatisfaction has increased among healthcare workers, who report increasingly high levels of feelings of exhaustion caused by increased administrative work, such as documentation via Electronic Health Record (EHR), which takes time away from providing patient care (Sinsky et al. 2016; Shanafelt and Noseworthy 2017). These healthcare workers are burned out due to a lack of proper alignment between clinical values and institutional priorities, which emphasise productivity and profit at the cost of the care relationship dynamics (Linzer et al. 2009; Shanafelt et al. 2010). Other issues providers face includes reduced autonomy resulting from strict protocols, as well as heightened stress due to cognitive overload from restricted decision-making resources (Maslach and Leiter 2016; Ariely and Lanier 2016). Though EHRs were created to improve workflow, Sinsky et al. (2016) and Shanafelt et al. (2016) found a paradoxical rise in physician stress and a decrease in job satisfaction. Healthcare workers devote two hours to office work for every hour spent in direct patient care and often spend additional hours after work completing clerical tasks (Sinsky et al. 2016). These consequences increase the sense of frustration of healthcare professionals, who are deprived of the time to devote to doctor-patient interaction for data entry, thus leading to undesirable effects that have increased stress (Shanafelt et al. 2016).

Burnout in healthcare professionals can be mitigated through the integration of AI technologies into healthcare workflows and can provide a promising solution to reduce administrative burdens like documentation, billing and repetitive interactions. AI offers several innovative opportunities, including digital scribes, AI-based communication tools and automated billing systems (Shanafelt and Noseworthy 2017; Topol 2019). Integrating AI within the organisation to address the problems of burnout and shortage among healthcare workforce is now a reality. Generative AI and significant advances in machine learning, notable results have been achieved in the development of accurate predictive models, advanced data analysis tools and sophisticated automation systems that simplify clinical and administrative tasks (Topol 2019; Davenport and Kalakota 2019; Sharma et al. 2022). For supporting the accuracy of the information in medical records, healthcare organisations can implement solutions such as medical scribes or voice recognition software that reduce administrative work related to documentation and allow physicians to focus more on interactions with patients. The inaccuracy can lead to communication problems, diagnostic discrepancies, perception by patients of inadequate care and the documentation errors itself has been identified as a major contributor to physician burnout (Bell et al. 2020; Gaffney et al. 2022). Moreover, AI represents an important tool to support healthcare workforce management, helping to reduce stress and fatigue associated with manual scheduling processes. For example, Leung et al. (2022) highlighted that the AI-based platform designed nursing shifts meeting both the most stringent requirements, including organisational and legal regulations and the most flexible ones, such as nurses' preferences.

Systematic Literature Review

This research is grounded in a systematic literature review (SRL) aimed at exploring the relationship between burnout, AI and communication within the healthcare sector.

As Denyer and Tranfield (2009) explain, a SLR is a structured and rigorous method for identifying, selecting, critically appraising and synthesizing existing research within a defined field. Its purpose is to establish the current state of knowledge and to highlight gaps that warrant further investigation. The importance of systematic reviews has been pointed out by Elsbach and van Knippenberg (2020), who acknowledge their contribution in providing structure to scattered literature as it aids in formulating coherent frameworks to facilitate and define future research.

Snyder (2019) points out the importance of SLRs in synthesizing the findings of multiple studies for a more integrated interpretation of insights. Hulland and Houston (2020) and Paul and Criado (2020) also emphasize the important role of SLRs in shaping future research agendas, particularly by uncovering inconsistencies and identifying gaps in the existing body of knowledge – key elements in developing explanatory frameworks. Tranfield et al. (2009) further stress the methodological rigor of SLRs, describing them as "scientific instruments" rather than simple literature reviews. SLRs provide a transparent and systematic selection process with reduced bias, thereby increasing trust in the synthesized knowledge and bolstering empirical and theoretical contributions to research (Petticrew 2019; Cronin and Cronin 2019; The Campbell Collaboration 2019). Kitchenham et al. (2009) also notes the importance of meticulous research frameworks that guarantee replicability and authenticity, thus placing the SLR at the very foundation of academic evidence synthesis.

A SLR diverges from a traditional literature review in that it has a distinctly scientific framework designed to evaluate theories and hypotheses, therefore minimizing error and maximizing accuracy in scholarly reasoning (Moher et al. 2009; Petticrew 2019; The Campbell Collaboration 2019).

In this research study, the PRISMA framework (Preferred Reporting Items for Systematic Reviews and Meta-Analyses) was selected. This approach offers a flow diagram depicting the stages of identification, screening and eligibility assessment and is considered a key element within systematic bibliographic research. PRISMA ensures that all relevant research studies are rigorously collected and evaluated.

The SLR process for this research was split into two primary phases: first, data collection which included the sourcing of records from scholarly databases; second, data analysis which included a detailed descriptive analysis of the assembled dataset (Gundolf and Filser 2013).

Data Collection

The first phase of data collection is finding a reliable academic source that comprises peer-reviewed journal articles, scholarly books and conference proceedings. For a systematic literature review, one of the leading academic databases SCOPUS was selected. A search string was built based on relevant key terms to the topic, which comprised "communication*" (including "interaction*"), "burnout" (including "work stress", "job stress" and "exhaustion") and healthcare (including "hospital*", "nurs*", "doctor*" and "medic*"). These were applied in the title, abstract and keyword fields. As of April 2025, this query produced an initial set of 71 relevant documents. The PRISMA methodology was followed to ensure robustness and relevant rigor for the review which is laid out in Figure 1. Specific inclusion-exclusion criteria were established in order to reduce bias and improve the quality of the dataset. First, records published in non-English languages were excluded (n = 3). Followed by removing publications that did not align with study core themes, which included communication, burnout and AI (n = 32), as they lacked direct relevance to the research objectives or did not provide substantive contributions to the identified focus areas. The remaining dataset comprised 36 publications that were eligible for complete analysis. The selection of eligible records for the final dataset was performed using human sensitivity-based coding.

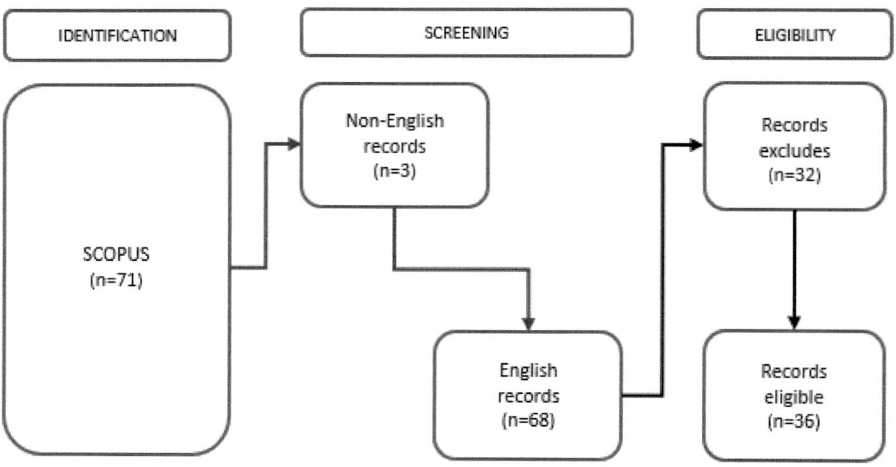

Figure 1. PRISMA flow diagram illustrating the selection process of the reviewed literature.

Data Analysis

The second step, Dataset Analysis, is a descriptive review of the 36 publications sample to capture information on publication patterns across years (Figure 2), document types (Figure 3) and countries (Figure 4).

The trend presented in Figure 2 illustrates the sustained increased scholarly attention on the relationship between communication, AI and burnout in the healthcare industry.

Figure 3 shows the distribution of sources available in the original dataset indicating most of the records are journal articles with 26 records (72%). This is followed by review articles with 7 records (19%), conference papers with 2 records (6%) and contributions in edited volumes with 1 record (3%).

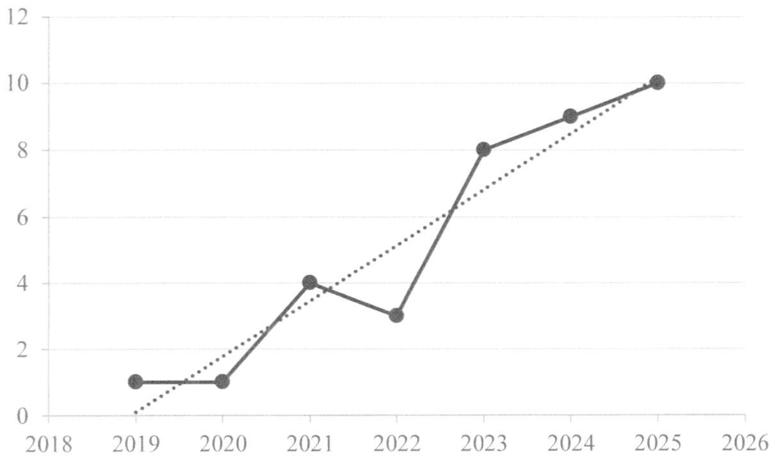

Figure 2. Document by years.

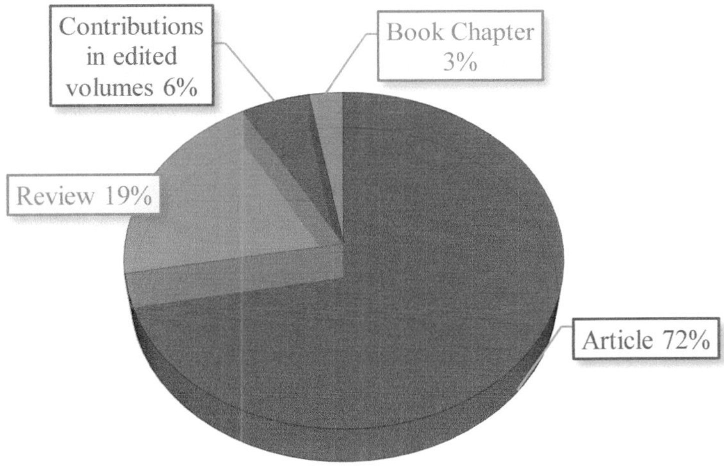

Figure 3. Document by type.

With respect to the communication, AI and burnout intersections in the health care industry, the SLR focuses on the United States (18 records), the United Kingdom (6 records) and Canada (4 records) as primary countries and territories of concern. In addition, four other countries contributed two records each: China, Finland, India and South Korea. The following countries contributed one record each: Australia, Brazil, Denmark, Japan, Malaysia, Netherlands, Pakistan, Poland, Portugal, Singapore, Sweden, Switzerland and Taiwan.

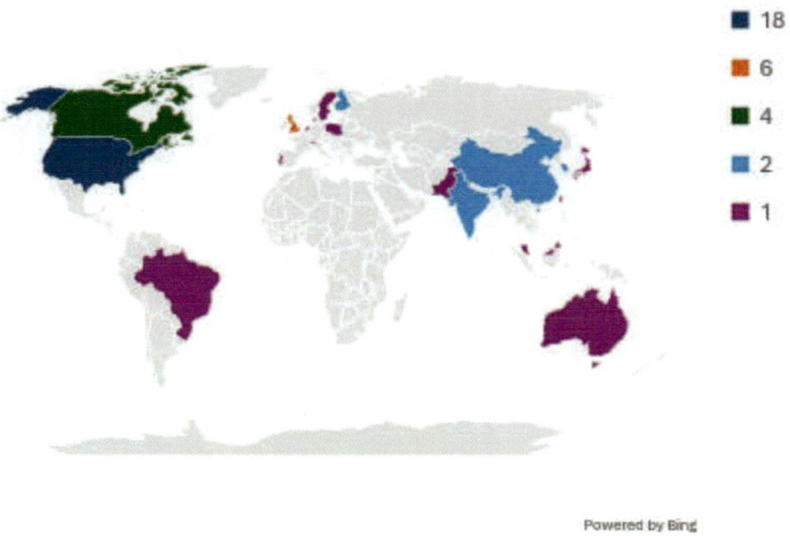

Figure 4. Documents by country.

Results

Building on literature about the origins of burnout – such as role overload, emotional labour and the absence of supportive structures (Maslach and Jackson 1981; Karasek and Theorell 1990; Demerouti et al. 2001), we identified three interrelated thematic areas: (1) cognitive and workflow overload (Section 4.1), (2) communication intensity and emotional strain (Section 4.2) and (3) lack of empathetic leadership and organisational misalignment (Section 4.3) as summarized in Table 1.

Cognitive and Workflow Overload

In organisational studies, workflow intensity and operational complexity have been identified as key antecedents of employee strain. These are framed within the Job Demand-Control and Job Demands-Resources (JD-R) frameworks (Demerouti et al. 2001) where the administrative burden, volatility of schedules and overload of information are seen as fundamental job demands. These demands are energy depleting factors that result in disengagement or increase burnout alongside insufficient resources. The energy-eroding demands require to be balanced with opportunities such as autonomy, social support, competent fulfilment of job roles, or escrows of qualitative feedback.

In contemporary healthcare systems, these stressors converge around three interdependent operational domains: clinical documentation, workforce rostering and alert management. These domains have become key tests for AI interventions, which – when carefully integrated – have the potential to rebalance the demand – resource equation central to the JD-R model.

Table 1. The macro-areas identified on communication, burnout and AI in the healthcare sector.

Macro-Area	**Description**	**Author/s**
Cognitive and workflow overload	Burnout is driven by excessive cognitive demands, including documentation load, unpredictable schedules and information overload. These stressors deplete mental energy, especially when not offset by adequate resources.	Basei de Paula et al. 2025; Dawa et al. 2025; Bindal et al. 2025; Moryousef et al. 2025; Roth et al. 2025; Kelly et al. 2025a; Michalowski et al. 2025; Kelly et al. 2025b; Liu et al. 2024; De Souza et al. 2024; Johnvictor et al. 2024; Jonathan 2024; Tiase et al. 2024; Kernberg et al. 2024a; Dhala et al. 2023; Choudhury and Asan 2023; Leung et al. 2022; Chen and Cheng 2022; de Pennington et al. 2021; Morey et al. 2021; Ali et al. 2020; Khavandi et al. 2023
Communication intensity and emotional strain	Persistent exposure to high volumes of digital communication without control over timing or content leads to cognitive fatigue, emotional exhaustion and blurred work-life boundaries, all of which contribute to burnout.	Cavalier et al. 2025; Kobayashi et al. 2023; Bett et al. 2023; Yoo and Lee 2022; Steitz et al. 2021; Rousseau et al. 2019
Lack of empathetic leadership and organisational misalignment	The absence of emotionally supportive and responsive leadership increases burnout by reducing psychological safety, weakening team cohesion and depriving staff of relational resources needed to cope with daily stressors	Baek and Cha 2025; Howick et al. 2024; Liu et al. 2024; Chen et al. 2024; Jackson-Triche et al. 2023; Watts et al. 2023; Marlicz et al. 2023; Alabi et al. 2021

Recent advances demonstrate these opportunities, including the Dora Project (Khavandi et al. 2023), which utilises an autonomous virtual assistant for the handling of low-complexity cases, freeing personnel to provide more valuable caregiving. Likewise, automated documentation systems such as Whisper (Basei de Paula et al. 2025) and digital medical scribes (Bindal et al. 2025) ameliorate the clerical burden and cognitive workload, aiding in the patient care attention shift. Ambient scribe systems, which transcribe spoken consultations to structured documents, facilitate a reduction in documentation time from thirty to fifty percent (Basei de Paula et al. 2025; Bindal et al. 2025). This enables clinicians to better manage their schedules and also enhances cognitive load and autonomy, improving focused professional self-management. Reductions in documentation burden after hours may be achieved concurrently with increased clinician engagement and enhanced patient satisfaction as evidenced by the Net Promoter Scores (Basei de Paula et al. 2025). Moreover, the ability to create structured medical notes, such as SOAP (subjective, objective, assessment, plan) notes, linked to the proximity of the medical visit, significantly reduces the documentation workload and combines speech recognition with large language models (LLM) could represent an additional strength (Goss et al. 2019).

As Bakker and Demerouti (2007) identified, these changes create feedback cycles termed "resource-gain spirals". In conjunction with this development, AI-based analytics such as RNteract utilise system data to generate strategic workload indicators (Tiase et al. 2024). Algorithmic scheduling via open-source optimisation can rapidly calculate fair nurse schedules that are constrained by safety, legal and personal preferences (Leung et al. 2022).

AI-enabled stroke triage systems (e.g., Viz-LVO) improve diagnostic processes by enhancing speed and accuracy alongside the reduction of false-positive technostress, thus addressing the overload of ambiguous alerts (Morey et al. 2021). At the clinical encounter level, Spotlight-AQ has been demonstrated to both streamline consultation time and capture key psychosocial priorities for patients. As demonstrated in the research by Kelly et al. (2025), clinical trials have reported improvements in functional health, mental well-being and reduced provider burnout. In addition, LCBuddy has been developed, which utilises smartphone-based image analysis for the triage of lactation consultations (De Souza et al. 2024). In the domain of dentistry, an entropy-informed neural network has been employed for the purpose of predicting the severity of burnout. The findings indicate that the utilisation of digital tools serves as a personal resource, contingent upon the presence of attention, control and perceived effectiveness. The observations presented herein are in alignment with the JD-R framework (Dawa et al. 2025). Another tool based on AI for improving work performance is Qventus. This software predicts the flow of hospital patients, suggesting better resource allocation and better task balance. In US hospitals, the integration of this tool has shown measurable results, including a 30% reduction in waiting times and improved staff well-being (Qventus 2021; Topol 2019).

Communication Intensity and Emotional Strain

Clinicians routinely engage with patient grief, uncertainty and the demands of self-rehabilitation, producing a form of high-intensity emotional labour that, over time, depletes mental reserves and increases susceptibility to compassion fatigue, depersonalisation and burnout (Brotheridge and Grandey 2002). These dynamics are exacerbated by a structural misalignment between communication volume and the resources available to manage it, an increasingly central concern in organisational studies on information and communication overload.

Managerial literature has long recognised that communication, while essential to coordination and engagement, can also function as a job demand. According to O'Reilly (1980), "communication load" can lead to role strain. The concept has found support in subsequent literature. Exposed to high amounts of information through digital channels, employees demonstrate cognitive fatigue, decreased task performance and increased emotional exhaustion (Karr-Wisniewski and Lu 2010). As posited by Mazmanian et al. (2013), boundary theory further illustrates that constant connectivity erodes distinctions between work and recovery time, fuelling ongoing resource depletion. More recent empirical studies confirm that "digital communication intensity" is now a distinct predictor of burnout across sectors, particularly when workers lack control over communication rhythms and content

(Fonner and Roloff 2012; Ter Hoeven et al. 2016). In healthcare, the exponential rise of secure patient portals and internal messaging platforms has far outpaced scheduled clinical capacity, creating a persistent mismatch between communication demands and attention resources. LLM assistants that generate draft responses and assign triage labels have emerged as a pragmatic solution. One of the most well-known tools in this field is ChatGPT-4, developed by OpenAI. This cutting-edge LLM (November 2022) generates coherent and articulated text based on natural language input and, thus, it can provide, for example, immediate response to patient requests, automating prior authorizations of insurance companies and producing differential diagnoses (Dahmen et al. 2023; Lewis et al. 2017).

Cavalier et al. (2025) refer to this process as "digital buffering", the transferring of low-level, repetitive mental tasks to AI to protect cognitive capacity for higher-order, relational work that requires active engagement and deep thinking. The purpose of these buffers is to triage low-complexity communications and draft replies. Automating low-value communications shields clinicians' attention, allowing them to focus on relational, high-value encounters and thereby reducing emotional strain. Steitz et al. (2021) provided evidence using natural language processing that approximately two-thirds of the intra-oncology messaging volume consists of logistical rather than clinical work. This supports Daft and Lengel's (1986) media richness theory, which posits that communication effectiveness is determined by the relationship between a message and its corresponding channel. It has been demonstrated that messages which are unclear, formless, open-ended and easy to misinterpret are sent the fastest and with the least effort through high information and feedback channels with multimodal cues. Conversely, the transmission of structured and comprehensible messages can be effective even when utilising low-level richness, such as asynchronous feedback modulated by textual means. Indeed, the utilisation of AI tools is designed for staff members, which provide immediate assistance by means of chatbots or telepresence robots. They provide assistance in an efficient and timely manner, thereby ensuring that the burden on existing services is minimised. In Korean isolation wards, mobile robots and AI-enabled video systems served a dual function: reducing infection exposure while also delivering emotional reassurance to patients, an intervention that lowered stress levels among nurses (Yoo and Lee 2022). In a separate initiative, video analytics were employed to provide personalised coaching on how clinicians utilised eye contact, physical gestures and adjust speech to show empathy, resulting in improved self-reported outcomes of empathy (Kobayashi et al. 2023).

Lack of Empathetic Leadership and Organisational Misalignment

The absence of empathetic leadership has consistently been linked to burnout in the workplace. Leaders who care about their employees, listen to them and are emotionally responsive facilitate psychological safety. In other words, employees are able to recover from daily stressors and draw upon emotional reserves to sustain engagement (Edmondson 1999). In turn, indifference from managers has been shown to lead to emotional exhaustion and depersonalisation. Specifically, the lack of social support and emotionally available leaders is strongly associated with burnout (Maslach and Leiter 2008). The theory of the conservation of resources explains this situation, stating that the lack of relational resources, such as caring and supportive relationships, increases the proliferation of stress and emotional depletion (Hobfoll 1989). There is evidence that when empathetic leadership (that is, compassionate, authentic and constructive) is absent, organisational morale suffers, turnover intention escalates and burnout (emotional exhaustion, cynicism and reduced personal efficacy) becomes a normative phenomenon (Laschinger et al. 2009). Emerging studies highlight the impact of leadership approaches on the organisational capacity for empathy. Howick et al. (2024) show that frontline compassion is not merely an individual trait, but rather sculpted by factors such as environmental design, managerial modelling and the strategic integration of technology. These findings extend Edmondson's (1999) concept of psychological safety into the realm of digital health. Take, for instance, a randomized controlled trial that took place in Korea in which nurses were subjected to a two-week regimen of AI-tailored psychological treatments, which included mindfulness, acceptance–commitment therapy, reflective writing and laughter therapy and were administered based on individual stress profile data. Those in the AI-personalised group reported much greater reductions in client-related and personal burnout compared to those in self-selection or control conditions (Baek and Cha 2025).

Watts et al. (2023)'s review highlighted that compassionate leadership affects not just burnout, risk of malpractice but also the sentiments resulting from digitalised interventions. Telehealth and AI systems, depending on the manner of their application, can either enhance or diminish the quality of relationships in care. Such broader measures along with other systemic organisational changes might be viewed as creating a form of a digital psychological-support scaffold. To illustrate this point, Chen et al. (2024) analysed responses provided to cancer patients by tools such as GPT-3.5, GPT-4, and Claude AI. Their results showed that the best-performing chatbot, Claude AI, showed significantly greater empathy than the responses provided by doctors, as well as sincerity and readability. Jackson-Triche et al. (2023) documented how the Cope chatbot, through natural language understanding, enabled the monitoring of emotional distress among healthcare workers during COVID-19. This served both to identify early signs of burnout and to direct struggling workers to timely solutions. Meanwhile, an increasing number of studies indicate that the impacts, both beneficial and otherwise, for the use of digital tools are most evident when they are exercised, rather than when given attention by leadership (Marlicz et al. 2023; Howick et al. 2024). Indeed, Marlicz et al. (2023) suggest that new digital technologies such as training simulators, telemedicine, robotic services and AI do not alleviate the persistent issue of physician burnout associated with clinical practice: without a change in the organisational culture and a "new spirit" of trust, supportive and collaborative care, the technology will tend to add to the stress instead of relieving it.

Conclusions

This study is aimed at understanding the state-of-art of the current literature on burnout, communication, and AI within the healthcare sector. Findings provide some preliminary insights to scholars and practitioners who are interested to examine these issues. Regarding the research question, this contribution offers a broad overview on the relevant literature, with the objective of achieving a better understanding on the knowledge development in this field.

We collected and analysed 36 publications distinguishing them by year, by type, by country. As result of our analysis, we found that the number of articles in this research stream is increasing exponentially since 2020. The analysis of the publications trends and of the contributions in the dataset indicates this topic is current and especially relevant for researchers and practitioners in management, information systems, and healthcare fields. Moreover, our SLR revealed a growing body of literature on the topic, and we identified the existence of three main domain: (1) cognitive and workflow overload; (2) communication intensity and emotional strain; (3) lack of empathetic leadership and organisational misalignment.

These findings reinforce the notion that AI operates as a rebalancing lever within the JD–R framework when it is embedded in an environment that amplifies resources while containing demands. Nonetheless, the growing attention to AI's technical dimensions tend to shift focus away from the consequences of its use on human involvement, personal absorption and health. These factors fundamentally define the role of AI as either a support tool or an additional source of stress (Clegg 2000; Sittig and Singh 2010).

The implementation of ambient scribing systems and shift-optimisation algorithms has been demonstrated to initiate resource-gain spirals, thereby returning high-quality clinical time to professionals and enhancing their decision-making autonomy. In a similar manner, LLM that triage and draft responses function as digital buffers, thereby shielding clinicians' cognitive bandwidth so that they can concentrate on higher-value, relationship-centred encounters. Nonetheless, current platforms such as ChatGPT-4 are discouraged for direct clinical use due to serious privacy and regulatory concerns (Kernberg et al. 2024b), indicating the need for governance models and robust feedback loops to ensure safe and effective socio-technical integration. As AI becomes increasingly adopted in the healthcare industry, potential impacts regarding privacy, transparency, fairness and patient inclusion must be assessed from an ethical standpoint. There is a need for powerful AI governance policies to be in place along with compliance to higher order regulations and equitable access to these technologies facilitating the streamline operations of the systems. This could actively alleviate the digital divides while involving patients and clinicians in the co-design processes of the AI systems. Moreover, the lack of transparency in the decision-making processes of many deep learning algorithms (the so-called "black boxes") represents a further critical element, compromising doctor-patient communication and mutual trust (Rajkomar et al. 2018; Chen et al. 2020)

Embracing an AI-solution focused on a singular technical performance metric, neglecting a human-centred perspective, would severely erode trust, compromise relationship quality and diminish cooperation during clinical decision-making. Thus, it is essential to maintain a human-centered vision where healthcare providers are able to justify AI recommendations offered on their behalf to guarantee that therapeutic relationships remain sympathetic, candid and cooperative (Davenport and Kalakota 2019). Indeed, the increase or decrease in clinician burnout does not seem to stem from the algorithm itself but rather the organisational environment in which the AI operates. Using socio-technical systems theory and Kotter's (1996) change management principles, it is clear that an integration of AI tools with the culture and hierarchy at a given level is critical. For instance, Liu et al. (2024) showed that burnout associated with frequent AI use was significantly moderated by workload and user acceptance, with organisational climate playing a pivotal role in mitigating technostress (Liu et al. 2024). The efficacy of these technologies is contingent upon the quality of leadership, with the absence of empathetic guidance risking the transformation of innovation into a source of strain. AI-supported decision aids have been demonstrated to exert an influence on trust and cognitive workload, with clinicians' situation awareness and perceived cognitive effort serving as mediators in technology adoption (Choudhury and Asan 2023). This underscores the necessity for a comprehensive consideration of both structural and psychological dimensions in the context of technological fit. In the field of oncology, scoping studies have demonstrated that resilience training is most effective when digital workload management tools are integrated systemically (Alabi et al. 2021), thus underscoring the significance of a supportive infrastructure for maintaining well-being. In order to implement these insights, it is recommended that organisations integrate LLM functions directly into the electronic health record. This approach would facilitate data entry and enable clinicians to dictate or review notes rather than typing them.

Moreover, the success of technology is contingent upon the presence of empathetic leadership. It is evident that managers who practise compassionate leadership, aided by real-time well-being dashboards that flag early signs of strain, are better placed to respond before overload becomes burnout. When this vigilance is coupled with the provision of straightforward, stigma-free access to psychological support, organisations are able to infuse the workplace with the social resources and psychological safety that act as a shield for staff against the pressures of high-stakes care. Failing to recognise AI as a socio-technical change risks creating new job demands instead of the anticipated benefits. Organisations that adopt technical perspective often miss the opportunity to optimise cognitive load management and communication norms. In contrast, those that approach AI implementation through a broad socio-technical lens are more likely to harness its full potential for enhancing well-being, fostering sustainable improvements that realign job demands with available resources (Watts et al. 2023; Khavandi et al. 2023). Digital innovation, workflow redesign and leadership have been shown to converge in this way, thus restoring equilibrium between job demands and the resources available to meet them. In this sense, Marlicz et al. (2023) highlighted the need for the application of AI with compassionate leadership and collaborative care. Improving well-being at work could only be achieved through the promotion of a blame-free policy, an open discussion on mental health and caring attitudes from managers; without such a context, even the most sophisticated systems would represent ineffective or even harmful solutions for doctors who intend to participate (Marlicz et al. 2023).

This literature review has some limitations. The reliance on Scopus exclusively may have missed important clinical studies that are indexed only in PubMed or IEEE Xplore, which likely undermined the comprehensiveness of the records. The considerable heterogeneity in burnout measurement tools and AI interventions by automation type across included studies restricted the possibility for a robust quantitative synthesis and accurate comparative analysis. Finally, it is important to note that the findings based on data collected up to April 2025 are unlikely to fully reflect the implications or capabilities of newer models due to the rapid advancement in generative AI, which further complicates the analysis. These limitations underscore the mounting imperative for empirically and conceptually advanced integrated studies to AI technologies and clinical practices, which are undergoing incessant transformations.

Future research could consider the strategic alignment of AI projects with organisational missions, professional ethics and care cultures to evaluate whether the incorporation of AI enhances organisational integration and care quality, or worsens professional alienation, stress and burnout. Furthermore, research should analyse the consequences of adopting AI on organisational design, particularly focusing on workflow redesign, role change, hierarchy of authority and the impact these changes have on clinician freedom, cognitive burden and continuity of care. There is a need for longitudinal studies to examine how organisations cultivate certain dynamic capabilities such as adaptive learning, distributed leadership and collective resilience in response to the need for continuous adaptation to AI systems, as well as how these mechanisms, in the long run, sustain clinician well-being. In this sense, follow-up studies are important to evaluate the effectiveness of the implemented strategies considering the reality of burnout as a complex, multifactorial issue. Remedial efforts, including those aimed at mitigating burnout, are difficult to observe until significant time has elapsed. Finally, assessing proactive organisational surveillance systems designed for early detection of clinician strain, role distortion, or other emerging risks will provide timely information for ongoing adjustment and optimization of AI health-supporting strategies.

References

Alabi, R. O., Hietanen, P., Elmusrati, M., Almangush, A. and Mäkitie, A. A. 2021. Mitigating burnout in an oncological unit: a scoping review. Frontiers in Public Health 9: 677915.

Ali, F., Hamid, U., Zaidat, O., Bhatti, D. and Kalia, J. S. 2020. Role of artificial intelligence in telestroke: an overview. Frontiers in Neurology 11: 559322.

Amann, J., Blasimme, A., Vayena, E., Frey, D. and Madai, V. I. 2020. Explainability for artificial intelligence in healthcare: a multidisciplinary perspective. BMC Medical Informatics and Decision Making 20(1): 1–9. https://doi.org/10.1186/s12911-020-01332-6.

Ariely, D. and Lanier, J. 2016. The Future of Work: Robots, AI and Automation. TED Books.

Baek, G. and Cha, C. 2025. AI-assisted tailored intervention for nurse burnout: a three-group randomized controlled trial. Worldviews on Evidence-Based Nursing 22(1): e70003.

Bakker, A. B. and Demerouti, E. 2007. The job demands-resources model: State of the art. Journal of Managerial Psychology 22(3): 309–328.

Balch, C. M. and Shanafelt, T. D. 2011. Combating stress and burnout in surgical practice: a review. Advances in Surgery 45: 12–23. https://doi.org/10.1016/j.yasu.2011.06.003.

Basei de Paula, P. A., Bruneti Severino, J. V., Berger, M. N., Roeder, E. A. and Marques, G. L. 2025. Improving documentation quality and patient interaction with AI: a tool for transforming medical records—an experience report. Journal of Medical Artificial Intelligence 8: 19.

Bell, K. M., Topaz, M., Ibrahim, S., White, M. and Kang, Y. 2020. Documentation burden in nursing: A scoping review. Journal of the American Medical Informatics Association 27(6): 957–965. https://doi.org/10.1093/jamia/ocaa036.

Bett, E. S., Frommeyer, T. C., Reddy, T. and Johnson, J. 2023. Assessment of patient perceptions of technology and the use of machine-based learning in a clinical encounter. Intelligence-Based Medicine 7: 100096.

Bindal, R., Dewangan, P., Walambe, R., Ramanna, S. and Kotecha, K. 2025. Framework for digital medical scribe technology for healthcare documentation. Engineered Science 33: 1377.

Brotheridge, C. M. and Grandey, A. A. 2002. Emotional labor and burnout: Comparing two perspectives of "people work". Journal of Vocational Behavior 60(1): 17–39.

Cacciamani, G. E., Sanford, D. I., Chu, T. N., Kaneko, M., Abreu, A. L. D. C., Duddalwar, V. et al. 2023. Is artificial intelligence replacing our radiology stars? Not yet!. European Urology Open Science 48: 14–16.

Cavalier, J. S., Goldstein, B. A., Ravitsky, V., Poon, E. G. and Chowdhury, A. 2025. Ethics in patient preferences for artificial intelligence-drafted responses to electronic messages. JAMA Network Open 8(3): e250449.

Center, C., Davis, M., Detre, T., Ford, D. E., Hansbrough, W., Hendin, H. et al. 2003. Confronting depression and suicide in physicians: a consensus statement. Jama 289(23): 3161–3166.

Chen, C.-H. and Cheng, C.-M. 2022. Potential next-generation medications for self-administered platforms. Journal of Controlled Release 342: 26–30.

Chen, D., Parsa, R., Hope, A., Heesters, A. M. and Raman, S. 2024. Physician and artificial intelligence chatbot responses to cancer questions from social media. JAMA Oncology 10(7): 956–960.

Chen, J. H., Asch, S. M. and Bates, D. W. 2020. AI and the path to clinical implementation. JAMA 323(6): 509–510. https://doi.org/10.1001/jama.2019.21552.

Choudhury, A. and Asan, O. 2023. Impact of cognitive workload and situation awareness on clinicians' willingness to use an artificial intelligence system in clinical practice. IISE Transactions on Healthcare Systems Engineering 13(2): 89–100.

Clegg, C. W. 2000. Sociotechnical principles for system design. Applied Ergonomics 31(5): 463–477. https://doi.org/10.1016/S0003-6870(00)00009-0.

Cronin, P. and Cronin, B. 2019. Undertaking a literature review: A step-by-step approach.

Daft, R. L. and Lengel, R. H. 1986. Organizational information requirements, media richness and design. Management Science 32(5): 554–571.

Dahmen, J., Cook, M., Fellows, R. and Bi, J. 2023. ChatGPT in Healthcare: A Taxonomy and Systematic Review. arXiv preprint, arXiv:2305.05733. https://doi.org/10.48550/arXiv.2305.05733.

Davenport, T. and Kalakota, R. 2019. The potential for artificial intelligence in healthcare. Future Healthcare Journal 6(2): 94–98. https://doi.org/10.7861/futurehosp.6-2-94.

Dawa, H., Neves, J. and Vicente, H. 2025. Evaluating the impact of digital tool utilization in dentistry on burnout syndrome among dentists: an entropy analysis and ai-driven approach. Eng 6(3): 47.

de Pennington, N., Mole, G., Lim, E., Xue, K. and Meinert, E. 2021. Safety and acceptability of a natural language artificial intelligence assistant to deliver clinical follow-up to cataract surgery patients: Proposal. JMIR Research Protocols 10(7): e27227.

De Souza, J., Chamberlain, K. and Wang, E. J. 2024. LCBuddy: Towards a smartphone-based self-assessment tool for postpartum patients with breast pain. *In*: Conference on Human Factors in Computing Systems - Proceedings, p. 215.

Demerouti, E., Bakker, A. B., Nachreiner, F. and Schaufeli, W. B. 2001. The job demands-resources model of burnout. Journal of Applied Psychology 86(3): 499.

Denyer, D. and Tranfield, D. 2009. Producing a systematic review. pp. 671–689. *In*: Buchanan, D. A. and Bryman, A. (eds.). The Sage Handbook of Organizational Research Methods. London: Sage Publications.

Dhala, A., Fusaro, M. V., Uddin, F., Alegria, J. and Masud, F. 2023. Integrating a virtual ICU with cardiac and cardiovascular ICUs: Managing the needs of a complex and high-acuity specialty ICU cohort. Methodist DeBakey Cardiovascular Journal 19(4): 4–16.

Dyrbye, L. N., Shanafelt, T. D., Sinsky, C. A., Cipriano, P. F., Bhatt, J., Ommaya, A. et al. 2017. Burnout among health care professionals: a call to explore and address this underrecognized threat to safe, high-quality care. NAM Perspectives.

Edmondson, A. 1999. Psychological safety and learning behavior in work teams. Administrative Science Quarterly 44(2): 350–383.

Elsbach, K. D. and van Knippenberg, D. 2020. Creating high-impact literature reviews: An argument for 'integrative reviews'. Journal of Management Studies 57(7): 1277–1289. https://doi.org/10.1111/joms.12581.

Esteva, A., Kuprel, B., Novoa, R. A., Ko, J., Swetter, S. M., Blau, H. M. et al. 2017. Dermatologist-level classification of skin cancer with deep neural networks. Nature 542(7639): 115–118.

Fang, X., Ma, C., Liu, X., Deng, X., Liao, J. and Zhang, T. 2025. Burnout crisis in Chinese radiology: will artificial intelligence help?. European Radiology 35(3): 1215–1224.

Fonner, K. L. and Roloff, M. E. 2012. Testing the connectivity paradox: Linking teleworkers' communication media use to social presence, stress from interruptions and organizational identification. Communication Monographs 79(2): 205–231.

Freudenberger, H. J. 1974. Staff burnout. Journal of Social Issues 30(1): 159–165. https://doi.org/10.1111/j.1540-4560.1974.tb00706.x.

Gaffney, A., White, D. B., Dine, C. J. and Halpern, S. D. 2022. Physician burnout and the electronic health record: Finding the signal in the noise. NEJM Catalyst 3(3). https://doi.org/10.1056/CAT.22.0039.

Gold, K. J., Sen, A. and Schwenk, T. L. 2013. Details on suicide among US physicians: data from the National Violent Death Reporting System. General Hospital Psychiatry 35(1): 45–49. https://doi.org/10.1016/j.genhosppsych.2012.08.005.

Goss, F. R., Zhou, L. and Weiner, S. G. 2019. Incidence of documentation errors in electronic health record clinical notes. Academic Emergency Medicine 26(5): 492–500. https://doi.org/10.1111/acem.13614.

Gundolf, K. and Filser, M. 2013. Management research and religion: A citation analysis. Journal of Business Ethics 112(2): 177–185. https://doi.org/10.1007/s10551-012-1240-7.

Gupta, M. D., Bansal, A., Sarkar, P. G., Girish, M. P., Jha, M., Yusuf, J. et al. 2021. Design and rationale of an intelligent algorithm to detect BuRnoUt in HeaLthcare workers in COVID era using ECG and artificiaL intelligence: The BRUCEE-LI study. Indian Heart Journal 73(1): 109–113.

Hobfoll, S. E. 1989. Conservation of resources: a new attempt at conceptualizing stress. American Psychologist 44(3): 513.

Howick, J., de Zulueta, P. and Gray, M. 2024. Beyond empathy training for practitioners: Cultivating empathic healthcare systems and leadership. Journal of Evaluation in Clinical Practice 30(4): 548–558.

Hulland, J. and Houston, M. B. 2020. Why systematic review papers and meta-analyses matter: An introduction to the special issue on generalizations in marketing. Journal of the Academy of Marketing Science 48(3): 351–359.

Jackson-Triche, M., Vetal, D., Turner, E.-M., Dahiya, P. and Mangurian, C. 2023. Meeting the behavioral health needs of health care workers during COVID-19 by leveraging chatbot technology: development and usability study. Journal of Medical Internet Research 25: e40635.

Johnvictor, A. C., Poonkodi, M., Sankar, N. P. and Thinesh, V. S. 2024. TinyML-Based lightweight AI healthcare mobile chatbot deployment. Journal of Multidisciplinary Healthcare 17: 5091–5104.

Jonathan, S. 2024. Nursing in the digital age: the importance of health technology and its advancement in nursing and healthcare. pp. 283–296. *In*: Digital Technology in Public Health and Rehabilitation Care: COVID Era.

Karr-Wisniewski, P. and Lu, Y. 2010. When more is too much: Operationalizing technology overload and exploring its impact on knowledge worker productivity. Computers in Human Behavior 26(5): 1061–1072.

Kelly, R. C., Holt, R. I. G., Price, H., Lizoain, A. and Barnard-Kelly, K. 2025a. Cost-effective quality of life improvement while reducing health care professional burnout with an AI-driven intervention for personalized medicine. Journal of Diabetes Science and Technology. [Article in press].

Kelly, R. C., Price, H., Phiri, P., Mendez, O. and Barnard-Kelly, K. 2025b. Delivering biopsychosocial health care within routine care: Spotlight-AQ pivotal multicenter randomized controlled trial results. Journal of Diabetes Science and Technology 19(1): 91–97.

Kernberg, A., Gold, J. A. and Mohan, V. 2024a. Using ChatGPT-4 to create structured medical notes from audio recordings of physician-patient encounters: comparative study. Journal of Medical Internet Research 26(1): e54419.

Kernberg, P., Nassour, M., McMurry, T. L. and Denton, G. D. 2024b. Large language models and medical education: Opportunities and challenges. Academic Medicine, epub ahead of print. https://doi.org/10.1097/ACM.0000000000005432.

Khavandi, S., Zaghloul, F., Higham, A., Lim, E., de Pennington, N. and Celi, L. A. 2023. Investigating the impact of automation on the health care workforce through autonomous telemedicine in the cataract pathway: protocol for a multicenter study. JMIR Research Protocols 12(1): e49374.

Kitchenham, B., Pearl Brereton, O., Budgen, D., Turner, M., Bailey, J. and Linkman, S. 2009. Systematic literature reviews in software engineering – A systematic literature review. Information and Software Technology 51(1): 7–15.

Kobayashi, M., Katayama, M., Hayashi, T., Une, S. and Honda, M. 2023. Effect of multimodal comprehensive communication skills training with video analysis by artificial intelligence for physicians on acute geriatric care: a mixed-methods study. BMJ Open 13(3): e065477.

Kotter, J. P. 1996. Why Transformation Efforts Fail. Harvard Business Review.

Kristensen, T. S., Borritz, M., Villadsen, E. and Christensen, K. B. 2005. The Copenhagen Burnout Inventory: A new tool for the assessment of burnout. Work and Stress 19(3): 192–207. https://doi.org/10.1080/02678370500297720.

Lasalvia, A., Bonetto, C., Bertani, M., Bissoli, S., Cristofalo, D., Marrella, G. et al. 2009. Influence of perceived organisational factors on job burnout: Survey of community mental health staff. The British Journal of Psychiatry 195(6): 537–544. https://doi.org/10.1192/bjp.bp.108.060871.

Laschinger, H. K. S., Wong, C. A. and Grau, A. L. 2012. The influence of authentic leadership on newly graduated nurses' experiences of workplace bullying, burnout and retention outcomes: A cross-sectional study. International Journal of Nursing Studies 49(10): 1266–1276.

Leung, F., Lau, Y.-C., Law, M. and Djeng, S.-K. 2022. Artificial intelligence and end user tools to develop a nurse duty roster scheduling system. International Journal of Nursing Sciences 9(3): 373–377.

Leung, J., Gutierrez, M., Zheng, K. and Melnick, E. R. 2022. Optimizing nurse scheduling using artificial intelligence: A socio-technical perspective. Journal of Nursing Management 30(3): 558–567. https://doi.org/10.1111/jonm.13579.

Lewis, T. L. and Wyatt, J. C. 2017. mHealth and mobile medical apps: A framework to assess risk and promote safer use. Journal of Medical Internet Research 16(9): e210. https://doi.org/10.2196/jmir.3133.

Linzer, M., Visser, M. R., Oort, F. J., Smets, E. M., McMurray, J. E. and De Haes, H. C. 2001. Predicting and preventing physician burnout: results from the United States and the Netherlands. The American Journal of Medicine 111(2): 170–175.

Linzer, M., Manwell, L. B., Williams, E. S., Bobula, J. A., Brown, R. L., Varkey, A. B. et al. 2009. Working conditions in primary care: physician reactions and care quality. Annals of Internal Medicine 151(1): 28–36.

Liu, H., Ding, N., Li, X., Bao, H. and Xue, H. 2024. Artificial intelligence and radiologist burnout. JAMA Network Open 7(11): e2448714.

Liu, Y., Awang, H. and Mansor, N. S. 2024. Exploring potential applications of generative artificial intelligence in future healthcare: the case of sora. *In*: 2024 7th International Conference on Internet Applications, Protocols and Services (NETAPPS 2024).

Marlicz, W., Koulaouzidis, A., Charisopoulou, D., Rydzewska, G. and Koulaouzidis, G. 2023. Burnout in healthcare - the Emperor's New Clothes. Przeglad Gastroenterologiczny 18(3): 274–280.

Maslach, C. and Jackson, S. E. 1986. Maslach Burnout Inventory Manual. 2nd ed. Palo Alto: Consulting Psychologists Press.

Maslach, C. and Leiter, M. P. 2008. Early predictors of job burnout and engagement. Journal of Applied Psychology 93(3): 498.

Maslach, C., Jackson, S. E. and Leiter, M. P. 1996. Maslach Burnout Inventory Manual. 3rd ed. Palo Alto: Consulting Psychologists Press.

Maslach, C., Schaufeli, W. B. and Leiter, M. P. 2001. Job burnout. Annual Review of Psychology 52(1): 397–422. https://doi.org/10.1146/annurev.psych.52.1.397.

Mazmanian, M., Orlikowski, W. J. and Yates, J. 2013. The autonomy paradox: The implications of mobile email devices for knowledge professionals. Organization Science 24(5): 1337–1357.

Michalowski, M., Topaz, M. and Peltonen, L. M. 2025. An AI-enabled nursing future with no documentation burden: a vision for a new reality. Journal of Advanced Nursing. [Article in press].

Mijakoski, D., Karadzinska-Bislimovska, J., Stoleski, S., Minov, J. and Zafirova, B. 2018. Workplace psychosocial characteristics as determinants of burnout in hospital nurses. Archives of Industrial Hygiene and Toxicology 69(3): 265–273. https://doi.org/10.2478/aiht-2018-69-3176.

Mohammadi, F. G. and Sebro, R. 2024. Artificial intelligence impact on burnout in radiologists—alleviation or exacerbation?. JAMA Network Open 7(11): e2448720–e2448720.

Moher, D., Liberati, A., Tetzlaff, J. and Altman, D. G. 2009. Preferred reporting items for systematic reviews and meta-analyses: The PRISMA statement. BMJ 339: b2535. https://doi.org/10.1136/bmj.b2535.

Morey, J. R., Zhang, X., Yaeger, K. A., Tuhrim, S. and Fifi, J. T. 2021. Real-world experience with artificial intelligence-based triage in transferred large vessel occlusion stroke patients. Cerebrovascular Diseases 50(4): 450–455.

Moryousef, J., Nadesan, P., Uy, M., Matti, D. and Guo, Y. 2025. Assessing the efficacy and clinical utility of artificial intelligence scribes in urology. Urology 196: 12–17.

O'Reilly III, C. A. 1980. Individuals and information overload in organizations: is more necessarily better?. Academy of Management Journal 23(4): 684–696.

Parikh, R. B., Obermeyer, Z. and Navathe, A. S. 2019. Regulation of predictive analytics in medicine. Science 363(6429): 810–812. https://doi.org/10.1126/science.aaw0029.

Paul, J. and Criado, A. R. 2020. The art of writing literature review: What do we know and what do we need to know? International Business Review 29: 101717. https://doi.org/10.1016/j.ibusrev.2020.101717.

Petticrew, M. 2019. Systematic Reviews in the Social Sciences: A Practical Guide. Oxford: Wiley-Blackwell.

Qventus, 2021. Case Study: Reducing ED Wait Times with AI-Driven Flow Management. [online] Available at: https://www.qventus.com/resources/case-study-reducing-ed-wait-times/ [Accessed April 21, 2025].

Rajkomar, A., Oren, E., Chen, K., Dai, A. M., Hajaj, N., Hardt, M. et al. 2018. Scalable and accurate deep learning with electronic health records. NPJ Digital Medicine 1(1): 18.

Roth, J., Thunga, S. and Yoo, J. 2025. Assessing the landscape of artificial intelligence-powered patient documentation in dermatology. Journal of Drugs in Dermatology 24(1): 64–69.

Rousseau, J. F., Ip, I. K., Raja, A. S., Schuur, J. D. and Khorasani, R. 2019. Can automated retrieval of data from emergency department physician notes enhance the imaging order entry process?. Applied Clinical Informatics 10(2): 189–198.

Shanafelt, T. D. and Noseworthy, J. H. 2017. Executive leadership and physician well-being: Nine organizational strategies to promote engagement and reduce burnout. Mayo Clinic Proceedings 92(1): 129–146. https://doi.org/10.1016/j.mayocp.2016.10.004.

Shanafelt, T. D., Balch, C. M., Bechamps, G., Russell, T., Dyrbye, L., Satele, D. et al. 2010. Burnout and medical errors among American surgeons. Annals of Surgery 251(6): 995–1000.

Shanafelt, T. D., Hasan, O., Dyrbye, L. N., Sinsky, C., Satele, D., Sloan, J. et al. 2015, December. Changes in burnout and satisfaction with work-life balance in physicians and the general US working population between 2011 and 2014. pp. 1600–1613. In Mayo Clinic Proceedings (Vol. 90, No. 12). Elsevier.

Shanafelt, T. D., Dyrbye, L. N. and West, C. P. 2012. Addressing physician burnout: the way forward. JAMA 317(9): 901–902. https://doi.org/10.1001/jama.2017.0076.

Sinsky, C., Colligan, L., Li, L., Prgomet, M., Reynolds, S., Goeders, L. et al. 2016. Allocation of physician time in ambulatory practice: a time and motion study in 4 specialties. Annals of Internal Medicine 165(11): 753–760.

Snyder, H. 2019. Literature review as a research methodology: An overview and guidelines. Journal of Business Research 104: 333–339. https://doi.org/10.1016/j.jbusres.2019.07.039.

Steitz, B. D., Sulieman, L., Warner, J. L., Davis, A. L. and Unertl, K. M. 2021. Classification and analysis of asynchronous communication content between care team members involved in breast cancer treatment. JAMIA Open 4(3): ooab049.

Swensen, S., Kabcenell, A. and Shanafelt, T. 2016. Physician-organization collaboration reduces physician burnout and promotes engagement: The Mayo Clinic experience. Journal of Healthcare Management 61(2): 105–127. https://doi.org/10.1097/00115514-201603000-00007.

Ter Hoeven, C. L., van Zoonen, W. and Fonner, K. L. 2016. The practical paradox of technology: The influence of communication technology use on employee burnout and engagement. Communication Monographs 83(2): 239–263.

The Campbell Collaboration. 2019. Campbell Collaboration systematic reviews: Policies and guidelines.

Tiase, V. L., Sward, K. A. and Facelli, J. C. 2024. A scalable and extensible logical data model of electronic health record audit logs for temporal data mining (RNteract): Model conceptualization and formulation. JMIR Nursing 7: e55793.

Toderi, S., Balducci, C., Edwards, J. A., Sarchielli, G. and Broccoli, M. 2015. La valutazione del clima psicosociale e organizzativo nei luoghi di lavoro: una proposta metodologica. Risorsa Uomo 21(3): 313–326. https://doi.org/10.3280/RU2015-003005.

Topol, E. 2019. Deep Medicine: How Artificial Intelligence Can Make Healthcare Human Again. New York: Basic Books.

Tranfield, D., Denyer, D. and Smart, P. 2003. Towards a methodology for developing evidence-informed management knowledge by means of systematic review. British Journal of Management 14(3): 207–222.

Wallace, J. E., Lemaire, J. B. and Ghali, W. A. 2009. Physician wellness: a missing quality indicator. The Lancet 374(9702): 1714–1721. https://doi.org/10.1016/S0140-6736(09)61424-0.

Watts, E., Patel, H., Kostov, A., Kim, J. and Elkbuli, A. 2023. The role of compassionate care in medicine: toward improving patients' quality of care and satisfaction. Journal of Surgical Research 289: 1–7.

West, C. P., Huschka, M. M., Novotny, P. J., Sloan, J. A., Kolars, J. C., Habermann, T. M. et al. 2006. Association of perceived medical errors with resident distress and empathy: a prospective longitudinal study. Jama 296(9): 1071–1078.

Yoo, H. J. and Lee, H. 2022. Critical role of information and communication technology in nursing during the COVID-19 pandemic: A qualitative study. Journal of Nursing Management 30(8): 3677–3685.

Chapter 9

Data-augmented Venture Firms

AI in Venture Capital Decision-making

Sanguineti Francesca[1,*] and *Previtali Pietro*[2]

Introduction

Artificial intelligence (AI) is widely seen as a transformative force, with the potential to enhance or even replace traditional decision-making processes across diverse sectors (Tursunbayeva and Gal 2024). In industries such as healthcare, logistics, and finance, organizations are increasingly leveraging AI to generate insights, automate tasks, and improve outcomes. Venture capital (VC), however, represents a more complex terrain. Known for its reliance on "gut feeling," trust-based relationships, and expert judgment (Hisrich and Jankowicz 1990), VC has been slower to adopt AI despite operating under conditions of high uncertainty and information asymmetry, the kind of environment where AI could offer meaningful support. This tension between promise and hesitation sets the stage for a deeper investigation into how AI is reshaping the field.

Venture capital has grown into a global engine for innovation, even amid recent macroeconomic uncertainties. Global VC investment reached $368.3 billion in 2024, up from $349.4 billion in 2023 (KPMG 2025). Much of this growth has centered on AI ventures (Gil and Perrault 2025; Tricot 2021). Indeed, late 2024 saw record-breaking funding rounds for AI startups (e.g., Databricks with $10 billion; OpenAI with $6.6 billion) (KPMG 2025). Industry reports indicate that VC firms are "doubling

[1] Assistant Professor in Organization Studies, University of Pavia.
[2] Full Professor in Organization Studies, University of Pavia.
* Corresponding author: francesca.sanguineti@unipv.it

DOI: 10.1201/9781003535393-9

down" on AI investments despite a general market slowdown (Ernst and Young 2024; Struta 2024). In other words, VCs are heavily investing in AI startups, yet paradoxically few have integrated AI tools into their own decision processes. A 2021 Gartner report observed that < 5% of VC investment decisions used data science or machine learning at that time (with a predicted rise to 75% by 2025) (Rimol and Costello 2021). Even in 2020, industry leaders admitted they had not adopted AI yet, though they expected to soon (Sanchez 2020). Surveys by 2022 likewise found only a handful of firms proactively using AI (Scabbio 2022; Röhm et al. 2022). This slow adoption reflects VC's unique challenges – decisions are highly people-driven and relationship-based, and unlike public markets, data on nascent startups is scarce and qualitative. In short, that "gut feel" and personal networks still dominate VC decision-making, raising questions about how and when AI tools can meaningfully contribute.

Nonetheless, pressure to leverage AI in VC is growing. Some pioneering VC firms have begun experimenting with AI to gain a competitive edge. For instance, tech-focused funds like SignalFire[1] built proprietary AI-driven sourcing platforms to optimize deal flow. Meanwhile, new third-party AI solutions tailored to investors have lowered barriers to adoption (Röhm et al. 2022). The hype surrounding generative AI (e.g., ChatGPT) further demonstrated AI's potential for tasks like market research, writing, and pattern recognition, spurring further interest in VC applications. Some practitioners even speculate about an upcoming era of "agentic AI," autonomous AI agents that could execute complex tasks on behalf of investors. A recent industry report envisions that such agentic AI could eventually reshape the venture landscape, forcing limited partners and VCs to fundamentally rethink how they operate (Fairview 2024). While this scenario remains futuristic, it stresses the transformative potential of AI in the investment world.

Academic research on AI in venture capital is still nascent and has largely been conceptual or quantitative. Several studies have demonstrated in theory that machine learning models could support venture investment decisions; for instance, by predicting startup success or screening opportunities (Arroyo et al. 2019; Mishra et al. 2017; Ross et al. 2021; Setty et al. 2024). However, there seems to be a notable gap in understanding the real-world organizational adoption of AI within VC firms. Existing literature tends to focus on technical algorithms rather than in-depth case evidence. As a result, we have identified the need for more qualitative, firm-level research to clarify the business implications of AI adoption in venture capital.

This chapter begins to address such a gap through an in-depth case study of a VC firm that has embraced AI. NEVA SGR[2] – one of Italy's leading venture capital firms – has been identified as a best-case scenario for AI implementation in VC. Founded in 2019 as the venture arm of Intesa Sanpaolo (Italy's largest banking group) NEVA SGR operates at the intersection of traditional finance and high-tech entrepreneurship.

[1] https://www.signalfire.com/ai-lab.

[2] https://www.nevasgr.com/content/neva/en.html.

Venture Capital and AI Applications: A Brief Analysis

Venture capital firms perform a series of activities in their investment lifecycle, from deal sourcing and screening, through due diligence and deal selection, to post-investment monitoring and exit (Kaplan and Strömberg 2001; Wright and Robbie 1998). Each of these stages involves intensive information processing and judgment under uncertainty. Traditionally, VC firms gain an edge by leveraging the experience and networks of their partners, for example, tapping personal connections to source promising startups, or drawing on pattern recognition refined through years of investing to identify which business models are likely to succeed (Gompers et al. 2016). The VC decision process has often been described as much an "art" as a science, where intuition, qualitative assessments of founders, and informal signals (the so-called "gut feeling") are as important as hard data (Hisrich and Jankowicz 1990). In a well-known survey of private equity and venture investors, Gompers and colleagues (2016) found that qualitative factors like the management team's capabilities and the firm's network were consistently highlighted as key determinants in investment decisions. However, as data availability has exploded in recent years—with startups leaving digital footprints across databases and the internet—opportunities have emerged to bring more analytical rigor into this process.

AI technologies, particularly those under the umbrella of machine learning and data analytics, offer tools to process large volumes of structured and unstructured data far more quickly than human analysts. In principle, AI could assist VC firms at every stage of the investment value chain. For deal sourcing, algorithms can scan vast online data (news, social media, startup databases, and patent filings) to spot emerging companies or trends that might not yet be on any investor's radar (Jo et al. 2024). For example, InReach Ventures,[3] a London-based VC founded in 2015, spent three years building a proprietary software platform called "DIG" that continuously crawls the web for new startups and then filters them for potential interest. Similarly, the San Francisco firm SignalFire[4] developed an AI-driven real-time data platform ("Beacon") to analyze market signals (hiring data, web traffic, and so on) and flag promising ventures. These examples illustrate how AI can extend the reach of VCs in the sourcing stage.

In due diligence, AI and advanced analytics could help make sense of complex information about a target startup's market, technology, and financial projections (Jo et al. 2024). Natural language processing (NLP) algorithms can rapidly summarize industry reports or technical documents. Predictive models might forecast a startup's growth trajectory based on patterns learned from thousands of past companies. In portfolio management, AI tools can monitor key performance indicators of portfolio companies in real time or even predict which companies might be heading toward trouble, allowing VCs to intervene early. AI could also assist in identifying potential

[3] https://www.inreachventures.com.

[4] https://www.signalfire.com/ai-lab.

exit opportunities by matching companies with likely acquirers based on strategic fit. It is important to note that AI in this context is not a single technology but rather spans a vast range of capabilities – from relatively simple algorithmic screening rules to more sophisticated machine learning models and, most recently, generative AI and agentic AI.

Agentic AI refers to AI systems equipped with a level of autonomy to take actions or make recommendations based on goals, effectively acting as intelligent "agents" on behalf of human users (Stryker 2023). Unlike traditional software that follows predefined instructions, an agentic AI can dynamically design its own workflow to achieve an objective, using tools and querying data as needed. For example, an AI agent might be tasked with evaluating a new investment in a particular sector: it could autonomously gather up-to-date market data, consult relevant scientific literature, ask and answer intermediate questions, and ultimately produce an investment memo draft. Such systems have "agency" in that they make intermediate decisions (which sources to consult, which hypotheses to test) without constant human direction. As Purdy (2024) notes, agentic AI could enable scenarios like AI-powered financial analysts that proactively research and optimize portfolios in response to real-time events. In the VC domain, one can imagine agentic AI assistants that handle many of the routine analytical tasks and even interact with entrepreneurs or other agents to negotiate terms—a significant advancement from today's tools.

While these possibilities are compelling, it is of fundamental importance to consider them in the organizational context of VC firms. Venture capital is a high-stakes business where decision quality directly impacts financial returns, and where trust and reputation matter. The introduction of AI tools thus raises practical questions: How comfortable are investors with relying on algorithmic outputs? How can AI insights be integrated into existing decision workflows? What about data security and confidentiality, given that VC firms deal with sensitive information from startups? These questions highlight why studying real adoption is important. The success of AI in VC likely depends not just on the technology's capabilities, but on how humans use and govern it.

Literature Review

Academic literature on the use of AI in venture capital (VC) is still expanding, reflecting the relatively recent convergence of these fields. Broadly, existing studies can be grouped into two interrelated streams. The first stream focuses on AI's technical potential in VC decision-making, often by building predictive models on venture datasets. The second, smaller stream examines organizational and behavioral aspects of AI adoption in VC firms, including the determinants and implications of integrating AI tools into the VC investment process. This section reviews both streams, incorporating recent contributions that shed light on the phenomenon of AI in VC and its key drivers.

AI's Technical Potential in VC Decision-Making

The first stream emphasizes AI's technical capabilities in supporting VC decision-making, primarily through predictive modeling. Many studies have proposed quantitative models to assist VCs in screening and selecting startups, demonstrating that machine learning can uncover patterns in large datasets and help predict venture outcomes. For example, Arroyo and colleagues (2019) demonstrated that machine learning algorithms effectively forecast startup success by analyzing data from over 120,000 early-stage companies, highlighting predictive analytics' potential for risk assessment and opportunity identification. Similarly, Corea et al. (2021) developed a data-driven investment framework using the Crunchbase database, identifying 21 key features that predict startup success – notably a startup's social media visibility, the reputations of its existing investors, and the amount of prior funding. These technical studies underscore that large-scale venture data, when analyzed with AI, can in theory improve risk assessment and opportunity identification for investors.

A number of studies have reported impressive predictive performance of AI models on historical venture data. Mishra et al. (2017), for instance, developed a Bayesian-based multi-criteria decision model that simulates VC decision-making, emphasizing the structured analytical process used by investors. Ross et al. (2021) introduced CapitalVX, a machine learning model trained on a big dataset of VC financings and startups. CapitalVX could predict startup outcomes (such as successful exit or follow-on funding) with 80–89% out-of-sample accuracy, suggesting that VC firms might potentially leverage machine learning to evaluate prospective investments with publicly accessible information.

Other studies echo these findings. Caruso and colleagues (2015) applied a deep neural network to predict valuation step-ups in follow-on financing rounds of VC-backed companies. Their model outperformed traditional linear regression in forecasting which startups would achieve higher valuations. More recently, Maurer et al. (2024) extended this perspective by practically implementing an AI-Augmented Screening System, tailoring the system using a Design Science methodology to address specific user challenges. Setty and colleagues (2024) trained cost-sensitive machine learning models on data about 10,000 Israeli startups to predict investment success. In contrast to conventional methods, they claim that these models greatly decreased investment risk and even enabled VCs to customize forecasts to suit their risk tolerance. In a related vein, Wang and Xue (2022) explored decision tree algorithms for early-stage project screening, and Lyonnet and Stern (2022) used a large French dataset to see if algorithmic predictions could identify high-potential ventures that VCs might otherwise overlook. Interestingly, Lyonnet and Stern (2022) found that algorithmic predictions could uncover overlooked high-potential ventures, although human investors sometimes ignored these insights, indicating a need for improved investor integration with AI tools.

Interestingly, some studies have directly compared algorithmic investors to human investors. Retterath (2020) benchmarked an XGBoost machine learning model against 111 VC professionals in picking promising startups. In a controlled experiment, the algorithm outperformed the median VC by about 25% (and the average VC by 29%) in identifying successful ventures. Importantly, Retterath does not suggest replacing investors with algorithms; instead, he recommends an augmented approach wherein "intelligent algorithms narrow down the upper part of the deal-flow funnel" (Retterath 2020, p.5) and human VCs then focus their effort on the most promising opportunities (Retterath 2020). Even the most optimistic studies acknowledge that algorithms work best as decision support tools rather than standalone decision-makers.

Therefore, this first stream of literature demonstrates that AI and machine learning can model certain aspects of VC decision-making with accuracy. These works serve as valuable proofs-of-concept, indicating that data-driven approaches could improve the efficiency of screening or the consistency of evaluations. However, most such studies are retrospective, trained on historical data, and thus may not reflect the realities of real-time investing. They often assume the availability of large, high-quality datasets (thousands of labeled startup outcomes), which individual VC firms may not possess. Moreover, purely algorithmic models may overlook qualitative factors (e.g., founder chemistry, market timing) that seasoned investors consider. As a result, while technical results are encouraging, their practical validity is still being tested. As a matter of facts, a recurring theme is that algorithmic tools are complements to, not replacements for, human judgment in venture capital. For instance, Ross et al. (2021) suggested that automating preliminary analyses could free up VCs' time for human-centric activities like founder relationship-building. Huang and Rust (2018) similarly argue that AI's highest value is in augmenting professionals – taking over routine analytical tasks so experts can focus on creative and strategic thinking. In short, the literature to date portrays AI as a means to amplify the VC investor's capabilities, by systematically crunching numbers and flagging patterns that might otherwise go unnoticed.

Adoption of AI in VC Firms: Organizational and Behavioral Insights

The second stream of literature addresses if and how VC organizations are actually adopting AI tools, and what factors influence this integration. Here, recent studies suggest that AI adoption in venture capital is underway but still cautious and uneven. Early surveys and interviews indicated that only a handful of VC firms had begun experimenting with AI. For example, Corea (2019) examined AI applications in 13 Venture Capital firms, identifying which variables influence a company's likelihood of success or fundraising, categorized as human and team attributes, financial factors, and business qualities. Around the same time, Trocha (2019) reported the emergence of 83 venture firms that claimed to use data analytics, AI, or proprietary software in their investment processes, hinting that a subset of "data-driven VCs" was emerging. However, these numbers were small relative to the thousands of VC firms worldwide, and in most cases, the AI usage was limited to specific tasks (such as sourcing deals via algorithmic scanning of databases). An extensive review by Scabbio (2022) of 92 cases of VC firms revealed that AI usage in VC was still at a *very early stage*. Only a small number of firms had proactively implemented AI and data-driven approaches in their workflows, and even those tended to use AI for narrow functions. In Scabbio's (2022) assessment, the vast majority of VCs were merely exploring or learning about AI tools in principle, rather than deeply integrating them into decision-making. This underscored the conservative culture of venture investing: firms were waiting to see proven successes before overhauling their traditional, intuition-driven methods.

Recent qualitative studies provide deeper insight into the mindset of VC practitioners regarding AI. Röhm and colleagues (2022) conducted 17 interviews with early-stage VC investors and academics, mapping the current challenges and opportunities of AI along the VC investment funnel. They found that most VCs were not yet using AI in 2022, although those who did were primarily applying it to make front-end processes like deal sourcing and initial screening more efficient. Investors expressed hope that algorithmic tools could help widen their opportunity set and reduce human biases (for example, by surfacing startups outside their personal networks or mitigating affinity bias in evaluating founders). Importantly, the interviewees predicted a significant increase in VCs' AI adoption in the coming years, driven by emerging third-party software providers offering affordable AI tools designed for VCs (Röhm et al. 2022). This expectation was echoed by Sanchez (2020), who found in interviews with senior management of VC/PE funds a widespread belief that AI adoption was "inevitable" in the industry, despite virtually none of those firms using it at the time. In other words, by 2020 there was a general excitement about AI in venture capital, but it appears to have been more talk than action.

Several recent studies also highlight how AI adoption can shift and enhance VC investment patterns. For example, Rossi (2023) (via interviews with 25 VCs and AI experts) reported a generally positive attitude: VCs felt AI could improve decision-making by handling large data analysis, reducing cognitive bias, and aiding in portfolio monitoring. However, they also emphasized that AI's outputs must be interpreted by experienced investors – here again, human intuition and trust play a critical role, especially in qualitative judgments like assessing a founder's leadership potential (Rossi 2023).

By 2023–2025, some empirical evidence began to confirm a rise in adoption. Ronco and Barontini (2025) surveyed 31 European VCs and observed that AI usage in VC increased markedly after 2022, following the emergence of affordable, off-the-shelf AI tools. Deal sourcing and screening were reported as the most common applications of AI – for instance, using algorithms to scan databases or social media for promising startups, or to automatically filter pitch decks. Their statistical analysis found that VC firms with employees who have strong IT or data science backgrounds were significantly more likely to adopt AI, suggesting that human capital is a key determinant of organizational readiness. Interestingly, respondents noted that while AI tools had noticeably reduced the time spent on due diligence (by automating data gathering and analysis), the overall impact on investment performance remained unclear (Ronco and Barontini 2025). In other words, AI was making the VC workflow faster and potentially more objective, but there wasn't yet evidence that it was leading to better portfolio returns or "smarter" investment choices. This caution aligns with the earlier point that only long-term outcomes will reveal whether AI-assisted decisions outperform purely human decisions in venture investing.

Corroborating this, Bhatia and Dushnitsky (2023) compared the behavior of "data-driven VCs" versus traditional VCs. In their analysis of 20 U.S. VC funds, they found that data-driven VCs (defined as VC organizations explicitly using AI or data analytics in sourcing or evaluation) funded one-third more female-led startups than their traditional peers and backed fewer founders from "elite" educational backgrounds. At the same time, both data-driven VCs and traditional VCs had similar geographic focus (around half of investments in major startup hubs). These findings suggest that algorithmic tools may help venture investors reach beyond some of their inherent biases or network limitations – for example, surfacing strong startups founded by under-represented groups or outside the insiders' club – without fundamentally changing other aspects of their strategy. In a related study, Crumling (2024) provides evidence that adopting data analytics can literally expand a VC's horizons. She found that after VC firms adopt AI or data-driven techniques, they become more likely to invest in startups outside the traditional tech hubs, and notably, those out-of-hub investments show higher success rates (more frequent IPOs or unicorn valuations) compared to the firms' usual in-hub deals. Moreover, by identifying promising startups in emerging regions, these data-savvy VCs helped stimulate more VC activity in those regions over time.

Therefore, the literature on AI adoption in VC paints a picture of a gradual but accelerating change. As of the mid-2020s, AI is no longer an abstract theory but a nascent part of the VC toolkit, primarily used to augment front-end processes like deal sourcing, scouting, and preliminary screening. The consensus across studies is that AI, at its current stage, is best used to complement and support human decision-making, rather than to autonomously pick investments. Many VCs remain cautious, adopting AI one step at a time and rigorously evaluating its outputs against their own judgment. Key determinants of adoption include internal capabilities (having data-savvy team members or a culture open to quantitative methods) and external offerings (the availability of reliable third-party AI platforms tailored to VC needs). There are also persistent challenges noted: data quality and availability can be a constraint, transparency of AI recommendations is often lacking (leading to trust issues), and organizational inertia or "gut feeling" investing traditions can pose resistance (Rossi 2023). Nonetheless, the trajectory is clear. As AI tools continue to improve and success stories emerge, more VC firms are likely to integrate these technologies. Industry analysts even predicted that by 2025, the majority of VC and private equity firms would be using AI in some part of their decision process (Rimol and Costello 2021). While that specific prediction remains to be validated, it is evident that the conversation has shifted from "will AI be used in VC?" to "how AI is being used, and what does it mean for the industry?"

To further summarize the literature and recent contributions, Table 1 presents a selection of the studies on AI's role in VC, along with their key findings.

Thus, while these studies collectively advance our theoretical and practical understanding, there remains a gap regarding detailed, firm-level AI implementation analyses within venture capital settings. Existing studies often lack empirical, context-rich examinations due to difficulties of accessing internal VC processes and proprietary information. Yet such case evidence is crucial to validate and contextualize

Table 1. Key findings from extant literature.

Author(s)	**Year**	**Key Findings**
Arroyo et al.	2019	Machine learning classifiers can predict medium-term success levels of early-stage ventures with up to 82% accuracy and promising precision for high-gain outcomes, offering VC investors a valuable, though potentially biased, tool for portfolio construction.
Bathia and Dushnitsky	2023	Algorithmic sourcing tools can broaden the profile of funded entrepreneurs (more gender and educational diversity) without sacrificing deal quality
Caruso et al.	2015	Deep learning significantly outperforms traditional methods to make investment decisions.
Corea	2019	AI can support venture capital by identifying key predictors of startup success or fundraising likelihood, categorized into personal/team characteristics, financial considerations, and business features.
Corea, Bertinetti and Cervellati	2021	Identified 21 predictive features for startup success (e.g., social media presence, reputation of prior investors, funding amount), demonstrating that machine learning models can highlight key success factors for VCs
Crumling	2024	After adopting AI/data analytics, VCs became more likely to invest in startups outside traditional tech hubs, and those outside-hub investments had higher success rates (more IPOs or unicorn outcomes) than in-hub deals.
Gompers et al.	2020	VC decision-making still relies mostly on human judgment (e.g., emphasis on management team and market) with minimal use of AI or quantitative algorithms as of 2018, indicating data-driven investing was only just beginning to emerge
Jo et al.	2024	AI is presented as a transformative yet ethically complex tool that complements VC decision-making across the investment cycle.
Lyonnet & Stern	2022	Algorithmic tools can support VC investment decisions by reducing cognitive biases and enhancing decision quality, while also introducing new risks and challenges.
Kaplan and Strömberg	2001	Venture capitalists mitigate principal-agent problems through sophisticated contracts, intensive pre-investment screening, and active post-investment monitoring, aligning incentives and control rights with performance contingencies to support venture success.
Maurer et al.	2024	Practical system implementation tailored to VC needs. It boosts VC efficiency by accurately auto-rejecting low-potential founders, reducing workload while maintaining high recall.
Mishra et al.	2017	Analytical process reflects evolving global VC decision-making patterns.
Rettarath	2020	Recommends an augmented model where AI handles initial screening (deal filtering) and human VCs focus on final evaluation, leveraging AI to improve efficiency without replacing human judgment.
Röhm et al.	2022	AI primarily used for sourcing/screening; predicts accelerated adoption.
Ronco and Barontini	2025	Increased AI use, primarily for deal screening. AI enhances early-stage investment decisions by increasing deal flow efficiency and supporting—but not replacing—human judgment in VC processes
Ross et al.	2021	VCs use AI to enhance decision speed and consistency, but remain cautious about over-reliance due to trust, control, and interpretability concerns.
Rossi	2023	Positive views of AI; emphasizes human intuition's ongoing role.
Sanchez	2020	AI is valued for portfolio firms but underused internally in PE/VC, with growing awareness of its future potential and data-driven advantages.
Scabbio	2022	Early-stage exploration prevalent among VC firms.
Setty et al.	2024	Customization significantly reduces investment risk. AI enables more inclusive and data-driven VC funding, helping reduce biases and expand access for underrepresented founders.

the optimistic models proposed in the literature. This chapter addresses this gap by providing an in-depth case study of NEVA SGR, thus grounding theoretical discussions in concrete organizational practices.

Research Design and Methodology

To investigate the impact of AI on the VC investment decision-making process, a qualitative case study design was adopted, following the principle of "extreme case sampling" (Patton 2015, p. 230), which emphasizes the value of information-rich cases that offer strong manifestations of the phenomenon under study. The case of NEVA SGR was selected due to its pioneering experimentation with AI tools in the Italian venture capital landscape.

Four semi-structured interviews were conducted between December 2024 and April 2025 with key informants from NEVA SGR directly involved in the strategic adoption and operational implementation of AI. Participants included Mario Costantini (Chief Executive Officer), Matteo Colombo (ESG Team Manager and Research and Innovation), and Pietro Previtali (former member of the Board of Directors). Each provided detailed insights into NEVA's AI strategy and usage. All interviews were conducted in Italian, lasted between 45 and 90 minutes, and were recorded with participants' informed consent. The audio recordings were subsequently transcribed verbatim.

To complement and triangulate the primary data, a range of secondary sources was reviewed, including press coverage in business journals (e.g., Il Sole 24 Ore), the official NEVA SGR website, corporate presentations, and industry news articles. These documents provided context on the VC firm and its public positioning regarding AI.

Table 2 provides an overview of the interviews, including informant names, roles, dates and places of the interviews.

To ensure linguistic and conceptual accuracy, a back-translation procedure was implemented (Brislin 1970; Son 2018), translating relevant quotations into English and verifying semantic consistency across languages. This framework provides a structured way to examine where AI tools are being applied. Prior studies suggest that the screening phase might be the most receptive to AI support, followed by

Table 2. Overview of conducted interviews.

Interviewee	Role	Number of interviews	Duration	Where
Mario Costantini	CEO	1	75 min	Officine Grandi Riparazioni - Torino
Matteo Colombo	ESG Manager, R&I	1	90 min	Officine Grandi Riparazioni - Torino
Pietro Previtali	Former Board Member	2	45 min - 60 min	University of Pavia - Pavia Officine Grandi Riparazioni - Torino

elements of deal sourcing and evaluation. For instance, Jain (2018) analyzed each of the six steps for AI feasibility and concluded that deal selection (sourcing/screening) is the phase most suited for AI usage, followed by valuations/due diligence, then post-investment value-add, then sourcing, exits, and lastly deal structuring. In other words, the front-end of the funnel (selecting which startups to consider) ranked highest for AI potential, whereas negotiations and deal structuring, which are highly interpersonal and case-specific, ranked lowest.

The interview protocol covered each stage of the investment process, asking NEVA's team where (if at all) they employ AI, what tools are used, and what benefits or challenges have emerged. We also explored broader questions such as the motivation behind adopting AI, how the team was trained or educated on these tools, what internal policies govern their use, and how AI outputs are integrated with human decision-making.

The analysis followed a grounded theory approach (Glaser and Strauss 2017; Charmaz 2006), iteratively analyzing the data through open, axial, and selective coding phases. The goal was to inductively identify recurring themes, contrasts, and explanatory patterns related to AI's role in the VC investment process. Codes were both data-driven and literature-informed, allowing to align emerging insights with prior theoretical contributions.

As an organizing structure, the VC investment process was decomposed into six stages, following a model adapted from Kaplan and Strömberg (2001) and Wright and Robbie (1998). These stages are presented in Figure 1 and include: (1) Deal Sourcing & Generation, (2) Deal Screening, (3) Evaluation & Due Diligence, (4) Deal Approval & Structuring, (5) Monitoring & Assisting, and (6) Exit.

This structure informed both the interview design and the coding scheme, facilitating a systematic exploration of where and how AI tools are integrated into the investment process. Prior studies suggest that the screening phase might be the most receptive to AI support, followed by elements of deal sourcing and evaluation. For instance, Jain (2018) analyzed each of the six steps for AI feasibility

Figure 1. Stages of the Venture Capital Investment Process (adapted from Kaplan and Strömberg 2001; Wright and Robbie 1998).

and concluded that *deal selection* (sourcing/screening) is the phase most suited for AI usage, followed by valuations/due diligence, then post-investment value-add, then sourcing, exits, and lastly deal structuring. In other words, the front-end of the funnel (selecting which startups to consider) ranked highest for AI potential, whereas negotiations and deal structuring, which are highly interpersonal and case-specific, ranked lowest.

The interview protocol covered each stage of the investment process, asking NEVA's team where (if at all) they employ AI, what tools are used, and what benefits or challenges have emerged. We also explored broader questions such as the motivation behind adopting AI, how the team was trained or educated on these tools, what internal policies govern their use, and how AI outputs are integrated with human decision-making.

The Case Study: NEVA SGR

As the venture capital subsidiary of Intesa Sanpaolo, NEVA SGR sits at the intersection of a traditional banking group and the fast-moving startup world. The firm was established in 2019 and launched its first fund (Neva First) in 2020 with €250 million in assets under management, focusing on investments in innovative sectors such as life sciences, energy transition, digital transformation, advanced manufacturing, and aerospace – areas aligned with Intesa's strategic interest in supporting key industries of the future. By 2024, NEVA SGR had fully invested this first fund's capital across a portfolio of startups and had begun raising new funds (Neva II and Neva II Italia) targeting a combined €500 million. This rapid scaling underscores NEVA's ambition: as President Luca Remmert stated in an interview, the firm aspires to move from being a leading player in Italy to being a significant VC investor at the European level (D'Ascenzo 2024).

NEVA's heritage and leadership help explain its strong orientation toward innovation and technology adoption. The CEO, Mario Costantini, holds an engineering degree with a specialization in neural networks and robotics, and spent two decades driving digital innovation projects before transitioning into venture capital. He led Intesa Sanpaolo's Innovation Center from 2014 to 2019, which involved scouting new technologies and fostering innovation within the banking group. In that capacity, Costantini was exposed to cutting-edge developments globally, forging connections in tech hubs like Israel and Silicon Valley, and cultivating an appreciation for how emerging technologies could reshape large organizations. When NEVA was formed, he "*guided the constitution of Neva SGR*" (Costantini, interview) and the design of its funds, effectively embedding this innovation-driven mindset into the DNA of the new VC firm. It comes as little surprise, then, that NEVA's leadership began exploring the use of AI from the very inception of the firm. As Costantini noted in our interview, "*Surely artificial intelligence allows you to profoundly review organizations. The development of AI agents in particular makes it possible to classify and target tasks very specifically, and in effect the goal can be to gradually replace activities that before were done naturally by people.*"

Such a mindset illustrates NEVA's receptivity to agentic AI. Rather than viewing AI as just a fancy spreadsheet or a static tool, NEVA's CEO sees it as something that could potentially take on roles within the organization. At the same time, NEVA's approach is moderated by a realistic understanding of organizational challenges and responsibilities. Costantini acknowledged that whenever there is a technological transition, *"people must add new value... as technology's added value increases, it forces the human added value to be higher."* In other words, adopting AI requires upskilling and shifting human roles rather than eliminating the human element. He stressed that in large organizations (like Intesa San Paolo), introducing such novelties can be difficult, citing the need to navigate labor relations and the inertia of established processes. This perspective likely influenced how NEVA chose to implement AI, with careful steps, ensuring that the team is prepared and that the technology is brought in as a partner to humans, not an overnight replacement.

Given NEVA's intimate connection with a leading European bank, another background factor is data security and compliance. Financial institutions are typically cautious about data governance, and NEVA SGR has strict rules on how confidential information (such as deal memos or client data) is handled. This context made NEVA aware from the start that using cloud-based AI services could pose risks if not managed properly. Thus, NEVA SGR entered the world of venture capital with an unusual blend of characteristics: a new firm with a mandate to be innovative, backed by a large, traditional financial institution; a leadership team deeply knowledgeable about technology; and a set of strategic priorities (target sectors, global outreach) requiring it to stay at the forefront of trends. This combination set the stage for NEVA to be an early adopter of AI in its operations.

Motivation and Early Vision

From the outset, NEVA's leadership viewed AI as a transformative force that could redefine how the firm operates. NEVA's CEO stated that the idea of introducing AI emerged quite naturally as they were setting up the firm's processes. Given his previous experience driving innovation at a large bank, Costantini was well aware of AI's growing capabilities and did not want NEVA to fall behind. He remarked that *"today an organization must ask itself: in the various operational and business areas I oversee, how can AI agents replace the activities being done by people? It's not just a legitimate question – it's a necessary one"* (Costantini, interview). This comment exemplifies a proactive approach: NEVA did not wait for external pressure or vendor pitches to try AI. Instead, its CEO pushed the idea internally that the company should pursue AI applications to stay ahead of the curve.

It is important to note that Costantini's motive was *not* to eliminate human roles per se, but rather to augment the team's capabilities and efficiency. He framed AI adoption as an opportunity to *"rethink work to add more value,"* freeing up his investors so they could focus on higher-order tasks. Costantini gave an example that resonated strongly with his team: using AI could *"lighten the solitude of those who have to make a decision"* by providing a kind of intelligent sounding board or second opinion. In other words, venture investors often make tough calls under uncertainty, and it can be a lonely judgment call. AI, in the form of a conversational analytics agent, could serve as a partner to bounce ideas off. Indeed, Costantini described how an investor could interact with such an AI agent during decision-making: *"you can even play by saying [to the AI] that you are Warren Buffett, and… ask it to make the negative case, ask for the positive case, ask it to pose questions to you. The key point is how good you are at interacting so it's not a one-way question-and-answer, but a real dialogue."* In practice, he noted, the quality of insights from these tools depends on the user's skill in prompting and probing. Essentially, an emerging new skill set for investment professionals. NEVA's leadership thus saw AI not as an autopilot, but as a *"copilot"* that could challenge and enhance a human investor's thinking.

Crucially, Costantini also conveyed this vision in a way that inspired urgency. In our interview, he put it like this "[…] *not using AI in today's venture market would be like choosing a rowboat when others have motorboats."* By this he meant that ignoring AI tools would leave a VC painfully slow and disadvantaged compared to competitors turbocharged with technology. NEVA's team took this message to heart, with one board member humorously remarking that Costantini's stance resembled a "*masterclass*" capable of motivating any cautious investors into action (Previtali, interview).

Implementation Approach: Two Platforms for Two Data Worlds

Having decided to pursue AI, NEVA faced strategic choices on *how* to implement it. A key decision was whether to build proprietary AI systems in-house or leverage external solutions. NEVA SGR made a strategic decision to split their AI toolkit into two distinct environments, each handling a different "*world*" of data: public data versus private data. This dual approach was central to their strategy and is a defining feature of the case.

Costantini explained: *"We realized we needed essentially two platforms – one that works on public data, and one on sensitive data – with two similar but different purposes."* The logic was as follows. The first one works with public data (external), it is a platform that would leverage powerful external AI services (like large language model tools available via the cloud) to scrutinize and analyze information that is publicly available or non-confidential. It was conceived as an "*augmented Google*" (Costantini, interview) – a supercharged research assistant for the investment team. The tasks for this platform include exploring market trends, mapping emerging technologies, gathering competitive intelligence on sectors, scanning news and scientific publications for signals relevant to NEVA's investment themes, and generally helping formulate investment theses. Essentially, this AI platform acts as the firm's radar, continuously surveying the vast external environment for insights that could inform where and how NEVA invests. Because it deals with open information, using an external cloud-based AI (like OpenAI's GPT-4 or similar) is acceptable; there is no risk if these queries become part of the AI model's training data, since they contain no proprietary secrets. Colombo noted that on this public side, *"you definitely have nothing confidential… if you identify, say, the cybersecurity market and want evidence on forecasts or key players – these things are published; nothing is secret."* In practice, NEVA's team would use this platform by inputting prompts or questions about industries or technologies of interest and receiving synthesized analyses.

The second platform is instead for private data. Parallel to the above, NEVA is training a secure, internal AI system to handle any information that is sensitive, confidential, or proprietary. This includes internal documents (e.g., detailed due diligence reports, investment committee memos, legal documents from deals), data from startups that might be shared under NDA, and paid databases or market research that NEVA subscribes to. The purpose of this internal platform is to allow NEVA's team to query and analyze their *private knowledge base* with the assistance of AI, without any risk of that data leaking to outsiders or being used to train external models. To create this, NEVA set up what Costantini described as *"a big data folder… a repository of documents that is reserved and secure, with controlled access."* This folder is situated in a contained environment – a third-party solution with guarantees of data isolation. By feeding all relevant internal documents into this system, NEVA enables sophisticated search and natural-language querying over their own data. A concrete early application of this was automating parts of the *investment memorandum writing*. When NEVA makes an investment, they produce a formal write-up documenting the decision and rationale. Colombo noted that since these memos contain confidential company information, they use the internal platform to assist in drafting them. The AI can produce a first draft or outline based on the data provided, which the team then edits. This has started to "*simplify the production of minutes and reports*," freeing up investor time for deeper thinking.

Between these two platforms, NEVA essentially covers the spectrum of their informational needs, external intelligence gathering and internal knowledge management. Importantly, the two are connected in workflow. The firm envisions a phase 1 where the public-data AI helps them gather external insights and identify what they do not know, followed by a phase 2 where internal and expert sources fill those gaps. Costantini gave an illustrative scenario. Suppose NEVA is exploring a new investment trend (e.g., quantum computing applications). In phase 1, the team uses the external AI tool to learn the basics (state of the market, recent developments, key players) by querying it and obtaining a concise overview. This helps them formulate specific questions and identify what further information is needed. Then, as he said, *"pretend I went to the University of Pavia and got answers to the questions I had,"* meaning the team might consult domain experts or purchase a detailed study (bringing human expertise into the loop). All those findings, including reports or datasets obtained, then go into the confidential repository. At that point, in phase 2, NEVA can use the internal AI to dig deeper: *"I can take those answers, put them in a database of confidential information, add also legal docs, paid databases, etc., and then use an AI tool that does not access the internet but works exclusively on the data I've given it… I interact with it in natural language, and it makes the information usable and more correlated"* (Costantini, interview).

Through this two-step process, NEVA maximizes the strengths of both external and internal AI. The external AI is excellent for broad discovery and ideation. It is like casting a wide net into the ocean of global information. The internal AI is excellent for precision and depth on the information NEVA truly cares about, including the confidential details of potential investments. The outputs of both ultimately feed into the *human decision-making* stage.

To operationalize this dual-platform approach, NEVA had to establish clear policies and training. Colombo emphasized that one of their first actions was to create an internal AI usage policy, which, while confidential in detail, covered key principles. The policy instructs team members on issues such as not entering any confidential or personal data into the external AI tools to avoid inadvertent leakage; using strong authentication and access control for the internal system; awareness of AI limitations like the possibility of hallucinating incorrect facts; and verifying AI-generated content. Essentially, NEVA trained its staff to approach AI output critically. They also ensured compliance with privacy regulations, given Europe's stringent GDPR; for example, if any personal data were to be analyzed, it must be done in line with privacy rules (Colombo mentioned attention to personal data as part of their precautions).

One notable aspect of NEVA's implementation is the collaboration with external vendors/partners to build these platforms. Although NEVA did not publicly disclose specific vendor names (and Colombo noted internal policies could not be shared externally), the interview hints that NEVA used solutions from "*primary vendors*" for advanced features like deep search and AI agents. It is likely that NEVA partnered with a major cloud provider or AI company to set up the internal LLM environment, possibly using a framework that allows fine-tuning or deploying models on NEVA's data while ensuring isolation. By leveraging such partnerships, NEVA avoided having to hire a large in-house AI engineering team; instead, they focused on configuring and using the tools to suit their needs. This underscores the earlier point about moving away from purely internal builds. NEVA didn't try to code their own language model from scratch; they stood on the shoulders of giants but in a way tailored to their context.

Use Cases

As of 2025, NEVA SGR has two primary AI use cases in active operation, with more on the horizon. The first use case revolves around investment thesis development and trend analysis which essentially translates into deal sourcing and generation. The second is in operational efficiency for documentation, like drafting investment memos (as mentioned) and potentially other administrative text generation.

Investment thesis research and trend analysis are considered NEVA's *core business application* of AI, in Costantini's words. Before even looking at individual deals, NEVA spends time identifying the right *"trends of the moment to intercep*t." For example, determining which sub-sectors in biotech or fintech are most promising given current technological trajectories. To do this, the investment team traditionally would read extensively, attend conferences, consult experts, and iterate on hypotheses. Now, with their AI tools, they can accelerate that process. NEVA's public-data AI platform will allow the team to perform deep research in a fraction of the time. An investor can prompt the AI with a broad question like, "What are emerging problems and solutions in the field of autonomous vehicle safety?" and get a synthesized report drawing on recent articles, industry news, and even technical blogs. They can then drill down: "Who are the top 5 startups in Europe working on this?" The AI can list names and what is publicly known about them. Previously, gathering that information might require manually searching many sources and piecing it together. NEVA has effectively given each team member a powerful research assistant. The AI can also be used for forecasting and data analysis on public info. Colombo gave an example that if they want market size projections or to identify key players, the AI can often pull that together from reports (though if a source is behind a paywall, they might need to obtain the report and then feed it to the internal system).

One particularly creative way NEVA intends to use AI is as a collaborative partner in decision-making processes. Costantini described how an investor might engage in a dialogue with the AI, asking it to critique an investment idea. By shifting perspectives, the AI assists the human in considering viewpoints they might have overlooked, effectively simulating a debate. Costantini emphasized that the capacity to produce both a "negative version" and a "positive version" of the scenario, as well as to have the AI pose tough questions to the investor, is extremely valuable. It pushes the team to enhance their investment rationale and to recognize potential biases.

The second use case in active use is leveraging AI on NEVA's internal documents. After making several investments, NEVA accumulates a lot of knowledge – company reports, meeting minutes, performance data, and so on. The internal AI platform allows them to tap into this repository quickly. A concrete example is preparing the *minutes of investment committee meetings*. Colombo mentioned that after they make an investment decision, formal minutes need to be written for governance purposes, which summarize the discussion and reasons. This can be somewhat formulaic and time-consuming for the team to write from scratch each time. With their AI system, they can input bullet points or transcripts of the meeting and have the AI generate a well-structured draft of the minutes. Because this content is sensitive (containing names, financial details, etc.), it is done entirely in the secure internal environment. The output still gets reviewed and polished by a human, but it significantly cuts down the editing time. Over multiple iterations, the AI will also learn NEVA's preferred writing style or terminology, becoming more accurate in how it formulates these documents.

While the above are initial focuses, NEVA clearly sees many more applications. As Costantini puts it, *"the number of things that can be done with these agents can touch truly every corner of the organization."* By late 2024, NEVA had consciously prioritized the two use cases (thesis research and document drafting) as starting points, but with an intent to "*progressively see what else can be tested and pushed*" (Colombo, interview). This iterative approach – pick a couple of high-impact, manageable applications first, then expand – seems to be working well for them. Colombo noted that *"today we have chosen these two, and then gradually we'll see what else to test,"* reflecting a methodical scaling up rather than trying to do everything at once.

NEVA's experience also highlights how AI can alter the pace of venture work. Decisions that might have taken weeks of back-and-forth can potentially be made faster because information gathering is faster. However, NEVA has been careful not to rush critical decisions; the AI speeds up the preparation, giving more time for the team to deliberate on the implications. In practice, they might still take the same amount of time to make an investment decision, but a larger portion of that time is now spent on high-level analysis and discussion, rather than low-level research drudgery.

Perhaps most importantly, NEVA's case illustrates a mindset change. AI is not viewed with fear or as a gimmick, but as an inevitable and valuable evolution of the venture capital toolkit.

The VC Investment Phases

All interviewees agreed that the primary purpose of NEVA's AI applications is to increase operational efficiency in handling deal flow. In practical terms, AI enables the team to filter through far more information and opportunities than they otherwise could, focusing investor attention on a narrower set of high-potential deals. Another benefit is that the AI can proactively recommends deals that align with the VC's strategy. Thus, the technology helps NEVA *"keep their specialization"* by not wasting time on off-thesis deals.

In line with prior literature, the AI's impact has therefore been most present in the deal sourcing and screening phases. NEVA's external AI tools can scan the environment for new startups and relevant developments. For instance, the AI collects general information on companies from websites and public data, information from LinkedIn or news, data on funding rounds and patents from databases, and even sentiment or market interest from social media or web trends. All this happens automatically in the background, creating profiles on many startups. The investment team then can receive these AI-curated prospects and can quickly decide which ones warrant a closer look. In such cases, the only way to pursue the deal is through personal connection – which NEVA's partners then initiate. Costantini highlighted this interplay: the AI can surface a hidden gem, but *"the only chance to actually get that deal is if you have personal connections with the founders."* Thus, even in sourcing, AI and human networks complement each other.

During deal screening, NEVA's AI assists in evaluating the initial fit of opportunities. As soon as basic data on a startup is available, NEVA's internal database (augmented by AI) will match it against the firm's criteria and also compare it with historical cases. Thus, at the screening stage, the AI functions like an analyst who has meticolously reviewed all available info to inform the investors. Still, the decision to move a deal forward remains with the investors, based on their understanding and expertise.

In the evaluation and due diligence phase, NEVA's internal AI system, once properly trained and available, will come into play more. When the team enters detailed due diligence on a company, they accumulate a lot of documents and notes (i.e., financial models, technical reviews). The AI will be employed to organize and summarize this information. By late-stage due diligence, however, the involvement of AI will diminish. The decision relies on nuanced judgments of the founder's character, the VC's intuition regarding market timing, or the negotiation of terms, none of which are directly handled by AI.

Figure 2. Stages of the Venture Capital Investment Process – NEVA SGR AI's use case.

NEVA has not yet applied AI in the deal approval and structuring, in the post-investment monitoring and assisting phases, nor in the exit phase. Figure 2 reports the Stages of the Venture Capital Investment Process applied to NEVA SGR case.

Discussion

NEVA SGR's implementation of AI offers several insights that both reinforce and challenge the emerging narratives in the literature about AI in venture capital.

One clear theme from NEVA's case is that AI has been used to augment human decision-making, not to replace it. This aligns with the prevailing view among scholars and practitioners that AI in professional domains works best as a *complement* to human expertise (Huang and Rust 2018). At NEVA, every step of AI use ultimately loops back to human judgment. This resonates with the widespread idea that AI handles an expanded workload of analysis and information processing, allowing humans to focus on synthesizing insights and making nuanced judgments. In NEVA's own framing, the AI "*lightens the solitude*" of decision-makers but does not make the decision for them.

The literature has often debated whether algorithms might replace venture capitalists (some provocative articles ask, "Will AI be the next VC?"), but NEVA's experience underscores that *contextual understanding and strategic decision-making remain human domains*. Even as the AI produces trend analyses or risk lists, it is the team's collective experience and vision that decide which opportunities to pursue.

NEVA's two-platform architecture exemplifies a middle path between fully in-house AI and fully outsourced AI. This is an important contribution to the discussion on how organizations implement AI. Early adopters like SignalFire built everything internally for competitive secrecy, whereas some newer funds might lean on generic tools entirely. NEVA shows a hybrid model: use external AI where it's generic and powerful (taking advantage of billions of parameters trained on internet data), but create an internal custom-made system, leveraging on a third-party AI expert or provider, for what is unique to the firm.

The literature review noted that the dominant narrative of recent years was the rise of proprietary VC algorithms and the eclipse of gut instinct. NEVA's case provides a nuanced counterpoint. Yes, data and algorithms are playing a bigger role (NEVA certainly is far more data-driven now than a comparable firm would have been a decade ago). But this has not eradicated intuition or personal judgment; rather, it has shifted their timing and role. NEVA's use of AI in deal sourcing might reduce some of the bias of only seeing deals through personal networks (a common limitation of traditional VC). They are now exposed to a more global set of opportunities flagged by AI scanning. In that sense, it moves them away from a purely network-driven, internal deal flow model towards a more open, thesis-driven model. That challenges a long-standing norm in venture capital that personal referrals dominate sourcing. If AI can help find promising companies beyond one's immediate network, it could lead to a more meritocratic deal flow and potentially more diversity in what gets funded. However, NEVA's approach also shows respect for the qualitative elements. After the AI will find or analyze something, the team will still engage in deep discussion, applying their experience, and seeking human experts (like academics) for validation. This indicates a blended model of decision-making rather than a wholesale replacement of "gut feel" with "data." It might be described as *informed intuition*: the intuition is still there, but it's informed by a greater breadth of data.

Finally, the NEVA case provides a reality check on some of the more futuristic visions, such as fully autonomous VC decision-making or "agentic AI" investors (Fairview 2024). While it's tempting to imagine an AI that could run a VC fund on its own, NEVA's experience suggests we are quite far from that scenario. When asked about the possibility of an AI making independent investment decisions, Costantini was skeptical not on technical grounds, but on strategic ones. He believes that even if an AI could crunch all numbers, it would lack the *strategic narrative* sensemaking and the trust-building ability with founders that a good VC has. Moreover, in a competitive market, if everyone had the same AI, differentiation would again come down to human elements, who can, for example, persuade a founder to accept their term sheet. NEVA's stance is that AI will increasingly handle the analytical heavy-lifting and perhaps even some transactional processes, but the art of venture investing which includes intuition, creativity, and relationships will remain human for the foreseeable future. Put in other words, the winners will be those who effectively combine AI strengths with human strengths.

That said, NEVA is keeping an eye on developments in agentic AI. If AI agents become capable of autonomously conducting tasks like sourcing deals, conducting due diligence conversations, or negotiating, it could disrupt aspects of the VC job. NEVA's proactive approach suggests they would probably experiment with such agents early. Indeed, Costantini's quote about AI agents replacing tasks shows he is thinking along this direction. The firm anticipates a progressive evolution. Initially, AI would help in analysis (current state), then it might assist in decision simulations (e.g., scenario testing), and eventually it could undertake more responsibilities when deemed reliable.

The NEVA case confirms key observations about AI in venture capital: it is promising for sourcing and screening, yet adoption remains limited and human judgment still dominates. At the same time, NEVA adds nuance by illustrating a hybrid implementation strategy, the cultural challenges of adoption, and how AI may raise expectations for human performance. It offers a concrete example of an AI-augmented VC firm, highlighting both practical benefits and obstacles. From a theoretical standpoint, it shows that the traditionally heuristic-driven VC decision process can integrate algorithmic support without losing its core character. Classic VC decision-making models could be updated to show how AI insights inform each stage. It doesn't rewrite the process, but it changes the information environment at each stage.

Conclusion

Artificial Intelligence is no longer a distant prospect or mere buzzword in the venture capital industry; it is a present reality that forward-looking firms are actively dealing with. This chapter examined how AI is being implemented in VC through an in-depth case study of NEVA SGR, offering a grounded perspective on what AI can and cannot do in this domain. NEVA's experience demonstrates that AI can substantially improve the efficiency of deal sourcing, screening, and analysis, enabling investors to handle more opportunities with greater speed and information. Through a hybrid approach of external and internal AI systems, NEVA was able to harness advanced tools while safeguarding its proprietary knowledge, charting a practical path that other VC firms might emulate. Interestingly, the introduction of AI at NEVA did not alter the fundamentals of venture investing. Human judgment, shaped by experience and personal relationships, remains the decisive factor in deals. AI serves as an augmenting force, providing data-driven inputs and drafts that enhance the humans' capabilities.

This chapter opens avenues for further research. A single case study, no matter how detailed, is but one data point. It would be valuable to examine other VC firms, perhaps in different regions or of different sizes, to see how they approach AI. Quantitative research could also be done in the future to correlate AI adoption with performance metrics like deal sourcing efficiency, due diligence time, or portfolio returns (though the latter would require multi-year data). There is also room to study the *human* side: how does the role of a VC analyst or partner change when AI is introduced? Does it require new skills (as NEVA's case suggests, skill in interacting with AI becomes important)? Are there generational differences in adoption (perhaps younger investors adapt faster)? These questions can be explored through interviews or surveys across the industry.

In conclusion, the integration of AI into venture capital, as exemplified by NEVA SGR, appears to be a path of evolution rather than revolution. An evolution where the fundamental goals of VC remain the same, such as finding and funding great startups, but the tools and methods to achieve them are significantly enhanced. NEVA's case demonstrates that embracing AI can lead to a more informed, efficient, and potentially foresighted investment process, without discarding the qualitative insights and relationships that define venture capital. For the venture capital industry at large, the message is clear. AI is here to stay, and those who learn to harness it – thoughtfully and ethically – will shape the future of investing.

References

Arroyo, J., Corea, F., Jimenez-Diaz, G. and Recio-Garcia, J. A. 2019. Assessment of machine learning performance for decision support in venture capital investments. IEEE Access 7: 124233–124243.

Bhatia, A. and Dushnitsky, G. 2023. The future of venture capital? Insights into data-driven VCs. Calif. Manage. Rev. 65: 5–22.

Caruso, C., Enriquez, F., Oshotse, A. and Pradeep, G. 2015. Algorithmic venture capital: Predicting valuation step-up multiple in venture backed companies through deep learning techniques. Available at: http://cs230.stanford.edu/projects_fall_2020/reports/55791766.pdf.

Charmaz, K. 2006. Constructing Grounded Theory: A Practical Guide Through Qualitative Analysis. SAGE Publications, London.

Corea, F. 2019. AI and venture capital. In An Introduction to Data, Studies in Big Data, Vol. 50. Springer Cham.

Corea, F., Bertinetti, G. and Cervellati, E. M. 2021. Hacking the venture industry: An early-stage startups investment framework for data-driven investors. Mach. Learn. Appl. 5: 100062.

Crumling, M. 2024. Breaking network barriers in the era of data-driven venture capitalists. SSRN Working Paper No. 4941953.

D'Ascenzo, M. 2024. Neva Sgr lancia due nuovi fondi da 500 milioni di euro. Il Sole 24 Ore. Retrieved on 15th April 2025. Available at: https://www.ilsole24ore.com/art/neva-sgr-lancia-due-nuovi-fondi-500-milioni-euro-AFDUjGzD.

Ernst and Young. 2024. Large AI deals boost investment in 2024 VC market. Retrieved on April 9th, 2025. Available at: https://www.ey.com/en_us/insights/growth/venture-capital-investment-trends.

Fairview. 2024. Preparing for the agentic AI era in venture capital. Retrieved from: https://fairview.cdn.prismic.io/fairview/Zw7p3YF3NbkBXe02_Fairview-PreparingfortheAgenticAIErainVentureCapital.pdf.

Gil, Y. and Perrault, R. 2025. Artificial Intelligence Index Report 2025. Stanford University. https://hai-production.s3.amazonaws.com/files/hai_ai_index_report_2025.pdf.

Glaser, B. G. and Strauss, A. L. 2017. Discovery of Grounded Theory: Strategies for Qualitative Research. Routledge, Abingdon.

Gompers, P. A., Gornall, W., Kaplan, S. N. and Strebulaev, I. A. 2020. How do venture capitalists make decisions? J. Financ. Econ. 135: 169–190

Gompers, P. A., Kaplan, S. N. and Mukharlyamov, V. 2016. What do private equity firms say they do? J. Financ. Econ. 121(3): 449–476.

Hisrich, R. D. and Jankowicz, A. D. 1990. Intuition in venture capital decisions: An exploratory study using a new technique. J. Bus. Venturing 5: 49–62.

Huang, M. H. and Rust, R. T. 2018. Artificial intelligence in service. J. Serv. Res. 21: 155–172.

Jain, C. 2018. Artificial intelligence in venture capital industry: Opportunities and risks. Doctoral dissertation, Massachusetts Institute of Technology. http://hdl.handle.net/1721.1/118544.

Jo, H., Juarez, A., Rossi, A., Strauss, C. and Ressler, L. 2024. The impact of artificial intelligence on venture capital sourcing and due diligence. Glob. J. Entrep. 8(Special Issue 1): 11–31. ISSN: 2574-0415.

Kaplan, S. N. and Strömberg, P. 2001. Venture capitalists as principals: Contracting, screening, and monitoring. Am. Econ. Rev. 91(2): 426–430. https://www.jstor.org/stable/2677802.

KPMG. 2025. Venture Pulse Q4 2024. Retrieved 9th April 2025. Available at: https://kpmg.com/xx/en/our-insights/operations/venture-pulse-q4-2024.html.

Lyonnet, V. and Stern, L. H. 2022. Venture capital (mis)allocation in the age of AI. In Proc. EUROFIDAI-ESSEC Paris December Finance Meeting.

Maurer, M., Buz, T., Dremel, C. and de Melo, G. 2024. Design and evaluation of an AI augmented screening system for venture capitalists. Paper Presented at the Eur. Conf. Inf. Syst. (ECIS 2024), Paphos, Cyprus.

Mishra, S., Bag, D. and Misra, S. 2017. Venture capital investment choice: Multicriteria decision matrix. J. Priv. Equity 20(2): 52–68.

Patton, M. Q. 2015. Qualitative Research & Evaluation Methods: Integrating Theory and Practice. SAGE Publications, Thousand Oaks.

Purdy, M. 2024. What is agentic AI, and how will it change work? Harvard Bus. Rev. Retrieved from: https://hbr.org/2024/12/what-is-agentic-ai-and-how-will-it-change-work.

Retterath, A. 2020. Human versus computer: Benchmarking venture capitalists and machine learning algorithms for investment screening. SSRN Working Paper No. 3706119.

Rimol, M. and Costello, K. 2021. Gartner says tech investors will prioritize data science and artificial intelligence above "gut feel" for investment decisions by 2025. Gartner Press Release. Retrieved from: https://www.gartner.com/en/newsroom/press-releases/2021-03-10-gartner-says-tech-investors-will-prioritize-data-science-and-artificial-intelligence-above-gut-feel-for-investment-decisions-by-20250.

Ronco, U. and Barontini, R. 2025. Artificial intelligence in venture capital operations: An empirical analysis. Sant'Anna Sch. Adv. Stud. Inst. Manag. Pap. Ser., Winter Issue.

Ross, G., Das, S., Sciro, D. and Raza, H. 2021. Capital VX: A machine learning model for startup selection and exit prediction. J. Finance Data Sci. 7: 94–114.

Rossi, I. 2023. The role of AI in accelerating venture capital decision-making. Digit. Transform. Admin. Innov. 1(1): 46–54.

Röhm, S., Bick, M. and Boeckle, M. 2022. The impact of artificial intelligence on the investment decision process in venture capital firms. *In*: Degen, H. and Ntoa, S. (eds.). Artif. Intell. HCI, Lect. Notes Comput. Sci., Vol. 13336. Springer.

Sanchez, O. 2020. The Role of Artificial Intelligence in Investment Decision Making: A Study of Senior Management Perceptions Within Private Equity and Venture Capital Firms. Doctoral dissertation, National College of Ireland.

Scabbio. 2022. Exploring the adoption of artificial intelligence in venture capital: Current status and opportunities. Master's thesis. Copenhagen Business School. https://research-api.cbs.dk/ws/portalfiles/portal/92143006/1518505_MT_Scabbio_148657.pdf.

Setty, R., Elovici, Y. and Schwartz, D. 2024. Cost-sensitive machine learning to support startup investment decisions. Intell. Syst. Account. Finance Manag. 31(1): e1548.

Struta, I. 2024. How top VCs are placing their growing AI bets. S&P Global Market Intell. https://www.spglobal.com/market-intelligence/en/news-insights/research/how-top-vcs-are-placing-their-growing-ai-bets.

Stryker, C. 2023. Agentic AI: 4 reasons why it's the next big thing in AI research. IBM Think Blog. Retrieved from: https://www.ibm.com/think/insights/agentic-ai.

Sun, W., Zhao, Y. and Sun, L. 2020. Big data analytics for venture capital application: Towards innovation performance improvement. Int. J. Inf. Manag. 50: 557–565.

Tricot, R. 2021. Venture capital investments in artificial intelligence. OECD Digit. Econ. Pap. 319: 1–46.

Trocha, B. 2019. Data-driven VCs: How 83 venture capital firms use data, AI & proprietary software to drive alpha returns. Medium. Retrieved from: https://medium.com/hackernoon/winning-by-eating-their-owndogs-food-83-venture-capital-firms-using-data-ai-proprietary-da92b81b85ef.

Tursunbayeva, A. and Gal, H. C. B. 2024. Adoption of artificial intelligence: A TOP framework-based checklist for digital leaders. Bus. Horiz. 67: 357–368.

Wang, Y. M. and Xue, L. 2022. Application of decision tree algorithm in early entrepreneurial project screening. Sci. Program. 2022(1).

Wright, M. and Robbie, K. 1998. Venture capital and private equity: A review and synthesis. J. Bus. Finance Account. 25(5–6): 521–570.

Chapter 10

How AI Tools could Transform Research Methods in Organization, Business, and Management

A Review of Techniques and Emerging Trends

*Riccardo Coda, Arianna Ciabattoni** and *Francesca Ricciardi*

Introduction

Artificial Intelligence (AI) has rapidly evolved from a niche area of computer science into a pervasive and transformative force across the scientific and organizational landscape. Its roots trace back to the early computational theories of the 20th century, grounded in formal logic, algorithmic modeling, and the ambition to replicate or simulate human reasoning through machines. Over the decades, AI has diversified into a wide range of paradigms, including symbolic reasoning, statistical learning, biologically inspired algorithms, and, more recently, neural and generative models (Rojas 2013). Today, AI is not only a suite of computational techniques but also a conceptual shift that challenges how research is conducted, interpreted, and disseminated.

Recent advancements such as Large Language Models (LLMs), including tools like GPT-4, have further accelerated the relevance of AI by demonstrating its

Department of Management "Valter Cantino", University of Turin, Italy.
* Corresponding author: arianna.ciabattoni@unito.it

DOI: 10.1201/9781003535393-10

ability to generate coherent textual outputs, synthesize large corpora, and assist in the formulation of research hypotheses. These tools exemplify the paradigm shift in which machines are no longer just analytical engines but active cognitive partners. As noted by LeCun (2025), AI applications have already transformed disciplines such as biomedicine, materials science, and environmental modeling, offering superior capabilities in data interpretation, forecasting, and pattern recognition.

Despite these promising developments, the field of Organization, Business, and Management Studies – hereafter Management Studies – has been slower in embracing AI tools within its research methodologies. This cautious engagement is partly due to the inherently interdisciplinary nature of Management Studies, which often balances between qualitative interpretive frameworks and more quantitative, econometric approaches. The integration of AI, with its computational demands and unfamiliar conceptual lexicon, appears at odds with traditional paradigms and epistemological preferences.

One of the main deterrents lies in the technical opacity and methodological heterogeneity of AI itself. The term "AI" encompasses a broad family of techniques, each with its own assumptions, data requirements, and interpretive constraints. Neural networks, support vector machines, genetic algorithms, and generative models, for example, are grounded in fundamentally different logics and often serve distinct research purposes. This diversity, while a strength of the field, creates a steep learning curve for scholars lacking a computational background or access to interdisciplinary collaboration (Putka et al. 2018).

Moreover, the prevalence of highly specialized jargon and the lack of methodological transparency in many AI-based studies reinforce the perception that AI is inaccessible or even incompatible with the epistemological orientations of Management Studies. For example, scholars trained in grounded theory or ethnography may find it difficult to reconcile their paradigms with algorithmic decision-making processes or black-box models. This disconnect has important implications for methodological innovation, as it risks reinforcing disciplinary silos and preventing the cross-fertilization of ideas.

At the same time, the increasing accessibility of AI tools – thanks to open-source platforms, user-friendly interfaces, and extensive online documentation – offers an opportunity to democratize their use. The proliferation of platforms like TensorFlow, Keras, and Hugging Face, coupled with the integration of AI functionalities into software such as Excel or SPSS, is making it increasingly feasible for management researchers to experiment with AI without requiring deep technical knowledge. This evolving ecosystem warrants a shift in perception: AI should no longer be seen as a domain exclusive to data scientists but as a toolkit with interdisciplinary utility.

In response to these challenges and opportunities, this chapter provides a structured, functionally oriented overview of AI techniques relevant to Management Studies. It seeks to demystify the field, offering researchers a practical taxonomy of 17 AI tools that can support a range of empirical activities, from classification and prediction to simulation, optimization, and creative content generation. In doing so, the chapter contributes to a more pluralistic and integrative methodological landscape, fostering a spirit of experimentation and reflexivity.

This effort is positioned within the tradition of "taking stock" reviews, as articulated by Krlev et al. (2025). Such reviews are not merely descriptive but analytical, aiming to organize knowledge and establish foundations for future research. By synthesizing empirical studies and technical documentation, this chapter offers a map of the AI territory that is both grounded in current practice and aspirational in scope. The objective is not only to summarize what is already known but to invite new inquiries, bridge conceptual divides, and stimulate methodological innovation.

To develop the taxonomy, the authors adopted a rigorous two-phase approach. The first phase involved an exploratory scan of academic literature, technical manuals, course syllabi, and open-access materials to identify a wide range of techniques that had demonstrable relevance to data analysis in management contexts. The second phase entailed an expert validation process involving recursive consultations with a software developer experienced in AI implementation. This iterative design ensured both theoretical soundness and practical relevance, balancing technical rigor with operational feasibility.

The inclusion of techniques in the final taxonomy was based on three criteria: (i) visibility in peer-reviewed academic literature, particularly in high-quality journals; (ii) functional applicability to empirical research tasks, such as clustering, sentiment analysis, or simulation; and (iii) methodological representativeness across different computational paradigms. Importantly, the selection is not restricted to widely adopted methods. On the contrary, the taxonomy highlights underutilized yet promising techniques, advocating for their broader incorporation into management research. This includes tools that, while not mainstream in business research, have demonstrated strong results in adjacent fields such as operations research, behavioral science, and computational sociology.

A significant motivation for this work stems from the current imbalance in the types of AI tools used in Management Studies. Research in the field remains heavily skewed toward text-based analysis, due in part to the ubiquity of unstructured data in business contexts – estimated to constitute over 80% of available organizational data (Kobayashi et al. 2018). As a result, techniques such as Large Language Models, Natural Language Processing, and supervised classifiers receive disproportionate attention, while other powerful tools remain marginalized. This pattern reflects both a path dependency and a need for broader methodological education.

The chapter addresses this imbalance by grouping techniques according to their primary research function – classification and prediction, clustering and complexity reduction, simulation and modeling, optimization, text and time-sequence analysis, and generative content production. Each technique is described succinctly and paired with two examples: a canonical use case and a more novel or unexpected application. These examples are drawn exclusively from peer-reviewed journal articles to ensure scientific rigor and exclude grey literature such as preprints or conference proceedings.

Another central objective is to make the material accessible without compromising depth. To this end, the chapter avoids excessive technicality and limits the use of acronyms. Terminology is explained where necessary, and no assumption of prior coding or machine learning expertise is made. The emphasis is on functional understanding and practical decision-making: what a technique does, when it is useful, and how it can be integrated into existing research designs. Particular attention is given to matching techniques with different types of research questions and data structures, enabling researchers to make more informed methodological choices.

The methodological steps adopted in this study are presented in detail in the section *Methodology*, while the reviewed techniques are systematically illustrated through both canonical and alternative use cases in the section *Findings*. A comprehensive synthesis is also provided in the final *Discussion* and *Conclusion* section, which includes a summary table aligning techniques, research functions, and application domains.

The overall structure of the chapter reflects this intention. Following this introduction, the methodology section provides a step-by-step account of the literature review, keyword design, article selection, and expert validation procedures. The findings section presents the taxonomy itself, detailing the 17 techniques with definitions and real-world examples. The discussion and conclusion section reflects on key insights, addresses the systemic barriers to AI adoption in the field, and outlines possible trajectories for methodological innovation in Management Studies. In particular, it emphasizes the importance of interdisciplinary collaboration, open access to computational resources, and critical engagement with the ethical dimensions of AI use in research.

In summary, this chapter aims to be more than a catalog of AI methods. It offers a conceptual and practical bridge between AI's technical sophistication

Table 1. Summary of key conceptual and methodological publications on AI in Management Studies.

Author(s) (Year)	AI focus	Area of Application	Specific Contribution
Rojas (2013)	Various AI paradigms	General AI foundations	Outlines the historical development and theoretical traditions of AI, including symbolic reasoning, neural networks, and optimization methods.
LeCun (2025)	AI in scientific research	Cross-disciplinary research	Highlights AI's role in accelerating data analysis, predictive modelling, and hypothesis generation across sciences.
Putka et al. (2018)	Modern prediction methods	Organizational research	Discusses complexity of AI models and challenges for adoption in management studies.
Krlev et al. (2025)	Review methodology	Management & organization research	Defines 'taking stock' reviews and their role in synthesizing and organizing knowledge for future research.
Kobayashi et al. (2018)	Text mining	Organizational research	Analyzes dominance of textual data (80%) in management studies and potential of AI-based text mining.
Fecher et al. (2025)	Large Language Models	Science system studies	Examines implications of LLM adoption on research practices and the scientific system.

and the empirical realities of management research. By equipping scholars with a clearer understanding of AI's potentials and limitations, it seeks to promote a more strategic, inclusive, and critical engagement with computational tools. In doing so, it contributes to shaping a research environment that is not only technologically competent but also epistemologically diverse and socially responsive, aligned with the broader evolution of scientific inquiry in the digital age.

Table 1 summarizes a selection of key publications that address the use of Artificial Intelligence in Management Studies research. It includes both conceptual and methodological contributions, illustrating the variety of AI techniques, application areas, and research outcomes forming the background for this chapter.

Methodology

This is an exploratory, qualitative study aimed at mapping and categorizing AI techniques used in empirical research, through a structured literature scan and taxonomy development process. To make a research contribution as "robust and consistent" as possible, the literature review must be carefully planned, and the entire process clearly described (Brocke et al. 2009). To systematically conduct the study, after identifying the need for a detailed and reasoned survey of the main AI techniques recently featured in journals within the field of Management Studies, a step-by-step process divided into six stages was adopted, as reported in Table 2. The approach aligns with the 'taking stock' review methodology proposed by Krlev et al. (2025), which is particularly suited for emerging interdisciplinary domains lacking consolidated taxonomies.

Step 1: *Construction of a taxonomy*. An expert panel was formed consisting of the authors and an external contributor with programming expertise in the field (Walter Mantovani). The goal was to identify, based on their own experiences and the technical literature, a broad and representative classification of AI-related techniques. These techniques also had to meet the additional requirement of being potentially usable for data analysis in Management Studies. To avoid reaching premature conclusions "just because there is some evidence that seems to lead in an interesting direction" (Massaro et al. 2016), the group worked iteratively, making recursive adjustments to define an initial taxonomy of AI techniques.

Table 2. Overview of the methodological process and resulting outputs.

Step	Description	Output
1	Expert-based taxonomy construction	Initial AI technique list
2	Query design	32 search strings
3	Literature scan via Scopus	6,155 articles
4	Filtering based on abstracts	872 empirical studies
5	Taxonomy refinement and description	17 core techniques
6	Trend and growth analysis	Identification of adoption patterns

Step 2: *Definition of a set of search expressions*. Based on the taxonomy from the first phase, a set of 32 search expressions was defined, each corresponding to a specific technique. Special care was taken to disambiguate between similar or overlapping techniques to ensure comprehensive and consistent coverage of the terminology. These expressions were crafted to reflect the terminology typically used in keywords across relevant scientific literature. Following this, a normalization process was applied, which involved removing punctuation, capitalization, and hyphens, as suggested in Uysal and Gunal (2014).

Step 3: *Literature search*. The search expressions were used to query the Scopus database, restricting the search to the title, abstract, and keyword fields of English-language articles. To focus on recent contributions, the time frame was set to the last five years. To further narrow the scope to the area of interest, the search was limited to the BUSINESS subject area. A generic search query was structured as follows:

TITLE-ABS-KEY ("PLACEHOLDER" AND (ORGANIZATION OR MANAGEMENT OR BUSINESS)) AND PUBYEAR > 2019 AND PUBYEAR < 2026 AND (LIMIT-TO (DOCTYPE , "ar")) AND (LIMIT-TO (SUBJAREA, "BUSI")) AND (LIMIT-TO (LANGUAGE , "English"))

In each iteration, the term PLACEHOLDER was replaced by one of the following 32 search expressions: Agent Based Modelling, Ant Colony Optimization, Artificial Neural Network, Autoencoders, Bayesian Networks, Convolutional Neural Networks, Decision Trees, Deep Learning, Differential Evolution, Evolutionary Strategies, Federated Learning, Few Shot Learning, Generative Adversarial Networks, Genetic Algorithms, Genetic Programming, K-Means Clustering, Large Language Models, Machine Learning, Natural Language Processing, Neuroevolution, Particle Swarm Optimization, Principal Component Analysis, Random Forest, Recurrent Neural Networks, Reinforcement Learning, Self Supervised Learning, Simulated Annealing, Supervised Learning, Support Vector Machines, Transformers, Unsupervised Learning, Zero Shot Learning.

The 32 searches returned a total of 8,641 results. Since some results included more than one *search expression*, duplicates were removed, resulting in a final count of 6,155 items.

Step 4: *Selection of relevant contributions*. To ensure methodological rigor, specific inclusion and exclusion criteria were applied during the screening of the retrieved articles. The inclusion criteria required that the articles: (1) be published in peer-reviewed journals indexed in the Scopus database; (2) be written in English; (3) fall within the BUSINESS subject area; (4) be published between 2020 and 2025; and (5) employ at least one of the 32 identified AI techniques in empirical research applications. Articles were considered empirical if they used AI tools for data collection, analysis, classification, prediction, clustering, or dimensionality reduction in real-world organizational, managerial, or business contexts.

Conversely, exclusion criteria were applied to filter out theoretical, conceptual, or exploratory contributions that did not rely on empirical datasets or failed to employ AI tools beyond a conceptual framework. Articles focusing exclusively on technical developments or algorithmic refinements without application to management-related research were also excluded. Moreover, to preserve a consistent level of academic rigor, conference proceedings, working papers, and grey literature were not considered.

Each abstract was independently reviewed and categorized by the authors. In cases of disagreement, a consensus was reached through discussion. This process ensured that only studies demonstrating a clear application of AI techniques within a research design aimed at producing actionable insights or theoretical contributions in the management field were retained. These filtering operations resulted in a refined corpus of 872 articles that formed the basis for the final taxonomy and subsequent trend analysis. From the set of retrieved articles, a preliminary screening of abstracts was conducted to retain only those contributions relevant to the objectives of this work. Theoretical, exploratory, or conceptual papers were excluded, while articles that used AI techniques to support empirical analyses were included. This filtering led to a final dataset of 872 articles, which formed the empirical basis of the research.

Step 5: *Generation of the final taxonomy*. From the analysis of the empirical articles, a final taxonomy was created, focused on identifying techniques that are effectively used in scientific practice. A clean-up process was performed to remove terms that had supported the search process but did not actually represent techniques, as well as techniques deemed too specialized or marginal for inclusion.

A technical description was developed for each remaining technique, seeking a balance between technical accuracy and clarity. Where possible, illustrative examples of how and where the technique was applied in empirical research were extracted. These examples were drawn from the identified corpus, filtered using the Academic Journal Guide 2024 (AJG_2024) to include only articles published in journals rated above 0. When no suitable example was found, working papers and conference proceedings were not considered.

Step 6: *Identification of emerging trends and unexplored possibilities*. The analysis of the 872 selected articles revealed a clear prevalence of certain AI techniques within empirical literature in Management Studies. In absolute terms, Artificial Neural Networks were the most frequently used (53 occurrences), followed by Principal Component Analysis (48) and Genetic Algorithms (44). These findings suggest a preference for techniques that, although structurally complex, are well documented, widely supported by software, and adaptable to a variety of research problems, such as classification, prediction, and dimensionality reduction.

However, beyond absolute frequency, the analysis also highlighted significant trends. Some techniques with currently limited use are showing notable growth. Large Language Models, for instance, although applied in only 21 cases, experienced a 58% increase in usage between 2020 and 2024, indicating progressive adoption driven by improved maturity and accessibility. A similar pattern was observed for Generative Adversarial Networks, which, despite limited applications, grew by 48% in the same period.

In contrast, older techniques that are more complex to implement, such as Simulated Annealing or Bayesian Networks, remain marginal both in frequency and growth. This suggests that the adoption of AI techniques is influenced not only by theoretical robustness but also by operational accessibility and the availability of established use cases. These findings invite broader reflection on the balance between methodological innovation and practical feasibility in empirical management research.

The techniques identified and selected through this six-step process are explored in depth in the *Findings* section, which categorizes them according to their primary function and illustrates their empirical application with canonical and alternative examples.

Findings: Map of Categories

Based on the research conducted and the analysis of the data collected in the previous stages, a consolidated list of 17 techniques has been identified (Table 3), which will be outlined and illustrated below. This list was developed from the initial taxonomy and subsequently validated through the process detailed in the methodology section.

To provide a guide tailored toward practical application and to facilitate navigation among the various possible uses, each technique is described and grouped according to its primary function or typical application area. Given the inherent flexibility of these techniques, where applicable, two application examples are

Table 3. Taxonomy of AI techniques emerged from our literature review.

Main Function Performed	Technique
Classification and Prediction	Artificial Neural Network
	Decision Trees
	Random Forest
	Support Vector Machines
Clustering and Complexity reduction	K-Means Clustering
	Principal Component Analysis
Complex Systems Modeling and Simulation	Agent-Based Modelling
	Bayesian Networks
Content Generations and Creative Models	Generative Adversarial Networks
	Large Language Models
Solution optimizations	Ant Colony Optimization
	Differential Evolution
	Genetic Algorithms
	Particle Swarm Optimization
	Simulated Annealing
Text and Time sequences Analysis	Convolutional Neural Networks
	Recurrent Neural Networks

provided – one showcasing conventional usage and the other an alternative or less common implementation.

The classification of AI techniques presented in Table 3 builds upon our literature review and identifies six main functional clusters, enabling researchers to align methodological choices with research objectives.

In the following paragraphs, this chapter provides a technique-by-technique description, highlighting both canonical and alternative use cases derived from this review. Each technique is presented with a descriptive overview and two illustrative applications drawn from the literature. The first example demonstrates a typical or canonical use of the technique – namely, its original or most frequent application. The second example highlights a less conventional or innovative use case. For each case, the dataset used, the application method, and the outcomes achieved are specified.

This structured overview of AI techniques and their applications provides a reference framework for scholars aiming to integrate AI methods into empirical research, while also encouraging reflection on unconventional or cross-disciplinary uses that may open up new methodological frontiers.

Clustering and Complexity Reduction

K-Means Clustering

K-Means Clustering is a classification technique used to divide a dataset into k homogeneous clusters. The underlying principle of the algorithm is to group similar observations by minimizing the distance between each observation and the centroid of its corresponding cluster. The centroid represents the average observation and serves as the most representative element of the group.

This technique is widely employed for segmentation, classification, pattern discovery, and exploratory data analysis. Application areas include customer segmentation, financial risk profiling, and the categorization of individuals based on organizational behavior patterns.

Canonical use case: Based on sociological data such as individual preferences and environmental factors, K-Means Clustering was used to group individuals into behavioral clusters representing different boundary management styles between work and personal life (Kashive et al. 2023).

Alternative use case: Using OECD indicators (e.g., agricultural knowledge and innovation, inspection and control, infrastructure development, and public stockholding costs), K-Means Clustering was applied as a tool for systemic exploration to model complex relationships among countries for comparative and interpretive analysis (Dobrovolska et al. 2024).

Principal Component Analysis

Principal Component Analysis Principal Component Analysis (PCA) is a data decorrelation technique that reduces and orders the informative components of observations based on their relative importance. The method identifies correlated variables and replaces them with a smaller set of uncorrelated principal components.

PCA is commonly used to synthesize complex data, explore latent structures, conduct preprocessing and data visualization, and enhance the performance of predictive models.

Canonical use case: Using primary data alongside secondary data from statistical research institutes on household wealth, a Wealth Index was derived through PCA. The technique also enabled the construction and comparison of sub-indices (Kumar et al. 2025).

Alternative use case: Based on responses from 300 decision-makers, PCA was used in an exploratory analysis to identify seven key clusters among 48 variables related to supply chain efficiency. The resulting framework guided supply chain managers in identifying critical success factors (Bambrick et al. 2023).

Classification and Prediction

Artificial Neural Network

Artificial Neural Networks (ANNs) are computational models inspired by the workings of the biological brain and form the conceptual foundation for all other neural network-based architectures. They are composed of numerous simple, independent computational units, called artificial neurons, which are organized in layers and interconnected. The connections between external inputs, various internal layers, and final outputs are modulated by weights – known as synaptic weights – that determine the strength of transmitted signals. Each neuron individually processes the received information and transmits it to subsequent neurons. Through an iterative training process, where inputs are presented multiple times until an optimal set of weights is achieved, the system is said to have learned, and knowledge becomes embedded in the weight values.

Artificial Neural Networks are particularly effective when data exhibit nonlinear relationships that are difficult to model using traditional approaches. They are widely employed in classification, regression, and prediction tasks.

Canonical use case: To forecast the likelihood of business formation and abandonment during the first five years of a new business's life cycle, data were used on activities carried out by entrepreneurs during the gestation phase, including the number, concentration, and timing of actions taken to start the business. Among the models examined, ANNs proved effective in correctly classifying entrepreneurs who pursued their ventures through the early stages. The networks were trained on these data to recognize complex, nonlinear patterns associated with business success or failure. The output consisted of predictive probabilities of survival or market exit, thus offering a useful tool to guide targeted interventions in support of entrepreneurship (Bhatti et al. 2022).

Alternative use case: In the context of university performance evaluation in Canada, an integrated framework combining Data Envelopment Analysis (DEA) – a non-parametric quantitative technique for assessing the relative efficiency of homogeneous units – and ANNs was employed. Data on financial resources, number of faculty, publications, and teaching performance across 16 institutions were analyzed to measure efficiency in teaching and research. ANNs were then trained on the DEA results to predict future university efficiency, thereby supporting strategic decision-making in higher education (Jauhar et al. 2023).

Decision Trees

A Decision Tree is an algorithm used for both classification and regression tasks. It is structured as a tree, where each node represents a decision based on a variable and each leaf corresponds to a prediction. Data are recursively divided according to variables, and the resulting structures are generally more interpretable than those generated by other algorithms. Decision Trees can be applied to user classification, risk prediction, behavioral forecasting, and decision support.

Canonical use case: Data on consumer behavior – based on clothing searches, weather conditions, and promotional activity – were analyzed using a Decision Tree. The algorithm determined the relative importance of various factors in consumer decision-making, leading to predictive segmentation of consumer behavior (Oh 2024).

Alternative use case: Based on different types of operational risk in supply chain finance, a Decision Tree was employed to assess and understand these risks. In this context, the algorithm served as both an explanatory and prescriptive tool to support preventive strategies (Ma 2024).

Random Forest

Random Forest is an ensemble learning algorithm that combines the outputs of multiple Decision Trees to generate a single, aggregated prediction. Each tree is trained on a random subset of the data and evaluates a random subset of features at each split. This design reduces overfitting and improves generalization.

It is widely used for both classification and regression tasks on large datasets with many features and complex interactions. It also provides estimates of feature importance. However, it is less interpretable than a single Decision Tree.

Canonical use case: To estimate the probability of listing survival on Airbnb, various predictive models were tested. The Random Forest algorithm yielded the best predictive performance and identified the most relevant features for predicting survival (Hu et al. 2025).

Alternative use case: A Random Forest classifier was applied to survey data on ERP system usage in healthcare to identify key factors influencing adoption. The analysis combined Random Forest with partial least squares modeling to enhance robustness (Reyes et al. 2025).

Support Vector Machine

Support Vector Machines (SVMs) are supervised learning algorithms used to classify data by finding the hyperplane that best separates data points into distinct classes. The algorithm identifies support vectors – the data points closest to the hyperplane – which determine its optimal position.

SVMs are especially effective for small to medium-sized datasets with high-dimensional feature spaces. They are commonly used for text classification, sentiment analysis, diagnostics, behavior detection, and forecasting.

Canonical use case: An SVM was used to classify 438 university students based on their perceptions, identifying four main explanatory variables: value for money, ethical values and social responsibility, social networks, and university rankings (Alcaide-Pulido et al. 2024).

Alternative use case: An SVM was applied to the textual content of mission statements from non-profit organizations to classify them by service area. The algorithm successfully identified organizations involved in Housing and Shelter, even uncovering previously unclassified ones (Lee et al. 2023).

Solutions Optimizations

Ant Colony Optimization

This optimization algorithm is inspired by how certain species of ants find optimal paths between their colony and food sources. The problem is represented through a weighted graph, with scores assigned to the paths connecting nodes. In each iteration, the graph is traversed while keeping track of both the best previous and current solutions, seeking the optimal path. Applications include logistics and production process optimization, resource management, and strategic decision-making support.

Canonical use case: To determine the optimal route for transporting raw materials from collection centers to a dairy processing facility, routes were modeled considering both economic efficiency and environmental impact. An Ant Colony Optimization algorithm was employed to select the optimal route (Jabir et al. 2022).

Alternative use case: In analyzing the factors influencing companies' preference for adopting Circular Economy and Internet of Things technologies, an Ant Colony Optimization algorithm was applied to reduce the number of influencing factors from 79 to 39, thereby enhancing modeling robustness. The output was subsequently used as an intermediate step in the overall analytical process (Jinil Persis et al. 2021).

Differential Evolution

Differential Evolution is an iterative optimization technique. Each possible solution is viewed as an individual with specific characteristics. These individuals are combined using basic operations such as addition, subtraction, and elimination until an optimal solution emerges. This method is particularly suitable when the optimization problem cannot be represented by a continuous function – for instance, stepwise discount policies in pricing problems.

Canonical use case: In managing an electric power distribution system, a Differential Evolution algorithm was used to identify the optimal combination of generation unit schedules and energy demand allocation among operational units. Discrete operational states (e.g., Active, Inactive, Stand-by) introduced discontinuities into the model (Tsalavoutis et al. 2021).

Alternative use case: A dataset of over 150,000 reminder emails sent to marketing panelists was analyzed to study the hidden costs of excessive solicitation – measured through ignored emails or unsubscribes. A Differential Evolution algorithm refined the reminder strategy across various scenarios (Ferecatu et al. 2024).

Particle Swarm Optimization

This algorithm is inspired by the collective behavior of bird flocks or fish schools searching for food. Each "particle" occupies a position in the search space, associated with specific parameters and a velocity. The search process updates iteratively based on the best individual solution, the best solution among neighbors, and the global best solution. It is well-suited to continuous, non-linear optimization problems involving complex solution spaces with numerous local minima.

Canonical use case: To minimize total joint costs for a pharmaceutical company and its retailers, parameters such as deterioration rates, holding costs, and stockout shortages were optimized using a Particle Swarm Optimization algorithm (Dwivedi 2025).

Alternative use case: In optimizing the supply and sales cycle for hypermarket chains, a mathematical model was developed to reduce procurement costs and boost profits. The model was optimized using a Particle Swarm Optimization algorithm, integrated with time series forecasting to estimate demand (Riazi et al. 2024).

Simulated Annealing

Simulated Annealing is a probabilistic optimization technique that mimics the annealing process in metallurgy. By heating a material, atoms are excited, and during cooling, they settle into optimal positions. The algorithm simulates this by modifying variables while the objective function's value decreases. It occasionally accepts worse solutions based on a probability determined by a parameter called Temperature. As the algorithm progresses, Temperature gradually decreases, leading to convergence at a global minimum. This method is particularly effective for functions with many local minima and complex combinatorial problems.

Canonical use case: At the tactical planning level, a model was developed to reduce high operating costs in the forestry sector. It accounted for cutting costs, road construction, and timber transport. Using data from three forests – covering lot locations, road networks, costs, and constraints – the Simulated Annealing algorithm searched for optimal solutions (Naderializadeh et al. 2022).

Alternative use case: To meet triage objectives in healthcare, a discrete event simulation model was built, incorporating patient categories, staffing configurations, demand and flow, and current performance to identify an optimal configuration of medical staff. Simulated Annealing was used to explore the solution space, improving the main performance metric by 38% (Chen et al. 2020).

Genetic Algorithms

These algorithms are inspired by natural evolution and aim to identify optimal solutions to complex, often multi-objective problems. Each solution is encoded as a chromosome – a numerical string. At each iteration, a population of solutions is generated, evaluated, and the best individuals are selected for reproduction via crossover, mutation, and selection, continuing until an optimal solution is achieved.

This technique is particularly effective for complex combinatorial problems with large search spaces, where analytical solutions are unavailable or impractical.

Canonical use case: In medical waste management, a multi-objective model addressed a complex Location Routing Problem with time windows, waste types, capacity limits, and multi-period planning. The Genetic Algorithm effectively solved large-scale instances, demonstrating its reliability as a decision support tool in realistic, operational contexts (Palomino-Perez et al. 2024).

Alternative use case: In planning maintenance for safety-critical production systems, a methodology combining Functional Resonance Analysis Method (FRAM) – used to analyze function interactions – and a Genetic Algorithm was developed to optimize resource allocation. Applied to the aerospace sector, the technique resulted in significant man-hour savings, establishing itself as an innovative decision-making tool for managing complex socio-technical systems (Patriarca et al. 2025).

Content Generations and Creative Models

Large Language Models

Large Language Models are complex neural network architectures, composed of multiple layers, designed to generate text iteratively and coherently. Textual inputs are first converted into numerical tokens, based on linguistic distributions, and encoded through embedding techniques that transform words and phrases into semantic vectors. After being trained on large textual datasets, the model generates plausible and contextually relevant text by combining statistical prediction with semantic coherence – producing new content one token at a time. These models are used for generating textual content, supporting creativity and ideation, conducting semantic analysis and classification, and synthesizing large volumes of information.

Canonical use case: Due to the rapid growth of e-commerce, textual reviews and product ratings have become critical in consumer decision-making. However, many reviews provide misleading or incomplete feedback. To address this, a framework was developed to generate more reliable and informative reviews using a Large Language Model, based on user ratings and structured reviews. The generated reviews were shown to be highly readable, accurate, and complete – difficult to distinguish from those written by humans (Pandey and Singh 2025).

Alternative use case: Large Language Models have been widely adopted by businesses to support users in diverse open-ended tasks, including creative work. However, their optimal role in enhancing business outcomes remains uncertain. To investigate the effects of human-LLM collaboration, an LLM was used to generate text in two modes: as a ghostwriter (primary content creation) and as a sounding board (providing feedback on user-created content). The outputs were published and evaluated based on user click-through rates (Chen and Chan 2024).

Generative Adversarial Networks

Generative Adversarial Networks (GANs) use two competing neural networks – the generator and the discriminator. The generator creates synthetic data from random inputs, while the discriminator attempts to distinguish between generated and real data. Each network learns from the output of the other until the discriminator can no longer reliably tell the difference. GANs are typically employed when real data cannot be used, due to scarcity or privacy issues. They are used to produce text, images, or realistic scenarios for business simulations and strategic decision-making.

Canonical use case: In training image-based machine learning systems, input generation using conventional generative models can become monotonous, as class semantics are fixed and noise is artificially defined. To address this, two cascading Generative Adversarial Networks were employed to generate more representative and discriminative visual features (Liu et al. 2022).

Alternative use case: Not available.

Text and Time Sequences Analysis

Convolutional Neural Networks

Convolutional Neural Networks are a specific architecture of Artificial Neural Networks designed to analyze data structured in sequential form, such as text, signals, time series, and similar types. Inspired by the behavior of the animal visual cortex, they operate by locally scanning (convolving) the data to extract relevant patterns and identify recurring relationships. They are especially effective when applied to data with spatial or sequential structures, allowing for the automatic extraction of features. CNNs are used for tasks such as textual data classification, pattern detection, and behavior analysis over time.

Canonical use case: To enhance the user experience in omnichannel marketing, an intelligent chatbot was developed that integrates across iOS, Android, and web platforms. Convolutional Neural Networks were selected for their ability to analyze combined visual and textual data, such as product images and reviews. The aim was to provide personalized services and support precision marketing. Tested in a shared kitchen scenario, the system demonstrated applicability to other consumer contexts as well (Chiu and Chuang 2021).

Alternative use case: Images are an increasingly widespread means of communication and, like other forms of data, often require preprocessing. Image dehazing improves visual quality by restoring pixels distorted by poor lighting or environmental factors. A Convolutional Neural Network was trained to perform these corrections and accurately restore damaged pixels (Dai 2024).

Recurrent Neural Network

Recurrent Neural Networks, like CNNs, are designed to process data sequences in which order is significant – where subsequent data strongly depend on prior inputs. RNNs maintain a memory of previously processed input, enabling them to learn temporal dependencies. They are especially useful when predicting future events based on past data, such as in log file analysis, user behavior modeling, time series forecasting, text classification, and scheduling in dynamic environments.

Canonical use case: Estimated Time of Arrival (ETA) is critical in logistics and transportation, helping businesses and individuals optimize time management and improve operational efficiency. Based on historical data, preprocessed into vector format, a graph-structured Recurrent Neural Network was applied to estimate ETA. Both online and offline experiments confirmed its effectiveness (Su et al. 2025).

Alternative use case: To develop an automated real-time analysis method for large volumes of user reviews in the online clothing sector, 23,486 reviews were collected. A sentiment analysis tool was developed using a Long Short-Term Memory Recurrent Neural Network to detect emotions and behavioral patterns, focusing on ten characteristic variables. The model classified reviews in real time as positive or negative, achieving 92% accuracy and specificity (Nawaz et al. 2021).

Complex Systems Modeling and Simulation

Bayesian Network

Bayesian Networks combine Bayesian statistics with graph theory, enabling uncertainty to be modeled in a transparent and interpretable way. They are effective for representing dependency relationships among random variables. Each network is structured as a graph, where nodes represent variables and arcs indicate conditional dependencies. Since each node represents a random variable, the connections express which variables influence others and to what degree. Learning can occur either through expert knowledge – manually structuring the network – or through automated algorithms. Bayesian Networks are used for probabilistic inference to update beliefs in light of new evidence, and are particularly suited to complex decision-making contexts such as risk management, diagnostics, and decision support systems.

Canonical use case: In sustainable product design, it is difficult to predict deviations from expected risks after launching a new product. A Bayesian Network was used to evaluate the probability of risks affecting a product's performance throughout its life cycle. The model enabled predictive and diagnostic inferences and supported risk mitigation and scenario evaluation (Enyoghasi and Badurdeen 2023).

Alternative use case: To explore the relationship between the United Nations Sustainable Development Goals (SDGs) and business risks, Bayesian Networks were combined with Structural Equation Modeling (SEM) in a hybrid model. Using national sustainability performance and risk assessment datasets, the analysis identified dependencies among risks, reduced uncertainty for businesses, and highlighted parameters to enhance business environment resilience (Qazi et al. 2023).

Table 4. Summary of AI techniques and related empirical studies.

Technique	Author(s) (Year)	Application
Clustering and Complexity Reduction		
K-Means Clustering	Kashive et al. (2023)	Grouping individuals into behavioral clusters regarding boundary management between work and personal life.
K-Means Clustering	Dobrovolska et al. (2024)	Systemic exploration to model complex relationships among countries in agriculture.
Principal Component Analysis	Kumar et al. (2025)	Deriving a Wealth Index and sub-indices from primary and secondary household wealth data
Principal Component Analysis	Bambrick et al. (2023)	Identifying seven key clusters related to supply chain efficiency.
Classification and Prediction		
Artificial Neural Network	Bhatti et al. (2022)	Predicting venture success or abandonment in early-stage entrepreneurship.
Artificial Neural Network	Jauhar et al. (2023)	Predicting future efficiency of universities using DEA results.
Decision Trees	Oh (2024)	Segmenting consumer behavior based on clothing searches, weather, and promotions.
Decision Trees	Ma (2024)	Assessing operational risks in supply chain finance and suggesting preventive measures.
Random Forest	Hu et al. (2025)	Predicting survival of Airbnb listings and identifying key predictive factors.
Random Forest	Reyes et al. (2025)	Identifying factors influencing ERP adoption in healthcare institutions.
Support Vector Machines	Alcaide-Pulido et al. (2024)	Classifying university students based on perceptions and identifying key variables.
Support Vector Machines	Lee et al. (2023)	Classifying mission statements of Non-Profit Organizations in the housing and shelter field.
Solution Optimizations		
Ant Colony Optimization	Jabir et al. (2022)	Selecting optimal routes for raw material transport to a dairy facility considering cost and environmental impact.
Ant Colony Optimization	Jinil Persis et al. (2021)	Reducing factors in Circular Economy and IoT adoption modeling.
Differential Evolution	Tsalavoutis et al. (2021)	Optimizing scheduling and energy demand distribution in electric power systems.
Differential Evolution	Ferecatu et al. (2024)	Refining reminder email strategies to reduce subscriber attrition.
Particle Swarm Optimization	Dwivedi (2025)	Inventory cost optimization in pharmaceutical supply chains.
Particle Swarm Optimization	Riazi et al. (2024)	Planning optimization for hypermarket supply and sales cycles.
Simulated Annealing	Naderializadeh et al. (2022)	Optimizing costs in forestry operations (cutting, roads, transportation).
Simulated Annealing	Chen et al. (2020)	Optimizing medical staff allocation in emergency departments.

Table 4 contd. ...

...Table 4 contd.

Technique	Author(s) (Year)	Application
Genetic Algorithms	Palomino-Perez et al. (2024)	Solving multi-objective medical waste management location-routing problems
Genetic Algorithms	Patriarca et al. (2025)	Optimizing maintenance planning in aerospace systems using FRAM.
Content Generation and Creative Models		
Large Language Models	Pandey and Singh (2025)	Generating reliable and complete product reviews in e-commerce.
Large Language Models	Chen and Chan (2024)	Comparing ghostwriting vs. sounding board modes for business content generation.
Generative Adversarial Networks	Liu et al. (2022)	Generating more representative and discriminative visual features for machine learning.
Generative Adversarial Networks	Not available	Not available.
Text and Time Sequences Analysis		
Convolutional Neural Networks	Chiu and Chuang (2021)	Developing an intelligent chatbot integrating visual and textual data for precision marketing.
Convolutional Neural Networks	Dai (2024)	Restoring image pixels altered by poor lighting using image dehazing.
Recurrent Neural Networks	Su et al. (2025)	Estimating ETA in logistics using graph-structured RNNs.
Recurrent Neural Networks	Nawaz et al. (2021)	Real-time sentiment analysis of online clothing reviews.
Complex Systems Modeling and Simulation		
Bayesian Networks	Enyoghasi and Badurdeen (2023)	Predicting and diagnosing risks in sustainable product design.
Bayesian Networks	Qazi et al. (2023)	Linking sustainability-related risks to business risks in a hybrid model.
Agent-Based Modelling	Zapata-Roldan and Sheikh (2022)	Simulating organizational design behavior in new product development.
Agent-Based Modelling	Liu et al. (2024)	Modeling dynamics of user involvement in product development.

Agent Based Modelling

Agent-Based Modeling is a simulation technique that replicates the behavior of autonomous agents within a defined environment. Agents change their states in response to environmental conditions and interactions with other agents, guided by individual rules that shape local behaviors. These interactions are simulated step-by-step, and results can be observed at individual, collective, and system levels. This technique captures complex phenomena that emerge from multiple interacting entities, often hard to predict with aggregated models. Agent-Based Modeling is used to simulate social behaviors like consumer or organizational decision-making, to analyze flows such as movement of people or goods, or to model production processes in complex systems.

Canonical use case: To support strategic organizational decision-making in new product development, an agent-based model simulated the behavior of a design function comprising four autonomous agents. The model, calibrated using questionnaire data from manufacturing and service firms, assessed how variations in customer satisfaction influenced sales over time. Validated with real data from an electronics company, the model provided insights into configuring development teams, planning customer feedback, and enhancing responsiveness in design processes (Zapata-Roldan and Sheikh 2022).

Alternative use case: In the same context of new product development, user involvement is increasingly recognized as key to performance improvement. An Agent-Based simulation was developed to model both indirect user involvement (information exchange, psychological investment) and direct involvement (interaction with the product). The model identified critical factors such as social networks, past experiences, product attachment, and user–product fit. These findings offer practical guidance for managers seeking to effectively engage users (Liu et al. 2024).

To enhance the accessibility of this work, the following table presents a concise overview of each technique analyzed, indicating the corresponding article reference and the specific way in which the technique has been applied.

Discussion and Conclusion

This chapter has provided a structured and systematic overview of Artificial Intelligence techniques that are currently accessible and applicable within the field of Management Studies. Drawing from a corpus of 872 peer-reviewed empirical articles, it has proposed a taxonomy of 17 AI techniques, organized by their primary function and illustrated with practical examples. This taxonomy is intended to serve as both a conceptual map and a practical guide, enabling scholars in Management Studies to navigate the increasingly complex landscape of AI applications and to identify the most appropriate tools for their research objectives.

The main contribution of this work lies in its effort to bridge the gap between the growing sophistication of AI methodologies and their limited adoption in Management research. While AI techniques have gained significant traction in various scientific disciplines, their integration into business and management scholarship remains uneven. This is not due to a lack of applicability, but rather to several systemic barriers: the complexity of the mathematical and computational models, the predominance of highly technical language in the literature, and the limited availability of clear, contextualized examples tailored to the specific needs of management researchers.

By providing concise explanations, functional classifications, and grounded examples, the chapter addresses these barriers and encourages more inclusive engagement with AI. Moreover, it highlights the rich potential of underutilized techniques – such as Simulated Annealing, Recurrent Neural Networks, Ant Colony Optimization, Differential Evolution, and Generative Adversarial Networks – which remain on the periphery of current academic practice despite their versatility and demonstrated relevance in other domains. These methods, though less prevalent in the literature, offer promising pathways for exploring complex organizational phenomena, optimizing strategic processes, and modeling non-linear or emergent behaviors.

A distinctive and original contribution of this chapter lies in its meta-analytical approach, which not only synthesizes existing empirical work but also introduces a cross-comparative logic to identify patterns of methodological preference and neglect across the field. By juxtaposing canonical and alternative use cases, the chapter brings to light the multiple roles each AI technique can play – ranging from prediction and classification to optimization, simulation, and creative content generation – thus highlighting their epistemic versatility. Unlike existing reviews that remain confined to narrow technological scopes, this chapter opens up a broader horizon, advocating for methodological agility and adaptive research design.

Furthermore, the chapter proposes a novel classification framework that links AI techniques to research functions rather than disciplines of origin. This shift allows management scholars to reframe AI not as a foreign body imported from computer science, but as an evolving set of instruments capable of enriching their own epistemological toolkit. The pairing of function with real-world application also serves to demystify technical complexity, enabling a more pragmatic and problem-driven approach to methodological innovation.

To further illustrate this alignment, the following table presents an integrated visual summary of the techniques covered in this chapter, cross-referenced with their primary function and common application domains. This synthesis offers a clearer guide for scholars aiming to select techniques that best suit their research goals.

At the same time, the findings of this chapter underscore a notable imbalance in the current use of AI within Management Studies. Techniques such as Artificial Neural Networks, Principal Component Analysis, and Genetic Algorithms dominate the field – not necessarily because they are universally more effective, but because they are supported by established software environments, better documentation, and a larger repository of use cases. This pattern suggests that adoption is often influenced more by accessibility and familiarity than by methodological fit. Consequently, future research should aim to democratize access to lesser-known but equally powerful techniques by providing open-source tools, practical tutorials, and interdisciplinary training initiatives.

This chapter also offers several broader reflections on the methodological evolution of Management Studies. First, it emphasizes the importance of moving beyond a "one-size-fits-all" mindset when selecting analytical tools. The diversity of AI methods allows for highly customized research designs capable of addressing both structured and unstructured data, modeling complex interdependencies, or simulating dynamic environments. Second, the chapter invites scholars to think critically about the balance between methodological innovation and usability. The most advanced techniques are not necessarily the most appropriate for every research question; similarly, the simplest techniques may not fully capture the richness of managerial realities. Researchers must weigh interpretability, robustness, and computational cost when making their methodological choices.

Table 5. Summary table AI techniques in Management Research.

AI Technique	**Primary Function**	**Common Application Domains**	**Canonical Use Case Present?**
Artificial Neural Networks	Classification	Marketing, HR, Operations	Yes
Recurrent Neural Networks	Prediction	Logistics, Behavioral Analysis	Yes
Convolutional Neural Networks	Pattern Recognition	Omnichannel Commerce, Visual Data	Yes
Principal Component Analysis	Complexity Reduction	Strategic Decision-Making	Yes
Genetic Algorithms	Optimization	Waste Management, Maintenance Planning	Yes
Ant Colony Optimization	Path Optimization	Supply Chain, Circular Economy	Yes
Differential Evolution	Parameter Optimization	Energy Management, Digital Marketing	Yes
Particle Swarm Optimization	Cost Minimization	Inventory, Forecasting	Yes
Simulated Annealing	Discrete Optimization	Forestry, Healthcare Operations	Yes
Bayesian Networks	Probabilistic Modeling	Risk Analysis, Sustainability	Yes
Agent-Based Modeling	Simulation	Product Development, User Involvement	Yes
Large Language Models	Text Generation	Review Generation, Collaboration Tools	Yes
Generative Adversarial Nets	Scenario Generation	Image Data, Strategic Simulation	Yes

It is important to acknowledge certain limitations of the study. The analysis is based exclusively on literature indexed in the Scopus database and uses a curated set of 32 search expressions. As a result, certain relevant techniques – especially those broadly labeled (e.g., "Deep Learning" or "Machine Learning") or that fall under highly specific terminologies – may not be fully represented. Furthermore, the decision to exclude working papers and conference proceedings, while ensuring quality, may also limit the visibility of cutting-edge or emerging uses of AI.

Despite these limitations, the chapter provides a foundational reference point for scholars wishing to integrate AI tools into their research. It aims not only to inform but also to inspire: to promote methodological pluralism that welcomes experimentation, interdisciplinary dialogue, and the hybridization of traditional and computational approaches. As AI technologies continue to evolve – becoming more powerful, more user-friendly, and more embedded in organizational life – the responsibility of Management researchers is not simply to adopt these tools, but to shape their use in ways that are ethically sound, analytically rigorous, and theoretically meaningful.

In conclusion, this chapter advocates for a more widespread, informed, and strategic integration of Artificial Intelligence in Management Studies. It offers an accessible entry point into a complex domain, while also providing a call to action: to expand the repertoire of methods used in the field, to reduce the cognitive and technical barriers to AI adoption, and to embrace AI not merely as a computational solution, but as a catalyst for new forms of knowledge production and organizational inquiry.

Ackonwledgement

We gratefully acknowledge Walter Mantovani for his relevant contribution to the Expert Panel and the data analysis process.

References

Alcaide-Pulido, P., Gutiérrez-Villar, B., Carbonero-Ruz, M. and Alves, H. 2024. Four key variables for determining the image of higher education institutions: A cross-national analysis based on undergraduate students. Journal of Marketing for Higher Education 34(2): 692–710. https://doi.org/10.1080/08841241.2022.2056671.

Bambrick, S., Vafadarnikjoo, A., Reid, I. and Bamford, D. 2023. Unpacking critical success factors to improve supply chain effectiveness, efficiency and performance: A 7Vs framework for consideration. Production Planning and Control 1–15. https://doi.org/10.1080/09537287.2023.2286282.

Bhatti, O. K., Irfan, M., Öztürk, A. O. and Maham, R. 2022. Organizational inclusion through interaction of work meaningfulness and servant leadership: An artificial neural network approach. Cogent Business & Management 9(1): 2059828. https://doi.org/10.1080/23311975.2022.2059828.

Brocke, J. vom, Simons, A., Niehaves, B., Niehaves, B., Reimer, K., Plattfaut, R. et al. 2009. Reconstructingc the giant: On the importance of rigour in documenting the literature search process. ECIS 2009 Proceedings 161: 14.

Chen, W., Guo, H. and Tsui, K.-L. 2020. A new medical staff allocation via simulation optimisation for an emergency department in Hong Kong. International Journal of Production Research 58(19): 6004–6023. https://doi.org/10.1080/00207543.2019.1665201.

Chen, Z. and Chan, J. 2024. Large language model in creative work: the role of collaboration modality and user expertise. Management Science 70(12): 9101–9117. https://doi.org/10.1287/mnsc.2023.03014.

Chiu, M.-C. and Chuang, K.-H. 2021. Applying transfer learning to achieve precision marketing in an omni-channel system – a case study of a sharing kitchen platform. International Journal of Production Research 59(24): 7594–7609. https://doi.org/10.1080/00207543.2020.1868595.

Dai, C. 2024. Image dehazing network based on improved convolutional neural network. International Journal of Manufacturing Technology and Management 38(4/5): 302–320. https://doi.org/10.1504/IJMTM.2024.139491.

Dobrovolska, O., Schmidtke, K., Lastovchenko, P., Odnoshevna, O. and Tkachenko, O. 2024. Clustering countries of the world according to their business practices in agriculture. Problems and Perspectives in Management 22(2): 352–364. https://doi.org/10.21511/ppm.22(2).2024.27.

Dwivedi, V. 2025. Enhancing pharmaceutical supply Chains in health crises: Integrating fuzzy logic and particle swarm optimization. Journal of Industrial and Management Optimization 21(3): 2211–2239. https://doi.org/10.3934/jimo.2024170.

Enyoghasi, C. and Badurdeen, F. 2023. Bayesian belief network-based risk likelihood assessment for sustainable product design decision making. Journal of Cleaner Production 425: 138909. https://doi.org/10.1016/j.jclepro.2023.138909.

Ferecatu, A., De Bruyn, A. and Mukherjee, P. 2024. Silently killing your panelists one email at a time: The true cost of email solicitations. Journal of the Academy of Marketing Science 52(4): 1216–1239. https://doi.org/10.1007/s11747-023-00992-w.

Hu, M., Yang, L., Park, J. and Liu, M. 2025. Survival determinants and prediction for Airbnb listings. International Journal of Hospitality Management 128: 104132. https://doi.org/10.1016/j.ijhm.2025.104132.

Jabir, E., Panicker, V. V. and Sridharan, R. 2022. Environmental friendly route design for a milk collection problem: The case of an Indian dairy. International Journal of Production Research 60(3): 912–941. https://doi.org/10.1080/00207543.2020.1846219.

Jauhar, S. K., Zolfagharinia, H. and Amin, S. H. 2023. A DEA-ANN-based analytical framework to assess and predict the efficiency of Canadian universities in a service supply chain context. Benchmarking: An International Journal 30(8): 2734–2782. https://doi.org/10.1108/BIJ-08-2021-0458.

Jinil Persis, D., Venkatesh, V. G., Raja Sreedharan, V., Shi, Y. and Sankaranarayanan, B. 2021. Modelling and analysing the impact of Circular Economy; Internet of Things and ethical business practices in the VUCA world: Evidence from the food processing industry. Journal of Cleaner Production 301: 126871. https://doi.org/10.1016/j.jclepro.2021.126871.

Kashive, N., Sharma, B. and Khanna, V. T. 2023. Work from home: Understanding boundary management profiles using boundary-fit perspective. International Journal of Organizational Analysis 31(5): 1776–1801. https://doi.org/10.1108/IJOA-04-2021-2695.

Kumar, S., Chakraverty, S. and Sethi, N. 2025. Assessing changes in wealth index using primary survey data. Socio-Economic Planning Sciences 98: 102115. https://doi.org/10.1016/j.seps.2024.102115.

Lee, H., Wang, X. and Dull, R. B. 2023. Designing a classifying system for nonprofit organizations using textual contents from the mission statement. Journal of Information Systems 37(3): 33–58. https://doi.org/10.2308/ISYS-2021-033.

Liu, J., Fu, L., Zhang, H., Ye, Q., Yang, W. and Liu, L. 2022. Learning discriminative and representative feature with cascade GAN for generalized zero-shot learning. Knowledge-Based Systems 236: 107780. https://doi.org/10.1016/j.knosys.2021.107780.

Liu, Y., Onggo, B. S. and Busby, J. 2024. Agent-based modelling of user engagement in new product development. Technovation 135: 103062. https://doi.org/10.1016/j.technovation.2024.103062.

Ma, C. 2024. Study on operational risks and preventive measures of supply chain finance. International Journal of Electronic Business 19(4): 407–419. https://doi.org/10.1504/IJEB.2024.141862.

Massaro, M., Handley, K., Bagnoli, C. and Dumay, J. 2016. Knowledge management in small and medium enterprises: A structured literature review. Journal of Knowledge Management 20(2): 258–291. https://doi.org/10.1108/JKM-08-2015-0320.

Naderializadeh, N., Crowe, K. A. and Rouhafza, M. 2022. Solving the integrated forest harvest scheduling model using metaheuristic algorithms. Operational Research 22(3): 2437–2463. https://doi.org/10.1007/s12351-020-00612-3.

Nawaz, Z., Zhao, C., Nawaz, F., Safeer, A. A. and Irshad, W. 2021. Role of artificial neural networks techniques in development of market intelligence: a study of sentiment analysis of eWOM of a Women's clothing company. Journal of Theoretical and Applied Electronic Commerce Research 16(5): 1862–1876. https://doi.org/10.3390/jtaer16050104.

Oh, J. 2024. Classification and regression tree approach for the prediction of the seasonal apparel market: Focused on weather factors. Journal of Fashion Marketing and Management: An International Journal 28(5): 893–910. https://doi.org/10.1108/JFMM-12-2022-0266.

Palomino-Perez, Y., Rojas, M. and Amaya-Mier, R. 2024. Design of a reverse logistics network for medical waste considering location and routing decisions. Journal of Cleaner Production 474: 143592. https://doi.org/10.1016/j.jclepro.2024.143592.

Pandey, P. and Singh, J. P. 2025. Generating product reviews from aspect-based ratings using large language models. Journal of Retailing and Consumer Services 84: 104244. https://doi.org/10.1016/j.jretconser.2025.104244.

Patriarca, R., Lovaglio, L. and Simone, F. 2025. Functional resonance analysis via a genetic algorithm to ensure cost-effective maintenance planning. International Journal of Production Economics 281: 109516. https://doi.org/10.1016/j.ijpe.2025.109516.

Qazi, A., Simsekler, M. C. E. and Al-Mhdawi, M. K. S. 2023. Exploring network-based dependencies between country-level sustainability and business risks. Journal of Cleaner Production 418: 138161. https://doi.org/10.1016/j.jclepro.2023.138161.

Reyes, E. G. A., Ong, A. K. S., Andrada, M. F., Diaz, J. F. T. and Gumasing, Ma. J. J. 2025. Examining factors influencing the adoption of enterprise resource planning systems in secondary healthcare institutions. Journal of Health Organization and Management. https://doi.org/10.1108/JHOM-07-2024-0316.

Riazi, H., Doroodian, M. and Afshar-Nadjafi, B. 2024. Improving the sales process of profitable perishable goods: An inventory control strategy in a planned economy. International Journal of Retail and Distribution Management 52(6): 721–735. https://doi.org/10.1108/IJRDM-07-2023-0453.

Su, X., Alatas, B. and Sohaib, O. 2025. An express management system with graph recurrent neural network for estimated time of arrival. Journal of Organizational and End User Computing 37(1): 1–26. https://doi.org/10.4018/JOEUC.370912.

Tsalavoutis, V. A., Vrionis, C. G. and Tolis, A. I. 2021. Optimizing a unit commitment problem using an evolutionary algorithm and a plurality of priority lists. Operational Research 21(1): 1–54. https://doi.org/10.1007/s12351-018-0442-x.

Uysal, A. K. and Gunal, S. 2014. The impact of preprocessing on text classification. Information Processing & Management 50(1): 104–112. https://doi.org/10.1016/j.ipm.2013.08.006.

Zapata-Roldan, F. and Sheikh, N. J. 2022. A design management agent-based model for new product development. IEEE Transactions on Engineering Management 69(5): 2026–2038. https://doi.org/10.1109/TEM.2020.2995141.

Chapter 11

Artificial Intelligence and Human Resource Management

Insights and Challenges through a Bibliometric Literature Review

Danila Scarozza,[1,*] *Isabella Bonacci,*[2] *Maria Menshikova*[2] and *Emanuele Gabriel Margherita*[1]

Introduction

Human Resource Management (HRM) modernization has experienced a grand evolution, as digitization breaks into the several processes that exist within its respective operations. From earlier inventions like the computer and the internet, HRM has always found a way to navigate these advancements to increase productivity, cost effectiveness, efficacy, and market competition (Hmoud and Várallyai 2020). In more recent years, the adoption of techniques employing advanced artificial intelligence (AI) tools has seen an emergence of their applications across all industries and professions, and HRM is no exception (Prikshat et al. 2023).

HRM activities comprise several routine and time-consuming tasks, while they are also subject to human perception, subjectivity, or biases. For these reasons, HRM is viewed as a fertile ground for the use of AI (Rodgers et al. 2023). The use of AI in HRM is being developed, tested, analyzed, and investigated empirically in various research domains (Meijerink et al. 2021; Prikshat et al. 2023). There is

[1] Università degli Studi Link (Rome, Italy).
[2] Universitas Mercatorum (Rome, Italy).
Emails: isabella.bonacci@unimercatorum.it, maria.menshikova@unimercatorum.it, e.margherita@unilink.it
* Corresponding author: d.scarozza@unilink.it

DOI: 10.1201/9781003535393-11

a strong indication that the next normal in HRM practices will be characterised by high digitalization and increased virtualization, aided by AI technologies for attaining sustainable competitive advantage based on superior human capital and HRM practices that embrace industry 4.0 (Mefi and Asoba 2021). Despite this recent surge, research investigating the integration between HRM and AI is still underdeveloped, and there is limited evidence of extensive review of literature on HRM that systematically conceptualises the context and content of this integration. A comprehensive review of state-of-the-art literature concerning AI and HRM research suggests that such research started in the early 1990s (Lawler and Elliot 1996) and has gained much traction over the last couple of years (Budhwar et al. 2022; Malik et al. 2023; Mori et al. 2023).

The amount of organizational, personnel, and task-oriented data HR leads to the incorporation of AI in many HR processes, as it enhances sustainable business models (Di Vaio et al. 2020). However, this evolution and growth in capabilities come with a responsibility of understanding the current state of AI within HRM activities and practices, requiring both academics and practitioners to dive into existing literature in order to understand the more recent developments and the current state of the art within the HR discipline and practice. AI applications in the area of HRM, in fact, are still in the investigation phase (Bujold et al. 2024). Previous studies (Kaushal et al. 2023) have revealed that in the development of HRM, the usage of AI technology can reduce repetitive administrative tasks of HR managers by helping them: (i) make decisions, and (ii) predict employee behavior at work. AI technology is used mainly in recruitment, training, employee engagement, and employee retention, which helps to reduce cost, save time, and complete HR tasks more accurately (Pillai and Sivathanu 2020). Enhancing HRM productivity through AI technology execution has prompted an imperative inclination in the future progress of this operational area. However, in research on HRM, there is still a deficiency of an inclusive AI framework, combined with a detailed scope for HRM to examine its specific application (Van Esch et al. 2019; Zehir et al. 2020).

Literature reviews leading up to this chapter have provided a foundational understanding of where AI exists within HRM (Di Vaio et al. 2020; Qamar et al. 2021; Vrontis et al. 2022). However, these extensive reviews have failed to consider how AI applications are integrated with HRM processes and practices. Identifying this deficiency, we seek to explore this consideration to provide the academic community and professional sector insight into where AI is potentially lacking and where it is thriving.

This chapter aims to contribute to the ongoing debate regarding the integration of Artificial Intelligence (AI) in Human Resource Management (HRM). While emerging technologies and AI have been discussed in the academic literature over recent years, research on AI-based technologies for HRM remains fragmented. Furthermore, the implications and impacts for organisational processes, practices, and structures have yet to be sufficiently theorised and empirically investigated (Budhwar et al. 2022).

Thus, we conduct a bibliometric literature review to provide a baseline to understand the status of AI and HRM integration within the literature and how it is represented most in the literature. Within this manuscript, we attempt to bridge this understanding by answering the following research questions: (i) How has the integration of AI and HRM literature evolved over time? (ii) What are the main authors, countries, and journals in the said field? (iii) What are the main keywords associated with AI and HRM research? (iv) What are the mature and emerging themes that the literature on AI and HRM revolves around?

As a contribution, the chapter tries to inform both the academic community and professional sector with insights into where AI is potentially lacking and where it is thriving in terms of geographical areas, research areas, HRM activities, and processes. This work, in fact, scientifically reviews existing literature, identifying what has been accomplished by integrating AI and HRM. Given the ever-evolving state of technology and emerging applications within HRM, the implications of this research are imperative for academics and practitioners to understand the direction research has taken with regard to AI and HRM.

Conceptual Framework

The evolution of AI within the domain of HRM has ushered in a transformative era, reshaping conventional practices and offering new avenues for strategic workforce management (Basnet 2024). Tracing the historical trajectory of AI in HRM unveils a journey from rudimentary automation to sophisticated systems, setting the stage for a nuanced exploration of its contemporary significance. The historical evolution of AI within HRM is a multifaceted journey deeply intertwined with technological advancements and scholarly insights. The origins of human resources automation date back to the late 1960s, as highlighted by IceHrm (2020). Initial endeavors in automation predominantly focused on rudimentary data processing and record retention, tasks conventionally delegated to computer systems (Spring et al. 2022). Over time, technological progress facilitated the ascendance of Human Resources Management Systems (HRMS) and Enterprise Resource Planning (ERP) systems during the 1990s, marking the mainstream adoption and heralding a transformative phase in the domain of human resources automation (Peretz 2013). The advent of automation in HR processes not only streamlined routine tasks but also initiated a paradigmatic shift towards more sophisticated AI applications (William et al. 2023). Scholars such as Pandey et al. (2023) argue that this early integration of automation laid the groundwork for a redefinition of HRM as a strategic function rather than merely an administrative one. The automation of routine tasks not only improved operational efficiency but also enabled HR professionals to pivot their focus towards more strategic initiatives, paving the way for the integration of AI-driven intelligence. The strategic importance of integrating AI into HRM extends beyond mere operational enhancements. AI is transforming HRM across all key areas (acquisition, development, and retention), resulting in shifts in the nature of work, workforce characteristics, and the working environment (Malik et al. 2023).

The exploration in the academic literature of AI integration in HRM involves a nuanced examination of the theoretical frameworks, methodological advancements, and empirical studies that underpin its current state (Rafiq et al. 2024). The theoretical foundations that explain the AI integration in HRM are deeply rooted in the Resource-Based View and the Dynamic Capability Theory (Chowdhury et al. 2023). The first theory underlines how AI applications and technologies can be considered strategic resources that provide a sustainable competitive advantage in the management of human capital (Samarasinghe and Medis 2020). The second theoretical contribution, on the other hand, highlights the organization's ability to adapt and innovate in response to changing technological landscapes, crucial in the context of AI integration (Talafidaryani 2023).

Moreover, methodological advancements in studying AI integration in HRM involve the application of advanced analytics and machine learning algorithms to assess the effectiveness of these technologies. Recent work by Birjali et al. (2021) utilizes natural language processing techniques to analyze textual data from employee surveys, uncovering hidden patterns in sentiment and engagement. This methodological approach provides a more granular understanding of the employee experience and the factors influencing AI adoption.

Concerning the empirical studies, several scholars have examined both the advantages and drawbacks of integrating AI into HRM strategies and practices (Radonjić et al. 2022; Nawaz et al. 2024). Among the notable benefits, researchers have highlighted that AI tools offer several operational, relational, and transformational advantages (Prikshat et al. 2023). AI's capability to enhance the quality of knowledge available to HR professionals leads to greater accuracy in tasks such as recruitment, selection, onboarding, training, performance analysis, talent acquisition, and retention (Kaushal et al. 2023). Increased automation facilitates more efficient processes, improving effectiveness while reducing time, costs, and errors in routine administrative tasks (Zehir et al. 2020; Nawaz et al. 2024). Furthermore, AI enhances decision-making by processing vast amounts of data, enabling HR managers to make not only data-driven choices that benefit the organisation but also to act as essential overseers in ensuring that decisions align with ethical standards and the organisation's culture and values (Rodgers et al. 2023).

However, alongside these benefits, scholars have raised significant concerns regarding the "dark sides" of this innovation assimilation (Pan and Froese 2023). One of the main challenges is the increased volume, velocity, and variety of data, which can complicate HR operations and overwhelm decision-makers. While AI tools can assist HR specialists in decision-making, there is a risk of losing control if decisions are made without human oversight and a clear audit trail. This underscores the importance of HR professionals applying their expertise during the development and implementation of AI technologies to ensure ethical outcomes and maintain control over HR processes (Rodger et al. 2023). Ethical concerns, particularly surrounding biases in AI algorithms, have also been widely discussed, as AI systems can inadvertently perpetuate or exacerbate existing biases (Prikshat et al. 2022).

Additionally, AI's limited capacity for emotional understanding presents challenges when managing tasks that require empathy and human interaction, which are critical in HR. Some studies highlight the importance of soft skills and emotional intelligence of HR professionals in adapting AI for effective HRM (Rathi 2018; Singh and Chouhan 2023). The potential for job and task displacement, as

AI systems automate roles traditionally held by humans, is another pressing issue discussed within the scientific community (Malik et al. 2020; Vrontis et al. 2022).

Understanding both the effects and the potential uses of AI in HRM is essential for ensuring ethical use, improving efficiency, and enhancing decision-making, while also addressing challenges such as data privacy, bias, and the evolving role of HR professionals in an AI-driven landscape (Suseno et al. 2023). Indeed, some studies argue that it is crucial to transform not only HR strategies and practices but also the profile of HR specialists within organisations. This shift ensures that HR professionals remain equipped to navigate the evolving landscape and effectively support organisational goals in an AI-influenced environment without damaging the organisational climate and the well-being of workers (Dulloo 2024). Moreover, the reskilling and upskilling of HR professionals, as well as the broader workforce, are becoming increasingly critical in the context of AI integration into organisational strategies and processes (Pradhan and Saxena 2023; Morandini et al. 2023; Nankervis and Cameron 2023).

The academic landscape surrounding AI integration in HRM is characterized by a synthesis of theoretical frameworks, methodological innovations, and several studies. The result is a multidimensional approach that advances our understanding of the current state of AI integration in HRM, laying the groundwork for future research and business best practices.

Materials and Methods

Our analysis was conducted from September 2024 to February 2025. Utilising the Scopus platform, we conducted a search for scientific documents using a query "Artificial Intelligence*" OR "AI" AND "human resource* management" OR "HRM" published from 2006 to February 2025. We used Scopus as a source because it is considered as a valid source for bibliometric analysis in business studies (Secinaro et al. 2020). Moreover, we selected these keywords because the scope of our research is to analyse the key discourses in the scientific literature that are developing within the intersections of these two areas (AI and HRM). Moreover, it was decided to analyse this time period because, for the first time in 2006, the number of published documents exceeded 10 units (11 documents in 2006), and the gradual growth of the number of documents was determined, reaching 469 published documents in 2024. In total, 2169 documents were published in this period from 2006 to February 2025. We then limited our analysis only to the type of documents defined as "articles" published in English. After applying these inclusion criteria, the database was composed of 671 documents. Figure 1 summarizes the literature search and analysis protocol. We started our study using bibliometric analysis to identify different visual outcomes presenting relationships between the key features of a certain literature stream (Za and Braccini 2017). Bibliometric techniques provide a subjective assessment of the literature as a quantitative approach (Centorrino et al. 2024). This type of analysis addresses certain limitations inherent in the literature review methodology by quantifying the existing body of literature, especially the literature review limitation on the identification of intellectual domains (Tranfield et al. 2003). The bibliometric analysis was performed on the 671 retrieved documents,

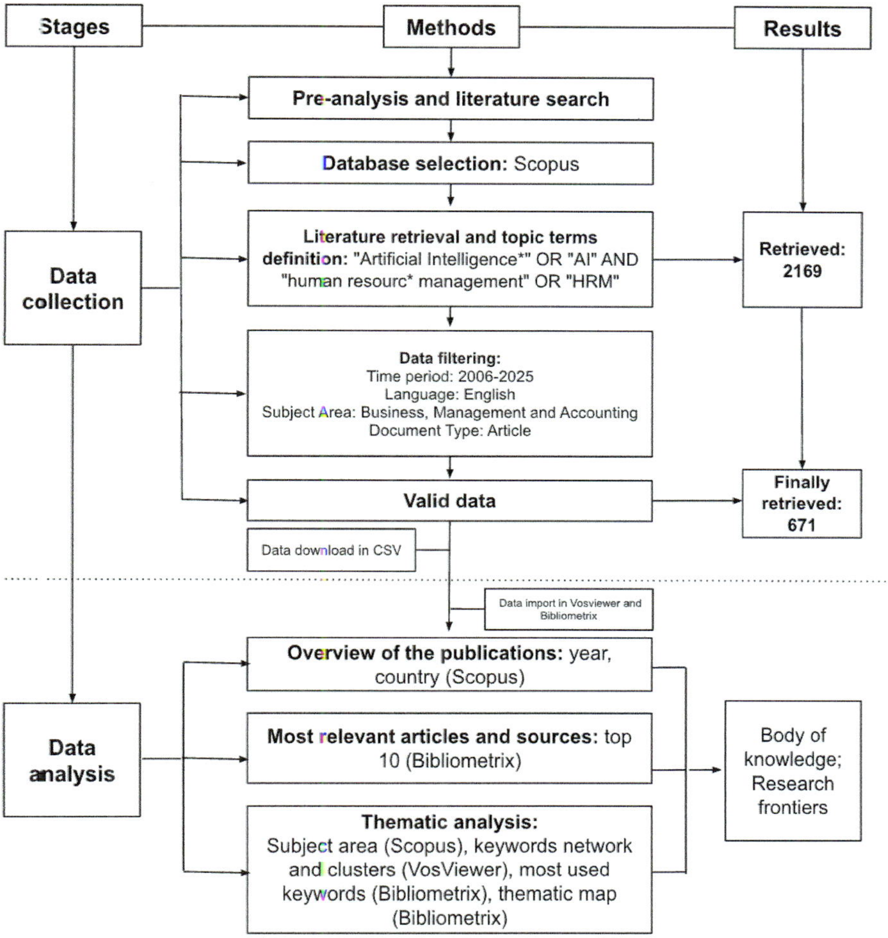

Figure 1. Literature search and analysis protocol (Source: Our elaboration).

also using the Social Network Analysis (SNA) tools, including software such as VOSviewer and Bibliometrix, into which we uploaded the documents downloaded from Scopus in CSV format, containing information on all the selected documents. Particularly, in this study, we use the following approaches to analyse the extracted dataset:

1. Descriptive statistics of the dataset by years, subject data, and countries.
2. Identification of the most relevant papers and sources.
3. Co-authorship analysis to identify the collaborations between authors and the relationships between their countries of affiliation for the identification of research hubs with the highest number of publications and relations in the research community.

4. Co-occurrence analysis of keywords to explore the present and future direction of the most diffused research focus.
5. Thematic map to explore emerging, declining, and central topics of the field.

Results

Descriptive Analysis

Our findings indicate a significant growth in the number of documents addressing this topic over the specified period, highlighting the multidisciplinarity of the field and a marked increase in scholarly interest within management and business areas, particularly over the last 7 years (notably from 2018 with 20 documents, with a significant increase in 2024 with 192 documents in Scopus (See Figure 2).

The study also highlights the most influential nodes in terms of countries, based on the network among countries (see Figure 3) and the number of documents published (see Figure 4). Figure 2 shows the distribution of documents published across various countries and territories. China stands out as the leading contributor with the highest number of published documents, closely followed by the United States. India ranks third, demonstrating a strong presence in terms of publications, while the United Kingdom, France, and Australia show moderate levels of contribution.

Figure 3 illustrates the distribution of documents contributed by various countries within the database, highlighting the presence of contributions from a wide

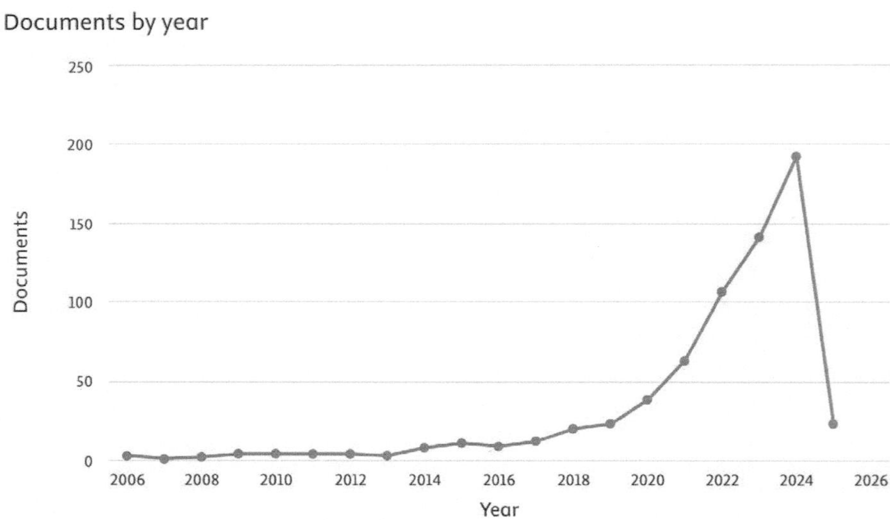

Figure 2. Distribution of documents by year (Source: Scopus).

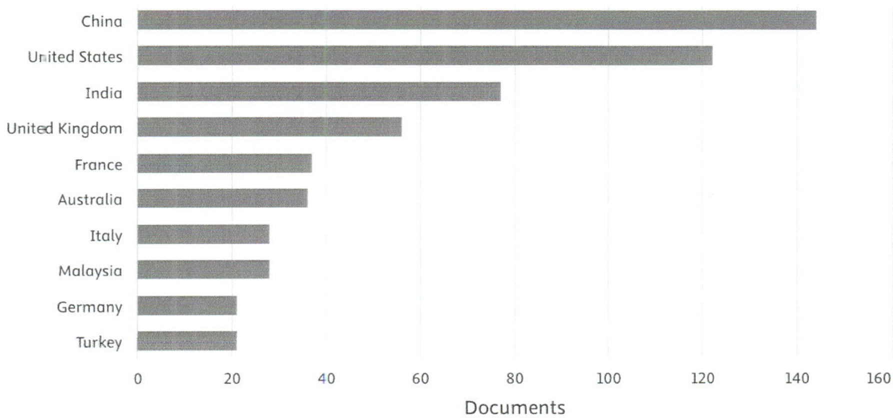

Figure 3. Distribution of documents by country/territory (Source: Scopus).

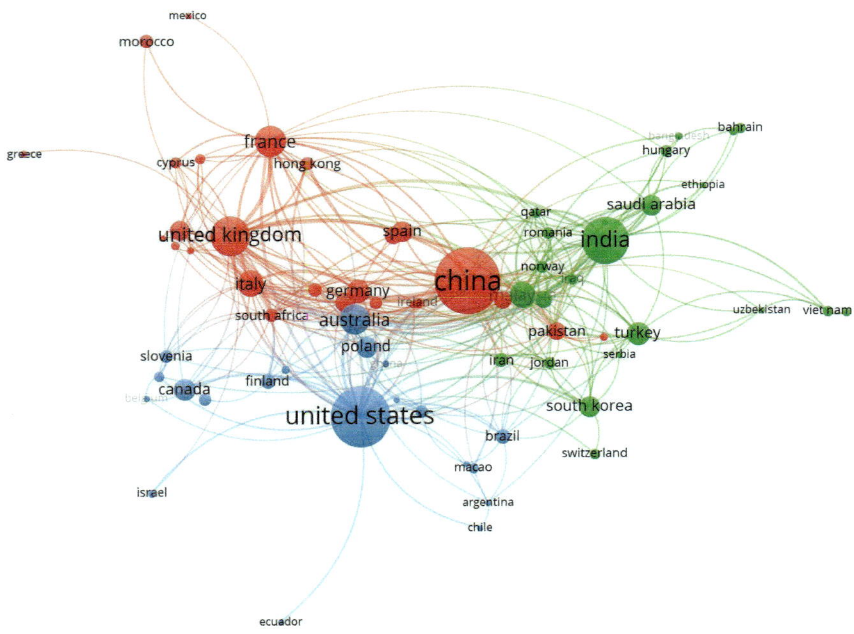

Figure 4. Visualisation of the network among countries (Source: Our elaboration through VOSviewer).

range of nations. This aspect reflects a broad and widespread interest in the analysed topic, indicating its global relevance and importance across different regions.

Figure 4 represents the network of connections among countries, highlighting their centrality and interaction density. The countries with the highest centrality and most dense connections are China, India, the United States, and the United Kingdom, as represented by their larger nodes and numerous interlinking edges. These nations act as major hubs within the network, fostering extensive collaboration and interaction with other countries. Moreover, countries like Australia, France, Saudi Arabia, and

Germany also display significant network activity, connecting to multiple partners, albeit to a slightly lesser extent than the primary hubs.

Table 1 shows the top 10 most influential articles in the database, distinguished by their high citation counts. The leading article, "Artificial intelligence in human resources management: Challenges and a path forward" by Tambe et al. (2019),

Table 1. Top 10 authors per number of citations (Source: Our elaboration).

Authors	Year	Title	Source title	Cited by
Tambe P., Cappelli P., Yakubovich V.	2019	Artificial intelligence in human resources management: Challenges and A path forward	California Management Review	568
Vrontis D., Christofi M., Pereira V., Tarba S., Makrides A., Trichina E.	2022	Artificial intelligence, robotics, advanced technologies, and human resource management: a systematic review	International Journal of Human Resource Management	524
Li C.Z., Xue F, Li X., Hong J., Shen G.Q.	2018	An Internet of Things-enabled BIM platform for on-site assembly services in prefabricated construction	Automation in Construction	330
Güngör Z., Serhadlioğlu G., Kesen S.E.	2009	A fuzzy AHP approach to personnel selection problem	Applied Soft Computing Journal	307
Chowdhury S., Dey P., Joel-Edgar S., Bhattacharya S., Rodriguez-Espindola O.; Abadie A., Truong L.	2023	Unlocking the value of artificial intelligence in human resource management through AI capability framework	Human Resource Management Review	306
Mercado J.E., Rupp M.A., Chen J.Y.C., Barnes M.J., Barber D., Procci K.	2016	Intelligent Agent Transparency in Human-Agent Teaming for Multi-UxV Management	Human Factors	276
De Mauro A., Greco M., Grimaldi M., Ritala P.	2018	Human resources for Big Data professions: A systematic classification of job roles and required skill sets	Information Processing and Management	254
Akhavian R., Behzadan A.H.	2016	Smartphone-based construction workers' activity recognition and classification	Automation in Construction	217
Pereira V., Hadjielias E., Christofi M., Vrontis D.	2023	A systematic literature review on the impact of artificial intelligence on workplace outcomes: A multi-process perspective	Human Resource Management Review	192
Sheng T.J., Islam M.S., Misran N., Baharuddin M.H., Arshad H., Islam M.R., Chowdhury M.E.H., Rmili H.; Islam M.T.	2020	An Internet of Things Based Smart Waste Management System Using LoRa and Tensorflow Deep Learning Model	IEEE Access	191
Pillai R., Sivathanu B.	2020	Adoption of artificial intelligence (AI) for talent acquisition in IT/ITeS organizations	Benchmarking	191

has been cited 568 times, reflecting its significant impact in the field. The 10th position is shared by two articles, "An Internet of Things-based smart waste Management System Using LoRa and Tensorflow Deep Learning Model" by Sheng et al. (2020) and "Adoption of artificial intelligence (AI) for talent acquisition in IT/ITeS organizations" by Pillai et al. (2020), each with 191 citations. The 10 most-cited articles in the table explore various critical themes at the intersection of AI and human resource management. These include the challenges and opportunities of integrating artificial intelligence into HRM processes, as well as more generally the analysis of the impact of some advanced technologies, such as robotics and IoT, in workplace management, and more specifically innovative methodologies for personnel selection and talent acquisition. Other key topics include frameworks for unlocking AI's value in HR, the transparency of intelligent agents in multi-agent teaming, the role of AI for sustainable initiatives, and the classification of skill sets for new professions.

Finally, Table 2 highlights the key sources examining the relationship between AI and HRM. The first two sources are HR journals, which likely present a managerial and HR-focused perspective on AI. In contrast, the subsequent journals, with an engineering focus, provide a more detailed view of AI development. Lastly, the eighth and ninth most significant sources focus on the innovation and adoption of AI in HRM.

Table 2. Top relevant sources by number of documents (Source: Our elaboration).

Sources	Number of documents
Human Resource Management Review	10
International Journal of Resource Management Review	9
Sustainability	8
IEEE Access	7
IEEE Transactions and Engineering Management	7
International Journal of Organizational Analysis	7
Sensor	7
Technological Forecasting and Social Change	7
Technology in Society	7
Asia Pacific Journal of Human Resources	6

Thematic Analysis

Additional insights emerged from the Social Network Analysis about the content of the analyzed publications. Concerning the distribution of contributions across various disciplinary areas, Figure 5 illustrates the interdisciplinary interest in the relationship between AI and HRM. The largest contributions come from Computer Science (20.1%), followed by Business and Management (19.0%) and Engineering (14.9%), reflecting strong interest from technical and managerial perspectives. Additionally, Social Sciences (10.4%), Decision Sciences (5.4%), and Mathematics (4.9%) provide significant input, showcasing analytical and societal viewpoints.

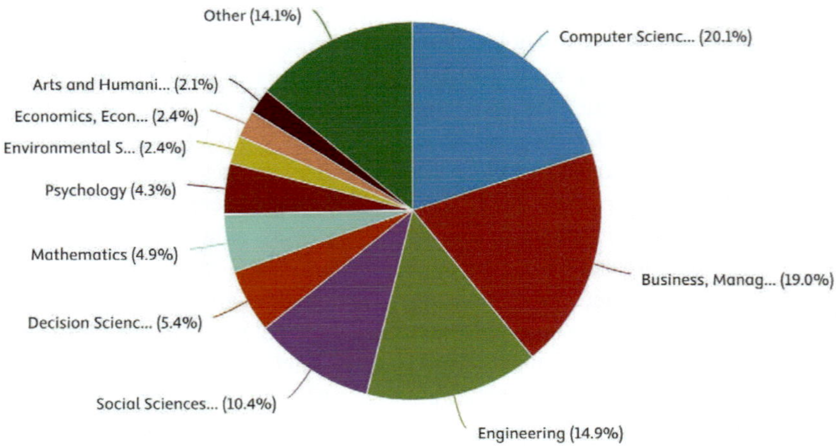

Figure 5. Distribution of documents by subject area (Source: Scopus).

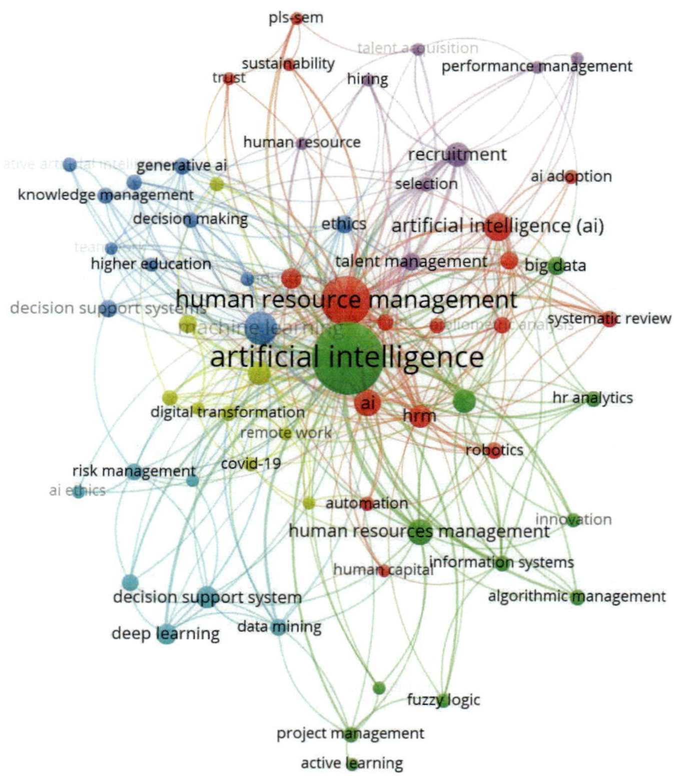

Figure 6. The keywords' network visualization (Source: Our elaboration through VOSviewer).

In order to provide a comprehensive overview of the literature on the relationship between AI and HRM and identify key areas of investigation within the scientific community, a co-occurrence analysis on the authors' keywords was conducted. We instructed the software (VOSViewer) to select the keywords that appear at least 5 times in the obtained database and to group them into clusters. As a result, we identified 64 keywords (items), which were organised into 6 clusters (See Figure 6).

Figure 7 illustrates the cumulative occurrences of the most frequently used keywords from 2006 to 2025. The top four keywords pertain to technologies utilised in HRM, namely artificial intelligence, big data, decision support systems, and deep learning. Following these, we identified keywords representing the application areas of these technologies, such as HRM in general, recruiting, and employee engagement in particular. The remaining keywords are broader in scope, including the term technology, the machine learning method, and finally, Industry 4.0, which serves as an umbrella term encompassing various digital technologies aimed at driving digital transformation within organisations. In addition, the keywords within each cluster have been analysed both in terms of content and occurrence in the database to identify the main focus and recurring themes within each cluster:

- *Green Cluster: AI and HRM Integration.* This cluster highlights the relationship between AI and HRM through keywords such as "innovation", "information systems", "algorithmic management", "big data", and "HR analytics". It illustrates how AI drives data-driven decision-making and innovation in HR practices.
- *Red cluster: automation and Industry 4.0.* Focusing on "AI adoption" and "robotics" within the "Industry 4.0" framework, this cluster explores how these technologies automate HR tasks while addressing ethical concerns such as "trust" and "sustainability".
- *Yellow cluster: digital transformation and the future of work.* This cluster emphasises the digital transformation of workplaces, using keywords like "future of work", "remote working", always with the "COVID-19" impact, while examining their role on "employee engagement" and "employee performance" in this new normal situation.
- *Dark Blue Cluster: Generative AI and collaboration tools.* Keywords such as "generative AI", "chatbots", and "teamwork" dominate this cluster, focusing on the role of AI in enhancing decision-making and knowledge management within collaborative working environments.
- *Light Blue Cluster: Data-driven decision support.* This cluster investigates "data mining", "deep learning", and "decision support systems", exploring their applications in "risk management" and analysing their ethical implications through the lens of "AI ethics".
- *Purple cluster: recruitment and talent acquisition.* This cluster centres on recruitment, selection, and hiring, with a special focus on talent acquisition, reflecting how AI optimises the HRM processes, relating to the first phase of the employee life cycle – that is, when people enter organisations.

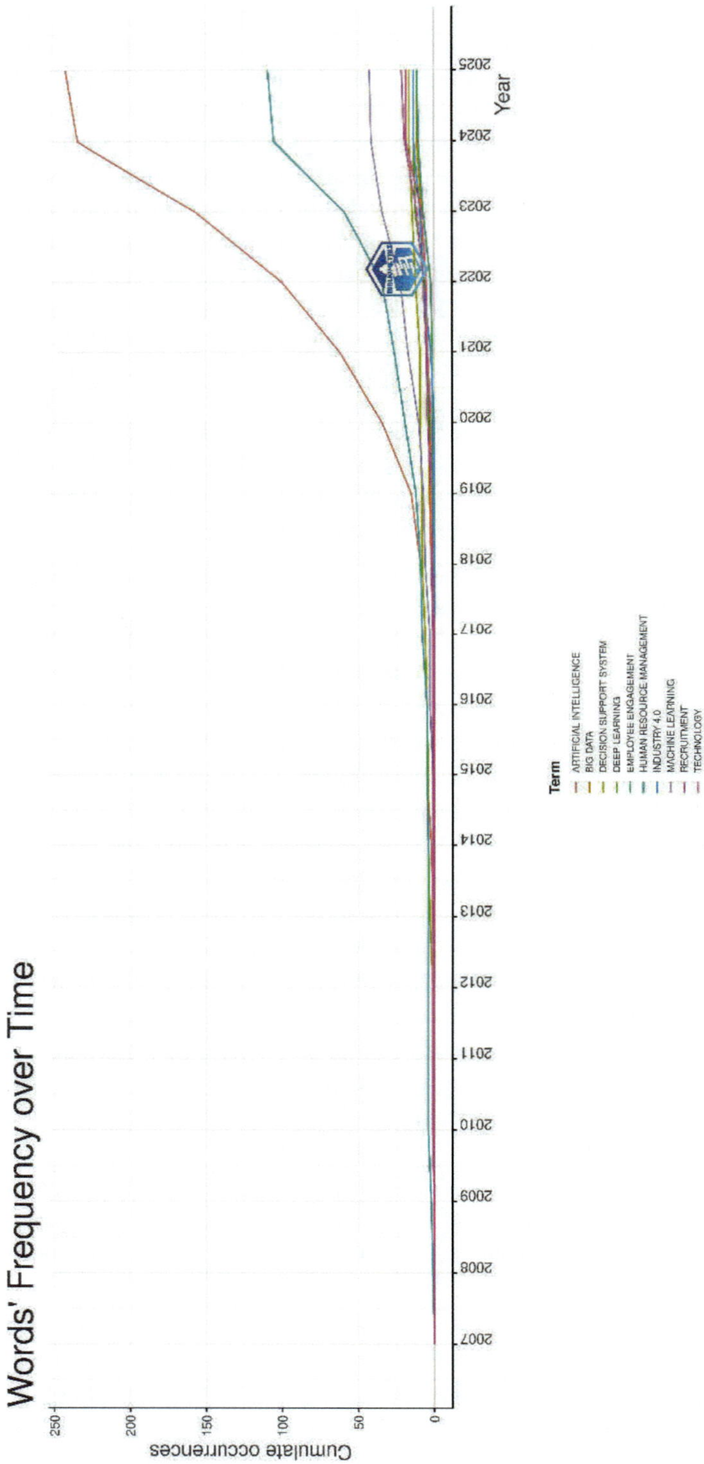

Figure 7. Most used keywords over time (Source: Our elaboration through Bibliometrix).

To further analyse the themes emerging from the database, thematic analysis using the software Bibliometrix was carried out.

Figure 8 presents a thematic map that shows keyword clusters and their interconnections within the dataset. These clusters were analysed based on two parameters: density, which measures the strength of internal connections within a cluster, and centrality, which indicates the significance of a cluster's external connections within the broader field of study. The results are organised into a diagram with four quadrants.

1. *Top right quadrant*: Well-established themes and central in the field.
2. *Top left quadrant*: Well-developed themes but marginally important.
3. *Bottom left quadrant*: Marginal and less consolidated themes potentially emerging or declining.
4. *Bottom right quadrant*: Relevant themes that are still in development.

The thematic map reveals that each quadrant contains two clusters. In the top-right quadrant, one cluster focuses on the challenges and opportunities of AI in HRM through a machine learning approach, while the other explores the use of generative AI, particularly ChatGPT, for knowledge management. The top-left quadrant includes studies on digital transformation and its relationship with the future of work, along with research on active learning techniques to enhance AI analysis. In the bottom-left quadrant, declining themes are observed, such as project management and similar technologies close to AI like decision support systems and

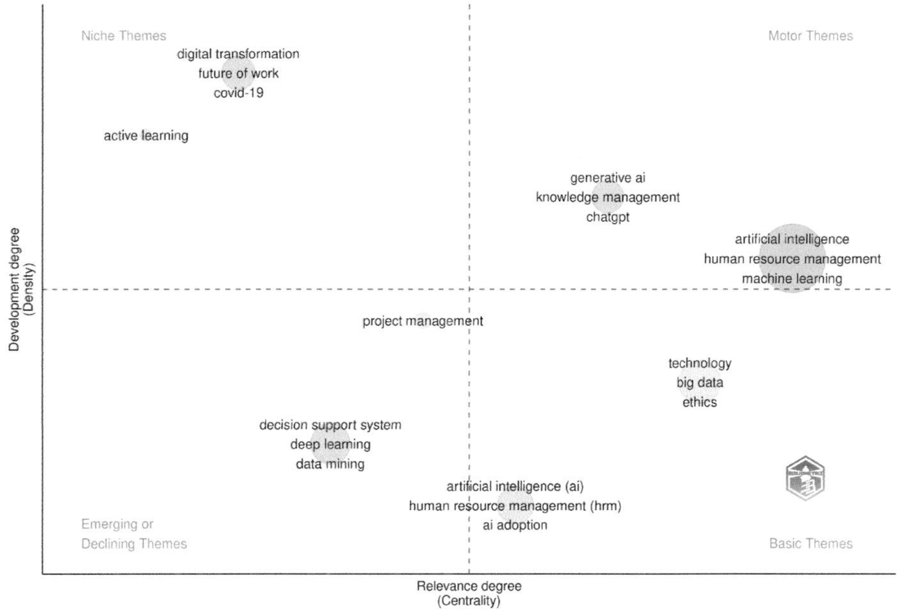

Figure 8. Thematic map (Source: Our elaboration through Bibliometrix).

data mining. Finally, the bottom-right quadrant highlights two developing clusters: the first examines the benefits of AI adoption in HRM, which the literature suggests is complex to achieve, while the second addresses ethical considerations regarding the use of big data in employee management.

Discussion

This study addresses a research call by Vrontis et al. (2022) to unravel the complex relationship between AI and HRM. To this end, we provide an in-depth bibliometric analysis of the existing body of knowledge in the field. This review also contributes to the literature by offering a broad perspective of AI and HRM while previous literature only relates to talent management and AI and decision making for HRM (Maghsoudi et al. 2024; Lawande 2024). Particularly, our review of AI and HRM literature trends highlights a growing publication trajectory since 2006, reaching 461 published articles by 2024. This growth underscores the importance of AI in HR functions, offering operational, relational, and transformational benefits (Prikshat et al. 2023), despite technological, organizational, and ethical challenges (Radonjić et al. 2022; Nawaz et al. 2024). Our analysis also reveals that researchers from China and the USA have contributed the most publications during the studied period. A key insight from the literature is the strong focus on AI's strategic application for HR managers (Vrontis et al. 2022). Indeed, Tambe et al. (2019) is the most cited study, and the authors explore the potential challenges that AI imposes on the HR function, along with mitigation mechanisms to overcome them.

Moreover, we continue the analysis of the various topics at the basis of AI and HRM by conducting an analysis of the keyword network. The analysis revealed six clusters. In the green cluster, studies analyze AI as an innovation for the HR function, adding to previous technologies such as big data and information systems. The integration of AI in HRM can lead to increased efficiency, better decision-making, and improved employee experience (Bharadwaj 2024). Still, Ercik and Kardaş report that the implications of AI on the HR function are immense, especially for organizations operating in the tourism sector. Indeed, this innovation has fundamentally transformed workforce dynamics and job descriptions, requiring employees and managers to learn new digital competencies, especially for strategic planning and data-driven decision-making (Kaur 2024). Still, Strohmeier and Piazza explore the potential of AI in six specific HRM scenarios, including turnover prediction, candidate search, staff rostering, sentiment analysis, resume data extraction, and employee self-service. The red cluster includes studies that examine how AI, in combination with Industry 4.0 technologies, may automate tasks. For instance, Yin (2024) explains how to integrate AI and robotics in a manufacturing firm to automate scheduling and human resource allocation for improved production efficiency and optimized workflows. In the yellow cluster, some studies explore the relationship between AI, digital technologies, and the future of work. Although some roles based on routine activities may disappear (Frey and Osborne 2017), new ones will emerge, especially related to the management of data and insight coming from advanced technologies (Kaur 2024). While the yellow cluster presents negative consequences of AI and digital technologies (Chin et al. 2025), the dark blue cluster underscores the possibility of using AI as a collaborative tool. In this case, AI, especially in the form of chatbots, may support HR operations when employees work in teams (Tambe et al. 2019). The light blue cluster includes several studies exploring how AI can be used for data analysis. This cluster first posits that AI can analyze large quantities of employee data. Complex AI analysis allows a better understanding of employee performance (Nie 2024). Additionally, AI can be used to make more data-driven decisions, especially in HR processes (Maghsoudi et al. 2024). For instance, organizations may set reachable goals, measure progress, and ensure accountability. However, the use of such data poses several ethical concerns for organizations (Zeir et al. 2020). Indeed, employee data with high granularity can also be used to monitor employees (Margherita and Braccini 2024). Therefore, organizations should develop policies for AI use that support ethical organizational behavior (Tursunbayeva 2024). The last cluster, the purple one, differs from the others as it summarizes a well-defined topic: the application of AI for recruiting and talent acquisition tasks. In this cluster, we found AI applications for streamlining CV screening operations (Khan et al. 2024). Indeed, AI may summarize large quantities of textual data from CVs, allowing HR specialists to conduct screening activities in less time and with greater depth (Lawande 2024).

Finally, thanks to the thematic map, we can better characterize these six clusters by identifying whether they represent well-developed, marginal, or emerging themes (Tennekes 2018). The central themes relate to the exploration of the challenges and opportunities of AI in HRM and talent management, as well as the use of AI for knowledge management. These themes overlap with the dark blue and purple clusters. Therefore, these results can be interpreted as a way to reflect on this new technology in a collaborative manner, considering both the potential benefits and drawbacks that AI can bring to HRM and knowledge management (Vrontis et al. 2022). Marginal themes relate to the future of work and AI, specifically the yellow and red clusters. This result is linked to the fact that AI is a unifying element in various studies that explore the negative impacts of automation provided by emerging technologies on job positions (Frey and Osborne 2017; Margherita and Braccini 2024). Emerging themes relate to the empirical benefits of AI adoption and the ethical considerations of AI use, represented by the green cluster. These themes may emerge due to the lack of empirical studies on AI in real-world contexts (Tambe et al. 2019). Still, marginal and less explored themes relate to the legacy technologies of AI, such as decision support systems, which characterize the light blue cluster. This decline is due to the hype of AI and its generative version (Chowdhury et al. 2024).

Conclusion

The purpose of this research was to review the integration of AI within HRM strategies, policies, processes, and practices. Based on the results analysis of our research, the integration of AI in HRM needs further exploration within academia in a variety of areas.

Considering the theoretical contributions this bibliometric literature review has provided to the existing literature, this chapter seeks to shine a light on the importance of AI in HRM practices. The prominent growth of digitalization within the workforce and the evolution of AI within HRM have helped improve areas like employee experiences and performance (Garg et al. 2021). Thus, our contribution highlights the importance of understanding where AI is best represented in HRM and the topic extensively explored by scholars. We sought to provide inductive insights to the current state of AI within HRM based on a literature-driven and systematic methodology that is repeatable for future research opportunities to come for both the researchers and the practitioners. Furthermore, in relation to the discourse on AI as an organizational resource, we contribute to this research stream by showing that AI can be understood as an umbrella term. However, organizations should adopt different types of AI according to their specific needs (Samarasinghe and Medis 2020). For example, generative AI may serve as a collaboration tool rather than a means to automate the recruitment process, which data mining techniques can instead support. Moreover, while the dominant narrative in the literature often presents AI as the primary resource for value creation, our findings highlight the importance of skilled HR managers in effectively leveraging these tools (Vrontis et al. 2022). A well-orchestrated socio-technical interaction can support the achievement of competitive advantage and lead to more effective HR practices (Vrontis et al. 2022).

Moreover, this study offers some practical implications, providing several recommendations for HR managers. Overall, organizations – particularly HR managers – should recognize that AI implementation presents challenges such as data limitations, fairness concerns, and employee resistance. Therefore, organizations should establish an organizational culture, based on trust as a key value, that fosters collaboration between managers, employees, and technologies. To this end, a key strategy should be the use of AI to augment employees' and managers' decision-making instead of using AI to replace or marginalize employee contributions. Moreover, HR managers may use AI for the recruitment and hiring process. Indeed, HR managers can reduce time spent on CV screening and interview analysis with AI software capable of summarizing large quantities of text. Some studies posit that AI use has ethical implications. Therefore, organizations may establish policies, procedures, or an ethics manager to address this issue. Finally, some studies pinpoint the use of different technologies in conjunction with AI, especially information systems and e-HRM. Therefore, organizations should hire or prepare IT specialists capable of integrating such technologies to develop large databases that AI may use for fine-grained analysis. Lastly, it is important to point out the limitations of our research and how future scholars can address these limitations. First, the analysis relies on Scopus as the primary scientific database. While Scopus is a reputable source for HR and management research, some relevant studies may have been omitted. Future research could extend this analysis by incorporating alternative databases such as Web of Science or EBSCO, providing a broader and more complementary perspective on the topic. Second, we used a broad range of keywords like "artificial intelligence" and "human resource management" within our search string to provide us with a wide coverage of topics in HR and AI. This may have inhibited our ability to gather insights from other authors, which may have emerged outside of the selected keywords used in our string. Furthermore, the findings of this study are influenced by the keyword selection process and the authors' interpretation.

Different keyword choices might have led to varying results, particularly during the hype period of AI, which is closely linked to the emergence of new technologies. Therefore, future studies may consider including related technologies to expand the scope of this analysis. Third, our study focuses exclusively on academic journal articles in English, excluding research published in other languages. To provide a more comprehensive overview of AI in HR, future studies could conduct a content analysis or systematic literature review of articles published in different languages. Through this study, we aim to lay the groundwork for advancing this research agenda and gain a deeper understanding of why the identified gaps exist within the literature and where professional and academic stakeholders can focus their attention to further grow the field. Moreover, future research could investigate the potential challenges and resolution mechanisms organizations employ to integrate HRM practices with AI, using case studies to explore this emerging phenomenon in depth. Another promising avenue is to examine the value AI generates in recruitment activities, particularly how organizations balance automated processes with human decision-making. Finally, quantitative studies could explore how AI simultaneously creates and eliminates job opportunities within the HR function, and whether these changes differ between operational and strategic job profiles.

References

Basnet, S. 2024. Artificial Intelligence and machine learning in Human Resource Management: Prospect and future trends. International Journal of Research Publication and Reviews 5(1): 281–287.

Bharadwaj, V. 2024. Integrating artificial intelligence in human resource management: A comprehensive overview. Journal of Management 11(3): 71–78.

Birjali, M., Kasri, M. and Beni-Hssane, A. 2021. A comprehensive survey on sentiment analysis: Approaches, challenges and trends. Knowledge-Based Systems 226: 107134.

Budhwar, P., Malik, A., De Silva, M. T. and Thevisuthan, P. 2022. Artificial intelligence–challenges and opportunities for international HRM: A review and research agenda. The International Journal of Human Resource Management 33(6): 1065–1097.

Bujold, A., Roberge-Maltais, I., Parent-Rocheleau, X., Boasen, J., Sénécal, S. and Léger, P. M. 2024. Responsible artificial intelligence in human resources management: A review of the empirical literature. AI and Ethics 4(4): 1185–1200.

Chin, T., Li, Q., Mirone, F. and Papa, A. 2025. Conflicting impacts of shadow AI usage on knowledge leakage in metaverse-based business models: A Yin-Yang paradox framing. Technology in Society 81: 102793.

Chowdhury, S., Budhwar, P. and Wood, G. 2024. Generative artificial intelligence in business: Towards a strategic human resource management framework. British Journal of Management 35: 1680–1691.

Chowdhury, S., Dey, P., Joel-Edgar, S., Bhattacharya, S., Rodriguez-Espindola, O., Abadie, A. et al. 2023. Unlocking the value of artificial intelligence in human resource management through AI capability framework. Human Resource Management Review 33(1): 10089.

Di Vaio, A., Palladino, R., Hassan, R. and Escobar, O. 2020. Artificial intelligence and business models in the sustainable development goals perspective: A systematic literature review. Journal of Business Research 121: 283–314.

Dulloo, R. 2024. The AI revolution in HR: Mapping automation, skills, and emerging roles in the evolving human resources landscape. Journal of Computational Analysis and Applications (JoCAA) 33(2): 742–753.

Ercik, C. and Kardaş, K. 2024. Reflections of digital technologies on human resource management in the tourism sector. Worldwide Hospitality and Tourism Themes 16(5): 646–663.

Frey, C. B. and Osborne, M. A. 2017. The future of employment: How susceptible are jobs to computerisation? Technological Forecasting and Social Change 114: 254–280.

Garg, R., Kiwelekar, A. W., Netak, L. D. and Ghodake, A. 2021. i-Pulse: A NLP based novel approach for employee engagement in logistics organization. International Journal of Information Management Data Insights 1(1): 100011.

Hmoud, B. I. and Várallyai, L. 2020. Artificial intelligence in human resources information systems: investigating its trust and adoption determinants. International Journal of Engineering and Management Sciences 5(1): 749–765.

IceHrm. 2020. Evolution of the human resource information system. IceHrm. Available at: https:// icehrm.com/blog/evolution-of-human-resource-information-system/ (Accessed: 11 February 2025).

Kaushal, N., Kaurav, R. P. S., Sivathanu, B. and Kaushik, N. 2023. Artificial intelligence and HRM: Identifying future research agenda using systematic literature review and bibliometric analysis. Management Review Quarterly 73(2): 455–493.

Kaur, R. 2024. Human resource management and artificial intelligence: Transformative effects and future prospects. International Journal of Education, Modern Management, Applied Science & Social Science 6(3): 89–98.

Khan, S., Faisal, S. and Thomas, G. 2024. Exploring the nexus of artificial intelligence in talent acquisition: Unraveling cost-benefit dynamics, seizing opportunities, and mitigating risks. Problems and Perspectives in Management 22(1): 462–476.

Lawande, N. 2024. Exploring the trends of artificial intelligence in recruitment: A bibliometric study. International Journal of Supply and Operations Management 11(3): 351–366.

Maghsoudi, M., Shahri, M. K., Kermani, M. A. M. A. and Khanizad, R. 2024. Mapping the landscape of AI-driven human resource management: A social network analysis of research collaboration. IEEE Access.

Malik, A., Budhwar, P. and Kazmi, B. A. 2023. Artificial intelligence (AI)-assisted HRM: Towards an extended strategic framework. Human Resource Management Review 33(1): 100940.

Malik, A., Srikanth, N. R. and Budhwar, P. 2020. Digitisation, artificial intelligence (AI) and HRM. pp. 88–111. *In*: Crashaw, J., Budhwar, P. and Davis, A. (eds.). Human Resource Management: Strategic and International Perspectives (3rd ed.). Sage Publications Ltd.

Margherita, E. G. and Braccini, A. M. 2024. Exploring tensions of Industry 4.0 adoption in lean production systems from a dialectical perspective. International Journal of Operations & Production Management 44(6): 1127–1157.

Meijerink, J., Boons, M., Keegan, A. and Marler, J. 2021. Algorithmic human resource management: Synthesizing developments and cross-disciplinary insights on digital HRM. International Journal of Human Resource Management 32(12): 2545–2562.

Nankervis, A. R. and Cameron, R. 2023. Capabilities and competencies for digitised human resource management: Perspectives from Australian HR professionals. Asia Pacific Journal of Human Resources 61(1): 232–251.

Nawaz, N., Arunachalam, H., Pathi, B. K. and Gajenderan, V. 2024. The adoption of artificial intelligence in human resources management practices. International Journal of Information Management Data Insights 4(1): 100208.

Nie, Q. 2024. Application of artificial intelligence in enterprise human resource management and employee performance evaluation. International Journal of Computer Applications in Technology 74(3): 186–196.

Secinaro, S., Brescia, V., Calandra, D. and Biancone, P. 2020. Employing bibliometric analysis to identify suitable business models for electric cars. Journal of Cleaner Production 264: 121503.

Tennekes, M. 2018. tmap: Thematic maps in R. Journal of Statistical Software 84(6): 1–39.

Tursunbayeva, A. 2024. Augmenting Human Resource Management with Artificial Intelligence. Springer. Cham.

Van Esch, P., Black, J. S. and Ferolie, J. 2019. Marketing AI recruitment: The next phase in job application and selection. Computers in Human Behaviour 90: 215–222.

Vrontis, D., Christofi, M., Pereira, V., Tarba, S. and Makrides, A. 2022. Artificial intelligence, robotics, advanced technologies and human resource management: A systematic review. International Journal of Human Resource Management 33(6): 1237–1266.

Zehir, C., Karaboğa, T. and Başar, D. 2020. The transformation of human resource management and its impact on overall business performance: Big data analytics and AI technologies in strategic HRM. Digital Business Strategies in Blockchain Ecosystems: Transformational Design and Future of Global Business 265–279.

Chapter 12

Understanding the Relationship between Artificial Intelligence and Stress within Organizations

Raffaele Silvestre, Mauro Romanelli* and *Maria Ferrara*

Introduction

The adoption of Artificial Intelligence (AI) technologies is rapidly expanding across a wide range of sectors, including business, medical-healthcare, educational-training and consumer services. Lee et al. (2023) stated that organizations are increasingly integrating Artificial Intelligence technologies into their operational processes and activities.

There are several definitions of AI. The IEEE guide (2017) provided a comprehensive definition in terms of "the combination of cognitive automation, machine learning, reasoning, hypothesis generation and analysis, natural language processing, and intentional algorithm mutation producing insights and analytics at or above human capability" (p. 12).

According to the European Commission (2024), with regards to the alignment with the Artificial Intelligence Act, "the term AI system is used in this communication for machine-based systems designed to operate with varying levels of autonomy and that may exhibit adaptiveness after deployment and that, for explicit or implicit objectives, infers, from the input it received, how to generate output such as content,

Department of Business and Economics, University of Naples 'Parthenope', Naples, Italy.
Emails: mauro.romanelli@uniparthenope.it, maria.ferrara@uniparthenope.it
* Corresponding author: raffaele.silvestre@collaboratore.uniparthenope.it

DOI: 10.1201/9781003535393-12

predictions, recommendations, or decisions, that can influence physical or virtual environments" (p. 2).

Rai et al. (2019) stated that "AI is typically defined as the ability of a machine to perform cognitive functions that we associate with human minds, such as perceiving, reasoning, learning, interacting with the environment, problem solving, decision-making, and even demonstrating creativity" (p. 3).

Recently, there is an increasing attention on AI in the academic literature. Zhang et al. (2024) examined the emotional expressions of chatbots to assess their influence on customer satisfaction. Hashem et al. (2024) investigated the potential for teacher burnout, resulting from the increasing integration of AI-technologies in the United Arab Emirates, and explored potential strategies to mitigate this issue. In the business sector, Sjödin et al. (2023) explored the extent to which AI-technologies may facilitate circular business model innovation among industrial firms.

Among the challenges associated with the implementation of Artificial Intelligence (AI), the phenomenon of technostress is increasingly recognized across various domains.

It constitutes a distinct variant of general stress, originating from the convergence of conventional stress factors with the use of technology, particularly those that are highly innovative and complex.

Beginning with the foundational concept of stress, Bhargava and Trivedi (2018), drawing on Selye's (1956) seminal definition, according to which "any external event or any internal drive which threaten to upset the organism equilibrium is stress" (Selye 1956), defined stress as "a condition or feeling experienced when a person perceives that demands exceed the personal and social resources the individual is able to mobilize" (Bhargava and Trivedi 2018, p. 109). Tarafdar et al. (2007) conceptualized stress as "a cognitive response that individuals experience when they anticipate their inability to respond adequately to the perceived demands of a given situation, accompanied by an anticipation of substantial negative consequences due to inadequate response" (p. 304).

Particularly noteworthy is the definition provided by McEwen (2012) who situated stress within a neurobiological framework linking the concept to the brain and characterizing it as "a state of the mind, involving both brain and body as well as their interactions; it differs among individuals and reflects not only major life events but also the conflicts and pressures of daily life that alter physiological systems to produce a chronic stress burden that, in turn, is a factor in the expression of disease" (p. 17180). This perspective emphasizes the complex interplay between psychological, physiological and environmental factors in shaping the experience and impact of stress.

When stress intersects with, and is amplified by, the use of technology, it can evolve into the specific phenomenon known as technostress, which manifests in both positive (techno-eustress) and negative (techno-distress) forms. This transformation is particularly evident in contexts where the use of technology becomes essential and unavoidable, as occurred during the COVID-19 pandemic in 2020 and continues to be observed in the post-pandemic era. In this sense, Tarafdar et al. (2014), defined technostress as "the stress caused by the use of IS in the workplace"

(p. 51). Expanding on this framework, Tarafdar et al. (2019) distinguished between two dimensions: techno-eustress and techno-distress. Techno-eustress describes situations in which "individuals appraise IS as challenging or thrilling, and experience consequent 'good' stress which motivates them to engage in coping behaviours that lead to positive outcomes" (Tarafdar et al. 2019, p. 13). In contrast, techno-distress refers to "the processes by which individuals appraise IS as a threat, experience consequent 'bad' stress, and are faced largely with detrimental outcomes" (Tarafdar et al. 2019, p. 13). Finally, Salanova et al. (2007) defined technostress as a "negative psychological state associated with the use or threat of ICT use in the future. This experience is related to feelings of anxiety, mental fatigue, skepticism and inefficacy" (p. 1).

Specifically, in the organizational contexts, technostress arises when individuals struggle to adapt to the continuous evolution of information and communication technologies and to meet the increasingly complex physical, social, and cognitive demands required for their effective use (Tarafdar et al. 2007). Nayak and Budhwar (2022) examined the technostress as a pervasive issue within contemporary organizations, focusing specifically on the stress induced by enterprise social networks and its associated consequences.

Given that technostress arises from the use of technologies, and considering that Artificial Intelligence technologies are among the most innovative, complex, and still relatively unfamiliar forms of technology, it becomes evident that their adoption contributes significantly to the emergence of technostress. Specifically, these technologies may influence various techno-stressors (techno-overload, techno-invasion, techno-complexity, techno-insecurity and techno-uncertainty) in similar ways to which the use of technologies in general, impacts on stress through effects on the same techno-stressors, as outlined by Tarafdar et al. (2007). Specifically, the deployment of advanced and complex technologies can lead to both techno-distress and techno-eustress, with consequential effects on productivity, job satisfaction, health and overall well-being among employees and managers. Tarafdar et al. (2007), Tarafdar et al. (2014), and Tarafdar et al. (2019) have extensively discussed these dynamics. Accordingly, it is reasonable to hypothesize that the integration of AI-technologies may likewise generate techno-distress, causing job dissatisfaction, reduced productivity, and/or psychological discomfort, as well as techno-eustress, which fosters enthusiasm for innovation and new opportunities, ultimately enhancing efficiency, performance, productivity, job satisfaction, and well-being. In this sense, Tarafdar et al. (2015) have demonstrated "that stress-creating conditions from the use of IS can manifest in adverse effects on outcomes that are technology-enabled and broader outcomes of the overall performance in the role (p. 105). With reference to AI-technologies and Responsible Artificial Intelligence, Verma et al. (2024) analyzed the stress induced by the principles of responsible artificial intelligence by focusing on the negative and positive consequences that their use can have in terms of technostress, also in psychological terms, and on the impact that this can have on workers' performance and well-being.

As emerged in the existing literature, the intersection between Artificial Intelligence and technostress, and the potential implications of this relationship for

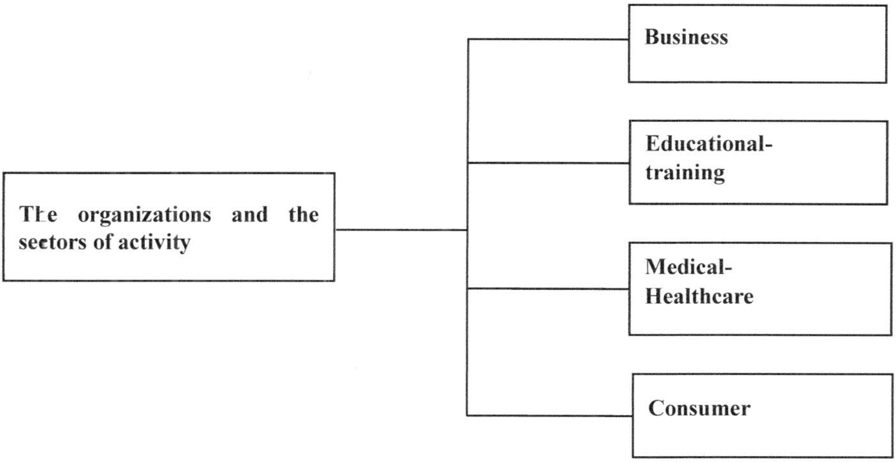

Figure 1. The organizations emerging in the literature according to the sector of activity.

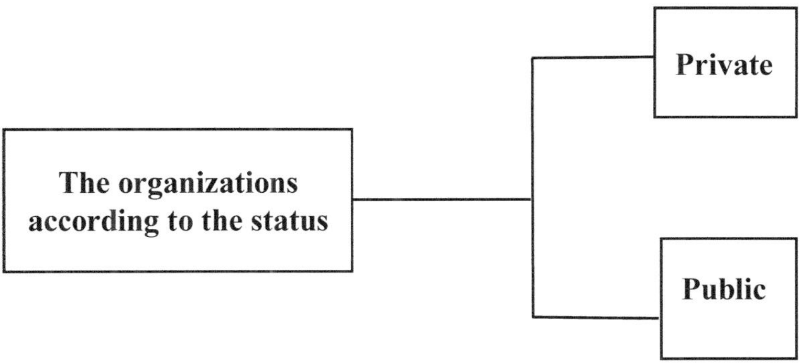

Figure 2. The organizations emerging in the literature according to the status.

productivity, job satisfaction and employee well-being, is emerging as a significant area of interest for organizations, with different status, across a wide range of sectors. Despite their diversity, these organizations share a common trend: the exponential increase in the adoption of AI-technologies, which has led to both beneficial and adverse outcomes that warrant deeper investigation. In particular, the analysis refers to public and private organizations emerging in the business, education and training, medical healthcare and consumer sectors as shown in Figures 1 and 2.

To provide the examples across the various sectors that emerged, Santos et al. (2024) focused on the consumer sector and examined the use of Artificial Intelligence in governmental contexts and its associated risks, identifying the presence of predominantly positive sentiments, alongside a minor proportion of negative reactions resulting from consumer interactions with AI. In the educational-training sector, Pagán-Garbín et al. (2024) have investigated the stress, the burnout, and the technostress among educators through the application of artificial neural networks. In the business sector, Kumar et al. (2023) have analyzed the organizational technostress induced by the adoption of machine learning and Artificial Intelligence technologies, and explored the coping mechanisms for navigating technostress with success. Lastly, in the medical-healthcare domain, Turja et al. (2020) "surveyed healthcare professionals' acceptance of robots and identified the factors that determine the intention to use robots specifically in the context of care for the elderly" (p. 2) and proposed "a new robot acceptance model for care (RAM-care) to be used in academic and workplace studies with an aim to statistically model acceptance of care robots among employees" (p. 2).

Considering the emerged findings, it is evident that there is a notable lack of studies that systematically model the relationships among AI-implementation, techno-distress and techno-eustress, considering the potential role of organizational support, and the potential impact on employee and managerial productivity. Developing such a model could prove valuable in assessing whether organizations that have adopted, or plan to adopt, AI-technologies, and consequently face potential technostress-related outcomes, align more closely with an ideal organizational typology that optimizes productivity. Moreover, this framework could inform the design of strategic pathways aimed at enhancing techno-eustress and mitigating techno-distress through targeted organizational support, thereby fostering improved performance, well-being and productivity across the workforce.

For these reasons, and with specific reference to private organizations operating within the business sector, the aim of this conceptual paper is to develop a model that explores the relationships between Artificial Intelligence and technostress in organizational contexts where Artificial Intelligence technologies are being implemented or are intended for future adoption. Drawing upon Typology Analysis and insights derived from the existing literature, the study seeks to enhance understanding of the potential effects arising from this intersection, as well as to examine the critical role that targeted organizational support may play in mediating these outcomes.

Therefore, the study has tried to answer the following research questions:

- **RQ1.** What are the relationships between AI-technologies, technostress and organizational support and their impact on productivity in business context?
- **RQ2.** What organizational typologies emerge and what is the ideal organizational typology that maximizes productivity, considering the interplay between Artificial Intelligence, technostress and organizational support?

The subsequent sections of this study are structured as follows. Firstly, the study examined the extant literature concerning private sector organizations engaged in business activities that are currently deploying, or planning to deploy, Artificial Intelligence (AI) technologies that may result in techno-eustress and techno-distress (Theoretical Background section). Thereafter, the study delineated the methodological framework employed, specifically a typology analysis, designed to identify the principal variables within these organizational contexts, elucidate the relationships among them, and evaluate the influence of independent variables on dependent ones. This process will facilitate the construction of a model (Typology

Model) comprising potential organizational typologies, derived from the observed values of the identified variables, within which the optimal typology for enhancing the dependent variable(s) will be possible to determine (Research Methodology and Results sections). Finally, the study provides a comprehensive analysis of the emergent organizational typologies; the theoretical and practical implications; the limitations inherent in the study, and avenues for future research (Discussion, Implications, Limitations, and Future Research sections).

Theoretical Background

The literature addressing the interrelations among Artificial Intelligence, techno-distress, techno-eustress, and organizational support within the business sector includes several contributions that provide valuable insights. Notably, a number of these studies examined the impact of emerging AI-technologies on the psychological responses of employees and managers, specifically in terms of techno-distress and techno-eustress. Furthermore, they explored how these responses may influence individual and organizational productivity, while also considering the potential mitigating role of targeted organizational support in enhancing positive outcomes and reducing adverse effects. In this sense, Choudrie et al. (2023) have identified a gap in the literature concerning the application of Artificial Intelligence within small and medium-sized enterprises (SMEs), and explored smartphones AI enabled functions in the context of a case study. In particular, their study focused on AI-enabled functionalities embedded in smartphones, specifically those associated with Apple's Hey Siri and Google's Google Assistant, examining their use within SMEs broadly and, more specifically, in the case of Camden Market in London, which was classified as a small or medium-sized enterprise. The findings revealed that several participants experienced cognitive, skill-based, and access-related divides, which contributed to the emergence of technostress, particularly techno-distress. For instance, some interviewees reported stress stemming from difficulties in processing natural language through these AI tools, while others cited delays and disruptions during usage that negatively affected productivity. Nonetheless, the study also highlighted instances of techno-eustress, wherein participants developed enhanced competencies that enabled more effective utilization of AI functionalities. This, in turn, led to improved task management and greater efficiency in performing organizational activities (Choudrie et al. 2023).

Focusing specifically on the positive and/or negative impact of Artificial Intelligence and the resulting technostress on productivity, Kumar et al. (2023), through an analysis of responses collected from semi-structured interviews with experts, have documented a particularly response from a senior executive at a travel services company. This individual emphasized that the implementation of Artificial Intelligence and Machine Learning technologies had significantly contributed to enhancing organizational productivity: "One of the use cases of ML and AI in our company is the chatbot. When customers come to our website, they are managed by the chatbot. Now, the chatbot is programmed to perform certain functions but cannot handle complex queries. This is where our agents come into the picture. Now, employee satisfaction and productivity are up as they spend more time on sales conversion. Such practices are a boost for the employees and the company" (Kumar et al. 2023, p. 12). It is evident that these organizations, as analyzed by Kumar et al. (2023), have already implemented, and continued to implement AI technologies whose use has been associated with the emergence of technostress. Following a comprehensive data analysis, they identified a range of techno-stressors as well as various organizational practices aimed at managing them. Specifically, the study revealed that the implementation of Machine Learning (ML) and Artificial Intelligence (AI) technologies within these organizations is perceived as stressful due to several factors: the inherent complexity of the technologies (techno-complexity); the uncertainty surrounding their use and management (techno-uncertainty); the frequent errors encountered during implementation (techno-reliability); concerns regarding their actual effectiveness in enhancing managerial performance (techno-utility); ambiguity about how these technologies may influence managerial roles and responsibilities (role ambiguity); and the job insecurity experienced by employees as a consequence of their deployment (job insecurity). Moreover, based on the data derived from the interviews, they identified five coping mechanisms that illustrate how organizations are attempting to respond to and manage the identified techno-stressors. Specifically, the analysis highlighted several key approaches: many organizations are actively promoting collaboration between AI-technologies and human resources, rather than pursuing full automation of work processes; the development of employee competencies is regarded as a critical factor in the effective management of technostress; fostering a positive perception of these emerging technologies is considered essential; cultural transformation and organizational change are viewed as necessary levers for facilitating the successful integration of AI-technologies; and, finally, the presence of robust strategic planning is deemed fundamental to ensuring the effective implementation and assimilation of these technologies within organizational contexts.

Finally, with regard to the role of organizational support, the literature underscored its significance in facilitating the effective implementation of AI-technologies and in managing technostress in ways that enhance productivity. Specifically, organizational support is instrumental in minimizing techno-distress while maximizing techno-eustress, thereby fostering a more positive and adaptive response to technological change. This perspective also encompasses the coping strategies that individuals may choose, or be encouraged, to adopt when confronted with technostress-inducing situations. In this sense, Cram et al. (2022), through their analysis of algorithmic control mechanisms affecting Uber drivers, namely gatekeeping algorithmic control and guiding algorithmic control, which correspond respectively to threat and challenge techno-stressors, argued that, at both organizational and managerial levels, "by enhancing challenge techno-stressors and minimizing threat techno-stressors, gig economy organizations can contribute to the cultivation of a more committed workforce" (p. 446).

Drawing upon the insights derived from the reviewed literature and employing typology analysis as the methodological approach, it was possible to construct a model for identifying the various potential organizational typologies within the business context. These typologies emerge from specific combinations of values associated with AI-implementation, techno-distress, techno-eustress, and organizational support, which are emerged, in the literature, as independent variables, although technostress itself is influenced by AI-implementation as well as other technological factors, while, productivity, consistent with existing literature, is conceptualized as the dependent variable within this framework.

In this study, organizational support is defined as the manner in which an organization provides material, immaterial, and emotional assistance to its employees and managers in the pursuit of their objectives, thereby fostering well-being, job satisfaction, and productivity. This definition is informed by the work of Eisenberger et al. (1986) who, in their formulation of perceived organizational support, posited that such support "would be influenced by various aspects of an employee's treatment by the organization and would, in turn, influence the employee's interpretation of or organizational reasons underlying that treatment. This implies that there will be agreement in the degree of support that the employee would expect of the organization in a wide variety of situations" (p. 501).

While, productivity, for the purposes of this study, is defined in accordance with Statt (2004) as "The rate of output of a worker or a machine" (p. 121).

Building upon these foundational insights from the literature, the subsequent sections will identify the key variables emerging within organizations that are currently implementing, or planning to implement, Artificial Intelligence technologies. Particular attention will be given to the phenomena of techno-eustress and techno-distress and to the impact that they can have, with Artificial Intelligence technologies, on productivity and the mediating or moderating role of organizational support. The principal relationships among these variables will be delineated, with a clear distinction drawn between independent and dependent variables. Finally, an organizational typology model will be developed and its components analyzed in detail.

Research Methodology

Drawing upon the existing literature, the study has developed a conceptual model aimed at describing, synthesizing and explaining the potential configurations that organizations, operating within the business sector, may assume when implementing, or intending to implement, Artificial Intelligence technologies, technologies that may give rise to techno-eustress and/or techno-distress. The model also considers the potential moderating role of organizational support and its impact on productivity of both employees and managers.

To construct this model, the Typology Analysis has been used, guided by the methodological frameworks proposed by Doty and Glick (1994) and Valbuena et al. (2008). Specifically, following the approach outlined by Valbuena et al. (2008), typologies of agents, also extendable to the case of organizational typologies according to Doty and Glick (1994), can be formulated through a series of structured phases: (1) "Agent Modelling Objectives", defining the purpose of the simplification process; (2) "Criteria Selection", identifying the criteria necessary for typology construction; (3) "Agent Type Definition", establishing agent types based on the selected criteria; (4) "Agent Type Parameterization", a critical step for distinguishing among the various typologies; (5) "Agent Type Allocation", assigning entities to the defined typologies; (6) "Validation/Verification", assessing the robustness and reliability of the identified typologies.

This structured approach enables the development of a typological model that captures the diversity of organizational responses to AI-implementation, technostress dynamics, and the influence of organizational support on productivity outcomes.

It should be noted that, according to Valbuena et al. (2008), there are different methods for defining the typologies, the choice of which is linked to the selected criteria and the type of data available, such as: the method based on qualitative analysis; the method based on quantitative analysis; the one based on attitudinal variables; the method based on socio-economic variables; the method based on scientific knowledge and finally the one based on participatory processes.

In light of these contributions, and with particular reference to the work of Sadeghi and Sadeghi (2012) on the development of typology models, the study aims at providing a comprehensive analysis of scholarly literature concerning organizations operating within the business sector. This analysis enabled us to identify cases of organizations that exhibit consistent patterns with respect to the variables examined and the relationships among them. Both independent and dependent variables were defined and described in order to elucidate the full range of interrelationships. Only after systematizing this body of information it is possible to construct the typology model by which to delineate several theoretical organizational typologies. In each typology, the dependent variable assumes a specific value; however, its maximization is achieved solely within the ideal organizational configuration.

As shown in Figure 3, the flow chart of the research methodology develops the following steps: the identification of different variables; the distinction between independent and dependent variables; the identification of relationships between dependent and independent variables; the development of the typology model for the dependent variable productivity; the identification of the ideal organizational typologies for maximization of productivity.

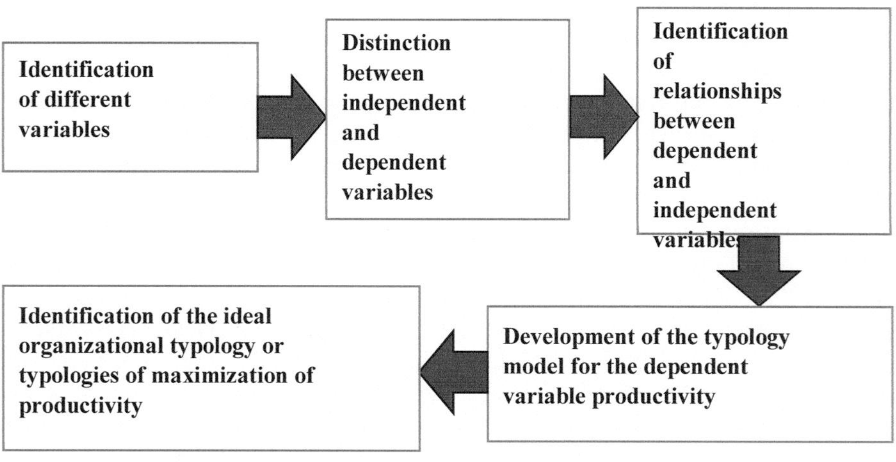

Figure 3. The flow chart of the research methodology.

Specifically, the research relies on analyzing the individual scholarly contributions on the topic in two databases online, Scopus and Web of Science. Subsequently, in relation to Phase 1 of the typology development process, defined in this study as "Organization Modelling Objectives", the primary aim is to identify organizational typologies pertaining to entities that are currently utilizing, or planning to adopt, Artificial Intelligence technologies from which phenomena of techno-eustress and techno-distress can derive. The objective is to provide managerial guidance for the formulation of effective strategies that optimize the deployment of these advanced and complex technologies, while also managing the dual dimensions of technostress in a manner that enhances organizational productivity.

Subsequently, in relation to Phase 2, "Criteria Selection", the criteria were identified in order to define the organizational typologies. Specifically, following a thorough review and analysis of the relevant literature, and considering the two principal central variables to the topic, Technostress and Artificial Intelligence, it was possible to determine the independent variables whose variation is presumed to influence the variation of the dependent variable. The independent variables identified are AI-implementation, techno-distress, techno-eustress and organizational support while the dependent variable is the productivity of workers and managers.

Proceeding to Phase 3, "Organization Type Definition", and with regards to the existing literature and the cases reviewed, it was possible to examine and interpret the nature of the relationships among these variables and the regularities they exhibit. This analysis provided the foundation for the identification of organizational typologies, each characterized by a distinct combination of high and low values assumed by the variables, as determined by the interrelationships observed among them.

Finally, having constructed a systematizing model to represent the identified typologies, the ideal configuration was determined, namely the typology that, based on specific values assumed by the independent variables, enables the maximization of the dependent variable, productivity. It is important to emphasize that, in this initial phase of the study, this analysis was limited to data derived exclusively from the existing literature.

Moreover, Phases 4 ("Organization Type Parameterization"), 5 ("Organizational Type Allocation"), and 6 ("Validation/Verification") are intended to be undertaken in subsequent research stages in order to complete the analytical framework. It should also be noted that each typology does not correspond to a fixed organizational category, but rather represents a specific typology toward which an organization may orient itself. This orientation is guided by the pursuit of the ideal typology through the implementation of targeted organizational policies and strategic initiatives.

Results

After careful reading and analysis of the papers emerged in the literature in Scopus and Web of Science until January 2024, the variables most frequently identified, concerning the relationship between Artificial Intelligence and technostress within organizations operating in the business sector, specifically those that have implemented or intend to implement AI-technologies, include AI-implementation, techno-eustress, techno-distress and organizational support as independent variables, and productivity as dependent variable to be maximized. Within this framework, discernible regularities were observed in the relationships among these variables.

In this study, the maximization of a variable is defined as the attainment of its highest possible value under the given conditions and based on the specified independent variables, beyond which further increases are not feasible without altering the structural parameters. Consequently, once this optimal level is reached, any attempt at further maximization, without modifying the underlying structural conditions, may result in an invariability or a decline in the dependent variable. This interpretation aligns with Varian's (2002) conceptualization of decreasing marginal productivity.

Specifically, an analysis of several cases presented in the literature has been conducted to identify the independent and dependent variables outlined above. Among the various contributions examined, the works that most significantly informed the conclusions, though not exclusively, include those by Kumar et al. (2023); Thunberg et al. (2023); Fu et al. (2022) and Choudrie et al. (2023). Through a critical reading of these studies, it was possible to discern, following an interpretative framework, the variables that they, implicitly or explicitly, treat as independent, the variable functioning as dependent outcome, the relationships among these variables and the regularities that characterize those relationships.

Based on these premises, and denoting by β and $1/\beta$ the extent to which a variable is changing as a function of other variables, the initial relationship identified pertains to the interplay between AI-implementation and technostress.

Technostress exhibits a positive dependence on AI-implementation, as these emerging and relatively unfamiliar technologies have the potential to influence various techno-stressors, namely, techno-overload, techno-invasion, techno-complexity, techno-insecurity and techno-uncertainty, from which technostress may originate. This dynamic is also noted by Tarafdar et al. (2007), in relation to technological systems more broadly. The deployment of AI-technologies may lead to heightened techno-distress when individuals perceive AI as a threat, and/or increased techno-eustress when AI is viewed as a source of challenge or excitement, as theorized by Tarafdar et al. (2019) in the context of general technological adoption. Furthermore, technostress may reciprocally influence AI-implementation: techno-distress may foster a negative disposition toward AI, perceived as a threat, whereas techno-eustress may promote a positive orientation, wherein AI is regarded as stimulating or exhilarating.

1. Technostress = $\delta + \beta$AI-implementation + ε

   While, the maximization of technostress is:

   max Technostress = δ + [max (βAI-implementation)] + ε
2. AI-implementation = δ + ($1/\beta$Techno-eustress-$1/\beta$Techno-distress) + ε

   While, the maximization of AI-implementation is:

   max AI-implementation = δ + [max ($1/\beta$Techno-eustress)] – [min ($1/\beta$Techno-distress)] + ε

The second relationship pertains to the variables AI-implementation and organizational support, wherein the latter is posited to exert a positive influence on the former by facilitating the attainment of desired organizational objectives. In the same way, AI-implementation may also positively affect the level of organizational support by stimulating the need to enhance support mechanisms aimed at optimizing the management of these technologies as their use becomes increasingly prevalent within the organization. This reciprocal dynamic is reflected in the findings of Fu et al. (2022).

3. AI-implementation = $\delta + 1/\beta$Organizational support + ε

   While, the maximization of AI-implementation is:

   max AI-implementation = δ + [max (1/βOrganizational support)] + ε

4. Organizational support = $\delta + \beta$AI-implementation + ε

   While, the maximization of organizational support is:

   max Organizational support = δ + [max (βAI-implementation)] + ε

The third relationship involves the variables organizational support, techno-distress, and techno-eustress in the context of AI utilization. Empirical evidence suggests a positive association between organizational support and techno-eustress and a negative association between organizational support and techno-distress, as demonstrated in the study by Cram (2022).

5. Techno-distress = δ + (-βOrganizational support) + ε

   While, the minimization of techno-distress is:

   min Techno-distress = δ - [max (βOrganizational support)] + ε

6. Techno-eustress = δ + (βOrganizational support) + ε

   While, the maximization of techno-eustress is:

   max Techno-eustress = δ + [max (βOrganizational support)] + ε

7. Organizational support = $\delta + 1/\beta$Technostress + ε

   While, the maximization of organizational support is:

   max Organizational support = δ + [max (1/βTechnostress)] + ε

Considering the relationship between productivity and AI-implementation, the literature indicates that productivity is positively influenced by the adoption of AI, given that such innovative technologies are likely to enhance operational efficiency. Moreover, when productivity gains attributed to AI are substantial, organizations are incentivized to pursue further implementation of these technologies to amplify productivity outcomes. This dynamic is supported by the findings of Kumar et al. (2023) as well as Choudrie (2023).

8. Productivity = $\delta + \beta$AI-implementation + ε

   While, the maximization of productivity is:

   max Productivity = δ + [max (βAI-implementation)] + ε

9. AI-implementation = $\delta + 1/\beta$Productivity + ε

   While, the maximization of AI-implementation is:

   max AI-implementation= δ + [max (1/βProductivity]] + ε

With regards to the relationship between productivity and technostress, the literature reveals a variable association contingent upon the nature of technostress. Specifically, with reference to techno-distress the link is negative as it tends to demotivate and discourage organizational actors, thereby exerting adverse effects on performance and so on productivity. Conversely, techno-eustress, by fostering a sense of challenge and heightened motivation, positively influences productivity by incentivizing engagement and effort. These dynamics are evidenced in the work of Tarafdar et al. (2007). Furthermore, it may be inferred that productivity itself can impact the experience of technostress. A highly productive organizational actor may be less susceptible to the detrimental effects of techno-stressors, thereby mitigating techno-distress and instead enhancing the potential for techno-eustress.

10. Productivity = δ + (-βtechno-distress) + ε

    While, the maximization of productivity is:

    max Productivity = δ - [min (βtechno-distress)] + ε

11. Productivity = δ + βtechno-eustress + ε

    While, the maximization of productivity is:

    max Productivity = δ + [max (βtechno-eustress)] + ε

12. Techno-distress = δ + (-1/βProductivity) + ε

    While, the minimization of techno-distress is:

    min Techno-distress = δ - [max (1/βProductivity)] + ε

13. Techno-eustress = δ + 1/βProductivity + ε

    While, the maximization of techno-eustress is:

    max Techno-eustress = δ + [max (1/βProductivity)] + ε

Finally, considering the relationship between productivity and organizational support, the literature highlights that support aimed at facilitating the effective management of AI-technologies and mitigating potential technostress exerts a positive influence on productivity of organizational actors, who are thereby incentivized and guided toward improved performance and so productivity. This relationship is evidenced in the work of Cram et al. (2022). Additionally, it may be inferred that productivity can, in turn, influence organizational support: higher levels of productivity may prompt increased investment in supportive measures which, if effectively implemented, could further enhance productivity outcomes.

14. Productivity = δ + βOrganizational support + ε

    While, the maximization of productivity is:

    max Productivity = δ + [max (βOrganizational support)] + ε

15. Organizational support = $\delta + 1/\beta$Productivity + ε

    While, the maximization of organizational support is:

    max Organizational support = δ + [max ($1/\beta$Productivity)] + ε

Building upon these interrelationships, emerged in the literature, and with a focus on maximizing productivity within organizations that have adopted or intend to adopt AI-technologies, potentially accompanied by experiences of techno-distress and/or techno-eustress, as well as varying degrees of organizational support, it is possible to develop a model in which productivity is treated as dependent variable while, the independent variables considered include AI-implementation, techno-eustress, techno-distress, and organizational support. For this reason, considering only these variables, to exemplify a complex reality, it is possible to deduce and posit that productivity is positively influenced by AI-implementation, techno-eustress, and organizational support, while being negatively affected by techno-distress. Accordingly, the multiple regression equation derived is as follows:

Productivity = δ + $\beta 1$AI-implementation + ($\beta 2$Techno-eustress – $\beta 3$Techno-distress) + $\beta 4$Organizational support + ε

where β indicates how much the dependent variable varies as a function of independent variables and the formula of maximization of productivity is:

max Productivity = δ + [max ($\beta 1$AI-implementation) + max ($\beta 2$Techno-eustress) – min ($\beta 3$Techno-distress)] + max ($\beta 4$Organizational support) + ε

Based on the aforementioned formula and relational dynamics, and considering productivity as dependent variable to be maximize, the following hypothesis is proposed:

H1: In order to maximize productivity, the organization under analysis must enhance AI-implementation, foster techno-eustress, and strengthen organizational support, while simultaneously mitigating techno-distress.

Subsequently, a typology model was emerging in order to delineate the various organizational profiles that may emerge from the intersection of theoretically high and low values assumed by both the independent and dependent variables within a four-dimensional space.

Discussion

Within the proposed Typology Model, based on the range of values that the variables may assume, sixteen distinct organizational typologies were identified, each corresponding to a specific level of productivity. Among these, only one represents the ideal typology in which productivity is maximized. Table 1 provides a summary of the principal characteristics associated with each organizational typology, as defined by the high and low values of the independent and dependent variables incorporated into the model.

Beginning with the first theoretical configuration termed "Zen Garden", it is possible to observe Low AI-implementation, Low techno-distress, Low techno-eustress and Low organizational support. It represents a hypothetical

Table 1. The organizational typologies.

	AI Implementation	Techno-distress	Techno-eustress	Organizational support	Productivity
Zen Garden	Low	Low	Low	Low	Low
Euphoric Mansion	Low	Low	High	Low	Medium-Low
Orchard Garden	Low	Low	Low	High	Low
Euphoric Mansion Carousel	Low	Low	High	High	High
Haunted Mansion	Low	High	Low	Low	Low
Haunted Euphoric Mansion Carousel	Low	High	High	High	Medium
Haunted Mansion Carousel	Low	High	Low	High	Low
Haunted Euphoric Mansion	Low	High	High	Low	Low
Cybernetic Jungle	High	High	Low	Low	Low
Cybernetic Carousel	High	High	Low	High	Medium-Low
Cybernetic Euphoric Jungle	High	High	High	Low	Medium
Cybernetic Euphoric Carousel	High	High	High	High	High
Automatic Home	High	Low	Low	Low	Medium-Low
Digital Zen Carousel	High	Low	Low	High	Medium-High
Technodelic Jungle	High	Low	High	Low	High
Futuristic Oasis	High	Low	High	High	High

organization that has either chosen not to adopt AI-technologies or has done so to a very limited extent. Consequently, both techno-eustress and techno-distress are either absent or present at minimal levels, and organizational support, aimed at managing these three variables, is similarly lacking or insufficient, particularly in anticipation of a potential future rise in techno-distress resulting from increased AI adoption. In this scenario, the organization promotes simplicity, minimalism and harmony, akin to the principles of a Zen garden. The emphasis is placed on maintaining an essential and balanced environment, free from the risks associated with high levels of AI-implementation. In this context, the organizational actors express satisfaction with the existing levels of productivity opting not to pursue further maximization efforts that might entail risk or disruption.

In the second theoretical configuration "Euphoric Mansion", the model reveals Low AI-implementation, Low techno-distress, High techno-eustress and Low organizational support. It represents a hypothetical organization that, as in a traditional house, and in similar to the previous case, has opted not to implement, or has implemented only minimally, AI-technologies. Nonetheless, a high level of techno-eustress is present, likely attributable to the use of other technological systems or influenced by additional contextual variables. Techno-distress remains low and organizational support, for managing the three variables, is either absent or insufficient. So, despite the limited adoption of AI, the organization exhibits a heightened sense of challenge and enthusiasm, yet lacks the structural mechanisms to channel this energy effectively or to mitigate possible future stressors. In this scenario, productivity is medium-low shaped by a combination of factors: negatively by the limited adoption of AI-technologies and the insufficient organizational support, and positively by the presence of high techno-eustress and low techno-distress. The overall performance of the organization reflects this complex interplay of inhibiting and enabling conditions.

In the third theoretical configuration termed "Orchard Garden", the model reveals Low AI-implementation, Low techno-distress, Low techno-eustress and High organizational support. It represents a hypothetical organization that, as a traditional garden, devoid of advanced technologies, yet abundant with orchards poised to bear fruit and supported by a robust organizational infrastructure, has chosen not to adopt, or has adopted only minimally, AI-technologies. As a result, techno-distress has not emerged or remains at a low level, and techno-eustress is similarly minimal or absent, so there isn't enthusiasm for cultivating and harvesting the potential benefits these orchards may yield in the future. However, the organization exhibits a high degree of support aimed at managing this configuration effectively. The elevated level of organizational support is directed toward several objectives: optimizing the management of the limited or absent AI-implementation; fostering the development of techno-eustress, particularly by encouraging engagement with technological challenges; and ensuring that techno-distress remains contained. In this context, productivity remains low, primarily due to the adverse effects associated with limited AI-implementation and the insufficient presence of techno-eustress. Nonetheless, the configuration also presents a noteworthy positive dimension: the low level of techno-distress, coupled with high organizational support, provides a promising foundation for future development.

In the fourth theoretical configuration "Euphoric Mansion Carousel", the model reveals Low AI-implementation, Low techno-distress, High techno-eustress and High organizational support. It represents a hypothetical organization that, as in a carousel situated within a traditional house and once again, has opted not to implement, or has implemented only minimally, AI-technologies. As a result, techno-distress has not emerged or remains at a low level. However, the organization exhibits a high degree of techno-eustress, generating a sense of enthusiasm and positive engagement. Furthermore, the presence of strong support structures ensures that the organization is well-positioned to sustain its current state of motivation and readiness, while maintaining psychological well-being and preparing for potential future technological transitions. Under these conditions, high levels of productivity are observed because, while the limited implementation of AI may pose constraints in the long term, the existing organizational support has the potential to foster increased adoption of such technologies. This environment can further enhance the positive effects of techno-eustress and sustain low levels of techno-distress, thereby exerting a favorable influence on both productivity and employee well-being.

In the fifth theoretical configuration, that refers to the "Haunted Mansion", the model reveals Low AI-implementation, High techno-distress, Low techno-eustress and Low organizational support. It represents a hypothetical organization that, as in a house with ghosts has chosen not to implement, or has implemented only minimally, AI-technologies. Nevertheless, the organization experiences elevated and phantasmagorical levels of techno-distress, which may be attributed to the use of alternative technologies or to other contextual variables. In this scenario, techno-eustress remains low, indicating a lack of enthusiasm, engagement and readiness to embrace new challenges. Moreover, organizational support is either absent or insufficient, thereby failing to facilitate the effective management of the limited AI-implementation, the mitigation of techno-distress, or the enhancement of techno-eustress. The overall organizational climate is thus characterized by stagnation, psychological strain, and a diminished capacity for innovation and adaptation. In such context, the negative impact on productivity, that is low, is closely associated with several interrelated factors: the limited implementation of AI-technologies, the detrimental effects of elevated techno-distress, the absence or insufficiency of techno-eustress and the lack of organizational support.

In the sixth theoretical configuration "Haunted Euphoric Mansion Carousel" reveals Low AI-implementation, High techno-distress, High techno-eustress and High organizational support. It represents a hypothetical organization that, as in a carousel in a traditional house in which certain organizational actors exhibit enthusiasm and vitality mixed to distress, once again, has opted not to implement, or has implemented only minimally, AI-technologies. Nevertheless, the organization experiences significant techno-distress, likely stemming from the adoption of alternative technologies or other contextual factors. Simultaneously, the organization demonstrates a high degree of techno-eustress, indicating a strong sense of enthusiasm and readiness to embrace new challenges. Importantly, this dynamic is supported by a robust level of organizational support, which facilitates the effective management of limited AI-implementation, mitigates the adverse effects of techno-distress and sustains the elevated techno-eustress. In this context, productivity is assessed as medium, resulting from the interplay of opposing forces: the negative impact of limited AI-implementation and heightened techno-distress, counterbalanced by the positive influence of elevated techno-eustress and substantial organizational support.

As the seventh theoretical configuration, the "Haunted Mansion Carousel" is characterized by Low AI-implementation, High techno-distress, Low techno-eustress and High organizational support. Within this framework, the organization in question, as a carousel situated within a traditional "haunted mansion", has either refrained from adopting AI-technologies or has done so only minimally. Nevertheless, a pronounced level of techno-distress is evident, likely attributable to the use of alternative technological systems or influenced by other contextual variables. Concurrently, the level of techno-eustress remains low, indicating a lack of the requisite enthusiasm and motivational energy necessary to embrace new challenges. Despite these constraints, the organization benefits from a high degree of support, which plays a critical role in managing the absence or limited integration of AI, mitigating the adverse effects of techno-distress and fostering conditions conducive to enhancing techno-eustress. In this configuration, overall productivity is low, primarily due to the detrimental effects of minimal AI-implementation, persistent techno-distress and insufficient techno-eustress. However, the initial presence of robust organizational support exerts a modestly positive influence, providing a foundation upon which future improvements may be built.

In the eighth theoretical organizational typology "Haunted Euphoric Mansion", the model reveals Low AI-implementation, High techno-distress, High techno-eustress and Low organizational support. It represents a hypothetical organization that, much like a traditional haunted mansion, has chosen not to adopt, or has adopted only minimally, AI-technologies. Nevertheless, the organization experiences a high level of techno-distress, likely stemming from the use of alternative technologies or other contextual factors. Simultaneously, a high level of techno-eustress is present, which partially offsets the negative effects of techno-distress by generating enthusiasm and motivational energy conducive to embracing new challenges. However, the organization lacks sufficient support structures to manage these dynamics effectively. The low level of organizational support undermines efforts to optimize the limited AI-implementation, mitigate techno-distress and sustain the positive momentum generated by techno-eustress. As a result, the absence of strategic guidance may hinder the organization's ability to translate its motivational potential into improved outcomes in the future. In this case, productivity is low due to the negative impact of limited AI-implementation, elevated levels of techno-distress and insufficient organizational support, despite the positive influence exerted by high levels of techno-eustress.

In the ninth theoretical configuration, the model reveals High AI-implementation, High techno-distress, Low techno-eustress and Low organizational support. This configuration corresponds to the theoretical organizational typology designated as "Cybernetic Jungle". It represents a hypothetical organization that, likely supported by substantial organizational investment in the past, has successfully implemented AI-technologies. However, this implementation has been accompanied by elevated levels of techno-distress. At present, both organizational support and techno-eustress are low, indicating a lack of enthusiasm, motivational energy and strategic guidance necessary to confront future challenges. The organization thus operates within a "Cybernetic Jungle", a complex and technologically advanced environment where the benefits of AI coexist with significant psychological strain. The absence of techno-eustress and the decline in organizational support exacerbate the situation, undermining the organization's capacity to reduce techno-distress and foster a more adaptive and resilient climate. It is precisely this imbalance, between technological advancement and insufficient human-centered support, that renders the organizational landscape a jungle, albeit one shaped by cybernetic systems. In this context productivity is notably low. While the implementation of AI contributes positively to operational capabilities, its benefits are offset by the detrimental effects of high techno-distress, low techno-eustress, and inadequate organizational support. These factors collectively diminish employee well-being and hinder overall performance.

In the tenth theoretical configuration "Cybernetic Carousel", the model reveals High AI-implementation, High techno-distress, Low techno-eustress and High organizational support. It represents a hypothetical organization that, likely benefiting from substantial organizational support both in the past and in the present, has adopted advanced AI-technologies. However, this implementation has been accompanied by elevated levels of techno-distress, manifesting in anxiety and demotivation, and by low levels of techno-eustress, indicating a deficiency in enthusiasm and motivational energy required to embrace new challenges. Despite the presence of high organizational support, which provides strategic guidance and the potential to mitigate techno-distress and foster techno-eustress, the organization remains caught in a paradoxical state. It operates on a carousel that is cybernetic in nature due to its technological sophistication, yet metaphorically "sad" owing to the psychological strain and lack of positive emotional engagement. The guidance is present, but the prevailing confusion and demotivation, coupled with insufficient euphoria, hinder the organization's capacity to fully capitalize on its technological investments. In this scenario, productivity tends is medium-low. While the implementation of AI contributes positively to operational capabilities, its benefits are counterbalanced by the adverse effects of high techno-distress and low techno-eustress. Nevertheless, the significant level of organizational support provides a critical resource for enhancing future productivity by enabling the reduction of techno-distress and the cultivation of techno-eustress over time.

The eleventh theoretical configuration, "Cybernetic Euphoric Jungle", reveals High AI-implementation, High techno-distress, High techno-eustress and Low organizational support. It reflects a hypothetical organization that, likely supported by substantial organizational investment in the past, has adopted advanced AI-technologies. This implementation has resulted in both high techno-distress, manifesting as anxiety and demotivation, and high techno-eustress, which signals the presence of enthusiasm and energy to engage with new challenges. However, the current low level of organizational support indicates a lack of strategic guidance necessary to mitigate techno-distress and to channel techno-eustress effectively. Thus, the organization operates within a cybernetic environment shaped by technological advancement, yet this environment resembles an euphoric jungle due to the coexistence of intense psychological strain and unmanaged motivational energy. The absence of adequate organizational support renders the euphoria and drive associated with techno-eustress directionless, while the negative consequences of techno-distress remain unaddressed. In this scenario, productivity is medium. It benefits from the positive effects of high AI-implementation and high techno-eustress, yet is simultaneously constrained by the detrimental impact of high techno-distress and insufficient organizational support.

In the "Cybernetic Euphoric Carousel", the twelfth theoretical configuration, the model reveals High AI-implementation, High techno-distress, High techno-eustress and High organizational support. It represents a hypothetical organization that, likely benefiting from sustained organizational support both historically and presently, has adopted advanced AI-technologies. This implementation has led to elevated levels of techno-distress, manifested in anxiety and demotivation, alongside high techno-eustress, which reflects a strong sense of enthusiasm and energy for engaging with new challenges. The concurrent presence of high organizational support provides essential guidance for alleviating techno-distress and for optimizing the benefits of techno-eustress moving forward. The organization thus operates within a cybernetic euphoric carousel, an environment characterized by technological dynamism and continuous motion. While the carousel metaphor captures the presence of strategic direction and motivational energy, it also conveys the underlying tension: the coexistence of euphoria, guidance and confusion, motivation and psychological strain. The high levels of techno-distress persist despite the supportive infrastructure and the energizing effects of techno-eustress. In this scenario, productivity is high, driven by the synergistic effects of robust AI-implementation, elevated techno-eustress and strong organizational support. Although techno-distress remains a significant challenge.

In the thirteenth theoretical configuration, the model reveals High AI-implementation, Low techno-distress, Low techno-eustress and Low organizational support. This configuration corresponds to the theoretical organizational typology designated as "Automatic Home". It represents a hypothetical organization that, likely supported by substantial organizational investment in the past, has successfully implemented AI-technologies. The low level of techno-distress suggests that this technological integration has not generated significant anxiety or demotivation among organizational actors. However, the concurrent low level of techno-eustress indicates a lack of enthusiasm and motivational energy to pursue new challenges, and the limited organizational support reflects an absence of strategic guidance for optimizing both techno-distress and techno-eustress in the future. Much like an automatic home, efficient and functional, yet emotionally neutral, this organization operates with technological sophistication but without the affective engagement or support structures necessary to fully leverage its potential. In this scenario, productivity is assessed as medium-low, shaped by the positive influence of high AI-implementation and low techno-distress, but constrained by the negative impact of low techno-eustress and insufficient organizational support.

Nonetheless, this configuration presents considerable opportunities for future improvement. By reversing the current trends in organizational support and techno-eustress, the organization may enhance its capacity for innovation, engagement and overall performance.

In the "Digital Zen Carousel" fourteenth theoretical configuration, the model identifies High AI-implementation, Low techno-distress, Low techno-eustress and High organizational support. It represents a hypothetical organization that, likely benefiting from substantial organizational support both historically and presently, has successfully integrated AI-technologies with minimal techno-distress, indicating an absence of anxiety or demotivation associated with technological adoption. However, the low level of techno-eustress suggests a lack of enthusiasm and motivational energy to embrace new challenges. Simultaneously, the high level of organizational support reflects the presence of strategic guidance capable of optimizing both techno-distress and techno-eustress in future organizational dynamics. The metaphor of the "Digital Zen Carousel" captures an organization that is technologically advanced and structurally supported, yet emotionally disengaged. It operates within a digital system, efficient and guided, where organizational actors are steered by institutional mechanisms rather than intrinsic motivation. These individuals experience neither distress nor excitement, functioning within a stable but affectively neutral environment. In this scenario, productivity is assessed as medium-high, driven by the positive effects of high AI-implementation, low techno-distress and robust organizational support, yet tempered by the absence of techno-eustress. The organization holds potential for further enhancement by fostering greater emotional engagement and challenge-oriented energy among its members.

In the "Technodelic Jungle", that refers to the fifteenth theoretical configuration, the model reveals High AI-implementation, Low techno-distress, High techno-eustress and Low organizational support. It represents a hypothetical organization that, likely supported by substantial organizational investment in the past, has successfully adopted advanced AI-technologies. The low level of techno-distress indicates that this technological integration has not generated significant anxiety or demotivation among organizational actors. Concurrently, the presence of high techno-eustress reflects a strong sense of enthusiasm and energy to embrace new challenges. However, the current low level of organizational support highlights a lack of strategic guidance necessary to sustain and optimize these psychological dynamics over time. The organization thus operates within a technodelic environment, characterized by intensive technological engagement, yet this environment resembles a jungle due to the unstructured and unmanaged nature of its emotional and motivational climate. While the absence of techno-distress is beneficial, the high level of techno-eustress, in the absence of adequate support, risks becoming directionless and unsustainable. In this scenario, productivity is currently high, driven by the positive effects of advanced AI-implementation, elevated techno-eustress and minimal techno-distress. However, these outcomes are tempered by the negative impact of insufficient organizational support, which may hinder the organization's ability to preserve and enhance these gains in the future.

The "Futuristic Oasis" is the sixteenth and final theoretical configuration of this Typology Model that is characterized by High AI-implementation, Low techno-distress, High techno-eustress and High organizational support. It represents a hypothetical organization that, likely benefiting from substantial organizational support both historically and presently, has successfully integrated advanced AI technologies with minimal psychological strain. The low level of techno-distress indicates an absence of anxiety or demotivation associated with technological adoption, while the high level of techno-eustress reflects a robust sense of motivation, enthusiasm, and readiness to embrace new challenges. Crucially, the concurrent presence of high organizational support ensures that both techno-distress and techno-eustress are effectively managed and optimized over time. The organization thus operates within a "futuristic oasis", a metaphorical space where technological advancement (high AI implementation) coexists harmoniously with psychological well-being (high techno-eustress and low techno-distress), underpinned by strategic and sustained organizational guidance. This configuration represents the theoretical ideal, wherein productivity are maximized. The synergistic effects of high AI-implementation, elevated techno-eustress, minimal techno-distress, and strong organizational support contribute not only to current performance but also to the long-term sustainability of these outcomes. The "Futuristic Oasis" thus embodies a model of organizational excellence in the age of AI.

Implications, Limitations and Future Research

This study provides valuable theoretical and practical implications. The typology model developed herein constitutes a meaningful advancement in the scholarly understanding of this topic and provides a foundation for the formulation of more effective management and organizational policies. Specifically, this framework invites future research aimed at refining or expanding the proposed model, given that only a limited set of variables and factors were considered in order to simplify the complexity of organizational reality. Scholars may pursue empirical investigations, such as surveys or interviews, to validate and apply the model in real-world contexts. Moreover, as this study focuses exclusively on organizations operating within the business sector and assumes a generalized cultural and organizational context, future research may extend its scope by examining other sectors, diverse cultural environments, and organizations characterized by distinct organizational cultures. Such extensions would enhance the model's applicability and contribute to a more nuanced understanding of AI implementation and its organizational dynamics.

In terms of practical implications, the model provides the managers a valuable diagnostic tool for identifying the organizational typology that most closely aligns with their current context, based on the observed levels of AI-implementation, techno-distress, techno-eustress, organizational support, and productivity. By situating their organization within this framework, managers can determine the strategic actions necessary to progress toward the ideal typology, "Futuristic Oasis", which represents the optimal configuration for maximizing productivity. To illustrate with a few examples, when an organization exhibits a typological configuration that diverges significantly from the ideal, managers can intervene by leveraging specific organizational mechanisms to facilitate the integration of AI technologies, while simultaneously minimizing techno-distress and enhancing techno-eustress.

This may be achieved through several strategic initiatives:

- establishing a dedicated department responsible for promoting AI implementation and addressing any concerns, uncertainties, or challenges associated with its use,
- organizing regular training programs aimed at increasing awareness of the potential benefits of AI technologies and enhancing the competencies of organizational actors who will engage with them;
- activating formal and informal mechanisms, such as regulatory frameworks or group dynamics, to support the harmonious integration of AI without generating adverse effects;

- promoting transparent and constructive communication channels that allow organizational actors to voice difficulties encountered in the adoption and use of AI-technologies;
- providing both tangible and intangible incentives to foster motivation and encourage a positive perception of AI, thereby transforming resistance into engagement;
- facilitating intergenerational knowledge exchange, whereby younger, technologically native employees, who possess greater familiarity and proficiency with AI, support and mentor older colleagues who may struggle to adapt due to their experience, having lived between two technological eras profoundly different.

Through these targeted interventions, managers can guide their organizations toward the "Futuristic Oasis" typology, thereby maximizing productivity and fostering a resilient, innovation-ready organizational culture.

It is evident that the aforementioned organizational initiatives, alongside numerous others, may exert a positive influence on key variables such as AI implementation, techno-eustress, and organizational support, while concurrently mitigating techno-distress. Collectively, these effects contribute to a substantial enhancement in productivity and, ultimately, in overall organizational performance.

Regarding limitations, the primary constraint pertains to the inherently dynamic nature of the subject matter, which necessitates ongoing revision and adaptation of the proposed framework. Moreover, this study represents an initial exploration that addresses only a limited set of variables and organizational contexts. It is therefore recommended that future research undertake empirical investigations to achieve a more comprehensive and nuanced understanding of the variables in question, across a broader spectrum of organizational settings. Additionally, scholars are encouraged to expand the scope of analysis by incorporating further dimensions, such as individual personality traits, personal factors, different cultural contexts and different organizational cultures.

AI-technologies are advancing at an unprecedented pace. In order to collaborate effectively with these systems, it is imperative to develop a comprehensive understanding of their functionalities, as well as their potential benefits and drawbacks. Equally important is the capacity to manage their integration by identifying and disseminating organizational practices that foster optimal synergy. Such practices can enable the maximization of productivity through a dynamic and transformative fusion of Artificial Intelligence and Human Intelligence.

References

Bhargava, D. and Trivedi, H. 2018. A study of causes of stress and stress management among youth. IRA-International Journal of Management & Social Sciences 11(03): 108–117.

Choudrie, J., Manandhar, N., Castro, C. and Obuekwe, C. 2023. Hey Siri, Google! Can you help me? A qualitative case study of smartphones AI functions in SMEs. Technological Forecasting and Social Change 189: 122375.

Cram, W. A., Wiener, M., Tarafdar, M. and Benlian, A. 2022. Examining the impact of algorithmic control on Uber drivers' technostress. Journal of Management Information Systems 39(2): 426–453.

Doty, D. H. and Glick, W. H. 1994. Typologies as a unique form of theory building: toward improved understanding and modeling. Academy of Management 19(2): 230–251.
Eisenberger, R., Huntington, R., Hutchison, S. and Sowa, D. 1986. Perceived organizational support. Journal of Applied Psychology 71(3): 500.
European Commission: COMMUNICATION TO THE COMMISSION. Artificial Intelligence in the European Commission (AI@EC). A strategic vision to foster the development and use of lawful, safe and trustworthy Artificial Intelligence systems in the European Commission. Brussels, 2024. In: https://commission.europa.eu/publications/artificial-intelligence-european-commission-aiec-communication_en.
Fu, S., Zheng, X. and Wong, I. A. 2022. The perils of hotel technology: The robot usage resistance model. International Journal of Hospitality Management 102: 103174.
Hashem, R., Ali, N., El Zein, F., Fidalgo, P. and Khurma, O. A. 2024. AI to the rescue: Exploring the potential of ChatGPT as a teacher ally for workload relief and burnout prevention. Research & Practice in Technology Enhanced Learning 19.
IEEE Corporate Advisory Group. 2017. IEEE guide for terms and concepts in intelligent process automation. 2755.
Issa, H., Jaber, J. and Lakkis, H. 2024. Navigating AI unpredictability: Exploring technostress in AI-powered healthcare systems. Technological Forecasting and Social Change 202: 123311.
Kumar, A., Krishnamoorthy, B. and Bhattacharyya, S. S. 2024. Machine learning and artificial intelligence-induced technostress in organizations: a study on automation-augmentation paradox with socio-technical systems as coping mechanisms. International Journal of Organizational Analysis 32(4): 681–701.
Lee, M. C., Scheepers, H., Lui, A. K. and Ngai, E. W. 2023. The implementation of artificial intelligence in organizations: A systematic literature review. Information & Management 60(5): 103816.
McEwen, B. S. 2012. Brain on stress: how the social environment gets under the skin. Proceedings of the National Academy of Sciences 109(supplement_2): 17180–17185.
Nayak, S. and Budhwar, P. 2022. Negative effects of enterprise social networks (ESNs) and technostress: empirical evidence from R&D centres operating in India. Aslib Journal of Information Management 74: 956–988.
Pagan-Garbín, I., Méndez, I. and Martínez-Ramón, J. P. 2024. Exploration of stress, burnout and technostress levels in teachers. Prediction of their resilience levels using an artificial neuronal network (ANN). Teaching and Teacher Education 148: 104717.
Rai, A., Constantinides, P. and Sarker, S. 2019. Next generation digital platforms: Toward human-AI hybrids. MIS Quarterly 43(1): iii–ix.
Sadeghi, D. and Sadeghi, S. 2012. A typology model for creativity managers based on reference points and their characteristics. Procedia - Social and Behavioral Sciences 47: 2219–2224.
Salanova, M., Llorens, S., Cifre, E. and Nogareda, C. 2007. El tecnoestres: Concepto, mediday prevencion [Technostress: Concept, measurement and prevention]. Nota Tecnica de Prevencion, 730. Madrid, Spain: INSHT.
Santos, R., Brandão, A., Veloso, B, and Popoli, P. 2024. The use of AI in government and its risks: lessons from the private sector. Transforming Government: People, Process and Policy.
Selye, H. 1956. The Stress of Life. New York: McGraw-Hill.
Sjödin, D., Parida, V. and Kohtamäki, M. 2023. Artificial intelligence enabling circular business model innovation in digital servitization: Conceptualizing dynamic capabilities, AI capacities, business models and effects. Technological Forecasting and Social Change 197: 122903.
Statt, D. A. 2004. The Routledge Dictionary of Business Management, 3rd edition, Routledge Publishing, Detroit.
Tarafdar, M., Cooper, C. L. and Stich, J.-F. 2019. The technostress trifecta - techno eustress, techno distress and design: Theoretical directions and an agenda for research. Information Systems Journal 29(1): 6–42.
Tarafdar, M., Pullins, E. B. and Ragu-Nathan, T. S. 2014. Examining impacts of technostress on the professional salesperson's behavioural performance. Journal of Personal Selling and Sales Management 34(1): 51–69.
Tarafdar, M., Pullins, E. B. and Ragu-Nathan, T. S. 2015. Technostress: Negative effect on performance and possible mitigations. Information Systems Journal 25(2): 103–132.

Tarafdar, M., Tu, Q., Ragu-Nathan, B. S. and Ragu-Nathan, T. S. 2007. The impact of technostress on role stress and productivity. Journal of Management Information Systems 24(1): 301–328.

Thunberg, S., Johonson, E. and Ziemke, T. 2024. Investigating healthcare workers' technostress when welfare technology is introduced in long-term care facilities. Behaviour & Information Technology 43(13): 3288–3300.

Turja, T., Aaltonen, I., Taipale, S. and Oksanen, A. 2020. Robot acceptance model for care (RAM-care): A principled approach to the intention to use care robots. Information & Management 57(5): 103220.

Valbuena, D., Verburg, P. H. and Bregt, A. K. 2008. A method to define a typology for agent-based analysis in regional land-use research. Agriculture, Ecosystems & Environment 128(1-2): 27–36.

Varian H. R. 2002. Microeconomia. Cafoscarina Editore.

Verma, S., Singh, V., Tudoran, A. A. and Bhattacharyya, S. S. 2024. Elevating employees' psychological responses and task performance through responsible artificial intelligence. Information Technology & People 37(7): 2551–2567.

Zhang, J., Chen, Q., Lu, J., Wang X., Liu, L. and Feng, Y. 2024. Emotional expression by artificial intelligence chatbots to improve customer satisfaction: Underlying mechanism and boundary conditions. Tourism Management 100: 104835.

Index

A

Adaptability 1, 3–5, 7, 8, 13, 14
Agentic AI 168, 170, 178, 186
AI Adoption 71–76, 78–81, 83–85
AI adoption (organizational) 170, 172
AI-technologies 235–240, 243, 244, 246–254, 256
Algorithmic governance 107
Algorithmic management 106, 108, 110
algorithms 4, 6, 18, 26, 29, 32, 33, 61, 64, 68, 75, 78–80, 83, 92, 93, 97–99, 105–108, 110–117, 120–122, 131, 144, 156, 159, 160, 168–175, 185–187, 190, 191, 195–198, 200–203, 205, 207, 209, 210, 217, 225, 234, 240
Artificial intelligence (AI) 1–4, 6, 7, 10, 13, 14, 18–34, 71–85, 88–90, 92–94, 96–100, 105–123, 128, 129, 131–138, 140–145, 147–161, 167–187, 190–198, 206, 208–211, 214–218, 222–225, 227–231

B

Behavioral implications of AI 106, 111
bibliometric analysis 218, 228
Burnout 147–161
Business Automation 89, 91
Business context 238, 240

C

Case study 40, 49, 168, 176, 178, 187
challenges 19–22, 24–26, 28–34
Chatbots in banking 129, 131, 134, 136, 142, 144
Classification 191, 192, 194–201, 203–206, 208–210
Cloud Computing 98, 100
Communication 148–160
complexity 21
Computing History 89
Coordination 75–77, 83, 84
Customer relationship management (CRM) 129, 132
Customer trust and loyalty 131
Customer–bank relationships 145

D

Data governance 179
Datafication of work 108
Deal screening 175, 177, 184
Deal sourcing 169, 173, 174, 177, 182, 184, 186, 187
Decision-making 88, 90, 93, 94, 96–99
Decision-making process 39–41, 43, 44, 48, 51
Deep Learning 88, 89, 98, 99
Digital Collaboration 2, 5, 7, 9, 14
Digital Evolution 39
digital government 23, 24
Digital literacy 1, 2, 5–10, 13, 14, 133, 135, 137, 139, 142, 145
Digital transformation 1, 23, 40, 90, 95, 96, 99, 110, 117, 139, 178, 225, 227
Digitalization of banking services 137–140
Due diligence 169, 173, 177, 178, 181, 184, 186, 187

E

emerging technologies 39, 41, 42, 178, 180, 215, 229, 240
Employability 1–5, 8, 13, 14
Employee autonomy 116, 122
Employee engagement 105, 111, 119, 120
Ethical use of AI 128, 142, 144
Expert Systems 94, 97, 99

F

Football 39–45, 48, 49, 51–54
Four-dimensional-Typology-Model 247

H

Healthcare 147–152, 154, 155, 157–159
Higher Education 1, 2, 6, 8
Human judgment 172, 175, 185, 187
human resources management 216, 222
Human-AI 30, 79, 83
Human-AI Collaboration 83
Human–AI interaction 132, 136, 140, 141
Hybrid leadership 113, 115
Hybrid service models (human–AI) 136, 142

I

Ideal organizational typology 238, 242
Information asymmetry 167
Information System 39
Innovation 2, 8, 9
Italy 45, 46, 49, 51, 61

L

Labour Market 6, 7, 9, 14, 15
Large language models 190, 192, 193, 195–197, 203, 207, 210

M

Machine learning 20, 67, 78, 90, 97–100, 107, 118, 120, 131, 150, 168–172, 175, 193, 195, 204, 207, 210, 217, 225, 227, 234, 237–240
Management studies 191–194, 196, 208, 209, 211
Maximization of productivity 242, 245–247, 256
Multichannel banking 130, 144

N

Neural Networks 97–99
NEVA SGR 168, 176, 178–180, 182, 185, 187

O

OpenAI Tools 1, 2, 4, 5, 9–12, 14
Operational Complexity 71, 72, 76–78, 80–82
opportunities 21, 22, 24, 28, 31–33
Optimization 191–193, 195, 197, 201, 202, 206, 208–210
Organization Design 76
organizational change 28, 29, 31, 40, 74, 89, 90, 240
Organizational context 236, 238, 240, 255, 256
Organizational Model 71, 76, 77, 80–82, 84
Organizational Structure 72, 75, 76, 80, 81, 84
organizational structure and design 8, 9, 13, 14, 28, 29, 72–76, 80, 81, 84, 85, 88, 89, 93, 94, 96, 99, 100, 110, 114, 207
Organizational support 238–256
Organizational Transformation 88–90, 95
Organizational typologies 238–243, 247, 248

P

Personalized banking services 128, 131, 132, 136, 137, 140, 144, 145
Prediction 191–193, 195–197, 199, 200, 203, 206, 209, 210
Productivity 236–256
Psychological contract 106, 108, 110, 111, 114
public sector 18–34
public value creation 25, 26

Q

qualitative meta-synthesis 19, 21, 22, 33

R

Reinforce 72, 76, 79, 80, 82–85
Relationship marketing 128, 129, 133, 135, 138–141, 145
Replace 72, 76, 79, 81–85
Research methods 190, 191
Resistance to technological change 119
Responsible marketing 128, 141, 145
Reveal 72, 76, 79, 80, 82–85

S

Self-Regulated Learning 2, 3, 6, 7
Simulation 191, 192, 197, 202, 204, 205, 207–210
SkillFusionLab 1–3, 5, 8, 9, 12–14
Socio-technical systems 72–74, 84, 107, 114
Soft Skills 2, 3, 5, 8, 9, 13–15
Sport 39–44, 51, 53, 54
Systematic Literature Review 147, 149, 151, 152

T

Task Complexity 76, 78, 80
Techno-distress 235, 236, 238–241, 243–256
Techno-eustress 235, 236, 238–241, 243–256
Technology adoption 95, 96, 99
Technostress 156, 160, 235–246
Text analysis 192, 197, 201, 204, 205, 207
Theoretical implications 239, 255
Trust in AI 106, 108, 110, 116, 118

Trust in banking 139
Typology Analysis 238, 240, 241

V

VC investment decision-making 176
Venture capital (VC) 167–170, 172–179, 184–187
Video Assistant Referee 39, 45, 49–52
VOSviewer 47

W

Work meaningfulness 107, 111, 113, 116, 117

Editors' Biographies

Eleonora Veglianti PhD is an Associate Professor of Business Organizations and Human Resource Management (HRM) at Kedge Business School, Paris campus, France. She teaches courses on human resource management, business organizations, intercultural management and organizational behavior. Prior to academia, she worked as a business consultant. Her primary research interests lie in work organization, human resource management, digital transformation, artificial intelligence and smart technologies. She serves as an anonymous reviewer for several international journals. She also serves on scientific committees, participates in academic associations, and is actively involved in editorial boards. She is Associate editor of the International Studies of Management & Organization journal.

Wendy Currie is a Professor of information systems at Audencia Business School, France. She holds a fractional post at the University of Bradford, UK, where she teaches qualitative research methods. She is a Co-Editor-in-Chief of the Journal of Information Technology and the Journal of Information Technology Teaching Cases. She is the founding Editor of Health Policy and Technology, published by Elsevier. The journal gained an impact factor within three years of its launch. Her current research projects focus on artificial intelligence regulation, digital technology transformation, and financial technologies, including crypto-assets and decentralized finance. She has held editorial board positions at MISQ, ISR, JIT, EJIS, JSIS, and I&M. She has published over 200 scientific papers in leading management, public administration, and information systems journals and conferences. Her scholarly contributions use institutional theory, stakeholder analysis, and decision theory. She holds a BSc in Sociology, a PhD in Management, and an HDR in information systems.

Luisa Varriale, PhD, is a Full Professor of Organization Theory (OT) and Human Resource Management (HRM) at the Department of Economics, Law, Cybersecurity, and Sports Sciences, Parthenope University of Naples (Italy). Her main research interests include mentoring, learning processes, knowledge creation and sharing, event management, e-HRM, artificial intelligence and its impact on organizational and HRM processes and policies, digital recruitment, the integration of digital and smart technologies into organizational dynamics, social inclusion, disability management, sustainability, and corporate social responsibility (CSR). She particularly focuses on these themes within service-oriented sectors such as educational institutions (school systems and universities), the tourism industry (hospitality and the cruise sector), cultural heritage organizations (museums), healthcare organizations, and related contexts. She also serves on scientific and organizing committees, participates in academic associations, and is actively involved in editorial boards.

For Product Safety Concerns and Information please contact our
EU representative GPSR@taylorandfrancis.com Taylor & Francis
Verlag GmbH, Kaufingerstraße 24, 80331 München, Germany